THE DOCUMENTARY HISTORY OF THE RATIFICATION OF THE CONSTITUTION

VOLUME I

Constitutional Documents and Records, 1776–1787

THE DOCUMENTARY HISTORY OF THE RATIFICATION OF THE CONSTITUTION

Volume I

Constitutional Documents and Records, 1776–1787

Edited by Merrill Jensen

———◆◆◆———

MADISON

STATE HISTORICAL SOCIETY OF WISCONSIN

1 9 7 6

Manufactured in the United States of America by
Worzalla Publishing Company, Stevens Point, Wisconsin

LIBRARY OF CONGRESS CATALOGING IN PUBLICATION DATA
Main entry under title:
The Documentary history of the ratification
of the Constitution.

Includes index.
CONTENTS: v. 1. Constitutional documents
and records, 1776–1787.
1. United States—Constitutional history—Sources.
I. Jensen, Merrill.
KF4502.D63   342'.73'029   75-14149
ISBN 0-87020-153-0

Foreword

In 1911 Max Farrand published in three volumes the *Records of the Federal Convention,* presenting with scholarly authority the documentary history of the writing of the Constitution. Farrand's achievement has long challenged American scholars to continue his work and to produce a similar documentary record of the ratification of the Constitution.

With the exception of Jonathan Elliot's *Debates, Resolutions, and Other Proceedings in Convention on the Adoption of the Federal Constitution,* now over one hundred and thirty years old, and the *Documentary History of the Constitution,* published by the Department of State in the nineteenth century, historians have limited their studies of the ratification of the Constitution to single states. Histories of ratification have not been written for all of the states. Of those which do exist, some contain fragmentary documentary material, but their obvious purpose has been to present an historical narrative of the particular state's share in ratification. In some cases, the history of ratification in a state is confined to a chapter or two in a book of broader scope. There is, however, no scholarly and comprehensive documentary history of the ratification process of the Constitution or of the first ten amendments for all of the states. The reason for this is obvious. Such a project was clearly much more than a one-man job, and it called for substantial financing. It is to be hoped that the publication of the present documentary history will encourage and provide materials for scholarly studies in the areas of ratification not yet covered by monographic works.

The establishment of the National Historical Publications Commission, created by the National Archives Act of 1934, brought together a group of prominent men, under the chairmanship of the Archivist of the United States, who were deeply interested in this kind of historical venture and whose official voice could command attention. At its first meeting in January 1935, the new Commission had placed before it a resolution adopted the month before by the council of the American Historical Association, urging early consideration of a program of publication of documentary material relating to the history of the Constitution. Such consideration was given. At the Commission's meeting in February 1936, one of its members, J. Franklin Jameson, a master statesman in promoting historical research, moved "that a scheme of publication respecting the adoption of the Constitution be recommended by the Commission to Congress." This motion was adopted unanimously, and on March 17, 1936, the Archivist, on behalf of the Commission, sent to both houses of Congress a report presenting and elaborating this proposal.

Emphasizing that only a small portion of the original documentary material relating to ratification had been collected, edited and published, the report encouraged a project to bring together this material from contemporary newspapers, magazines, pamphlets, and published and unpublished correspondence and state archives. The report stressed that the forces and issues involved in the state-by-state struggles over ratification could only be understood through such a publication. It emphasized that such historical scholarship would be a valuable service to scholars, lawyers, teachers and the general public and "would promote a more adequate comprehension of the significance of the Constitution on the part of the American people."

Endorsements of this report were forthcoming from numerous scholars and organizations throughout the nation. Bills authorizing the proposed documentary history of ratification and the first ten amendments were introduced in both houses of Congress in 1939, and a hearing was held by the House Committee on the Library. Although reported favorably, the House bill did not reach a vote before adjournment.

Because of World War II and its aftermath, little progress was made with respect to this enterprise for nearly a dozen years. The Federal Records Act of 1950, however, revived the National Historical Publications Commission by authorizing the creation of a staff to carry forward its work. The staff operations progressed under the able and imaginative leadership of Philip M. Hamer and his successor as Executive Director, Oliver W. Holmes. In December 1951, the Commission reaffirmed its earlier approval of publication, under the direct auspices of the Commission, of a documentary history of the ratification of the Constitution and the first ten amendments. The small but efficient staff of the Commission began at that time and carried on for several years the task of assembling the documents which would comprise such a work.

In the fall of 1957 the Ford Foundation made a grant of $125,000, which it was then believed would make possible the completion of such a documentary history within five years, and in from six to eight volumes. Work began on the *Documentary History of the Ratification of the Constitution and First Ten Amendments* in 1958, under the editorship of Robert E. Cushman, former President of the American Political Science Association and a recognized authority in the field of constitutional law and history.

As work progressed with the collecting of documents from numerous sources, it became clear that the original estimate of time and cost was inadequate and that additional volumes would be required to document thoroughly the story of ratification in the several states. In 1964, under Public Law 88-383, Congress authorized and funded a program of grants and allocations for the collection, reproduction, and publication of documentary source materials, under the auspices of the National Historical Publications Commission. Funds from this program have since largely supported the present work.

In the spring of 1969 the project was left, with the unfortunate death of Dr. Cushman, without an editor. His able leadership had guided the project through the early days of organization and through the many difficult problems associated with an historical endeavor of this scope.

At its meeting on December 13, 1969, the Commission selected Merrill Jensen, Vilas Research Professor of History of the University of Wisconsin, as editor of the project. A widely respected scholar with numerous publications relating to this early period of American history, Dr. Jensen was a former member of the advisory board of the ratification project and editor of the *Documentary History of the First Federal Elections,* a project also supported by the National Historical Publications Commission. The University of Wisconsin generously agreed to accept joint sponsorship with the Commission and in October 1970, the entire project with its accumulated records and files was transferred to Wisconsin.

Dr. Jensen and his staff have labored impressively, and the publication of this initial volume is a monument to their diligence and careful scholarship. The appearance of this volume is a result of a massive effort to collect documents from manuscript repositories, libraries, and private collectors all over the world. A careful search in thousands of collections has resulted in the discovery of an extraordinary number of documents illustrating the state controversies over the ratification question. Historians should find this and succeeding volumes a rich and fascinating source of documentation which will provide a greater understanding and appreciation of the origins of the United States Constitution.

JAMES B. RHOADS, *Chairman*
National Historical Publications
Commission

Introduction and Acknowledgments

By Robert E. Cushman

Before his death Robert E. Cushman prepared a first volume containing the official documents recording the action of the Confederation Congress on the Constitution and the ratification of the Constitution by Delaware and Pennsylvania. The change in editorship was followed by a major reorganization of the scope and content of the project. As a result Dr. Cushman's volume has been replaced by this volume of *Constitutional Documents and Records, 1776–1787*. However, as a tribute to Dr. Cushman's devoted labors, we are presenting here his introduction and his acknowledgments to the people who worked with him during his years as editor. [Ed.]

The Constitution of the United States is the greatest achievement of American creative statesmanship. This judgment of it has grown more firm and universal as the Constitution has proved adequate over the years to serve the needs of a great and growing nation.

The editors of this documentary history of the ratification of the Constitution, having examined the records which comprise that history, believe that the ratification of the Constitution, against the obstacles and uncertainties which it faced, stands out as a constructive political achievement second only to the drafting of the Constitution itself. The political maturity and statesmanship necessary to achieve ratification were not limited to a few outstanding leaders, but were exhibited by shrewd and tough-minded men all the way from New Hampshire to Georgia; the bitter controversies which had to be won were scattered up and down the Atlantic seaboard as well as in the back country; and, in the cases of North Carolina and Rhode Island, a good deal of time was necessary to achieve victory. If, however, the entire struggle for ratification is viewed as a whole, the fact that will emerge most conspicuously is the political maturity and wisdom shown both by those who favored ratification and by those who did not. Had this quality been lacking in the leaders as well as in the rank and file of citizens of the American states when they faced the issue to ratify or reject the new Constitution, the work of the Federal Convention might have gone for naught, and the hopes for a firm national government might have been frustrated for many years.

9

The modern reader of the Constitution of the United States (of whom there are far too few) may well wonder why the question of adopting or rejecting it should have caused the bitter and protracted struggles and debates which took place before ratification was achieved. A reading of the major documents which these volumes contain will give the reader a few guide lines which will not only sharpen and emphasize these issues, but will indicate also the ways by which politically experienced men were able to find peaceable solutions for them.

In recent years a number of scholars have made careful studies designed to state with precision the lines of cleavage in the American society of the 1780's which could reasonably explain the deep breach which separated the Federalists who strongly favored the Constitution, from the Antifederalists who opposed it with equal, if not greater, fervor. The editors, whose task has been to collect and arrange documents, and not write a history, have felt no obligation to pass judgment upon these analyses, nor to offer conclusions of their own. They have preferred to hide behind the wisdom of Professor McLaughlin as expressed in the following paragraph.[1]

It is quite impossible to classify accurately the opponents or the advocates of the Constitution. Economic influences of course played their part. If generalizations must be indulged in, it is probably correct to say that on the whole the well-to-do—especially the commercial elements of the population—favored ratification; the sections remote from the centers of trade were inclined to be opposed to it. But even this classification needs modification. Not all of the back-country—the region naturally less affected by government and in some instances bearing a traditional grudge against domination by the eastern section—was opposed to ratification; and by no means were all of the prosperous planters or men of property advocates of the new system. No attempt to draw lines sharply dividing the people into classes can be successful. Geographical and sectional conditions were of considerable influence in determining the attitudes of men; some differences of opinion were apparently due to special economic interests. If one thinks of the struggle in Virginia, where Washington and Mason represented opposite sides, the difficulty of classification is plain. Richard Henry Lee, after referring to debtors and also to aristocrats desirous of power, said: 'these two parties are really insignificant compared with the solid, free, and independent part of the community.' Though the areas favorable to ratification, in a number of instances, lay along routes of trade, it is quite possible, of course, that this attitude toward the Constitution was due, at least in a measure, to the fact that the people of those areas could be reached by information emanating from the east, and were not solely guided by economic influences or geographical environment.

Thus the differences between the two political groups in the American states long antedated the Constitution, and the debates on it merely intensified old conflicts and antagonisms. When the Antifederalists learned the membership of the Federal Convention, they were at once convinced that this body, heavily overweighted with conservatives, would produce no Constitution which they could support; their views were not likely to prevail. Most of the leaders in the Convention were known for their belief that a strong national government must be created. To many an Antifederalist it looked like a Federalist conspiracy.

When the Constitution was given to the public all these fears were realized. The Antifederalists were convinced that state autonomy and individual civil liberty would be heavily restricted, if not destroyed, under the new Constitution. It is well to bear in mind, in appraising these Antifederalist judgments, that most of our American history books in the earlier days were written with a strong Federalist bias. More recently we have been correcting this. It is not, however, accurate or fair to class the opponents of the Constitution as uneducated and stubborn people who could not or would not grasp an argument when presented to them. This documentary history, were evidence needed, completely refutes any such judgment that the views and arguments of the Antifederalists were stupid or frivolous. Those adjectives do not apply convincingly to men like George Mason and Patrick Henry in Virginia, George Clinton in New York, or Willie Jones in North Carolina.

The Antifederalists had, in fact, a very strong case, and one which was bound to have wide popular appeal. Only a few of its more important points can be mentioned. First, they would lose the power which they had enjoyed under the unanimity rule of the Articles of Confederation to block changes of which they disapproved in the basic structure and powers of the confederated government. Second, having escaped by separation from England the authority of an outside power to dictate to them in the management of their affairs, they were now to be placed in many important matters under the power of a strong national government. This national government could control their relations with their neighbors in matters of trade and commerce, and, of even greater importance, could move in and impose taxes upon persons, property, and interests, a power which had never existed before. More alarming than this was the creation of a Supreme Court with limited but important jurisdiction over the states, together with the power given to Congress to create inferior federal courts to which could be given jurisdiction over the individual citizen in criminal and civil actions.

Perhaps the most effective Antifederalist attack on the new Constitution was that it contained no bill of rights. It did have a very few clauses, such as those relating to jury trial and *ex post facto* laws, but there was no listing and safeguarding of the general civil rights of the people. This was the most effective weapon which the Antifederalists had in their arsenal, and it also gave many Federalists serious misgivings.

The Federalists stood on somewhat firmer ground. A number of their leaders had been educated in England and still valued their "rights of Englishmen," and many would have preferred the peaceful status of home rule under the British Crown had they not learned from bitter experience that this was impossible and that the only future for the American colonies lay in an independent union. That union, however, must be held together, and it must have the power to deal with national problems and to put up a united front against England and the rest of Europe. The Federalists were in closer touch with each other than were their Antifederalist opponents, since they had from the beginning built up the business and commercial centers along the Atlantic seaboard.

Even while this major struggle over the Constitution was going on, it was obvious that the Articles of Confederation, the only "union" of the states which existed, was gradually disintegrating. It had no assurance of being able to present a united front on anything, since any powers of real importance could be exercised only with the unanimous consent of all the states, which unanimity experience had proved virtually impossible to secure. The Continental Congress had been given only minor delegated powers, and so low had it fallen in public esteem that it was becoming increasingly hard for it to get a quorum to transact even its routine business. It was obvious that something would have to be done; and while the Constitution drafted at Philadelphia did not command the unqualified approval of any of the members of the Federal Convention, and a few refused to sign it or support it, it did create a strong centralized government with power to deal with national and interstate problems at home, and a government which could take its place with dignity in the family of nations. That, the Federalists believed, was to be its purpose and effect; and if mistakes had been made they could be corrected by the process of amendment.

Could the new Constitution be ratified in the face of all these fundamental differences of opinion? If ratified, could it be put into effect peaceably and be acquiesced in by those who had so strongly and ably opposed it? It was earlier suggested that the ratification of the Constitution stands as a tribute to the political maturity of the generation of Americans who achieved it. In speaking of the political wisdom and experience of the colonists on the Atlantic seaboard one is not referring to the political traditions and practices which had existed in England for so long and which the colonists brought with them as a matter of course when they settled in the new world. They had all been brought up to be familiar with the right (usually qualified) to vote, and with the electoral processes set up to make it effective. They had all learned that if you lose an election you accept the result peaceably, rather than try to organize an army and dislodge your successful competitor.

There were, however, two hallmarks of political maturity which were of the utmost importance in this critical situation. Without them ratification might well have failed. One of these was skill and effectiveness in debate. One cannot read the records presented in these volumes without being impressed with the penetration and thoroughness with which, in the more important conventions, every issue of importance was dissected and argued. Every man who had anything to say could say it, and he could argue at length with those who disagreed with him. The newspapers, of course, garnered in many of these discussions and printed them, attesting a public interest in political matters not always so apparent today. The debates on ratification did, in fact, change men's minds as the result of open discussion. Perhaps more important than anything else, however, in judging highly this measure of political maturity, was the long and practiced skill which those engaged in the ratification struggle had in the art of compromise. Without it deliberative bodies come to a standstill, and new programs are foredoomed by men's stubbornness. There is no finer example of this compromise in action than the day-by-day use of it in the Federal Convention of 1787. Without it we should have had no Constitution. Edmund Burke once wisely observed:[2] "However, it is a settled rule with me, to make the most of my *actual situation;* and not to refuse to do a proper thing, because there is something else more proper, which I am not able to do." This principle has guided British and American political leaders for many years. The records indicate many instances in the ratifying conventions of men who at first thought their own opinions were immutable and who later found themselves modifying those opinions as the result of argument and persuasion.

There was one compromise, however, which was of crucial importance to the success of ratification. As the conventions in the states swung into action, especially those in which there were sharp differences of opinion, there emerged a tendency, especially among the opponents of the Constitution, to urge that various amendments were needed, and that the ratification of the Constitution should be made conditional upon the acceptance of these amendments. In the Massachusetts convention the division of opinion was very intense. The point was reached at which a powerful group in the convention took the position that Massachusetts should ratify the Constitution, but only on the condition that a list of amendments which the convention had approved be adopted. The implications of this were obvious and serious. During the struggle over ratification 124 amendments were proposed by the various ratifying conventions. If the Constitution was not validly ratified until all these conditions had been met or considered, then the whole process would have had to be started over again, and a new convention called. Nothing would have been finally decided. By a skillful and subtle use of the method of compromise, the Federalist and Antifederalist leaders in Massachusetts were able to agree upon a decision by which Massachusetts should openly and firmly ratify the Constitution, with no strings attached to that ratification, but that the desired amendments should accompany the ratification as embodying the wishes of the people of Massachusetts. This proved to be the perfect solution, and from then on the policy was followed by those states in which the ratifying conventions proposed amendments to the Constitution. The new national government set up in 1789 gave consideration to these amendments, and our present first ten amendments are the result.

The purpose of this brief foreword has been to emphasize the political atmosphere in which the very close struggle for ratification took place, and to impress upon the reader of this documentary history the high measure of statesmanship which its final success represents; and also to emphasize the value which the documents here present, not only to the scholar, but to all who may wish to know how our Constitution came into force.

The editor of a work such as this is bound to feel both an obligation and a keen desire to make his acknowledgements and express his gratitude to institutions and persons who have given him assistance. Friends and colleagues have extended wise counsel and careful criticism; while libraries, archives, and other depositories have provided free access to documents and manuscripts, always with courtesy and cooperation. A glance through the pages of this single volume, with a dozen more to come, makes clear that these sources are too numerous to be listed individually in a prefatory note; and it is the hope of the editor that his gratitude to these many individuals and institutions may be acceptably expressed in footnotes.

The editor and his colleagues owe a heavy debt to two great national institutions, the National Archives and the Library of Congress. The offices of this project on ratification are located in the National

Archives Building, with all of its resources and services readily available. Thus the enterprise was begun and continued under the discerning eye of Dr. Wayne C. Grover, Archivist of the United States, and *ex officio* Chairman of the National Historical Publications Commission. His deep interest and shrewd counsel were constantly on tap to the date of his retirement in 1965. Equally helpful and cooperative have been the two men who have since succeeded him in the office of Archivist, Dr. Robert H. Bahmer and Dr. James B. Rhoads. Thanks are also due to the members of the staff of the National Archives who have helped generously in making manuscripts and other records available and have extended many other courtesies. Here special mention should be made of Miss Camille Hannon, Reference Librarian in the Archives, who lent constant and indispensable assistance.

The Library of Congress, located as it is in Washington, has made available its reference works, catalogs, manuscript and rare book collections, microfilms, and many other resources. The courtesy and assistance extended by its staff have been well beyond the call of duty.

Probably the most valuable single source of documentary material made available to the editors of this project has been the almost 2,000 roles of microfilm of Early State Records that the Library of Congress in association with the University of North Carolina prepared, and for which the Library in 1950 and 1951 published guides.[3] This material was located and filmed by Professor William S. Jenkins of the University of North Carolina over the course of more than twenty-five years. The collection includes, for the ratifying states, their records of the period, including the journals of legislative sessions which called the ratifying conventions, the journals and sometimes other records of these conventions, the state constitutions and laws, together with administrative and executive records such as governors' letter books and council minutes. These films, which are available at the Library of Congress, have placed at the disposal of the editors, not only the documents actually printed in this work, but other documents useful for background or biographical notes: access to this collection has been the next thing to setting up shop in the various state archives.

The editor wishes to make some special personal acknowledgements of indebtedness. The first of these are to Dr. Philip M. Hamer and Dr. Oliver W. Holmes, who have been the two Executive Directors of the National Historical Publications Commission in recent years; one could hardly exaggerate the importance of the aid and support they have extended in countless ways. The late Professor Carl B.

Swisher of Johns Hopkins University read critically a substantial part of the manuscript of this volume; while Professor John A. Munroe of the University of Delaware read the galley proof of the section dealing with the state of Delaware. Mr. John R. Fleming, a retired senior editor of *U.S. News & World Report,* upon his own generous offer, read the entire galley proof of Volume I. Penetrating and helpful suggestions and corrections came from members of the Panel of Advisors, to each of whom galley proof was sent. The editor is keenly grateful for all of this valuable assistance.

Grateful appreciation must be expressed in particular to those who have comprised the editorial staff of this documentary history either from its inception or for shorter periods. At the outset Leonard Rapport was appointed associate editor, but it became almost at once imperative to transfer his energies to the all-important task of visiting and searching archives, libraries and other depositories in quest of the manuscripts and documents relating to ratification not previously assembled. The amazing thoroughness and perception with which he has done, and is still doing, this work has placed this entire project under a heavy debt of gratitude to him. Marion Tinling was on the staff as an assistant editor for more than a year, rendering efficient service, while Leonard Faber was an assistant editor for a much longer period. Sybil Schaffrath, Jane Anderson, and Mary Darnall, over varying periods of time, were valuable colleagues and assistants, as Loretta Taple and Peggy Wehage are at present. Clarissa Fairchild Cushman, formerly a publishing house and magazine editor, has worked on this project from its beginning.

1. Andrew C. McLaughlin, *A Constitutional History of the United States* (New York, N.Y., 1935), 221–22.

2. Edmund Burke to Samuel Span, 23 April 1778, Thomas W. Copeland et al. (eds.), *The Correspondence of Edmund Burke* (9 vols., Cambridge, England and Chicago, Ill., 1958–1970), III, 434.

3. *A Guide to the Microfilm Collection of Early State Records* (Washington, D.C., 1950); *Supplement* (1951).

Contents

Foreword by *James B. Rhoads*   5

Introduction and Acknowledgments by *Robert E. Cushman*   9

* * * *

Introduction to

THE DOCUMENTARY HISTORY OF THE RATIFICATION OF THE CONSTITUTION

Introduction and Acknowledgments by *Merrill Jensen*   25

The Sources   30

Organization   39

Editorial Procedures   43

American Newspapers, 1787–1790: Short Title List   48

* * * *

CONSTITUTIONAL DOCUMENTS AND RECORDS, 1776–1787

Introduction   52

Symbols for Manuscripts, Manuscript Depositories,
Short Titles, and Cross-references   69

17

I. The Declaration of Independence

Introduction 72

The Declaration of Independence 73

Signers of the Declaration of Independence 76

II. The Articles of Confederation

Introduction 78

A. Draft of Articles of Confederation, 12 July 1776 79

B. Act of Confederation of the United States of America, 15 November 1777 86

III. Ratification of the Articles of Confederation by the States in Congress, 22 June 1778–1 March 1781

Introduction 96

A. Maryland, 22–23 June 1778 97

B. New Hampshire, 23 June 1778 101

C. Massachusetts, 23 June 1778 102

D. Rhode Island, 23 June 1778 105

E. Connecticut, 23 June 1778 109

F. New York, 23 June 1778 111

G. New Jersey, 23, 25 June 1778 113

H. Pennsylvania, 25 June 1778 118

I. Virginia, 25 June 1778 120

J. South Carolina, 25 June 1778 121

K. Eight States Sign the Articles of Confederation, 9 July 1778 124

L. North Carolina Signs, 21 July 1778   124

M. Georgia Signs, 24 July 1778   126

N. New Jersey Signs, 26 November 1778   128

O. Delaware Signs, 22 February 1779   130

P. Maryland Signs, 1 March 1781   135

IV. Amendments to the Articles of Confederation, Grants of Power to Congress, and Ordinances for the Western Territory, 3 February 1781–13 July 1787

A. Grant of Power to Collect Import Duties,
3 February 1781   140

B. Amendment to Give Congress Coercive Power over the
States and Their Citizens, 16 March 1781   141

C. Committee Report on Carrying the Confederation
into Effect and on Additional Powers Needed by
Congress, 22 August 1781   143

D. Grant of Temporary Power to Collect Import Duties
and Request for Supplementary Funds, 18 April 1783   146

E. Amendment to Share Expenses According to Population,
18 April 1783   148

F. Ordinance for the Government of Western Territory,
23 April 1784   150

G. Grant of Temporary Power to Regulate Commerce,
30 April 1784   153

H. Amendment to Grant Commercial Powers to Congress,
28 March 1785   154

I. Ordinance for the Sale of Western Lands,
20 May 1785   156

J. Amendments to the Articles of Confederation
    Proposed by a Grand Committee of Congress,
    7 August 1786   163

K. Ordinance for the Government of the Territory of
    the United States Northwest of the River Ohio,
    13 July 1787   168

V. The Calling of the Constitutional Convention,
21 January 1786–21 February 1787

                    Introduction   176

A. Virginia Calls Meeting to Consider Granting Congress
    Power to Regulate Trade, 21 January–23 February 1786   180

B. Proceedings and Report of the Commissioners at
    Annapolis, Maryland, 11–14 September 1786   181

C. Confederation Congress Calls the Constitutional
    Convention, 21 February 1787   185

D. James Madison, Notes of Debates in Congress,
    21 February 1787   188

VI. Appointments of Delegates to the Constitutional
Convention, 23 November 1786–15 September 1787

                    Introduction   192

A. New Jersey, 23 November 1786   195

B. Virginia, 4 December 1786   196

C. Pennsylvania, 30 December 1786   199

D. North Carolina, 6 January 1787   200

E. Delaware, 3 February 1787   203

F. Georgia, 10 February 1787   204

G. Massachusetts, 3 March 1787   205

H. New York, 6 March 1787   209

I. South Carolina, 8 March 1787   213

J. Connecticut, 17 May 1787   215

K. Maryland, 26 May 1787   216

L. New Hampshire, 27 June 1787   223

M. Rhode Island's Reasons for refusal to Appoint
Delegates, 15 September 1787   225

Delegates Who Attended the Constitutional Convention   230

VII. The Resolutions and Draft Constitutions of the
Constitutional Convention, 29 May–17 September 1787

Introduction   232

A. The Virginia Resolutions, 29 May   243

B. Charles Pinckney's Plan, 29 May   245

C. The Amended Virginia Resolutions, 13–19 June   247

D. The New Jersey Amendments to the Articles of
Confederation, 15 June   250

E. Alexander Hamilton's Plan, 18 June   253

F. Resolutions Submitted to the Committee of Detail,
24, 26 July   255

G. Draft Constitution by the Committee of Detail,
6 August   260

H. Amended Draft Constitution Submitted to the
Committee of Style, 10 September   270

I. Draft Constitution by the Committee of Style, as
Amended by the Convention, 12–17 September   284

Population and Constitution-Making, 1774–1792   297

VIII. The Report of the Constitutional Convention, 17 September 1787

Introduction   304

A. The President of the Convention to the President of
Congress, 17 September   305

B. The Constitution, 17 September   306

C. Resolutions of the Convention Recommending the
Procedures for Ratification and for the Establishment
of Government under the Constitution by the
Confederation Congress, 17 September   317

D. Transmittal of the Constitution from the Convention
in Philadelphia to the Confederation Congress in
New York, 17–20 September   318

IX. The Confederation Congress and the Constitution, 20–28 September 1787

Introduction   322

Members of Congress in Attendance, 20–28 September   324

A. Proceedings of Congress on the Constitution,
20–28 September   325

B. Commentaries by Members of Congress on the
Proceedings of Congress on 26–28 September   342

C. Public and Private Commentaries on the Proceedings
of Congress on 26–28 September   349

Index   355

Introduction

to

The Documentary History of the Ratification of the Constitution

Introduction and Acknowledgments

The Sources

Organization

Editorial Procedures

American Newspapers, 1787–1790: Short Title List

Introduction and Acknowledgments

The editing of *The Documentary History of the Ratification of the Constitution* involves tasks of a different order of magnitude than those involved in editing the papers of a person or a family. One task arises from the number of individuals involved. The thirteen state legislatures that called conventions to consider the Constitution contained a total of almost 1,700 members. In the state conventions, 1,071 men voted to ratify the Constitution and 577 voted to reject it —a total of 1,648 men. In addition to these men, there was an even greater number of local officials, and of influential men who held no public office but who, directly or indirectly, influenced the political decisions of the time. The great majority of these men did not leave letters or diaries, but enough of them did to provide a rich, if often perplexing, variety of facts and opinions.

A second task arises from the great variety of materials, in addition to personal letters and diaries, that relate to the ratification of the Constitution. There are three bodies of official material. The first consists of the Journals and other papers of the Confederation Congress which played an essential role in the establishment of the Constitution: on 21 February 1787 it called the Constitutional Convention; on 26–28 September 1787 it debated the Constitution and transmitted it to the states; and on 13 September 1788 it set the time for the election of the President, and the time and place for the meeting of the new government under the Constitution. The second body of official material consists of the journals, papers, and sometimes the debates of the thirteen state legislatures which considered the Constitution and called conventions to reject or ratify it. The third body of official material consists of the documents relating to the election of delegates to the state conventions and the journals, papers, and debates of those conventions.

Finally, there are the contemporary printed materials in the form of newspapers, pamphlets, and broadsides, which bulk larger than all other documents relating to ratification combined. The accumulation of nearly 40,000 items from newspapers alone illustrates the interest of contemporaries in and the intensity of the debate about the Constitution.

The Constitution was debated, for the most part, in ignorance of the proceedings of the Constitutional Convention. However, the objections of the few members of the Convention who opposed the Constitution were widely published in newspapers and pamphlets. Robert Yates and John Lansing, Jr. stated their objections in a letter to Governor George Clinton of New York, Elbridge Gerry gave his views in a letter to the Massachusetts legislature, George Mason's objections were widely circulated in manuscript as well as printed form, and Luther Martin provided the lengthiest unfavorable account of the Convention's proceedings in his "Genuine Information" to the Maryland legislature.

Such statements were overwhelmed in terms of quantity and circulation by publications supporting the Constitution. James Wilson's speech in the State House Yard in Philadelphia on 6 October was the most widely circulated of all the defenses. It became, in effect, the "official" Federalist interpretation of the Constitution, although that interpretation was at considerable variance with what Wilson and others had declared to be the purpose of the Constitution during the debates in the Convention.

While the men who debated the ratification of the Constitution knew little of the Convention, the debate took place in a context that extended back to colonial times. Many of the same men had been debating the issue of a central government best suited for the United States ever since the Declaration of Independence, and even before. Some of the most important leaders in 1787 had helped write the first constitution of the United States in 1776–1777, the Articles of Confederation. Afterwards, they had debated proposals for amending it and for increasing or limiting the powers of Congress. Hence in the debates in the Constitutional Convention, in the public prints, and in the state conventions many of the leaders were simply repeating old principles and discussing earlier constitutional proposals in a new context.

* * * *

The editor of any collection of documents always owes a debt to his predecessors. Such is notably the case with *The Documentary History of the Ratification of the Constitution*. The debt began in 1819 when John Quincy Adams edited and published the Journals of the Constitutional Convention for the first time. The debt mounted after 1951 when the staff of the National Historical Publications Commission, and in particular, H.B. Fant, James R. Masterson, and Leonard Rapport, began to collect sources concerning the history of writing and ratification of the Constitution. The obligation became even greater after Robert E. Cushman assumed the editorship in 1958. Between then and 1969 he and his staff continued the search for materials, carried on the never-ending task of organizing the growing mass of documents in manageable and intelligible order, and made plans for publication. In the course of his work Dr. Cushman recognized, as any editor does, that as documents accumulate their organization must constantly be reevaluated. Hence he made changes in the organization that he projected in *The Quarterly Legal Historian* in March 1962. The process begun by Dr. Cushman has continued, and the organization finally established is described immediately after this introduction.

The present editor of *The Documentary History of the Ratification of the Constitution* became involved in the project in 1966, when he became a member of Dr. Cushman's editorial board. At the same time he undertook to edit *The Documentary History of the First Federal Elections, 1788–1790,* a project which is essentially a continuation of the Ratification project. The editor and the staff of the Elections project began searching hitherto unsearched libraries and re-searching previously searched libraries for materials for Ratification and for the documentary history of the First Federal Congress, as well as for the First Federal Elections.

The editor had the unfailing support and sound advice of Oliver W. Holmes, Executive Director of the National Historical Publications Commission until his retirement in February 1972. Dr. Holmes arranged for the transfer of the Ratification project from the National Archives to the University of Wisconsin in 1970 in a way that overcame obstacles and smoothed the transition so that the work of editing could be carried on without a waste of time and energy. To him the editor owes a debt that mere words are inadequate to express. Oliver Holmes's successor, E. Berkeley Tompkins, has continued to give the same understanding and support. Throughout, other members of the Commission staff, and particularly Roger Bruns, H. Bartholomew Cox, Faye Kidd, and Fred Shelley, have cheerfully answered endless queries and located and provided copies of hitherto missing or new documents.

Many acknowledgments are due to others as well. Fred Harvey Harrington, then President of the University of Wisconsin, did much to establish the project at the University—as an administrator by providing funds, and as an historian, by his understanding of the significance of the documents relating to the ratification of the Constitution. Before the materials for Ratification were moved from the National Archives to the University of Wisconsin, John P. Kaminski and Gaspare J. Saladino added to the material and made a notable contribution in organizing them for the move. They are continuing their contribution as associate editors of the Ratification volumes.

Many others have contributed much to the work of searching for and helping to organize the material. Kenneth R. Bowling carried out extensive searches of libraries west of the Appalachian Mountains and in some eastern libraries while he was associated with the First Federal Elections project. Others who have helped in the search for documents—as volunteers while teaching, as graduate students doing research for theses, or as research assistants on the project—are LeGrand Baker, Robert Becker, Steven R. Boyd, Thomas Caulfield, Douglas E. Clanin, Kenneth Coleman, Gordon DenBoer, Joseph A. Ernst, Van Beck Hall, Richard H. Kohn, Richard Leffler, David Maas, and Jerome Nadelhaft.

As important as the search for documents has been the assistance of those who have helped prepare the documents for publication by transcribing them for printer's copy. The editor therefore owes an incalculable debt for the skill and patience of Esther Anken, Virginia Fiedler, Carole Foster, Judy Marberry, Karen Roubicek, Sylvia Sheridan, Ellen Story, Gail Walter, and Joan Westgate who have, at one time or another, engaged in the arduous work of transcription.

Any project such as this requires major financial help. This has been provided by the National Historical Publications Commission and by the University of Wisconsin. The Commission provides funds for staff salaries, for copying of documents, and travel; while the University of Wisconsin provides the editor's salary, office space, equipment, and supplies. In addition, the editor, as Vilas Research Professor of History, is provided with funds for research assistants, books, and travel by the Trustees of the Vilas Estate.

Apart from the many obligations to individuals and to certain institutions, there is a major one to hundreds of libraries and archives in the United States and Europe. The staffs of such libraries have given unstinting help to searchers, have answered letters of enquiry promptly and fully, and have given permission to print documents within their jurisdiction. When required, special permission for the publication of manuscripts has been given freely by individuals, families, and libraries. H. Bartholomew Cox has given permission to print Anthony Wayne's note of debates in the Pennsylvania Convention; the Shippen family to print letters of Dr. William Shippen, Jr., in the Shippen family papers on deposit in the Library of Congress; the Adams Manuscript Trust to print materials from the Adams family papers; and the Pinckney family for permission to print material from the Thomas Pinckney letterbook in the Library of Congress. The Archives Nationales of France has given permission to print the correspondence of French consuls in America contained in Affaires Étrangères, Series B, Correspondance Consulaires. The Archives du Ministère des Affaires Étrangères has given permission to print the dispatches from French diplomatic representatives contained in Correspondance Politique, États-Unis.

In the day-to-day work of editing, the librarians of the University of Wisconsin Memorial Library and of the University of Wisconsin Law School have been invariably helpful. Above all, the library of the State Historical Society of Wisconsin has been indispensable. For more than a century the Society has collected materials concerning the state and local history of all the states, as well as of the United States. As a result the Society library contains an unparalleled collection of nineteenth-century state, county, and town histories, and printed official records. Such local histories and records are invaluable in identifying hundreds of individuals significant during the ratification of the Constitution, and remembered for some decades thereafter, but forgotten today. Furthermore, the Society has one of the major collections of eighteenth-century newspapers, a collection it adds to as such newspapers become available on microfilm or microcard. The Society also purchases microfilm of manuscript collections as they become available. The willingness of the staff of the Society library to help the ratification staff equals the richness of the library in their charge. Our gratitude to the staff is correspondingly great for what they have done in the past and what we are confident they will do in the future as the publication of the documents concerning the ratification of the Constitution continues.

Finally, a word should be said about the members of the editorial board. They have done far more than lend their names. They are working members who have provided encouragement, answered questions, and given advice based on a wide range of knowledge and experience. Most valuable of all, they have been forthright in criticizing editorial plans and policies. The editor therefore owes a debt of gratitude beyond measure to Whitfield J. Bell, Jr., Librarian of the American Philosophical Society; Julian P. Boyd, editor of *The Papers of Thomas Jefferson;* Justice William J. Brennan, Jr., of the United States Supreme Court; Lyman H. Butterfield, editor of *The Adams Papers;* Judge Edward Dumbauld of the United States District Court: District of Western Pennsylvania; Oliver W. Holmes, former Executive Director of the National Historical Publications Commission; and James Morton Smith, Director of the State Historical Society of Wisconsin.

MERRILL JENSEN

The Sources

The sources for the history of the writing and ratification of the Constitution are located in hundreds of libraries and archives in the United States and in Europe, although the bulk of them are found in such institutions as the National Archives of the United States, the Library of Congress, and state archives and historical societies.

Despite the wealth of sources, the significance of the Constitution, and the ongoing debate about its interpretation, the publication of documents concerning its writing and ratification has been slow and remains incomplete today. The Journals and papers of the Constitutional Convention were not published until 1819, when Secretary of State John Quincy Adams, in conformity with a congressional resolution of the previous year, edited and published them as *Journal, Acts and Proceedings, of the Convention . . . Which Formed the Constitution of the United States* (Boston, Mass., 1819).

The Journals of the Convention provide only a bare, incomplete outline, and, most of the Convention's "loose papers" were destroyed by Secretary William Jackson before he delivered the Journals and a few papers to George Washington the evening of the last day of the Constitutional Convention. These records are now in the National Archives in Record Group 360: "Records of the Continental and Confederation Congresses and the Constitutional Convention." They are available on a single roll of microfilm (M-866), described in a pamphlet, *Records of the Constitutional Convention of 1787* (Washington, D.C., 1972).

The notes of debates kept by members of the Convention are essential for an understanding of its work. The first such notes, published two years after the Journals, were those of Robert Yates of New York *(Secret Proceedings and Debates of the Convention Assembled at Philadelphia in the year 1787 . . .* [Albany, N.Y., 1821]). Yates's notes report the debates only to 10 July, when he left the Convention because he opposed the direction it was taking.

Nineteen years elapsed between the publication of Yates's notes and the one indispensable source for the debates in the Convention— the voluminous notes taken by James Madison. Madison refused to allow anyone to see his notes during his lifetime. He usually told those who appealed to him for information that they should study the debates in the state conventions for an understanding of the meaning of the Constitution. Madison's notes and other papers were finally published four years after his death in 1836 (Henry D. Gilpin, ed., *The Papers of James Madison* . . . [3 vols., Washington, D.C., 1840–1841]).

Forty-two years elapsed between the publication of Madison's notes and the next important publication: George Bancroft's history of the Constitution. Half of the two volumes consist of contemporary letters and other documents, some of which had never been published before or were not readily available (*History of the Formation of the Constitution of the United States of America* [2 vols., New York, N.Y., 1882]).

In 1894 the Department of State began the publication of what was, up to then, the fullest documentary record of the history of the Constitution (*Documentary History of the Constitution of the United States of America 1786–1870* . . . [5 vols., Washington, D.C., 1894–1905]). The *Documentary History*, compiled from the records and manuscripts then in the Bureau of Rolls and Library of the Department of State, is divided into three groups: (1) official records such as the Journals and papers of the Constitutional Convention, the Journals of the Confederation Congress, and the state ratification certificates; (2) James Madison's notes of debates in the Constitutional Convention; and (3) contemporary letters and papers relating to the Constitution from December 1785 to January 1834.

The most complete record of the Convention is contained in Max Farrand, *The Records of the Federal Convention* (3 vols., New Haven, Conn., 1911). These volumes were reprinted in 1937 with a fourth volume of additional material and a general index. The first two volumes of the *Records* contain the Journals and papers of the Convention and the notes of debates taken by various delegates, which are placed after the Journal entry for each day. The third and fourth volumes contain variant texts of the plans submitted to the Convention, credentials of the delegates, and contemporary papers, letters, and newspaper items relating to the Constitution.

Since its publication, Farrand's *Records* has been the standard source for the proceedings of the Convention. The only significant addition to the material in the *Records* has been the publication of the notes of John Lansing, Jr., a New York delegate, who left the Convention with Robert Yates on 10 July (Joseph R. Strayer, ed., *The Delegate from New York* . . . [Princeton, N.J., 1939]).

The Congress under the first constitution of the United States, the

Articles of Confederation, played a pivotal role in constitution-making and revision from 1776 to 1787, and in the establishment of the new government under the Constitution. On 21 February 1787 Congress called the Convention to meet, and on 20 September it received the Constitution from the Convention. After a three-day debate, Congress transmitted the Constitution to the states on 28 September 1787. In July 1788, after Congress received official word that nine states had ratified the Constitution, it began a debate which lasted until 13 September 1788. On that date Congress adopted an ordinance setting the time for the election of presidential Electors, the time for the new government to meet, and the place where it was to meet.

The records of Congress from 1774 to 1789 are therefore essential for the history of constitution-making. The "Papers of the Continental Congress" are now in the National Archives in Record Group 360: "Records of the Continental and Confederation Congresses and the Constitutional Convention."

The basic records are the rough manuscript Journals of Congress. The Journals, however, are incomplete and need to be supplemented with the drafts of motions made in Congress, reports of committees, resolve books, dispatch books, and the letterbooks of the President and of the Secretary of Congress. The National Archives has microfilmed the "Papers" on 204 reels of film (M-247), described in a pamphlet, *Papers of the Continental Congress 1774–1789* (Washington, D.C., 1971). Nine additional reels of miscellaneous papers (M-323) are described in a pamphlet, *Miscellaneous Papers of the Continental Congress 1774–89* (Washington, D.C., 1962). The National Archives now has underway a massive index of the "Papers" which will, for the first time, make the wealth of material in them accessible.

Meanwhile, very little of the material in the "Papers," except for the Journals, has ever been published. Congress published its Journals from time to time between 1774 and 1789, but with many gaps and omissions. It was not until 1904 that the Library of Congress began the publication of a complete edition of the Journals, a task completed in 1937 (W.C. Ford, et al., eds., *Journals of the Continental Congress, 1774–1789* [34 vols., Washington, D.C., 1904–1937]).

The incomplete and often ambiguous record of the *Journals* is supplemented and amplified by Edmund C. Burnett's edition of the letters of the members of Congress between 1774 and 1789 (*Letters of Members of the Continental Congress* [8 vols., Washington, D.C., 1921–1936]). Since the completion of his edition, many additional letters have been located. The Library of Congress is now preparing a new edition of the letters of members of Congress which may extend to twenty volumes.

The states were the final arbiters whose decisions would either reject the work of the Constitutional Convention or establish the Constitution as the framework of a new government for the United States. Most of the records of state legislatures, state executives and administrative bodies, town and county governments, and state conventions are located in state and local archives. Such documents provide the essential framework for the history of ratification. They indicate how and when the state governments received the Constitution from the Confederation Congress, how and when the several governmental bodies in the states acted upon it, and how and when the state conventions ratified the Constitution.

The records of state legislatures consist of journals, debates, legislative papers, and acts and resolves. These legislative records are relatively complete, sometimes in both manuscript and printed form. However, the clerks of state legislatures differed greatly in keeping journals. The journals of the Pennsylvania General Assembly, for example, are very full, while those of the Connecticut General Assembly contain only a mere outline. However, even the most detailed journals are incomplete and do not always contain precise data such as roll calls, or even exact records of motions and resolutions.

The journals are supplemented in some states by reports of legislative debates. During the Confederation Period, legislatures did not employ official reporters but occasionally allowed private reporters to take notes. The only complete set of legislative debates are those of the Pennsylvania General Assembly, which were taken and published by Thomas Lloyd, a shorthand reporter. Lloyd's *Debates*, printed in four volumes, cover the four sessions of the Assembly between September 1787 and October 1788. Some newspapers reported legislative debates concerning the calling of state conventions. Examples of such reports are in the Philadelphia *Pennsylvania Herald*, 29 September and 2 October 1787, for the debates in the Pennsylvania General Assembly on 28 and 29 September; and in the Charleston *City Gazette* between 15 January and 1 February 1788 for debates in the South Carolina House of Representatives on 14, 16, 17, 18, and 19 January 1788. The latter were also published separately.

Loose legislative papers supplement the legislative journals. They consist of drafts of bills and resolutions and the various actions taken upon them. Committee reports are sometimes attached to these drafts. Some legislative papers also contain congressional and executive communications about the Constitution and petitions for or against it. There are extensive collections of such papers for Massachusetts, Virginia, and North Carolina.

Engrossed manuscripts of legislative acts and resolves, or contemporary printed versions of them, still exist for most of the states. Legislatures usually ordered their acts published; and, in special cases, such as legislation calling the state conventions, the acts or resolves were often printed as broadsides for public distribution.

Only a few states have kept records of executive and administrative actions. The most complete collections are those for Pennsylvania, Virginia, and North Carolina. The incoming and outgoing correspondence of the governors of Virginia and North Carolina is very full, as are the executive council journals of Pennsylvania and Virginia.

Town and county records are another group of official documents. The most complete local records are those of New England towns. For the most part, the minutes of town meetings give only the names of delegates elected to the state conventions, although occasionally the minutes contain information about a town's position on the Constitution, or instructions to its delegates. The most complete town records are those for Rhode Island. Several times between 1787 and 1790 the towns instructed their deputies to the General Assembly and to the state Convention on matters concerning the Constitution. For example, on 24 March 1788 Rhode Island held a referendum on the Constitution, and the votes and names of the voters for all but three of the thirty towns are extant. In some states, town and county meeings enabled the inhabitants to express their opinions on the Constitution. The reports of such meetings are often found in newspapers or in legislative papers in the form of petitions.

The records of the state conventions, like those of the legislatures, vary in extent and completeness. Except for Connecticut and Maryland, each convention kept a journal, and some were published at the time. The most detailed journals are those of the Massachusetts, New York, Pennsylvania, Virginia, and the first North Carolina conventions, while those for New Jersey and Georgia contain little information. Even the most detailed journals, however, provide only partial accounts of ratification.

Private reporters took notes of debates in several state conventions. The fullest newspaper reports are those of the Massachusetts Convention in the Boston *Independent Chronicle* and the Boston *Massachusetts Centinel,* which were later published separately. Francis Childs printed the debates of the New York Convention in his *Daily Advertiser,* although his reports for the second half of the Convention are less complete than those for the first half. Later he published the debates in book form. Alexander J. Dallas published very full notes of the Pennsylvania Convention debates of 27, 28, and 30 November in the *Pennsylvania Herald,* but political pressure stopped the publication of the debates that took place between 1 December and the end of the Convention. Thomas Lloyd printed speeches of Federalists James Wilson and Thomas McKean in one volume but did not report any Antifederalist speeches. The most complete debates, intended specifically for publication, are those of the Virginia and of the first North Carolina conventions, both taken by David Robertson.

In 1827 Jonathan Elliot began reprinting these contemporary printed debates and some additional material, such as the Journals of the Constitutional Convention. The second edition in 1836, entitled *The Debates in the Several State Conventions, on the Adoption of the Federal Constitution* . . . (4 vols., Washington, D.C.), was later reprinted with additional material. The work has remained, with a few exceptions, the principal source for the history of the ratification of the Constitution, despite the fact that it contains only a small percentage of the relevant material.

The notes taken by members of conventions often contain material not found in either the journals or the reports of debates. The notes of James Wilson, Anthony Wayne, and Jasper Yeates in the Pennsylvania Convention; Gilbert Livingston, Melancton Smith, John McKesson, Richard Harison, Robert R. Livingston, and Alexander Hamilton in the New York Convention; William Cushing in the Massachusetts Convention; and Theodore Foster in the Rhode Island Convention contain significant information.

Loose convention papers also fill some gaps. They consist largely of election certificates and drafts of motions and resolutions. Relatively complete sets of election certificates exist for the Massachusetts, New Hampshire, Virginia, and the two North Carolina conventions. The papers of the Virginia and first North Carolina conventions have material on disputed elections and records containing the per diem and travel expenses of each delegate.

Perhaps the most valuable set of convention papers are those for New York, which its clerk, John McKesson, kept among his own papers. In addition to his notes of debates, these papers include the rough manuscript journal of proceedings, drafts of motions and resolutions, drafts of proposed amendments to the Constitution, the manuscript of the report of the committee of the whole on 25 July 1788, and drafts of the New York Circular Letter of 26 July.

A large proportion of the official state material described above is in the microfilm collection entitled "Records of the States of the United States of America." It was brought together by William S. Jenkins under the auspices of the Library of Congress. The documents are described in William S. Jenkins and Lillian A. Hamrick, *A Guide to the Microfilm Collection of Early State Records* (Washington, D.C., 1950) and *Supplement* (1951). Since Jenkins did not film all state records, and usually copied contemporary printed versions rather than the manuscript versions, the archives of the thirteen original states have been searched for material not contained in the "Early State Records" microfilms. Official material has also been located in libraries, historical societies, newspapers, and printed histories.

The official sources, although they form the framework for the history of ratification, tell only part of the story. Hence the letters, notes, and diaries of contemporaries are indispensable. They reveal the writers' private thoughts about the nature of the Constitution, the prospects for ratification, and the characters of the individuals involved. To emphasize only the subjective aspects of letters and diaries would be a mistake, however, because they also contain information about events and people not obtainable elsewhere.

No documentary history of the ratification of the Constitution would be complete without James Madison's correspondence. On the same level of importance is the correspondence of George Washington, who was kept informed by prominent persons in every part of the Union. Other useful collections are the papers of John Adams, Jeremy Belknap, Tench Coxe, William Ellery, Alexander Hamilton, John Jay, Thomas Jefferson, Rufus King, Henry Knox, John Lamb, Richard Henry Lee, Benjamin Lincoln, George Mason, Benjamin Rush, and George Thacher.

The private correspondence relating to ratification in the several states varies greatly in terms of completeness and value. Among the most important collections are those for Massachusetts, Virginia, and New York, which are especially full during the meetings of the conventions in those states. The collection of letters for New York, although sparse for September–December 1787, is very extensive for 1788. There is extensive and informative private correspondence for North Carolina and Rhode Island, the states that ratified last. Pennsylvania, a state with voluminous official sources and printed material, has relatively little private correspondence describing the intense political activity from 17 September through December 1787. Other states for which there is little private correspondence are Delaware, Georgia, and New Jersey.

Although the official and private sources bulk large, they are slight compared to the volume of printed material. At one time or another between 17 September 1787 and the end of 1790, about 150 newspapers and magazines were published in the United States. Other printers specialized in books, pamphlets, and broadsides. Most newspapers were weeklies, but there was an increasing number of semiweekly, triweekly, and even daily papers. The printers were adept at distributing newspapers by various means, and they borrowed heavily from one another, so much so that certain news items and articles were reprinted by dozens of newspapers.

At least sixty-one of the eighty newspapers published in September and October 1787 printed the full text of the Constitution, and some printers issued it in broadside and pamphlet form. The newspapers also printed items about the course of ratification and the proceedings of legislative and executive bodies, local governments, town and county meetings, and state conventions.

In addition, newspapers published hundreds of items of varying length supporting or opposing the Constitution; praising or attacking the principal leaders on both sides of the question; and speculating about the attitude of the public toward the Constitution and the prospects of ratification. They printed statements of constitutional principles written by prominent advocates and opponents of the Constitution. Occasionally they also published the personal letters of political leaders. Furthermore, newspapers contained editorials, usually in the form of "letters to the editor."

The newspapers are therefore a significant source for the history of ratification, and Clarence S. Brigham has provided the basic guide to them. His *History and Bibliography of American Newspapers 1690–1820* (2 vols., Worcester, Mass., 1947) is supplemented by his "Additions and Corrections to *History and Bibliography of American Newspapers 1690–1820*," *Proceedings* of the American Antiquarian Society, LXXI, Part I (1961), 15–62.

The appearance of the Constitution was followed by the publication of a remarkable number of pamphlets attacking and defending the Constitution. Some pamphlets were original treatises about the merits or defects of the Constitution and the effect that ratification might have. Other pamphlets were anthologies of propaganda pieces previously published in newspapers. *The Federalist Papers* were printed first in newspapers, then in one volume, and finally in two volumes. Other essays were first published in pamphlet form and then reprinted in newspapers. A few pamphlets and books were reprints of works published before 17 September 1787 which were thought to be relevant to the principal constitutional issues under discussion.

Broadsides were also used during the ratification debates. Some broadsides were reprints of newspaper essays, while others, especially those in New York, presented the political platforms of the parties battling over the Constitution. Official proceedings, such as the Constitution, the resolutions of Congress and the state legislatures, the state conventions' certificates of ratification, slates of candidates, and executive proclamations, were also printed as broadsides to insure wide circulation.

Advocates and opponents of the Constitution often favored pamphlets and broadsides because they were easier to distribute than newspapers. Consequently, many thousands of copies of pamphlets and broadsides were printed in 1787 and 1788. For example, a total of four thousand copies, in four separate printings, of the first installment of the *Letters from the Federal Farmer to the Republican* were printed and distributed by the Antifederalists.

The wealth of material in contemporary printed sources, aside from newspapers, is recorded in Charles Evans, *American Bibliography* (12 vols., Chicago, Ill., 1903–1934) and Roger P. Bristol, *Supplement to Charles Evans' American Bibliography* (Charlottesville, Va., 1970). Evans' listings have been corrected; much new material has been added and is now available on microcard in Clifford K. Shipton, ed., *Early American Imprints, 1639–1800* (Worcester, Mass., 1955–1964) and *Early American Imprints, 1639–1800. Supplement* (Worcester, Mass., 1966———). This material is indexed in Clifford K. Shipton and James E. Mooney, eds., *National Index of American Imprints Through 1800: The Short-Title Evans* (2 vols., [Worcester, Mass.], 1969).

No search, especially for manuscripts, is ever completed since hitherto unknown manuscripts continue to appear from time to time. Conversely, over the years, manuscripts have been lost or sold to private collectors. Manuscripts obtained by collectors often do not reappear until they are either given to libraries or listed in auction catalogues when collectors or their heirs offer them for sale. Fortunately, many documents that have been lost or are now unavailable were published years ago in biographies, genealogies, state and local histories, monographs, auction catalogues, and printed collections of letters and other documents.

Such, then, are the many sources from which this documentary history has been constructed. The introduction to ratification in each state contains a detailed discussion of the official sources, private manuscripts, and printed sources for the state. It is impossible, of course, to print all of the material acquired, but its acquisition has made possible the editing in depth, and with a precision otherwise impossible, of the documents relating directly to the ratification of the Constitution by the thirteen states.

Organization

The Documentary History of the Ratification of the Constitution is divided into four groups of documents: (1) *Constitutional Documents and Records, 1776–1787;* (2) *Ratification of the Constitution by the States;* (3) *Commentaries on the Constitution: Public and Private;* (4) *Amendments to the Constitution: From Ratification by the States to the Proposal of a Bill of Rights by Congress.* Each of these groups is interrelated, and cross-references are made from group to group.

Constitutional Documents and Records, 1776–1787

This introductory volume to *The Documentary History of the Ratification of the Constitution* consists of constitutional documents and records from 1776 to 1787, beginning with the Declaration of Independence and concluding with documents describing the transmittal of the Constitution to the states by the Confederation Congress on 28 September 1787. The documents are arranged in chronological order within the following sections: (1) The Declaration of Independence; (2) The Articles of Confederation; (3) Ratification of the Articles of Confederation by the States in Congress; (4) Amendments to the Articles of Confederation, Grants of Power to Congress, and Ordinances for the Western Territory; (5) The Calling of the Constitutional Convention; (6) Appointment of Delegates to the Constitutional Convention; (7) The Resolutions and Draft Constitutions of the Constitutional Convention; (8) The Report of the Constitutional Convention; and (9) The Confederation Congress and the Constitution.

Ratification of the Constitution by the States

The documents relating to *Ratification of the Constitution by the States* are arranged as follows: (1) Pennsylvania; (2) Delaware; (3) New Jersey; (4) Georgia; (5) Connecticut; (6) Massachusetts; (7) First Session of the New Hampshire Convention; (8) Rhode Island Referendum; (9) Maryland; (10) South Carolina; (11) Second Session of the New Hampshire Convention; (12) Virginia; (13) New York; (14) First North Carolina Convention; (15) Second North Carolina Convention; (16) Rhode Island Convention.

With three exceptions, the states are placed in the order in which they ratified the Constitution. Pennsylvania is placed first, although Delaware ratified on 7 December, five days before Pennsylvania. The Pennsylvania Assembly was the first state legislature to receive the Constitution and to call a convention, and the means used to call it attracted nationwide attention. Furthermore, the Philadelphia press was for some time the principal source of material for the public debate on the Constitution.

The second exception is the placement of the first session of the New Hampshire Convention (13–22 February 1788) after Massachusetts, which ratified the Constitution on 6 February. The third exception is the popular referendum on the Constitution in Rhode Island on 24 March 1788, which is placed after the first session of the New Hampshire Convention. Thereafter, the states are arranged in the order in which their conventions ratified the Constitution.

The arrangement of documents in the order in which important events occurred is a more meaningful chronological order than one arbitrarily determined by the dates of ratification.

The documents for each state are arranged in the following order: (1) from the receipt of the Constitution after 17 September 1787 to the meeting of the state legislature which called the state convention; (2) the proceedings of the state legislature in calling the state convention; (3) from the legislature's call of the convention to the meeting of the convention; (4) the proceedings of the state convention day by day; (5) official letters transmitting the act of ratification to the Confederation Congress and to other states; and (6) post-convention documents.

Since the history of the ratification of the Constitution by each state is unique, the organization outlined above varies somewhat from state to state.

Ratification of the Constitution by the States: Microform Supplements

Much of the material for each state is repetitious or peripheral and is placed in microform supplements to the volumes of *Ratification of the Constitution by the States*. The documents in these supplements consist of consecutively numbered items arranged, for the most part, in chronological order.

The following is a list of the types of documents included in the microform supplements:

(1) Photographic copies of manuscripts such as notes of debates.

(2) Transcripts of certain letters which contain peripheral information about politics and social relationships.

(3) Newspaper items consisting of ongoing debates that repeat arguments, examples of which are printed in the volumes relating to ratification.

(4) Photographic copies of petitions with the names of signers.

(5) Pamphlets that circulated primarily within one state and which are not printed in either *Ratification of the Constitution by the States* or in *Commentaries on the Constitution.*

(6) Miscellaneous documents such as town records, election certificates, pay vouchers and financial records, attendance records, "recollections" of past events, etc.

Commentaries on the Constitution: Public and Private

The public debate and private commentary about a new government began before the Constitutional Convention met in the spring of 1787, continued during the Convention, and intensified after the Constitution was published in September 1787. The various forms of the public debate—newspapers, pamphlets, and broadsides which circulated in more than one state and throughout the nation—were read and referred to by men in and out of legislatures and conventions. Thus the Constitution was debated on a regional and on the national level as well as within each state. The purpose of these volumes is to place the ratification of the Constitution in this broad context.

These volumes also contain certain private letters. Most private letters were concerned with ratification in particular states and have been placed in *Ratification of the Constitution by the States.* However, other private letters were published and widely debated, gave mens' opinions of the Constitution in general, contained reports of ratification in more than one state, or discussed the means of securing or preventing ratification of the Constitution with or without amendments. Such documents, public and private, are an essential matrix of the history of ratification.

The documents are arranged in chronological order and are numbered consecutively throughout the volumes. A few of these documents are also printed in *Ratification of the Constitution by the States* because of their significance in the state of origin.

Amendments to the Constitution: From Ratification by the States to the Proposal of a Bill of Rights by Congress

The purpose of this selected group of documents is to bridge the gap between the ratification of the Constitution in each state and the proposal of a bill of rights in Congress on 8 June 1789. There is a basic continuity because the debate over the Constitution continued as actively in several states after ratification as it did before and during the state conventions. The debate centered upon the issue of amendments to the Constitution, and if amendments were needed, whether they should be proposed by a second constitutional convention or by the first Congress under the Constitution. These documents therefore provide the essential background for an understanding of the twelve amendments proposed by Congress on 26 September 1789.

This group of documents consists of materials in the following categories: (1) amendments adopted or rejected by state conventions; (2) amendments proposed by individuals and groups after the state conventions; (3) calls for a second constitutional convention; (4) the responses of state legislatures to calls for a second constitutional convention; (5) documents illustrating individual and group attitudes toward the Constitution after ratification; (6) examples of the continuing newspaper and pamphlet debate on the Constitution after ratification; (7) the role of the Confederation Congress in establishing the new government by setting the date for the first federal elections and the place for the first meeting of the government under the Constitution; (8) the first federal elections; (9) the debate over amendments in the first Congress under the Constitution; (10) the amendments proposed in and rejected by Congress; (11) the twelve amendments submitted to the states for consideration.

Editorial Procedures

Literal Reproduction of Official Documents

Official documents such as the Constitution, resolutions of the Confederation Congress, state acts calling conventions, forms of ratification, and proclamations are reproduced as literally as possible. A few other documents, because of their character or importance, are also reproduced as literally as possible. The literal reproduction of such documents is indicated by the symbol "LT" (i.e., literal transcript) in the footnote citation to the source.

Reproduction of Newspaper, Pamphlet, and Broadside Material

Eighteenth century printers sometimes used several varieties of type in a single item—large capitals, small capitals, and italics, as well as ordinary type. No attempt is made to reproduce varieties of type except when capital letters and italics were evidently used for emphasis by the author or the printer. In a few cases we have reproduced, so far as possible, the format of newspaper items.

Newspaper items are usually printed as separate documents, but occasionally more than one item from a single issue is printed under the title and date of the newspaper. In such cases the items are separated by asterisks.

Notes by Contemporaries

Contemporary footnotes and marginal notes are printed as footnotes after the document and immediately preceding editorial footnotes. Eighteenth-century symbols, such as asterisks, daggers, double daggers, etc., have been replaced by letters ("a," "b," "c," etc.), while Arabic numbers are used for editorial footnotes. Notes inserted in the text by authors remain in the text and are enclosed in parentheses.

Salutations, Closings, etc., of Letters

Endorsements, addresses, salutations, and complimentary closings of letters are omitted, except in cases where they provide information important for the understanding or identification of a letter. In such cases they are included in the editorial notes.

43

Excerpts and Elisions

Many documents, particularly letters, contain material such as family news, business affairs, and the like, which is not relevant to ratification. Hence, such material has been omitted. However, when longer excerpts or entire documents have been printed elsewhere, or are included in the microform supplements, this fact is noted.

Headings for Documents

All headings are supplied by the editors. They are as follows:

(1) Letters: Headings include the names of the writer and the recipient, and the place and date of writing.

(2) Newspaper essays, broadsides, and pamphlets: Headings are usually shortened versions of the full titles, which are given in editorial notes.

(3) Pseudonymous essays: Headings contain the pseudonym, title or short title, and the source if printed in a newspaper. Information and conjectures about the authors of such essays and full titles are placed in editorial notes.

(4) Untitled newspaper items: Headings consist of the short title of the newspaper and the date.

(5) Reports of public meetings: Headings consist of the name and date of such meetings with the source given in editorial notes.

Capitalization, Punctuation, and Italics in Manuscript Materials

Capital letters are used to begin each sentence. Random capitals and italics are removed except when they are evidently used by the author for emphasis. Periods are placed at the ends of sentences instead of dashes, colons, or no punctuation at all. Punctuation is altered within sentences if needed to clarify meaning.

Spelling

With one exception, spelling is made to conform to present-day practice. For example, "labour" and "foederal" are spelled "labor" and "federal." The exception to this rule is the spelling of names of individuals. While it is easy enough to correct the spelling of the names of a "Madison" or a "Washington," there are hundreds of legislators and other men whose names are spelled in various ways in document after document, and sometimes in the same document. The editors therefore follow the practice of the editors of such modern publications as the papers of Thomas Jefferson, John Adams, and Benjamin Franklin, who print the names as they are spelled in each document.

Abbreviations, Contractions, Superscripts, Numbers, Crossed-out Words, and Blank Spaces

Abbreviations such as those for place names ("Phila." for Philadelphia, for example) and military titles are spelled out. Contractions such as "can't," "tis," and "altho" are retained. Superscripts are lowered to the line. Archaic forms such as "yt" and "ye" are spelled out, "&c." is printed "etc.," and "&" is printed "and." Numbers are printed as they appear in the documents. Crossed-out words in documents, if they are significant, are placed in editorial notes. Otherwise they are not reproduced. Spaces intentionally left blank in documents are indicated by an underline.

Brackets

Brackets are used for the following purposes:
(1) Editorial insertions are enclosed in brackets: [Amendment].
(2) Conjectural readings are enclosed in brackets and followed by a question mark: [Amendment?].
(3) Illegible and missing words are indicated by dashes enclosed in brackets: [———].

Legislative Proceedings

The actions of state legislatures relating to ratification are printed under the headings "House Proceedings," "Senate Proceedings," or whatever the name of the "upper" or "lower" house may be, and are followed by the day and date. These proceedings consist primarily of excerpts from the journals of state legislatures but are supplemented by other sources.

When both houses acted on the same day, their actions are placed under the heading: "House and Senate Proceedings." In such cases the proceedings are arranged in the order of action by the two houses so that the progress of a report, a resolution, or a bill through the two houses can be followed in the order in which it occurred.

Messages, resolutions, and reports adopted by one house and sent to the other were often copied in the journals of the house to which they were sent. To avoid duplication in such cases, editorial notes enclosed in brackets are placed at appropriate places in the journals.

No attempt has been made to reproduce literally the *form* of printed or manuscript journals. Lists of names of members of committees, for example, which appear in column form, are printed as paragraphs, and each motion and resolution is set off as a paragraph.

When the first names of men making speeches or motions are not given, they are inserted without using brackets. The full names of speakers are set in italics. When a member is referred to in a general manner, the name is inserted in the proper place in brackets (i.e., "the member from Fayette [John Smilie] said").

We have included in the House and Senate proceedings only those actions relating to ratification. But it should be remembered that the legislatures which called state conventions also carried on their regular business during the same sessions, and usually spent far more time on such business than they did on ratification.

Convention Proceedings

The nature of the sources for the proceedings of state conventions varies from state to state, and sometimes from day to day within a state. In this *Documentary History* the proceedings of a convention, with some exceptions, are printed in the following order:

(1) Official convention journals.

(2) Accounts of convention debates by reporters.

(3) Notes of debates and proceedings by convention members (arranged alphabetically).

(4) Public and private commentaries on a day's proceedings.

In printing the convention journals and debates, the editorial procedures used in printing legislative journals and debates are followed, with some exceptions arising from the nature of the sources.

Cross-references

(1) Each volume of *The Documentary History of the Ratification of the Constitution* is divided into sections indicated by Roman numerals and subsections indicated by capital letters. Cross-references to documents within a single volume are indicated by the Roman numeral and the capital letter. For example: "II:B above," "III:C below," etc.

(2) Cross-references to documents in the first volume of *The Documentary History*, subtitled *Constitutional Documents and Records, 1776–1787*, are indicated by "CDR" followed by the relevant Roman numeral and capital letter. For example: "CDR:II, C."

(3) Cross-references to volumes in *The Documentary History*, subtitled *Ratification of the Constitution by the States*, are indicated by "RCS" followed by the abbreviation of the name of the state. For example: "RCS:Pa."

(4) Cross-references to documents in the microform supplements to *Ratification of the Constitution by the States* are indicated by "Mfm" followed by the abbreviation for the name of the state and the number of the document. For example: "Mfm:Pa. 36."

(5) Cross-references to documents in *Commentaries on the Constitution: Public and Private* are indicated by "CC" followed by the number of the document. For example: "CC:25."

References to Reprinting of Newspaper Items

Many items printed in a state's newspaper were reprinted by other newspapers in the same state and by newspapers in other states. When such reprinting appears significant, the distribution will be indicated in editorial notes.

American Newspapers, 1787–1790

Short Title List

The following short titles of selected newspapers, arranged alphabetically, are those used in editorial notes. The full titles and other information about all the newspapers of the period are contained in Clarence S. Brigham, *History and Bibliography of American Newspapers 1690–1820* (2 vols., Worcester, Mass., 1947), and in his "Additions and Corrections to *History and Bibliography of American Newspapers 1690–1820*," *Proceedings* of the American Antiquarian Society, LXXI, Part I (1961), 15–62. The notes on sources for each state in the volumes of *Ratification of the Constitution by the States* discuss a state's newspapers in more detail.

Albany Gazette, Albany, N.Y.

Albany Journal, Albany, N.Y.

American Herald, Boston, Mass. (Worcester, Mass., as of 21 August 1788)

American Mercury, Hartford, Conn.

Berkshire Chronicle, Pittsfield, Mass.

Boston Gazette, Boston, Mass.

Brunswick Gazette, New Brunswick, N.J.

Carlisle Gazette, Carlisle, Pa.

City Gazette, Charleston, S.C.

Columbian Herald, Charleston, S.C.

Connecticut Courant, Hartford, Conn.

Connecticut Gazette, New London, Conn.

Connecticut Journal, New Haven, Conn.

Country Journal, Poughkeepsie, N.Y.

Cumberland Gazette, Portland, Me.

Daily Advertiser, New York, N.Y.

Delaware Gazette, Wilmington, Del.

Essex Journal, Newburyport, Mass.

Evening Chronicle, Philadelphia, Pa.

Fairfield Gazette, Fairfield, Conn.

Fayetteville Gazette, Fayetteville, N.C.

Federal Gazette, Philadelphia, Pa.

Freeman's Journal, Philadelphia, Pa.

Freeman's Oracle, Exeter, N.H.

Gazette of the State of Georgia, Savannah, Ga.

Gazette of the United States, New York, N.Y.

Georgia State Gazette, Augusta, Ga.

Germantauner Zeitung, Germantown, Pa.

Hampshire Chronicle, Springfield, Mass.

Hampshire Gazette, Northampton, Mass.

Herald of Freedom, Boston, Mass.

Hudson Weekly Gazette, Hudson, N.Y.

Impartial Gazetteer, New York, N.Y. (*New York Weekly Museum* as of 20 September 1788)

Independent Chronicle, Boston, Mass.

Independent Gazetteer, Philadelphia, Pa.

Independent Journal, New York, N.Y. (*New York Daily Gazette* as of 29 December 1788)

Kentucke Gazette, Lexington, Ky.

Lancaster Zeitung, Lancaster, Pa.

Maryland Chronicle, Fredericktown, Md.

Maryland Gazette, Annapolis, Md.

Maryland Gazette, Baltimore, Md.

Maryland Journal, Baltimore, Md.

Massachusetts Centinel, Boston, Mass.

Massachusetts Gazette, Boston, Mass.

Massachusetts Spy, Worcester, Mass.

Middlesex Gazette, Middletown, Conn.

New Hampshire Gazette, Portsmouth, N.H.

New Hampshire Mercury, Portsmouth, N.H.

New Hampshire Recorder, Keene, N.H.

New Hampshire Spy, Portsmouth, N.H.

New Haven Chronicle, New Haven, Conn.

New Haven Gazette, New Haven, Conn.

New Jersey Journal, Elizabethtown, N.J.

Newport Herald, Newport, R.I.

Newport Mercury, Newport, R.I.

New York Journal, New York, N.Y.

New York Morning Post, New York, N.Y.

New York Museum, New York, N.Y.

New York Packet, New York, N.Y.

Norfolk and Portsmouth Journal, Norfolk, Va.

Edenton Intelligencer, Edenton, N.C.

North Carolina Gazette, New Bern, N.C.

Northern Centinel, Lansingburgh, N.Y. (*Northern Centinel* to January 1788; Albany *Federal Herald,* 11 February–14 April 1788; Lansingburgh *Federal Herald,* 28 April 1788———.)

Norwich Packet, Norwich, Conn.

Pennsylvania Chronicle, York, Pa.

Pennsylvania Gazette,
Philadelphia, Pa.
Pennsylvania Herald,
Philadelphia, Pa.
Pennsylvania Journal,
Philadelphia, Pa.
Pennsylvania Mercury,
Philadelphia, Pa.
Pennsylvania Packet,
Philadelphia, Pa.
Philadelphische Correspondenz,
Philadelphia, Pa.
Pittsburgh Gazette, Pittsburgh,
Pa.
Providence Gazette, Providence,
R.I.
Salem Mercury, Salem, Mass.
State Gazette of North Carolina,
New Bern, N.C. (Edenton
after August 1788)
State Gazette of South Carolina,
Charleston, S.C.
Trenton Mercury, Trenton, N.J.
United States Chronicle,
Providence, R.I.
Vermont Gazette, Bennington,
Vt.

Vermont Journal, Windsor, Vt.
Virginia Centinel, Winchester,
Va.
Virginia Gazette, Petersburg, Va.
*Virginia Gazette and
Independent Chronicle,*
Richmond, Va.
*Virginia Gazette and Weekly
Advertiser,* Richmond, Va.
Virginia Gazette, Winchester, Pa.
Virginia Herald, Fredericksburg,
Va.
Virginia Independent Chronicle,
Richmond, Va.
Virginia Journal, Alexandria,
Va.
Weekly Monitor, Litchfield,
Conn.
Western Star, Stockbridge, Mass.
Wilmington Centinel,
Wilmington, N.C.
Worcester Magazine, Worcester,
Mass. (April 1786–March
1788)

Constitutional Documents and Records
1776–1787

Introduction

Symbols
for Manuscripts, Manuscript Depositories, Short Titles, and Cross-references

Introduction

Throughout the Revolutionary Era, Americans engaged in a continuous debate about the need for and character of a central government. After 1763 there was mounting opposition, expressed in word and deed, to outside interference within each American colony, and by 1774 some Americans were denying the right and power of a central government—that of Great Britain—to control them in any way. Samuel Adams summed up that attitude the next year when he declared that each legislature "is and ought to be the sovereign and uncontrollable power within its own limits or territory."

At the opposite pole were other Americans who insisted that a central government was indispensable to regulate trade, to control finance, to direct military affairs, to suppress internal rebellions, and to prevent civil war among the colonies over lands and boundaries. This was the essence of Joseph Galloway's arguments in the First Continental Congress in 1774 when he proposed the creation of an American central government within the British Empire. Galloway's basic assumption was that "in every government, patriarchical, monarchical, aristocratical, or democratical, there must be a supreme legislature," and he argued that Americans should either create such a government or concede the necessary power to Parliament.

The opposing positions taken by Americans in the First Continental Congress in 1774 were maintained with remarkable continuity for years thereafter, and by some of the same men. Richard Henry Lee, Patrick Henry, and Samuel Adams opposed Galloway's plan in 1774, and thirteen years later they were leading opponents of the ratification of an unamended Constitution. John Rutledge, Edward Rutledge, James Duane, and John Jay supported Galloway's plan. Thirteen years later they were among the leading supporters of the ratification of the Constitution, and Jay was one of the authors of *The Federalist Papers*, which elaborated upon the issues raised by Galloway in 1774.

All told, ten of the forty-one surviving members of the First Continental Congress were elected to the Constitutional Convention, although Richard Henry Lee, Patrick Henry, and Richard Caswell refused to serve. The seven members of the First Congress who served in the Convention of 1787—John Dickinson, William Livingston,

Thomas Mifflin, George Read, John Rutledge, Roger Sherman, and George Washington—signed the Constitution and supported its ratification. Twenty of the surviving members of the First Congress were elected to the state conventions in 1787–1788, and the majority of them voted to ratify the Constitution.

Between 1774 and early 1776 the issue of a central government was subordinated to that of independence. The supporters of independence urged the creation of a confederation as one means of achieving it, while the opponents of independence opposed a confederation. When independence became inescapable, the latter reversed themselves and argued that a central government should be created before declaring independence.

On 7 June 1776 Richard Henry Lee, who supported independence, combined both issues when he moved that the colonies declare their independence and that Congress appoint a committee to prepare a "plan of confederation." On 12 June Congress elected a committee consisting of one delegate from each colony to prepare a constitution. The draft of articles of confederation, written by John Dickinson, was presented to Congress on 12 July.

Eight of the men who played key roles in the writing of the Articles of Confederation in 1776–1777 were members of the Constitutional Convention ten years later. They were George Clymer, John Dickinson, Benjamin Franklin, Elbridge Gerry, Robert Morris, George Read, Roger Sherman, and James Wilson. An even larger number of men who debated the Articles in 1776–1777 were not members of the Convention, but they were involved in the debate over the ratification of the Constitution. Among them were Samuel Adams, Samuel Chase, Abraham Clark, James Duane, John Hancock, Richard Henry Lee, and Benjamin Rush.

The Dickinson draft raised most of the issues which Americans debated between 1776 and 1787, and afterwards as well. In effect, it proposed the creation of a sovereign central government, for it gave broad powers to Congress and guaranteed very little power to the states. Thus while it provided that each state should retain "as much of its present Laws, Rights and Customs" as it saw fit, and reserve to itself the regulation of its "internal police," the guarantee was followed by a provision that negated its effect. The states were to retain such powers and rights only in "matters that shall not interfere with the Articles of this Confederation." Similar guarantees followed by similar limitations were scattered throughout the Dickinson draft.

The fundamental nature of the draft was at first ignored by Congress because it raised other issues of more immediate concern. One such issue was the balance of power between the large and the small states, an issue debated as heatedly in 1776 as it was in the Convention of 1787. Should each state have an equal vote in Congress or should voting be by population, wealth, amount of contributions to common expenses, or some combination of these?

The Dickinson draft also precipitated a confrontation between the Northern and the Southern states. The draft provided that the expenses of the central government should be apportioned among the states according to total population, except for Indians not paying taxes. Southern delegates argued that expenses should be shared according to white population alone because slaves were wealth and a species of personal property. Throughout the debates on the Articles of Confederation, New Englanders insisted that total population was the best index of wealth, but the Articles, as finally agreed upon, provided that expenses would be shared according to the value of land granted to or surveyed for individuals. New Englanders remained convinced that they would be exploited and that the South would escape payment of taxes on its slaves and its large areas of ungranted and unsurveyed lands.

A second issue raised between the North and the South during the dispute over the apportionment of expenses concerned the treaty-making power. Southern delegates argued that if slaves were to be taxed, so too should the commercial wealth of New England. As Edward Rutledge of South Carolina saw it, the New England States would become "the carriers for the Southern," and Southerners feared that future congresses might try to make commercial treaties granting Northern merchants a monopoly of the carrying trade. Therefore, shortly before the Articles were completed in November 1777, Southern delegates, led by Richard Henry Lee, secured the insertion of a restrictive provision. It forbade Congress to make commercial treaties which would prevent the states from levying the same duties on foreigners that their own citizens paid, or would prevent the states from prohibiting the exportation or importation of any goods whatsoever.

Another divisive issue, one which delayed ratification of the Articles of Confederation until March 1781, concerned the control of western lands. The Dickinson draft gave Congress the power to limit the boundaries of states whose colonial charters granted them land extending to the "South Seas," to fix boundaries of states where they seemed indefinite, and to create new states in the land separated from old states. Five states had definite western boundaries—Pennsylvania, Maryland, New Jersey, Delaware, and Rhode Island—and they supported such power. The states with charter claims extending to the "South Seas," led by Virginia, fought against and eliminated the provision. Furthermore, they added a provision to the Articles guaranteeing that "no State shall be deprived of territory for the benefit of the United States."

The question of the fundamental character of the proposed constitution came before Congress early in 1777 as the result of efforts to establish precedents for the exercise of congressional power over the states and their citizens. James Wilson, John Adams, and others proposed: (1) that Congress approve a convention of the New England States in order to establish the right to disapprove of state actions in the future; (2) that Congress ignore state governments and authorize constables and other state officials to seize deserters from the army; and (3) that Congress approve General Washington's proclamation requiring people who had taken an oath of allegiance to Great Britain to take an oath of allegiance to the United States, thus implying national citizenship.

The attempt to establish precedents was defeated by defenders of state sovereignty such as Samuel Adams, Richard Henry Lee, and Thomas Burke. Furthermore, these men acted positively to insure that the central government would be one of strictly delegated and limited powers. Burke proposed that an article be added declaring that "each State retains its sovereignty, freedom and independence, and every power, jurisdiction, and right, which is not by this confederation expressly delegated to the United States, in Congress assembled." Congress agreed, eleven states to one (Virginia) to what became Article II of the Articles of Confederation. It reversed the intent of the Dickinson draft and guaranteed the creation of a strictly federal government.

James Wilson summed up the significance of the Article when he told the Constitutional Convention in 1787 that "the original draft of Confederation" was based on the idea of Congress as a single state, and "the draft concluded on, how different!" Other American leaders were as aware as Wilson of the significance of Article II of the Confederation. In 1787 and 1788 every state that recommended amendments to the Constitution proposed that the language or the intent of the Article be added to the Constitution in order to limit and define the power of the central government.

After the Articles were submitted to the states in November 1777, various legislatures proposed amendments and suggested changes that reflected the debates during the writing of the Articles. Thus Maryland insisted that all ungranted western lands must be given to Congress and, with Delaware, proposed that Congress have the power to limit the boundaries of states claiming to extend to the "Mississippi or South Sea." Rhode Island, New Jersey, and Delaware proposed that the proceeds arising from the sale of western lands be for the benefit of all the states, although Rhode Island and New Jersey agreed that the states could retain jurisdiction over such lands within their boundaries.

Massachusetts expressed doubts about apportioning expenses according to the value of lands and improvements, and Connecticut proposed that common expenses be apportioned according to total population. Rhode Island urged that the value of land and improvements be established every five years, while South Carolina proposed that it be done every ten years. New Jersey asked for a census every five years as the basis for furnishing troops in wartime. Massachusetts, Pennsylvania, and New Jersey proposed that the quota of troops supplied by each state be based on the total population rather than on white population alone. Connecticut and New Jersey disapproved of standing armies. South Carolina proposed several amendments to guarantee greater state control of any troops raised at the request of Congress. New Jersey was the only state to propose that Congress have the exclusive power to regulate trade and that the money arising therefrom be used to build a navy and fortify the seacoast. South Carolina and Georgia wanted the guarantee of the privileges and immunities of the citizens of one state in any other state to be limited to "free white" inhabitants, not guaranteed to all free inhabitants.

The proposed amendments were rejected by Congress, and by 22 February 1779 all the states except Maryland had ratified the Articles of Confederation. From the beginning, Maryland refused to ratify unless Congress acquired the power to fix the western limits of states with charter claims extending to the "South Seas," and unless Congress recognized Maryland's demand for an equal share to the land "lying westward of the frontiers of the United States. . . ." However, Maryland exempted from her demand those areas which she defined as "the property of individuals" before the war. Maryland thus sought to protect the claims of the pre-war land speculators of the colonies with fixed western boundaries who had established claims within Virginia's charter limits by means of purchases from the Indians. The Virginia legislature responded in the fall of 1778 by declaring all such claims null and void.

Virginia continued to denounce the land speculators, but by the end of 1780 the state was ready to cede some of the territory within her charter limits. On 2 January 1781 the legislature ceded Virginia's claim to the territory northwest of the Ohio River—the "Old Northwest"—to Congress. But certain conditions were attached. At the same time that Virginia was moving toward a cession, Maryland was moving toward ratification of the Articles. Both states were impelled by British military victories in the South during 1780, by financial and

economic difficulties, and by the widespread hope that the final establishment of the Articles of Confederation might be helpful. The
Maryland legislature adopted an act of ratification on 2 February 1781,
and the Maryland delegates in Congress signed the Articles of Confederation on 1 March 1781.

* * * *

The establishment of constitutional government for the United States
in 1781 did not end the debate over the extent of power needed by
Congress to manage the affairs of the nation. Between 1781 and 1787
many individuals and some states suggested additional powers for
Congress, but most of the significant proposals for strengthening the
central government came from Congress itself. Furthermore, Congress
assumed powers and adopted measures that had a fundamental and
lasting impact on the future settlement and growth of the United
States.

Those measures concerned the national domain, the creation of
which was made possible by the Virginia cession of the Old Northwest in January 1781. In creating the national domain, and in
adopting ordinances for its government and the sale of land within
it, Congress exercised power for which there was no constitutional
warrant in the Articles of Confederation, but it was an exercise of
power accepted by political leaders of all shades of opinion. As James
Madison put it in the fall of 1787: "Congress had never scrupled
to recommend measures foreign to their constitutional functions,
whenever the public good seemed to require it; and had in several
instances, particularly in the establishment of the new western governments, exercised assumed powers of a very high and delicate
nature. . . ."

Americans in 1776 recognized that the territory west of the Ap-
palachians would eventually be divided into states, but they were
at odds from the beginning about how to create and to govern them.
The point of view of the states with claims extending beyond the
mountains was expressed in June 1776 by Thomas Jefferson in his
final draft of a constitution for Virginia. He provided that Virginia
would create new western colonies "free and independent of this
colony and of all the world." The point of view of the states with
definite western boundaries was expressed the next month in John
Dickinson's draft of articles of confederation. The draft gave Congress
power to limit the boundaries of states claiming lands to the "South
Seas," and the power to establish the boundaries of new states in the
area "within which Forms of Government are to be established on

the Principles of Liberty." The Articles of Confederation, as adopted, denied Congress such power, but the issue was revived by Maryland's refusal to ratify unless the Articles of Confederation were amended to give Congress control of western lands.

While Virginians were willing to cede some of Virginia's claims, they insisted that Congress must declare void all pre-war purchases from Indians as Virginia had done, while Maryland continued to insist that the land did not belong to Virginia, and that in any case, the pre-war claims must be validated.

In September 1780, in an effort to break the deadlock, Congress voted to ask the states to cede a portion of their western claims for the sake of the Union and asked Maryland to ratify the Articles of Confederation. Congress refused to consider the merits of the rival claims since Congress had declined to discuss them when "the Articles of Confederation were debated. . . ." Virginians then proposed specific policies for the future of the lands to be ceded and Congress agreed. Congress promised the states on 10 October 1780 that any land ceded (1) would be "disposed of for the common benefit of the United States"; (2) would be "settled and formed into distinct republican states, which shall become members of the federal Union, and have the same rights of sovereignty, freedom and independence, as the other states"; and (3) each state would not be "less than one hundred nor more than one hundred and fifty miles square, or as near thereto as circumstances will admit." However, Congress refused to guarantee the remaining claims of the ceding states or to declare invalid purchases from Indians within the areas to be ceded.

On 2 January 1781 the Virginia legislature ceded the territory northwest of the Ohio River to Congress. The legislature's resolutions incorporated the promises of Congress and, in addition, required Congress to void all pre-war purchases from Indians and to guarantee Virginia's territory south of the Ohio River to her.

Three years elapsed between the first Virginia cession in 1781 and the actual establishment of the national domain by the acceptance of the second Virginia cession on 1 March 1784. The delay was the consequence of the conditions attached to Virginia's first cession. That act required Congress, in effect, to nullify the claims of the Indiana Company south of the Ohio River and the Illinois-Wabash Company north of the river.

Powerful Maryland leaders such as Thomas Johnson, Samuel Chase, and Charles Carroll of Carrollton, and equally powerful Pennsylvania leaders such as Robert Morris and James Wilson were members of those companies, and they fought in Congress and out to prevent the acceptance of the Virginia cession with the conditions attached.

Land speculators argued that sovereignty over the West had "de-volved" from the British government upon Congress and that Virginia had no valid claim. James Wilson, as president of the Illinois-Wabash Company, was only one of the members of Congress who supported the speculators. The Virginians countered by demanding that each member of Congress declare his connection with the land companies whenever the Virginia cession came before Congress.

The end of the war in 1783 produced a change. Congress needed the money to be acquired from the sale of western lands; Virginia was selling land in the West; and people were settling on the land without paying anyone for it. The deadlock was broken on 13 September 1783. Congress adopted a report on the Virginia cession of 1781, which, James Madison said, "tacitly" excluded the claims of the land companies. Congress requested a new cession, and on 20 December 1783 the Virginia legislature ceded the Old Northwest to Congress a second time. The act embodied the general principles for the government of the West and its division into states, which Congress had promised on 10 October 1780 and reiterated on 13 September 1783.

Congress accepted the cession on 1 March 1784 and on 23 April adopted a plan for the government of the national domain. Thomas Jefferson was the chief architect of the ordinance, the broad outlines for which were established in October 1780 and made mandatory by the Virginia cession. The Ordinance divided the national domain into ten districts and provided for self-government by the people within them. The people were to create temporary governments, and whenever the population of a district equalled that of the smallest of the original thirteen states, the district was to be admitted to the Union as a state and as an equal partner of the original states.

On 20 May 1785 Congress adopted an ordinance for the survey of the Western Territory and the sale of the land surveyed. The Ordinance divided the national domain into townships each containing thirty-six square miles, with each square mile or "section" containing 640 acres. Four sections in each township were reserved for the United States, and one section was set aside for public schools. Once the land was surveyed, it was to be sold at public auction at not less than a dollar an acre.

The method prescribed for the survey and sale of land was soon ignored because of the slow pace of the survey, the rise of new speculative interests, and the growing demand for money to enable Congress to make payments on the national debt. The Ordinance required that seven ranges of townships be surveyed before land sales could begin, but only four ranges had been surveyed by 1787.

Meanwhile, a group of New Englanders, calling themselves the Ohio Company, appeared before Congress and offered to buy a million acres of land in the Northwest Territory beyond the seven ranges to be surveyed. Congress agreed to sell the land in July 1787. However, the division of the West into townships and sections set forth in the Land Ordinance of 1785 remained a permanent part of American land policy.

The abandonment of orderly land sales was accompanied by mounting opposition to the prospect of new western states and to the self-government provided for in the Ordinance of 1784. In December 1785 James Monroe reported to James Madison that the "most enlightened members" of Congress were doubtful about admitting even one new state into the Union, and that the Virginia cession should be revised to allow Congress to reduce the number of prospective western states.

On 24 March 1786 a committee reported that if the Western Territory were divided into states according to the Ordinance of 1784, many of the states would not soon, if ever, have enough inhabitants to form a government, would remain "without laws, and without order among them," and the Union would have no advantage from them. Therefore, Virginia should be asked to revise its cession, and the provision of the Ordinance of 1784 relating to the size of future states should be repealed.

On 10 May a second committee reported a plan of government to replace the Ordinance of 1784. The committee declared that a government should be established in the West before any lands were sold. Furthermore, instead of self-government by the inhabitants until a state was admitted to the Union, the West would be governed by officials appointed by Congress, including a governor with virtually dictatorial powers. The next day, James Monroe reported to Thomas Jefferson: "It is in effect to be a colonial government similar to that which prevailed in these states previous to the Revolution. . . ." The details of the plan contradicted Monroe's assurance to Jefferson that the most important principles of the Ordinance of 1784 were preserved.

Debate on the proposed ordinance was resumed in July, but by then Congress was involved in the power struggle between the Northern and Southern states over the proposed Jay-Gardoqui treaty, which provided for closing the Mississippi River to Americans for twenty-five years in exchange for commercial privileges for Northern merchants in Spanish ports. James Monroe was convinced that the purpose of the Northerners, and particularly of the New Englanders, was to break up the western settlements, prevent the admission of new states, keep population in the East, and increase the value of vacant lands in New York and Massachusetts. The ordinance was discussed again in September and then dropped until April 1787, when it became the basis for the Ordinance for the Western Territory adopted by Congress on 13 July 1787.

The spirit in which the Ordinance was written is indicated by the words of the men who wrote it. On 25 April 1787 a committee of Congress reported that the Ordinance of 1785 should be repealed. The sale of land would be too slow, and "discontented and adventurous" people were settling on the land, which would be lost "unless early measures are pursued for vesting a better kind of people with rights there." A second reason was that experience had proven that "private adventurers" would be willing to pay for surveys if allowed to choose the lands they wanted.

After the Ordinance was adopted, Nathan Dane of Massachusetts, its principal draftsman, reported that Congress was "rather pressed" because of the Ohio Company offer to buy a large tract of land, "and we wanted to abolish the old system. . . ." He thought that the requirement that a district have 60,000 free inhabitants before it could be admitted as a state was too small, but that it might not be important since the easternmost of the states "will no doubt be settled chiefly by Eastern people" who would likely adopt "Eastern politics." He was surprised that there was no opposition to forbidding slavery in the territory, but, as William Grayson of Virginia explained it, "the clause respecting slavery was agreed to by the Southern members for the purpose of preventing tobacco and indigo from being made on the North West side of the Ohio as well as for several other political reasons."

Richard Henry Lee, who had returned to Congress in time to be appointed to the committee which drafted the Ordinance, reported to George Washington after its passage that "it seemed necessary, for the security of property among uninformed, and perhaps licentious people as the greater part of those who go there are, that a strong toned government should exist, and the rights of property be clearly defined." A little later he wrote his brother William Lee: "The form of this government, as you will see by the enclosed paper, is much more tonic than our democratic forms on the Atlantic are."

The provisions of the Ordinance illustrate the spirit and intent of its creators. The Ordinance abolished the self-government provided for in the Ordinance of 1784. The first government in the national domain would be by a governor, a secretary, and three judges appointed by Congress. The governor, appointed for five years, must own 1,000 acres of land in the district; the secretary, appointed for four years, and the judges, appointed during good behavior, must each own 500 acres. The governor would be commander in chief of the militia and would appoint all officers below general rank. The governor had the power to appoint magistrates and civil officials, to lay out counties and townships, and, with the judges, to adopt any of the criminal and civil laws of the original states, which would remain in effect unless disapproved by Congress.

The Ordinance provided that when a district had 5,000 free male inhabitants, a legislature would be established. Representatives must own 200 acres of land and be citizens of one of the United States or residents of the district for three years. Voters must own 50 acres of land and be citizens of one of the United States or residents in the district for two years.

The power of the elected branch would be carefully controlled. Congress would appoint an upper house of five men for five years from ten names nominated by the elected branch, and each councillor must own 500 acres of land. Furthermore, the governor would retain great power. He would continue to appoint civil and military officers, have an absolute veto over legislation, and, like royal governors before 1776, have the "power to convene prorogue and dissolve the general assembly, when in his opinon it shall be expedient."

A "bill of rights" guaranteed freedom of religion, the right to a writ of habeas corpus, trial by jury, proportional representation, right to bail, freedom from cruel and unusual punishments; and slavery and indentured servitude were forbidden. The "bill" also provided for the protection of property: no law should ever be made "that shall in any manner whatever interfere with, or affect private contracts or engagements bona fide and without fraud, previously formed." Nor was the legislature of a district, or of the future states, to interfere with the sale of land by Congress, impose any tax on the property of the United States, or tax non-resident proprietors higher than the inhabitants.

The territory would be divided into not less than three nor more than five states. Whenever any district had 60,000 free inhabitants, it would be at liberty to form a constitution and state government and "be admitted by its delegates" to Congress on "equal footing with the original states. . . ."

The actions of Congress in adopting ordinances for the government and sale of the national domain were determined by political and economic realities, not by constitutional responsibilities or niceties. Even the final vote on the adoption of the Ordinance of 1787 ignored the requirement of the Articles of Confederation that no important question could be determined except by the approval of nine states. The states present in Congress voted unanimously for the Ordinance, but only eight states were represented.

* * * *

At the same time that Congress acted outside the bounds of the constitution by adopting ordinances for the national domain, Congress also sought to acquire strength within the constitutional framework by proposing amendments to the Articles of Confederation and temporary grants of power. None of the constitutional amendments or grants of power proposed between 1781 and 1786 had been approved by all the states before the Articles were replaced by the Constitution of 1787. Nevertheless, the debate over such proposals reflected the continuing concern of Americans with the nature and purpose of the central government.

The first serious effort to strengthen the central government was made in February 1781 shortly before the Articles of Confederation were ratified. Congress had the power to issue paper money and to borrow money, but it did not have the power to tax. It could issue requisitions on the states for money, but it did not have the power to force compliance. By the end of 1780 Congress had abandoned the paper money which had been issued to finance the first years of the War for Independence. By that time, too, men who believed in the creation of a powerful central government were becoming more influential in Congress. They argued that Congress must have the power to collect an independent revenue to finance the war and to pay the interest on the public debt.

The result was a proposal on 3 February 1781 that Congress be given power to collect import duties until the debts of the United States were paid. After the Articles of Confederation were ratified on 1 March, the proposal was regarded as an amendment to them, rather than a grant of power. By mid-1782 all the states had ratified except Rhode Island, which refused on the ground that the amendment would alter the fundamental character of the Articles of Confederation. Then, in December 1782, Virginia withdrew its ratification, thus blocking the effort to free Congress from financial dependence on the states.

Immediately after the ratification of the Articles of Confederation on 1 March 1781, Congress appointed a committee to make recommendations for carrying the Articles into effect. On 16 March a report written by James Madison stated that Congress had "a general and implied power" to force the states to comply with decisions which the Articles empowered Congress to make. However, since the Articles did not contain a "determinate and particular provision" to that effect, they should be amended to give Congress specific power to use military and naval force against the states, to seize the property of the states and their citizens, and to prohibit the states from trading with one another and with foreign countries unless they obeyed the decisions of Congress.

Congress refused to consider the amendment, which proposed a constitutional revolution, and turned the report over to another committee of which Edmund Randolph and Oliver Ellsworth were members. The new committee submitted a milder report on 22 August, but Congress ignored it. Six years later Randolph and Ellsworth were members of the Committee of Detail of the Constitutional Convention. On 6 August 1787 the committee presented a draft constitution which included many of the proposals contained in the committee report of August 1781.

By 1783 the men who wanted to create what they came to call a "national government" had been unable to secure approval of the states or of Congress for the measures they had proposed. They were faced with mounting opposition, and the end of the war destroyed their argument that independence could not be won without granting Congress more power. However, they made one more attempt to secure an independent income for Congress, but this time they placed a specific time limit on the request. On 18 April 1783 Congress asked the states for a twenty-five year grant of power to collect import duties and for a grant of supplementary funds from the states.

The request was accompanied by an amendment to the Articles of Confederation which proposed that the expenses of the central government be apportioned among the states according to population rather than according to the value of the land granted to or surveyed for individuals. As in 1776–1777, the issue of what population should be counted pitted the Northern against the Southern states. The dispute was compromised when Southern delegates, led by James Madison and John Rutledge, proposed that three-fifths of the slaves be counted in sharing expenses.

Four years later in the Constitutional Convention, the counting of three-fifths of the slaves became a central issue between the North and the South in the struggle over apportioning representation in Congress. Among the members of Congress in 1783 who debated the issue again as members of the Constitutional Convention in 1787 were Gunning Bedford, Jr., Daniel Carroll, Thomas FitzSimons, Nathaniel Gorham, Alexander Hamilton, James Madison, John Francis Mercer, Thomas Mifflin, John Rutledge, Hugh Williamson, and James Wilson.

The power to regulate trade was also a basic source of contention.

The need for such regulation was urged in the First Continental Congress in 1774 and was discussed briefly in the debate over the Articles of Confederation in 1776–1777. The issue was in abeyance during the war but was revived in 1783 when Britain closed its ports in the West Indies to American ships. The states began discriminating against British ships and goods, but merchants and proponents of a stronger central government insisted that Congress needed the power to establish uniform regulations. The result was a proposal on 30 April 1784 that Congress be given the power to pass "navigation acts" for a period of fifteen years.

Meanwhile, merchants continued to urge a permanent grant of power, and in March 1785 a committee of Congress reported an amendment to the Articles of Confederation. It would give Congress the power to levy duties and imposts on exports and imports as a part of its power to make commercial treaties. The committee concluded that a "temporary power" would be inadequate to serve the interests of the United States and of the individual states. Thirteen members of the Convention in 1787 were members of Congress in 1785 during the debate over the proposed amendment. They were Abraham Baldwin, Gunning Bedford, Jr., Elbridge Gerry, William C. Houston, William Houstoun, William Samuel Johnson, Rufus King, John Lansing, Jr., James McHenry, Charles Pinckney, Richard Dobbs Spaight, Hugh Williamson, and James Wilson.

The proposed amendment was not adopted by Congress in 1785 because of rivalry between the Northern and the Southern states. That rivalry created even more bitter dissension the next year when John Jay, Secretary for Foreign Affairs, attempted to negotiate a treaty with the Spanish minister, Don Diego de Gardoqui. Jay proposed to close the Mississippi River to Americans for twenty-five years in exchange for commercial privileges for American merchants in Spanish ports. Jay was supported by the delegates from all the Northern States, but late in August 1786 the five Southern States were able to defeat the proposed treaty because the Articles of Confederation required that nine states must approve treaties as well as all other important actions of Congress.

The dispute over commercial power between 1784 and 1786 was a rehearsal for the debates in the Constitutional Convention, where Southerners insisted that the "two thirds" requirement of the Articles for the adoption of all important measures be required for the regulation of trade and the approval of treaties and be embodied in the Constitution. Some Southerners wanted to require an even larger margin, while Northern delegates insisted that simple majorities should be enough in both cases.

*   *   *   *

By the end of 1785 most of the supporters of the Articles of Confederation agreed that Congress should have more power, and, in particular, the power to regulate trade. But, at the same time, they were alarmed at the growing demand for a constitutional convention and fearful that if one met, it would seek to overturn the Articles of Confederation.

The Massachusetts delegates in Congress summed up such fears in September 1785. The Massachusetts legislature had instructed them to move that Congress call a convention for the purpose of granting Congress power to regulate commerce. Rufus King, Elbridge Gerry, and Samuel Holten refused to obey and explained why in a letter to Governor James Bowdoin. They said that if a convention were called, it might overturn the government established at the beginning of the Revolution. "The great object of the Revolution," they declared, "was the establishment of good government," and the states and the federal government embodied republican principles. Nevertheless, plans had been laid, which if they had succeeded, "would inevitably have changed our republican governments into baleful aristocracies." Furthermore, if a convention were called, the "friends of an aristocracy" would send delegates who would promote a change in government. King, Gerry, and Holten agreed that Congress should have more power, but they warned "that every measure should be avoided which would strengthen the hands of the enemies to a free government. . . ." The Massachusetts legislature then dropped the idea of asking Congress to call a convention.

Members of Congress realized, however, that action was needed to strengthen the government, and during the early months of 1786 Congress appointed committees to report on the status of earlier requests for power to collect import duties and to regulate trade. Congress then encouraged the non-assenting states to comply. As a result, the states had taken the following actions by the middle of 1786:

(1) All states except New York had complied in one form or another with the proposal of 18 April 1783 giving Congress power to collect import duties for twenty-five years. New York ratified the request in August 1786 but refused to give Congress the power to remove state-appointed collectors. Congress therefore refused to accept New York's ratification.

(2) All the states except New Hampshire and Rhode Island had agreed to the amendment to the Articles which changed the basis for sharing expenses from the value of lands to population.

(3) All the states had granted Congress the power to pass navigation acts for a period of fifteen years, which Congress had requested on 30 April 1784. However, the states had approved the request

in various forms that needed to be reconciled before the grant of power could become effective.

During the spring of 1786, the intense and growing concern over the state of public affairs led to debates in Congress on ways to strengthen the government under the Articles of Confederation. Some delegates argued that a convention was the best method, but a majority insisted that Congress should proceed constitutionally by proposing amendments to the Articles and sending them to the states for the required unanimous ratification.

Eight of the men who debated these issues in 1786 were members of the Constitutional Convention in 1787 and supported ratification of the Constitution. They were William Blount, William Few, Nathaniel Gorham, William Houstoun, William Samuel Johnson, Rufus King, Charles Pinckney, and James Wilson. Also involved in the debates in 1786 were such opponents of the Constitution in 1787–1788 as Timothy Bloodworth, Nathan Dane, William Grayson, John Haring, Richard Henry Lee, Stephen Mix Mitchell, James Monroe, Charles Pettit, and Melancton Smith.

Early in May Congress agreed to sit as a committee of the whole to consider "the state of public affairs." After sitting from time to time as a committee, Congress appointed a "grand committee" on 3 July to "report such amendments to the Confederation and a draft of such resolutions as it may be necessary to recommend to the several states for the purpose of obtaining from them such powers as will render the federal government adequate to the ends for which it was instituted."

On 7 August the "grand committee" reported seven amendments to the Articles of Confederation, but by then Congress was so involved in the dispute between the North and the South over the proposed Jay-Gardoqui treaty that Congress never considered the amendments or submitted them to the states. Nevertheless, the amendments represented the views of men who in 1786 believed that a federal government was best for the United States. Such views were diametrically opposed to the views of most of the twelve men, representing five states, who met at Annapolis between 11 and 14 September 1786, only five weeks after the amendments were submitted to Congress.

The report of the Annapolis Convention and the call of a convention by the Confederation Congress on 21 February 1787 marked a crucial turning point in the debate over a central government that had been under way since 1774, but they did not mark an abandonment of the past.

The various plans presented to and debated by the Constitutional Convention in 1787 embodied, in substance or in principle, each of the constitutional documents that Americans had considered during the preceding decade. Furthermore, many men who had drafted those constitutional documents were members of the Convention in 1787. The documents had also been debated by still other leaders who were not members of the Convention but who played important roles, often as opponents of the ratification of the Constitution.

The principles explicit and implicit in the constitutional documents debated between 1776 and 1787 were debated in the Confederation Congress which transmitted the Constitution to the states on 28 September 1787 without approval or disapproval. Above all, those principles were debated in newspapers and pamphlets and in the state conventions called to reject or ratify the Constitution. Thus the constitutional documents written by Americans between 1776 and 1787 are an integral part of the record required for an understanding of the writing and the ratification of the Constitution of 1787.

To provide the constitutional context within which the men who debated the ratification of the Constitution were familiar, this volume presents the basic constitutional documents written by Americans between 1776 and 1787, the resolutions and draft constitutions showing the evolution of the Constitution in the Constitutional Convention, and the debates over the Constitution in the Confederation Congress before Congress transmitted the Constitution to the states. The reader will thus be able to refer to these documents as did the men who debated the ratification of the Constitution. This volume therefore serves as an introduction to each volume of *The Documentary History of the Ratification of the Constitution*.

Symbols

FOR MANUSCRIPTS, MANUSCRIPT DEPOSITORIES,
SHORT TITLES, AND CROSS-REFERENCES

Manuscripts

AD	Autograph Document
Dft	Draft
DS	Document Signed
f, ff	Folio, folios
FC	File Copy
LT	Literal Transcript
MS	Manuscript
RC	Recipient's Copy
Tr	Translation from Foreign Language

Manuscript Depositories[1]

Ct	Connecticut State Library, Hartford
CtHi	Connecticut Historical Society, Hartford
DLC	Library of Congress, Washington, D.C.
DNA	National Archives, Washington, D.C.
DNDAR	Daughters of the American Revolution, National Headquarters, Washington, D.C.
M-Ar	Archives Division, Secretary of State, Boston, Massachusetts
MHi	Massachusetts Historical Society, Boston
MNF	Forbes Library, Northampton, Massachusetts
N	New York State Library, Albany
Nc-Ar	North Carolina Department of Archives and History, Raleigh
NHi	New-York Historical Society, New York City
NN	New York Public Library, New York City
NNPM	Pierpont Morgan Library, New York City
PHi	Historical Society of Pennsylvania, Philadelphia
Sc-Ar	South Carolina Department of Archives and History, Columbia

Short Titles

Boyd   Julian P. Boyd, ed., *The Papers of Thomas Jefferson*
            (Princeton, N.J., 1950———).
Farrand   Max Farrand, ed., *The Records of the Federal Conven-*
            tion (3 vols., New Haven, Conn., 1911).
Hutchinson William T. Hutchinson, et al., eds., *The Papers of*
            James Madison (Chicago, Ill., 1962———).
JCC   Worthington C. Ford, et al., eds., *Journals of the*
            Continental Congress, 1774–1789 . . . (34 vols.,
            Washington, D.C., 1904–1937).
LMCC   Edmund C. Burnett, ed., *Letters of Members of the*
            Continental Congress (8 vols., Washington, D.C.,
            1921–1936).
PCC   Papers of the Continental Congress, 1774–1789 (Record
            Group 360, National Archives).
RCC   Records of the Constitutional Convention of 1787
            (Record Group 360, National Archives).
RG 11   United States Government Documents Having General
            Legal Effect, National Archives.
Rutland   Robert A. Rutland, ed., *The Papers of George Mason,*
            1725–1792 (3 vols., Chapel Hill, N.C., 1970).
Syrett   Harold C. Syrett, ed., *The Papers of Alexander Hamilton*
            (New York, N.Y., 1961———).

Cross-references

CC   *Commentaries on the Constitution: Public and Private*
Mfm   Microform Supplements to RCS
RCS   *Ratification of the Constitution by the States*

1. The symbols are those adopted by the Library of Congress: *Symbols of
American Libraries* (10th ed., Washington, D.C., 1969).

I

The Declaration of
Independence

Introduction

On 15 May 1776 Virginia instructed its delegates in Congress to move that the colonies declare themselves "free and independent states. . . ." In Congress, on 7 June, Richard Henry Lee moved a three-part resolution: that "These United Colonies are, and of right ought to be, free and independent states," that they should take measures to form foreign alliances, and that a "plan of confederation" should be prepared. Congress debated the issue of independence until 10 June, when it postponed further consideration until 1 July. On 11 June Congress appointed a commitee consisting of Thomas Jefferson, John Adams, Benjamin Franklin, Roger Sherman, and Robert R. Livingston to draft a declaration of independence.

The committee gave Jefferson the responsibility. He first submitted his draft to Adams and Franklin and then to the entire committee. The draft was read to Congress on 28 June, and Congress then ordered that it "lie on the table."

On 1 July Congress resumed debate on Lee's first resolution, and the next day all the colonies except New York voted for it. Congress then began to revise the draft declaration, a task completed the evening of the 4th. Congress ordered the Declaration of Independence printed and sent to civilian authorities in each colony and to officers commanding Continental troops. The next day, the printer presented to Congress a one-page broadside with the title: "A Declaration By the Representatives of the United States of America. In General Congress assembled."

New York agreed to independence on 9 July, and this action was reported to Congress on 15 July. Four days later Congress resolved "That the Declaration passed on the 4th, be fairly engrossed on parchment, with the title and stile of 'The unanimous declaration of the thirteen United States of America,' and that the same, when engrossed, be signed by every member of Congress."

On 2 August the engrossed Declaration was ready for signing. Some members signed that day and others later. Eventually fifty-six men signed the Declaration. However, the names of the signers were not made public at the time. It was not until 18 January 1777 that Congress ordered that a printed copy of the Declaration with the names of signers be sent to the states.

THE DECLARATION OF INDEPENDENCE[1]

In CONGRESS, July 4, 1776.

The unanimous Declaration of the thirteen united States of America,
When in the Course of human events, it becomes necessary for one
people to dissolve the political bands which have connected them
with another, and to assume among the powers of the earth, the
separate and equal station to which the Laws of Nature and of Nature's
God entitle them, a decent respect to the opinions of mankind requires that they should declare the causes which impel them to the
separation.—We hold these truths to be self-evident, that all men are
created equal, that they are endowed by their Creator with certain
unalienable Rights, that among these are Life, Liberty and the pursuit of Happiness.—That to secure these rights, Governments are instituted among Men, deriving their just powers from the consent of
the governed,—That whenever any Form of Government becomes destructive of these ends, it is the Right of the People to alter or to
abolish it; and to institute new Government, laying its foundation
on such principles and organizing its powers in such form, as to them
shall seem most likely to effect their Safety and Happiness. Prudence,
indeed, will dictate that Governments long established should not be
changed for light and transient causes; and accordingly all experience
hath shewn, that mankind are more disposed to suffer, while evils
are sufferable, than to right themselves by abolishing the forms to
which they are accustomed. But when a long train of abuses and
usurpations, pursuing invariably the same Object evinces a design
to reduce them under absolute Despotism, it is their right, it is their
duty, to throw off such Government, and to provide new Guards for
their future security.—Such has been the patient sufferance of these
Colonies; and such is now the necessity which constrains them to alter
their former Systems of Government. The history of the present King
of Great Britain is a history of repeated injuries and usurpations, all
having in direct object the establishment of an absolute Tyranny over
these States. To prove this, let Facts be submitted to a candid world.—
He has refused his Assent to Laws, the most wholesome and necessary
for the public good.—He has forbidden his Governors to pass Laws
of immediate and pressing importance, unless suspended in their operation till his Assent should be obtained; and when so suspended, he
has utterly neglected to attend to them.—He has refused to pass other
Laws for the accommodation of large districts of people, unless those
people would relinquish the right of Representation in the Legislature, a right inestimable to them and formidable to tyrants only.—He
has called together legislative bodies at places unusual, uncomfortable,

and distant from the depository of their public Records, for the sole
purpose of fatiguing them into compliance with his measures.—He
has dissolved Representative Houses repeatedly, for opposing with
manly firmness his invasions on the rights of the people.—He has refused for a long time, after such dissolutions, to cause others to be
elected; whereby the Legislative powers, incapable of Annihilation,
have returned to the People at large for their exercise; the State remaining in the mean time exposed to all the dangers of invasion from
without, and convulsions within.—He has endeavoured to prevent the
population of these States; for that purpose obstructing the Laws for
Naturalization of Foreigners; refusing to pass others to encourage their
migrations hither, and raising the conditions of new Appropriations
of Lands.—He has obstructed the Administration of Justice, by refusing
his Assent to Laws for establishing Judiciary powers—He has made
Judges dependent on his Will alone, for the tenure of their offices,
and the amount and payment of their salaries.—He has erected a
multitude of New Offices, and sent hither swarms of Officers to harrass
our people, and eat out their substance.—He has kept among us, in
times of peace, Standing Armies without the Consent of our legislatures.—He has affected to render the Military independent of and
superior to the Civil power.—He has combined with others to subject
us to a jurisdiction foreign to our constitution, and unacknowledged
by our laws; giving his Assent to their Acts of pretended Legislation:—
For Quartering large bodies of armed troops among us:—For protect-
ing them, by a mock Trial, from punishment for any Murders which
they should commit on the Inhabitants of these States:—For calling
off our Trade with all parts of the world:—For imposing Taxes on us
without our Consent:—For depriving us in many cases, of the benefits of
Trial by Jury:—For transporting us beyond Seas to be tried for pretended offences—For abolishing the free System of English Laws in
a neighbouring Province, establishing therein an Arbitrary government, and enlarging its Boundaries so as to render it at once an
example and fit instrument for introducing the same absolute rule
into these Colonies:—For taking away our Charters, abolishing our
most valuable Laws and altering fundamentally the Forms of our
Governments:—For suspending our own Legislatures, and declaring
themselves invested with power to legislate for us in all cases whatsoever.—He has abdicated Government here, by declaring us out of
his Protection and waging War against us.—He has plundered our seas,
ravaged our Coasts, burnt our towns, and destroyed the Lives of our
people.—He is at this time transporting large Armies of foreign Mer-
cenaries to compleat the works of death, desolation and tyranny, already begun with circumstances of Cruelty & perfidy scarcely paralleled

in the most barbarous ages, and totally unworthy the Head of a civilized nation.—He has constrained our fellow Citizens taken Captive on the high Seas to bear Arms against their Country, to become the executioners of their friends and Brethren, or to fall themselves by their Hands.—He has excited domestic insurrections amongst us, and has endeavoured to bring on the inhabitants of our frontiers, the merciless Indian Savages, whose known rule of warfare, is an undistinguished destruction of all ages, sexes and conditions. In every stage of these Oppressions We have Petitioned for Redress in the most humble terms: Our repeated Petitions have been answered only by repeated injury. A Prince, whose character is thus marked by every act which may define a Tyrant, is unfit to be the ruler of a free people. Nor have We been wanting in attentions to our Brittish brethren. We have warned them from time to time of attempts by their legislature to extend an unwarrantable jurisdiction over us. We have reminded them of the circumstances of our emigration and settlement here. We have appealed to their native justice and magnanimity, and we have conjured them by the ties of our common kindred to disavow these usurpations, which, would inevitably interrupt our connections and correspondence They too have been deaf to the voice of justice and of consanguinity. We must, therefore, acquiesce in the necessity, which denounces our Separation, and hold them, as we hold the rest of mankind, Enemies in War, in Peace Friends.—

We, therefore, the Representatives of the united States of America, in General Congress, Assembled, appealing to the Supreme Judge of the world for the rectitude of our intentions, do, in the Name, and by Authority of the good People of these Colonies, solemnly publish and declare, That these United Colonies are, and of Right ought to be Free and Independent States; that they are Absolved from all Allegiance to the British Crown, and that all political connection between them and the State of Great Britain, is and ought to be totally dissolved; and that as Free and Independent States, they have full Power to levy War, conclude Peace, contract Alliances, establish Commerce, and to do all other Acts and Things which Independent States may of right do.—And for the support of this Declaration, with a firm reliance on the protection of divine Providence, we mutually pledge to each other our Lives, our Fortunes and our sacred Honor.

1. Engrossed MS (LT), DNA.

Signers of the Declaration of Independence

[Engrossed documents such as the Declaration of Independence were signed in the traditional north-to-south order, beginning with New Hampshire and ending with Georgia. Signatures were first written in the right hand column. When that column was filled, a new column was started to the left of it. In the following list of signers, abbreviations of Christian names have been spelled out and the names of the states have been inserted.]

NEW HAMPSHIRE
  Josiah Bartlett
  William Whipple
  Matthew Thornton
MASSACHUSETTS
  John Hancock
  Samuel Adams
  John Adams
  Robert Treat Paine
  Elbridge Gerry
RHODE ISLAND
  Stephen Hopkins
  William Ellery
CONNECTICUT
  Roger Sherman
  Samuel Huntington
  William Williams
  Oliver Wolcott
NEW YORK
  William Floyd
  Philip Livingston
  Francis Lewis
  Lewis Morris
NEW JERSEY
  Richard Stockton
  John Witherspoon
  Francis Hopkinson
  John Hart
  Abraham Clark
PENNSYLVANIA
  Robert Morris
  Benjamin Rush
  Benjamin Franklin
  John Morton
  George Clymer

  James Smith
  George Taylor
  James Wilson
  George Ross
DELAWARE
  Caesar Rodney
  George Read
  Thomas McKean
MARYLAND
  Samuel Chase
  William Paca
  Thomas Stone
  Charles Carroll
    of Carrollton
VIRGINIA
  George Wythe
  Richard Henry Lee
  Thomas Jefferson
  Benjamin Harrison
  Thomas Nelson, Jr.
  Francis Lightfoot Lee
  Carter Braxton
NORTH CAROLINA
  William Hooper
  Joseph Hewes
  John Penn
SOUTH CAROLINA
  Edward Rutledge, Jr.
  Thomas Heyward, Jr.
  Thomas Lynch, Jr.
  Arthur Middleton
GEORGIA
  Button Gwinnett
  Lyman Hall
  George Walton

II

The Articles of
Confederation

Introduction

On 7 June 1776 when Richard Henry Lee moved that the colonies declare themselves "free and independent states," a part of the motion proposed that "a plan of confederation be prepared and transmitted to the respective colonies for their consideration and approbation." On 12 June Congress appointed a committee of one delegate from each colony to draft "a form of confederation." The members were: Josiah Bartlett, Samuel Adams, Stephen Hopkins, Roger Sherman, Robert R. Livingston, John Dickinson (chairman), Thomas McKean, Thomas Stone, Thomas Nelson, Joseph Hewes, Edward Rutledge, and Button Gwinnett. Francis Hopkinson was added to the committee on 28 June.

On 12 July the committee presented to Congress a draft of "Articles of confederation and perpetual union" in the handwriting of John Dickinson. Congress ordered eighty copies printed and instructed the printers and members of Congress not to divulge the contents. Congress debated and amended the document from 22 July to 20 August, when eighty copies of the amended articles were ordered printed for the delegates under the same restrictions as before.

The pressure of military disaster forced Congress to abandon the debate. On 8 April 1777, Congress voted to spend two days a week upon the plan of Confederation, but Congress was unable to move toward completion until October. Several disputed issues were soon settled, and on 10 November Richard Law, Richard Henry Lee, and James Duane were appointed to report additional amendments. The committee recommended seven amendments the next day, some of which were adopted or modified. On 13 November Richard Henry Lee, James Duane, and James Lovell were appointed to revise and arrange the Articles and prepare a circular letter to the states.

On 15 November Congress adopted the Articles of Confederation and ordered 300 copies printed. Congress then sent the Articles of Confederation to the states, accompanied by a circular letter. The letter described the difficulties involved in writing a constitution to satisfy so many differing interests and requested the state legislatures to authorize their delegates in Congress to be ready to approve the Articles on 10 March 1778.

A. DRAFT OF ARTICLES OF CONFEDERATION, 12 July 1776[1]

ARTICLES of Confederation and Perpetual Union, between the Colonies of New-Hampshire, Massachusetts-Bay, Rhode-Island, Connecticut, New-York, New-Jersey, Pennsylvania, the Counties of New-Castle, Kent and Sussex on Delaware, Maryland, Virginia, North-Carolina, South-Carolina, and Georgia.

Art. I. THE Name of this Confederacy shall be "THE UNITED STATES OF AMERICA."

Art. II. The said Colonies unite themselves so as never to be divided by any Act whatever, and hereby severally enter into a firm League of Friendship with each other, for their common Defence, the Security of their Liberties, and their mutual and general Welfare, binding the said Colonies to assist one another against all Force offered to or attacks made upon them or any of them, on Account of Religion, Sovereignty, Trade, or any other Pretence whatever.

Art. III. Each Colony shall retain and enjoy as much of its present Laws, Rights and Customs, as it may think fit, and reserves to itself the sole and exclusive Regulation and Government of its internal police, in all matters that shall not interfere with the Articles of this Confederation.

Art. IV. No Colony or Colonies, without the Consent of the United States assembled, shall send any Embassy to or receive any Embassy from, or enter into any Treaty, Convention or Conference with the King or Kingdom of Great-Britain, or any foreign Prince or State; nor shall any Colony or Colonies, nor any Servant or Servants of the United States, or of any Colony or Colonies, accept of any Present, Emolument, Office, or Title of any Kind whatever, from the King or Kingdom of Great-Britain, or any foreign Prince or State; nor shall the United States assembled, or any Colony grant any Title of Nobility.

Art. V. No two or more Colonies shall enter into any Treaty, Confederation or Alliance whatever between them, without the previous and free Consent and Allowance of the United States assembled, specifying accurately the Purposes for which the same is to be entered into, and how long it shall continue.

Art. VI. The Inhabitants of each Colony shall henceforth always have the same Rights, Liberties, Privileges, Immunities and Advantages, in the other Colonies, which the said Inhabitants now have, in all Cases whatever, except in those provided for by the next following Article.

Art. VII. The Inhabitants of each Colony shall enjoy all the Rights, Liberties, Privileges, Immunities, and Advantages, in Trade, Navigation, and Commerce, in any other Colony, and in going to and from the same from and to any Part of the World, which the Natives of such Colony enjoy.

Art. VIII. Each Colony may assess or lay such Imposts or Duties as it thinks proper, on Importations or Exportations, provided such Imposts or Duties do not interfere with any Stipulations in Treaties hereafter entered into by the United States assembled, with the King or Kingdom of Great-Britain, or any foreign Prince or State.

Art. IX. No standing Army or Body of Forces shall be kept up by any Colony or Colonies in Times of Peace, except such a Number only as may be requisite to garrison the Forts necessary for the Defence of such Colony or Colonies: But every Colony shall always keep up a well regulated and disciplined Militia, sufficiently armed and accoutred; and shall provide and constantly have ready for Use in public Stores, a due Number of Field Pieces and Tents, and a proper Quantity of Ammunition, and Camp Equipage.

Art. X. When Troops are raised in any of the Colonies for the common Defence, the Commission Officers proper for the Troops raised in each Colony, except the General Officers, shall be appointed by the Legislature of each Colony respectively, or in such manner as shall by them be directed.

Art. XI. All Charges of Wars and all other Expences that shall be incurred for the common Defence, or general Welfare, and allowed by the United States assembled, shall be defrayed out of a common Treasury, which shall be supplied by the several Colonies in Proportion to the Number of Inhabitants of every Age, Sex and Quality, except Indians not paying Taxes, in each Colony, a true Account of which, distinguishing the white Inhabitants, shall be triennially taken and transmitted to the Assembly of the United States. The Taxes for paying that Proportion shall be laid and levied by the Authority and Direction of the Legislatures of the several Colonies, within the Time agreed upon by the United States assembled.

Art. XII. Every Colony shall abide by the Determinations of the United States assembled, concerning the Services performed and Losses or Expences incurred by every Colony for the common Defence or general Welfare, and no Colony or Colonies shall in any Case whatever endeavor by Force to procure Redress of any Injury or Injustice supposed to be done by the United States to such Colony or Colonies in not granting such Satisfactions, Indemnifications, Compensations, Retributions, Exemptions, or Benefits of any Kind, as such Colony or Colonies may think just or reasonable.

Art XIII. No Colony or Colonies shall engage in any War without the previous Consent of the United States assembled, unless such Colony or Colonies be actually invaded by Enemies, or shall have received certain Advice of a Resolution being formed by some Nations of Indians to invade such Colony or Colonies, and the Danger is so imminent, as not to admit of a Delay, till the other Colonies can be consulted: Nor shall any Colony or Colonies grant Commissions to any Ships or Vessels of War, nor Letters of Marque or Reprisal, except it be after a Declaration of War by the United States assembled, and then only against the Kingdom or State and the Subjects thereof, against which War has been so declared, and under such Regulations as shall be established by the United States assembled.

Art. XIV. No Purchases of Lands, hereafter to be made of the Indians by Colonies or private Persons before the Limits of the Colonies are ascertained, to be valid: All Purchases of Lands not included within those Limits, where ascertained, to be made by Contracts between the United States assembled, or by Persons for that Purpose authorized by them, and the great Councils of the Indians, for the general Benefit of all the United Colonies.

Art. XV. When the Boundaries of any Colony shall be ascertained by Agreement, or in the Manner herein after directed, all the other Colonies shall guarantee to such Colony the full and peaceable Possession of, and the free and entire Jurisdiction in and over the Territory included within such Boundaries.

Art. XVI. For the more convenient Management of the general Interests of the United States, Delegates should be annually appointed in such Manner as the Legislature of each Colony shall direct, to meet at the City of Philadelphia, in the Colony of Pennsylvania, until otherwise ordered by the United States assembled; which Meeting shall be on the first Monday of November in every Year, with a Power reserved to those who appointed the said Delegates, respectively to recal them or any of them at any Time within the Year, and to send new Delegates in their stead for the Remainder of the Year. Each Colony shall support its own Delegates in a Meeting of the States, and while they act as Members of the Council of State, herein after mentioned.

Art. XVII. In determining Questions each Colony shall have one Vote.

Art. XVIII. The United States assembled shall have the sole and exclusive Right and Power of determining on Peace and War, except in the Cases mentioned in the thirteenth Article—Of establishing Rules for deciding in all Cases, what Captures on Land or Water shall be legal—In what Manner Prizes taken by land or naval Forces in the Service of the United States shall be divided or appropriated—Granting Letters of Marque and Reprisal in Times of Peace—Appointing Courts for the Trial of all Crimes, Frauds and Piracies committed on the High Seas, or on any navigable River, not within the Body of a County or Parish—Establishing Courts for receiving and determining finally Appeals in all Cases of Captures—Sending and receiving Ambassadors under any Character—Entering into Treaties and Alliances—Settling all Disputes and Differences now subsisting, or that hereafter may arise between two or more Colonies concerning Boundaries, Jurisdictions, or any other Cause whatever—Coining Money and regulating the Value thereof—Regulating the Trade, and managing all Affairs with the Indians—Limiting the Bounds of those Colonies, which by Charter or Proclamation, or under any Pretence, are said to extend to the South Sea, and ascertaining those Bounds of any other Colony that appear to be indeterminate—Assigning Territories for new Colonies, either in Lands to be thus separated from Colonies and heretofore purchased or obtained by the Crown of Great-Britain from the Indians, or hereafter to be purchased or obtained from them—Disposing of all such Lands for the general Benefit of all the United Colonies—Ascertaining Boundaries to such new Colonies, within which Forms of Government are to be established on the Principles of Liberty—Establishing and regulating Post-Offices throughout all the United Colonies, on the Lines of Communication from one Colony to another—Appointing General Officers of the Land Forces in the Service of the United States—Commissioning such other Officers of the said Forces as shall be appointed by Virtue of the tenth Article—Appointing all the Officers of the Naval Forces in the Service of the United States—Making Rules for the Government and Regulation of the said Land and Naval Forces—Appointing a Council of State, and such Committees and civil Officers as may be necessary for managing the general Affairs of the United States, under their Direction while assembled, and in their Recess, of the Council of State—Appointing one of their number to preside, and a suitable Person for Secretary—And adjourning to any Time within the Year.

The United States assembled shall have Authority for the Defence and Welfare of the United Colonies and every of them, to agree upon and fix the necessary Sums and Expences—To emit Bills, or to borrow Money on the Credit of the United Colonies—To raise Naval Forces—To agree upon the Number of Land Forces to be raised, and to make Requisitions from the Legislature of each Colony, or the Persons therein authorized by the Legislature to execute such Requisitions, for the Quota of each Colony, which is to be in Proportion to the Number of white Inhabitants in that Colony, which Requisitions shall be binding, and thereupon the Legislature of each Colony or the Persons authorized as aforesaid, shall appoint the Regimental Officers, raise the Men, and arm and equip them in a soldier-like Manner; and the Officers and Men so armed and equiped, shall march to the Place appointed, and within the Time agreed on by the United States assembled.

But if the United States assembled shall on Consideration of Circumstances judge proper, that any Colony or Colonies should not raise Men, or should raise a smaller Number than the Quota or Quotas of such Colony or Colonies, and that any other Colony or Colonies should raise a greater number of men than the Quota or Quotas thereof, such extra-numbers shall be raised, officered, armed and equiped in the same Manner as the Quota or Quotas of such Colony or Colonies, unless the Legislature of such Colony or Colonies respectively, shall judge, that such extra-numbers cannot be safely spared out of the same, in which Case they shall raise, officer, arm and equip as many of such extra-numbers as they judge can be safely spared; and the Officers and Men so armed and equiped shall march to the Place appointed, and within the Time agreed on by the United States assembled.

To establish the same Weights and Measures throughout the United Colonies.

But the United States assembled shall never impose or levy any Taxes or Duties, except in managing the Post-Office, nor interfere in the internal Police of any Colony, any further than such Police may be affected by the Articles of this Confederation. The United States assembled shall never engage the United Colonies in a War, nor grant Letters of Marque and Reprisal in Time of Peace, nor enter into Treaties or Alliances, nor coin Money nor regulate the Value thereof, nor agree upon nor fix the Sums and Expences necessary for the Defence and Welfare of the United Colonies, or any of them, nor emit Bills, nor borrow Money on the Credit of the United Colonies, nor raise Naval Forces, nor agree upon the Number of Land Forces to be raised, unless the Delegates of nine Colonies freely assent to the same: Nor shall a Question on any other Point, except for adjourning, be determined, unless the Delegates of seven Colonies vote in the affirmative.

No Person shall be capable of being a Delegate for more than three Years in any Term of six Years.

No Person holding any Office under the United States, for which he, or another for his Benefit, receives any Salary, Fees, or Emolument of any Kind, shall be capable of being a Delegate.

The Assembly of the United States to publish the Journal of their Proceedings monthly, except such Parts thereof relating to Treaties, Alliances, or military Operations, as in their Judgment require Secrecy—The Yeas and Nays of the Delegates of each Colony on any Question to be entered on the Journal, where it is desired by any Delegate; and the Delegates of a Colony, or any of them, at his or their Request, to be furnished with a Transcript of the said Journal, except such Parts as are above excepted, to lay before the Legislatures of the several Colonies.

Art. XIX. The Council of State shall consist of one Delegate from each C[o]lony, to be named annually by the Delegates of each Colony, and where they cannot agree, by the United States assembled.

This Council shall have Power to receive and open all Letters directed to the United States, and to return proper Answers; but not to make any Engagements that shall be binding on the United States—To correspond with the Legislature of every Colony, and all Persons acting under the Authority of the United States, or of the said Legislatures—To apply to such Legislatures, or to the Officers in the several Colonies who are entrusted with the executive Powers of Government, for occasional Aid whenever and wherever necessary—To give Counsel to the Commanding Officers, and to direct military Operations by

Sea and Land, not changing any Objects or Expeditions determined on by the United States assembled, unless an Alteration of Circumstances which shall come to the Knowledge of the Council after the Recess of the States, shall make such Change absolutely necessary—To attend to the Defence and Preservation of Forts and strong Posts, and to prevent the Enemy from acquiring new Holds—To procure Intelligence of the Condition and Designs of the Enemy—To expedite the Execution of such Measures as may be resolved on by the United States assembled, in Pursuance of the Powers hereby given to them— To draw upon the Treasurers for such Sums as may be appropriated by the United States assembled, and for the Payment of such Contracts as the said Council may make in Pursuance of the Powers hereby given to them—To superintend and controul or suspend all Officers civil and military, acting under the Authority of the United States— In Case of the Death or Removal of any Officer within the Appointment of the United States assembled, to employ a Person to fulfill the Duties of such Office until the Assembly of the States meet—To publish and disperse authentic Accounts of military Operations—To summon an Assembly of the States at an earlier Day than that appointed for their next Meeting, if any great and unexpected Emergency should render it necessary for the Safety or Welfare of the United Colonies or any of them—To prepare Matters for the Consideration of the United States, and to lay before them at their next Meeting all Letters and Advices received by the Council, with a Report of their Proceedings—To appoint a proper Person for their Clerk, who shall take an Oath of Secrecy, and Fidelity before he enters on the Exercise of his Office—Seven Members shall have Power to act—In Case of the Death of any Member, the Council shall immediately apply to his surviving Colleagues to appoint some one of themselves to be a Member thereof till the Meeting of the States, and if only one survives, they shall give immediate Notice, that he may take his Seat as a Councilor till such Meeting.

Art. XX. Canada acceding to this Confederation, and entirely joining in the Measures of the United Colonies, shall be admitted into and entitled to all the Advantages of this Union: But no other Colony shall be admitted into the same, unless such Admission be agreed to by the Delegates of nine Colonies.

These Articles shall be proposed to the Legislatures of all the United Colonies, to be by them considered, and if approved by them, they are advised to authorize their Delegates to ratify the same in the Assembly of the United States, which being done, the Articles of this Confederation shall inviolably be observed by every Colony, and the Union is to be perpetual: Nor shall any Alteration be at any Time hereafter made in these Articles or any of them, unless such Alteration be agreed to in an Assembly of the United States, and be afterwards confirmed by the Legislatures of every Colony.

1. Broadside (LT), PCC, Item 47, Articles of Confederation, ff. 21–28, DNA. For the manuscript of Dickinson's draft in his handwriting, see ibid., ff. 9–19. Dickinson wrote several "queries" on the margins of the manuscript. These are printed in JCC, V, 546–54 as notes to the printed copy of the draft.

B. ACT OF CONFEDERATION OF THE UNITED STATES OF AMERICA, 15 November 1777[1]

To all to whom these Presents shall come, we the under signed Delegates of the States affixed to our Names send greeting. Whereas the Delegates of the United States of America in Congress assembled did on the fifteenth day of November in the Year of our Lord One Thousand Seven Hundred and Seventy seven, and in the Second Year of the Independence of America agree to certain articles of Confederation and perpetual Union between the States of Newhampshire, Massachusetts-bay, Rhodeisland and Providence Plantations, Connecticut, New York, New Jersey, Pennsylvania, Delaware, Maryland, Virginia, North-Carolina, South-Carolina and Georgia in the Words following, viz, "Articles of Confederation and perpetual Union between the States of Newhampshire, Massachusetts-bay, Rhodeisland and Providence Plantations, Connecticut, New-York, New-Jersey, Pennsylvania, Delaware, Maryland, Virginia, North-Carolina, South-Carolina and Georgia.

Article I. The Stile of this confederacy shall be "The United States of America."

Article II. Each state retains its sovereignty, freedom and independence, and every Power, Jurisdiction and right, which is not by this confederation expressly delegated to the United States, in Congress assembled.

Article III. The said states hereby severally enter into a firm league of friendship with each other, for their common defence, the security of their Liberties, and their mutual and general welfare, binding themselves to assist each other, against all force offered to, or attacks made upon them, or any of them, on account of religion, sovereignty, trade, or any other pretence whatever.

Article IV. The better to secure and perpetuate mutual friendship and intercourse among the people of the different states in this union, the free inhabitants of each of these states, paupers, vagabonds and fugitives from Justice excepted, shall be entitled to all privileges and immunities of free citizens in the several states; and the people of each state shall have free ingress and regress to and from any other state, and shall enjoy therein all the privileges of trade and commerce, subject to the same duties, impositions and restrictions as the inhabitants thereof respectively, provided that such restriction shall not extend so far as to prevent the removal of property imported into any state, to any other state of which the Owner is an inhabitant; provided also that no imposition, duties or restriction shall be laid by any state, on the property of the united states, or either of them.

If any Person guilty of, or charged with treason, felony, or other high misdemeanor in any state, shall flee from Justice, and be found in any of the united states, he shall upon demand of the Governor or executive power, of the state from which he fled, be delivered up and removed to the state having jurisdiction of his offence.

Full faith and credit shall be given in each of these states to the records, acts and judicial proceedings of the courts and magistrates of every other state.

Article V. For the more convenient management of the general interests of the united states, delegates shall be annually appointed in such manner as the legislature of each state shall direct, to meet in Congress on the first Monday in November, in every year, with a power reserved to each state, to recal its delegates, or any of them, at any time within the year, and to send others in their stead, for the remainder of the Year.

No state shall be represented in Congress by less than two, nor by more than seven Members; and no person shall be capable of being a delegate for more than three years in any term of six years; nor shall any person, being a delegate, be capable of holding any office under the united states, for which he, or another for his benefit receives any salary, fees or emolument of any kind.

Each state shall maintain its own delegates in a meeting of the states, and while they act as members of the committee of the states.

In determining questions in the united states, in Congress assembled, each state shall have one vote.

Freedom of speech and debate in Congress shall not be impeached or questioned in any Court, or place out of Congress, and the members of congress shall be protected in their persons from arrests and imprisonments, during the time of their going to and from, and attendance on congress, except for treason, felony, or breach of the peace.

Article VI. No state without the Consent of the united states in congress assembled, shall send any embassy to, or receive any embassy from, or enter into any conferrence, agreement, alliance or treaty with any King prince or state; nor shall any person holding any office of profit or trust under the united states, or any of them, accept of any present, emolument, office or title of any kind whatever from any king, prince or foreign state; nor shall the united states in congress assembled, or any of them, grant any title of nobility.

No two or more states shall enter into any treaty, confederation or alliance whatever between them, without the consent of the united states in congress assembled, specifying accurately the purposes for which the same is to be entered into, and how long it shall continue.

No state shall lay any imposts or duties, which may interfere with any stipulations in treaties, entered into by the united states in congress assembled, with any king, prince or state, in pursuance of any treaties already proposed by congress, to the courts of France and Spain.

No vessels of war shall be kept up in time of peace by any state, except such number only, as shall be deemed necessary by the united states in congress assembled, for the defence of such state, or its trade; nor shall any body of forces be kept up by any state, in time of peace, except such number only, as in the judgment of the united states, in congress assembled, shall be deemed requisite to garrison the forts necessary for the defence of such state; but every state shall always keep up a well regulated and disciplined militia, sufficiently armed and accoutred, and shall provide and constantly have ready for use, in public stores, a due number of field pieces and tents, and a proper quantity of arms, ammunition and camp equipage.

No state shall engage in any war without the consent of the united states in congress assembled, unless such state be actually invaded by enemies, or shall have received certain advice of a resolution being formed by some nation of Indians to invade such state, and the danger is so imminent as not to admit of a delay, till the united states in congress assembled can be consulted: nor shall any state grant commissions to any ships or vessels of war, nor letters of marque or reprisal, except it be after a declaration of war by the united states in congress assembled, and then only against the kingdom or state and the subjects thereof, against which war has been so declared, and under such regulations as shall be established by the united states in congress assembled, unless such state be infested by pirates, in which case vessels of war may be fitted out for that occasion, and kept so long as the danger shall continue, or until the united states in congress assembled shall determine otherwise.

Article VII. When land-forces are raised by any state for the common defence, all officers of or under the rank of colonel, shall be appointed by the legislature of each state respectively by whom such forces shall be raised, or in such manner as such state shall direct, and all vacancies shall be filled up by the state which first made the appointment.

Article VIII. All charges of war, and all other expences that shall be incurred for the common defence or general welfare, and allowed by the united states in congress assembled, shall be defrayed out of a common treasury, which shall be supplied by the several states, in proportion to the value of all land within each state, granted to or surveyed for any Person, as such land and the buildings and improvements thereon shall be estimated according to such mode as the united states in congress assembled, shall from time to time direct and appoint. The taxes for paying that proportion shall be laid and levied by the authority and direction of the legislatures of the several states within the time agreed upon by the united states in congress assembled.

Article IX. The united states in congress assembled, shall have the sole and exclusive right and power of determining on peace and war, except in the cases mentioned in the sixth article—of sending and receiving ambassadors—entering into treaties and alliances, provided that no treaty of commerce shall be made whereby the legislative power of the respective states shall be restrained from imposing such imposts and duties on foreigners, as their own people are subjected to, or from prohibiting the exportation or importation of any species of goods or commodities whatsoever—of establishing rules for deciding in all cases, what captures on land or water shall be legal, and in what manner prizes taken by land or naval forces in the service of the united states shall be divided or appropriated—of granting letters of marque and reprisal in times of peace—appointing courts for the trial of piracies and felonies committed on the high seas and establishing courts for receiving and determining finally appeals in all cases of captures, provided that no member of congress shall be appointed a judge of any of the said courts.

The united states in congress assembled shall also be the last resort on appeal in all disputes and differences now subsisting or that hereafter may arise between two or more states concerning boundary, jurisdiction or any other cause whatever; which authority shall always be exercised in the manner following. Whenever the legislative or executive authority or lawful agent of any state in controversy with another shall present a petition to congress stating the matter in question and praying for a hearing, notice thereof shall be given by order of congress to the legislative or executive authority of the other state in controversy, and a day assigned for the appearance of the parties by their lawful agents, who shall then be directed to appoint by joint consent, commissioners or judges to constitute a court for hearing and determining the matter in question: but if they cannot agree, congress shall name three persons out of each of the united states, and from the list of such persons each party shall alternately strike out one, the petitioners beginning, until the number shall be reduced to thirteen; and from that number not less than seven, nor more than nine names as congress shall direct, shall in the presence of congress be drawn out by lot, and the persons whose names shall be so drawn or any five of them, shall be commissioners or judges, to hear and finally determine the controversy, so always as a major part of the judges who shall hear the cause shall agree in the determination: and if either party shall neglect to attend at the day appointed, without shewing reasons, which congress shall judge sufficient, or being present shall refuse to strike, the congress shall proceed to nominate three persons out of each state, and the secretary of congress shall strike in behalf of such party absent or refusing; and the judgment and sentence of the court to be appointed, in the manner before prescribed, shall be final and conclusive; and if any of the parties shall refuse to submit to the authority of such court, or to appear or defend their claim or cause, the court shall nevertheless proceed to pronounce sentence, or judgment, which shall in like manner be final and decisive, the judgment or sentence and other proceedings being in either case transmitted to congress, and lodged among the acts of congress for the security of the parties concerned: provided that every commissioner, before he sits in judgment, shall take an oath to be administered by one of the judges of the supreme or superior court of the state, where the cause shall be tried, "well and truly to hear and determine the matter in question, according to the best of his judgment, without favour, affection or hope of reward:" provided also that no state shall be deprived of territory for the benefit of the united states.

All controversies concerning the private right of soil claimed under different grants of two or more states, whose jurisdictions as they may respect such lands, and the states which passed such grants are adjusted, the said grants or either of them being at the same time claimed to have originated antecedent to such settlement of jurisdiction, shall on the petition of either party to the congress of the united states, be finally determined as near as maybe in the same manner as is before prescribed for deciding disputes respecting territorial jurisdiction between different states.

The united states in congress assembled shall also have the sole and exclusive right and power of regulating the alloy and value of coin struck by their own authority, or by that of the respective states—fixing the standard of weights and measures throughout the united states—regulating the trade and managing all affairs with the Indians, not members of any of the states, provided that the legislative right of any state within its own limits be not infringed or violated—establishing and regulating post-offices from one state to another, throughout all the united states, and exacting such postage on the papers passing thro' the same as may be requisite to defray the expences of the said office—appointing all officers of the land forces, in the service of the united states, excepting regimental officers—appointing all the officers of the naval forces, and commissioning all officers whatever in the service of the united states—making rules for the government and regulation of the said land and naval forces, and directing their operations.

The united states in congress assembled shall have authority to appoint a committee, to sit in the recess of congress, to be denominated "A Committee of the States," and to consist of one delegate from each state; and to appoint such other committees and civil officers as may be necessary for managing the general affairs of the united states under their direction—to appoint one of their number to preside, provided that no person be allowed to serve in the office of president more than one year in any term of three years; to ascertain the necessary sums of Money to be raised for the service of the united states, and to appropriate and apply the same for defraying the public expences—to borrow money, or emit bills on the credit of the united states, transmitting every half year to the respective states an account of the sums of money so borrowed or emitted,—to build and equip a navy—to agree upon the number of land forces, and to make requisitions from each state for its quota, in proportion to the number of white inhabitants in such state; which requisition shall be binding, and thereupon the legislature of each state shall appoint the regimental officers, raise the men and cloath, arm and equip them in a soldier like manner, at the expence of the united states, and the officers and men so cloathed, armed and equipped shall march to the place appointed, and within the time agreed on by the united states in congress assembled: But if the united states in congress assembled shall, on consideration of circumstances judge proper that any state should not raise men, or should raise a smaller number than its quota, and that any other state should raise a greater number of men than the quota thereof, such extra number shall be raised, officered, cloathed, armed and equipped in the same manner as the quota of such state, unless the legislature of such state shall judge that such extra number cannot be safely spared out of the same, in which case they shall raise officer, cloath, arm and equip as many of such extra number as they judge can be safely spared. And the officers and men so cloathed, armed and equipped, shall march to the place appointed, and within the time agreed on by the united states in congress assembled.

The united states in congress assembled shall never engage in a war, nor grant letters of marque and reprisal in time of peace, nor enter into any treaties or alliances, nor coin money, nor regulate the value thereof, nor ascertain the sums and expences necessary for the defence and welfare of the united states, or any of them, nor emit bills, nor borrow money on the credit of the united states, nor appropriate money, nor agree upon the number of vessels of war, to be built or purchased, or the number of land or sea forces to be raised, nor appoint a commander in chief of the army or navy, unless nine states assent to the same: nor shall a question on any other point, except for adjourning from day to day be determined, unless by the votes of a majority of the united states in congress assembled.

The congress of the united states shall have power to adjourn to any time within the year, and to any place within the united states, so that no period of adjournment be for a longer duration than the space of six Months, and shall publish the Journal of their proceedings monthly, except such parts thereof relating to treaties, alliances or military operations, as in their judgment require secresy; and the yeas and nays of the delegates of each state on any question shall be entered on the Journal, when it is desired by any delegate; and the delegates of a state, or any of them, at his or their request shall be furnished with a transcript of the said Journal, except such parts as are above excepted, to lay before the legislatures of the several states.

Article X. The committee of the states, or any nine of them, shall be authorized to execute, in the recess of congress, such of the powers of congress as the united states in congress assembled, by the consent of nine states, shall from time to time think expedient to vest them with; provided that no power be delegated to the said committee, for the exercise of which, by the articles of confederation, the voice of nine states in the congress of the united states assembled is requisite.

Article XI. Canada acceding to this confederation, and joining in the measures of the united states, shall be admitted into, and entitled to all the advantages of this union: but no other colony shall be admitted into the same, unless such admission be agreed to by nine states.

Article XII. All bills of credit emitted, monies borrowed and debts contracted by, or under the authority of congress, before the assembling of the united states, in pursuance of the present confederation, shall be deemed and considered as a charge against the united states, for payment and satisfaction whereof the said united states, and the public faith are hereby solemnly pledged.

Article XIII. Every state shall abide by the determinations of the united states in congress assembled, on all questions which by this confederation are submitted to them. And the Articles of this confederation shall be inviolably observed by every state, and the union shall be perpetual; nor shall any alteration at any time hereafter be made in any of them; unless such alteration be agreed to in a congress of the united states, and be afterwards confirmed by the legislatures of every state.

And Whereas it hath pleased the Great Governor of the World to incline the hearts of the legislatures we respectively represent in congress, to approve of, and to authorize us to ratify the said articles of confederation and perpetual union. Know Ye that we the undersigned delegates, by virtue of the power and authority to us given for that purpose, do by these presents, in the name and in behalf of our respective constituents, fully and entirely ratify and confirm each and every of the said articles of confederation and perpetual union, and all and singular the matters and things therein contained: And we do further solemnly plight and engage the faith of our respective constituents, that they shall abide by the determinations of the united states in congress assembled, on all questions, which by the said confederation are submitted to them. And that the articles thereof shall be inviolably observed by the states we respectively represent, and that the union shall be perpetual. In Witness whereof we have hereunto set our hands in Congress. Done at Philadelphia in the state of Pennsylvania the ninth Day of July in the Year of our Lord one Thousand seven Hundred and Seventy-eight, and in the third year of the independence of America.

On the part & behalf of the State of Delaware	{ Thos M:Kean Feby 22, 1779 { John Dickinson May 5th– 1779 { Nicholas Van Dyke,	Josiah Bartlett John Wentworth Junr August 8th 1778	} On the Part & behalf } of the State of } New Hampshire

| on the part and behalf of the State of Maryland | { John Hanson   March 1st, 1781
{ Daniel Carroll   do | John Hancock
Samuel Adams
Elbridge Gerry | } On the part and behalf
} of the State of
} Massachusetts Bay |

On the Part and Behalf of the State of Virginia — { Richard Henry Lee / John Banister / Thomas Adams / Jno Harvie / Francis Lightfoot Lee — Francis Dana / James Lovell / Samuel Holten

on the part and Behalf of the State of No. Carolina — { John Pènn, July 21st 1778 / Corns. Harnett / Jno. Williams — William Ellery / Henry Marchant / John Collins } On the part and behalf of the State of Rhode-Island and Providence Plantations

On the part & behalf of the State of South-Carolina — { Henry Laurens. / William Henry Drayton / Jno. Mathews / Richd. Hutson / Thos: Heyward Junr: — Roger Sherman / Samuel Huntington / Oliver Wolcott / Titus Hosmer / Andrew Adams } on the Part and behalf of the State of Connecticut

On the part & behalf of the State of Georgia — { Jno Walton   24th. July 1778 / Edwd. Telfair. / Edwd Langworthy. — Jas. Duane / Fras. Lewis / Wm: Duer. / Gouvr. Morris } On the Part and Behalf of the State of New York

Jno Witherspoon / Nathl. Scudder } On the Part and in Behalf of the State of New Jersey Novr. 26. 1778.—

Robt Morris. / Daniel Roberdeau / Jona: Bayard Smith. / William Clingan / Joseph Reed [22d.?] July 1778 } On the part and behalf of the State of Pennsylvania

1. Engrossed MS (LT), PCC, DNA. The engrossed document does not have a title. This heading is endorsed on the outside of the document. The title page of the printed pamphlet sent to the states reads "Articles of Confederation and Perpetual Union Between the States of," followed by the names of the states from New Hampshire to Georgia. For a careful analysis of the text of the engrossed Articles, see Julian P. Boyd, *The Articles of Confederation and Perpetual Union* (*Old South Leaflets*, Nos. 228–29 [Boston, Mass., 1960]).

III

Ratification of the Articles of Confederation by the States in Congress

22 June 1778–1 March 1781

Introduction

The Articles of Confederation sent to the states for their official consideration were in the form of a twenty-six page pamphlet signed by Henry Laurens, President of Congress. The pamphlet was accompanied by a letter, dated 17 November 1777, explaining the difficulties in writing the constitution, and requesting the state legislatures to authorize their delegates in Congress to be ready to ratify the Articles on 10 March 1778.

Nine states had ratified by 10 March, but some of them had also instructed their delegates to propose amendments. On that date Virginia was the only state prepared to ratify without qualification. The Maryland delegates presented their instructions and made it clear that Maryland would not ratify unless Congress were given control of western lands. The delegates from some states that had ratified had not yet received their instructions.

So few states were represented in March that Congress delayed action until 20 June, when it resolved that on 22 June the delegates would be called upon to present their instructions and powers, and that no amendments to the Articles of Confederation would be considered except those presented by a state.

Between 22 and 25 June, seven states offered amendments, but all of them were rejected by Congress. At the end of the debate on the 25th, Congress appointed a committee to draft a form of ratification to be placed at the end of the last article of the Confederation. The next day the form was approved, and the Articles were ordered engrossed on parchment. The engrossed document does not have a title, but it is endorsed: "Act of Confederation of The United States of America."

The delegates from eight of the ten states which had ratified signed the engrossed Articles on 9 July. Georgia, which had ratified on 26 February, and North Carolina, which had ratified on 25 April, were not represented on 9 July, but delegates from both states had signed by 24 July.

On 9 July Congress appointed Richard Henry Lee, Francis Dana, and Gouverneur Morris to prepare a circular letter to the three states which had not ratified. The New Jersey delegates signed on 26 November 1778 and one Delaware delegate on 22 February 1779.

Maryland, the last state, refused to instruct its delegates to ratify until 2 February 1781, and they signed on 1 March 1781. Congress then declared that "the Confederation of the United States of America was completed, each and every of the Thirteen United States from New Hampshire to Georgia, both included, having adopted and confirmed and by their delegates in Congress ratified the same."

The documents printed below are the formal acts of ratification by the states, which range all the way from legislative resolutions to formal laws, the instructions sent by the states to their delegates in Congress, and the actions of Congress upon amendments proposed by the states. The documents are arranged in the order in which the states presented their protests, amendments, and offers to ratify to Congress, followed by the dates on which the delegates from each state signed the engrossed Articles of Confederation.

A. MARYLAND, 22–23 June 1778

Instructions to Delegates in Congress, 22 December 1777[1]

The House, taking into consideration the report of the committee of the whole on the Articles of Confederation and perpetual Union, etc., came to the following resolutions thereon:

Resolved, That the delegates to Congress from the State of Maryland be instructed to endeavor to get an amendment of the fourth Article of the Confederation, by striking out the word "paupers" and inserting a provision, "that one state shall not be burthened with the maintenance of poor persons who may remove from another state."

Resolved, That the said delegates be instructed to use their endeavors to obtain an explanation of the eighth Article of the Confederation, which may be construed to comprehend those lands only which may be granted to or surveyed for any person at the time of ratifying the Articles of Confederation in the Congress of the United States; and to represent that all the lands within each state, thereafter granted to or surveyed for any person, with the buildings and improvements thereon, should from time to time be valued according to such mode as the United States in Congress assembled shall direct, to find the proportion in which each state ought to contribute towards the common expense, and supplying the treasury of the United States.

Resolved, That the delegates to Congress from this state be instructed to remonstrate to the Honorable Congress, that this state esteem it essentially necessary for rendering the Union lasting, that the United States in Congress assembled should have full power to ascertain and fix the western limits of those states that claim to the

Mississippi or South Sea. That this state consider themselves justly entitled to a right in common with the other members of the Union, to that extensive tract of country which lies to the westward of the frontiers of the United States, the property of which was not vested in or granted to individuals at the commencement of the present war. That the same hath been or may hereafter be gained from the king of Great Britain or the native Indians by the blood and treasure of all, and ought therefore to be a common estate to be granted out on terms beneficial to all the United States. And that they use their utmost endeavors to obtain, that an article to this effect be made part of the Confederation.

Instructions to Delegates in Congress, 20 June 1778[2]

This House having taken into consideration the report from a committee of the whole, relative to the Articles of Confederation and perpetual Union; also the particular instructions given to their delegates in Congress, during the last October session, have come to the resolutions herewith sent. . . .

Resolved, That this state hath, upon all occasions, shown her zeal to maintain and promote the general welfare of the United States of America; that, upon the same principles, this House is of opinion a confederation of perpetual friendship and union between the United States is highly necessary for the benefit of the whole; and this House is most willing and desirous to enter into a confederation and union, but at the same time such confederation, in their opinion, should be formed on the principles of justice and equity.

Resolved, That the delegates from this state to Congress consider themselves bound by the instructions given in October session last, and that they endeavor to procure from Congress an explicit answer to the propositions therein contained; but that they do not at any time consider themselves at liberty to ratify or confirm any confederation of perpetual friendship and union, until they have communicated such answer to the General Assembly of this state, and shall receive their express authority so to do.

Journals of Congress, 22 June 1778[3]

Congress proceeded to consider the objections of the states to the Articles of Confederation whereupon the delegates of Maryland read to Congress instructions they had just received from their constituents and moved,

That the objections of the State of Maryland to the Confederation be immediately taken up and considered by Congress, that the delegates of Maryland may transmit to that state with all possible dispatch the determination of Congress on those objections.[4]

Question put.

Resolved in the affirmative.

A motion was then made in behalf of Maryland: In Article 4 strike out the word "paupers" and after the words "or either of them" insert "That one state shall not be burthened with the maintainance [sic] of the poor, who may remove into it from any of the other in this union."

Question put.

Passed in the negative: one state only answering Aye.

Another amendment was moved in behalf of Maryland: Article 8th After the words "granted to or surveyed for" to insert "or which shall hereafter be granted to or surveyed for any person."

Question put.

Passed in the negative: four states answering Aye, eight answering No.

A third amendment was moved in behalf of Maryland: Article 9. After the words "shall be deprived of territory for the benefit of the united Unites [States]," insert "The united states in Congress assembled shall have the power to appoint commissioners, who shall be fully authorized and empowered to ascertain and restrict the boundaries of such of the confederated states, which claim to extend to the river Missisipi [sic] or South Sea."

After debate, Resolved, That the consideration thereof be postponed till tomorrow.

Adjourned to 10 o'clock tomorrow.

Journals of Congress, 23 June 1778[5]

Congress proceeded to consider the motion from Maryland under debate yesterday and after debate, Resolved, That the farther consideration thereof be postponed till the afternoon.

3 o'clock. Congress resumed the consideration of the motion from Maryland.

Question put.

Passed in the negative: four Ayes, five Noes.

Three other states coming in, a motion was made to reconsider the question just determined.

Question put.

Resolved in the affirmative.

The question being again put, Mr. Marchant required the yeas and nays.

New Hampshire			Pennsylvania		
Bartlett	no { no		Roberdeau	ay ⎫	
			Clingan	no ⎬ ay	
Massachusetts Bay			Jas. Smith	ay ⎭	
Hancock	no ⎫				
S. Adams	no		Delaware		
Gerry	no		M'Kean	ay { ay	
Dana	no ⎬ no				
Lovell	no		Maryland		
Holton	no ⎭		Plater	ay ⎫ ay	
			Carrol	ay ⎭	
Rhode Island					
Ellery	ay ⎫		Virginia		
Marchant	ay ⎬ ay		R. H. Lee	no	
Collins	ay ⎭		Banister	no ⎬ no	
			T. Adams	no ⎭	
Connecticut					
Sherman	no ⎫		South Carolina		
Huntington	no ⎬ no		Laurens	no ⎫	
Wolcot	no		Drayton	no	
Hosmer	no ⎭		Hutson	no ⎬ no	
			Matthews	no	
New York			Heyward	no ⎭	
Lewis	ay ⎫				
G. Morris	no ⎬ divided		Georgia		
			Langworthy	no { no	
New Jersey					
Witherspoon	ay ⎫				
Elmer	ay ⎬ ay				
Scudder	ay ⎭				

So it passed in the negative.

1. *Votes and Proceedings of the House of Delegates of the State of Maryland . . .* [31 Oct.–23 Dec. 1777] ([Annapolis, 1777]), 55. The Maryland legislature received copies of the Articles of Confederation on 3 December. On 13 December the House defeated a motion to delay consideration until the next session and four days later adopted three resolutions instructing the delegates to Congress. The Senate concurred on the 22nd.

2. *Votes and Proceedings of the House of Delegates of the State of Maryland . . .* [4–23 June 1778] ([Annapolis, 1778]), 129, 134. The House adopted the instructions on 18 June and accepted the instructions as amended by the Senate on 20 June.

3. PCC, Item 1, Rough Journals of Congress, DNA.

4. On 20 June Congress had resolved that the delegates would present their instructions beginning with New Hampshire and moving southward in the traditional order.

5. PCC, Item 1, Rough Journals of Congress, DNA.

B. NEW HAMPSHIRE, 23 June 1778

House of Representatives, 27 December 1777[1]

Voted, That the following words be printed at the bottom of the Articles of Confederation, and before the vote of the General Court relative to instructing the representatives, viz.:

"The foregoing Articles of Confederation, as formed by the honorable the Continental Congress, are printed and to be dispersed throughout this state, that every person may give their sentiment thereon. . . ."

House of Representatives, 24 February 1778[2]

The committee then proceeded to consider of the Articles of Confederation and perpetual Union, which being read and considered article by article, the committee agreed to the first, second, third, fourth, fifth, sixth and seventh articles; and the eighth Article being objected to and the arguments made pro and con, the committee adjourned to three o'clock afternoon—and then met according to adjournment, and resumed the consideration of the eighth Article of the Confederation and perpetual Union between the United States; and thereupon, reported, that the eighth Article be agreed to; also the ninth, tenth, eleventh, twelfth and thirteenth articles.

House of Representatives, 4 March 1778[3]

The House took under consideration the thirteen Articles of Confederation and perpetual Union between the thirteen United States of America, as agreed to by the Honorable Congress of said states, and came to the following resolution thereon, viz.:

Resolved, That we do agree to said Articles of Confederation, perpetual Union, etc. And do for ourselves and constituents engage that the same shall be inviolably observed by this state.

And the delegates of this state for the time being, at the Congress aforesaid are hereby empowered and instructed to ratify the same in behalf of this state.

Journals of Congress, 23 June 1778[4]

The delegates from New Hampshire, being called on for the report of their constituents upon the Confederation, informed Congress,

That the State of New Hampshire have, in their General Assembly, agreed to the Articles of Confederation as they now stand, and have empowered their delegates to ratify the same in behalf of their state.

1. Nathaniel Bouton, comp. and ed., *Documents and Records Relating to the State of New-Hampshire during the Period of the American Revolution, from 1776 to 1783* . . ., VIII (Concord, N.H., 1874), 758.

2. Ibid., VIII, 774. The committee mentioned was a joint committee of the House of Representatives and the Council.

3. Ibid., VIII, 778. Since there are no Council journals, the date of the Council's concurrence is unknown.

4. PCC, Item 1, Rough Journals of Congress, DNA.

C. MASSACHUSETTS, 23 June 1778

House of Representatives, 15 December 1777[1]

The House passed the following resolve, viz.:

Whereas the Honorable Congress have formed and proposed to the legislative body of this state Articles of Confederation and perpetual Union between the United States of America, and it is considered by this House as a matter of great importance, and beyond the usual course of business expected by their constituents at the election of their representatives, therefore,

Resolved, That it be recommended to the several towns in this state to instruct their representatives to act and do as they shall judge meet for the advantage of this and the other United States, relative to this matter.

House of Representatives, 19 January 1778[2]

Ordered, That the several members of this House (who are not empowered to act upon the proposed Articles of Confederation of the United States) be and they are hereby directed immediately to write to the selectmen of their respective towns, desiring them forthwith to call a meeting of their inhabitants, or at any meeting now subsisting, if they think proper, to empower their representatives to act upon the proposed Articles of Confederation aforesaid, and to furnish said representatives with a copy of their doings without delay.

And the members of this House are directed to furnish said selectmen with the resolve of this House passed the last session relative to the matter aforesaid.

Instructions to the Delegates in Congress, 10 March 1778[3]

THE General Court of the State of *Massachusetts-Bay*, having attentively considered the Articles of Confederation and Perpetual Union between the United States of *America*, recommended to our attention by the honorable Congress, do approve of them in general, as well calculated to secure the freedom, sovereignty and independence of the United States; perhaps no plan could have been proposed better adapted to the circumstances of all: We therefore the Council and House of Representatives of this State, in General Court assembled, do in the name and behalf of the good people of this State, instruct you their Delegates, to subscribe said Articles of Confederation and Perpetual Union, as they were recommended by Congress, unless the following alterations, or such as may be proposed by the other States, can be received and adopted, without endangering the Union proposed.

The first thing we desire your attention to, before you ratify and confirm these articles, is the mode of supplying the Continental treasury with money to defray the public expences, pointed out in the eighth article; in short, we conceive the Questions upon this article to be so difficult of solution without some experience of the effect, any method proposed may be attended with; that we apprehend provision ought to be made for varying the mode from time to time until experience has discovered which will be the most equitable plan, which when discovered and laid before the several States, will doubtless be confirmed:

The provision made in the sixth Paragraph of the Ninth Article, which makes the assent of *nine States* necessary to exercise the powers with which Congress are *vested*, does not give all that security to the States in these important matters which we think necessary, and which perhaps was intended by Congress; as the Paragraph now stands, it will put it in the power of the nine smallest States to give a Negative on the most important and necessary business, and as it is probable that a very small majority of the people of the United States, will be contained in the nine smallest States, nay perhaps less than half, it certainly ought not be in their power to give law in the important matters mentioned in this Paragraph; we apprehend it would be better to substitute in the room of *nine States,* these words, *ten States, or at least the Delegates for two thirds of the people of the United States of America represented in Congress.*

The Paragraph which determines the principle on which each State is to furnish its quota of the Army, demands your special attention, because it appears to be unequal, and consequently injurious, if the numbers to be furnished by each State to the Army, are to be rated in proportion to the number of Whites, it will be unequal, because those numbers are so, and will be injurious by operating as a Tax by the bounties necessary to be given, and by an unequal drain of the inhabitants, and consequently a diminution of the many advantages derived from their industry and labour, while other States who have a less number of Whites, tho' perhaps an equal, if not greater number of inhabitants are free from the burthen of the first, and the disadvantages arising from the last.

If any improper term of words now in any Article, or if any sentiment may in your Opinion be better expressed, you will propose and agree to have proper alterations made.

You will consider yourselves, also at liberty to consent to amendments proposed by other States, or their members, provided that such amendments are not materially repugnant to the Articles of Confederation, or the spirit of these Instructions.

Journals of Congress, 23 June 1778[4]

The delegates from Massachusetts Bay being called on for the report of their constituents upon the Confederation, read sundry objections transmitted to them by their constituents and thereupon moved,

That the eighth Article be reconsidered so far as relates to the criterion fixed on for settling the proportion of taxes to be paid by each state, that an amendment may be made, so that the rule of apportionment may be varied from time to time by Congress until experience shall have showed what rule of apportionment will be most equal and consequently most just.

Question put for reconsidering.

Passed in the negative: 2 Ayes, 8 Noes.

Another motion was made to reconsider the fifth section of the 9th Article so far as relates to the rule of apportioning the number of forces to be raised by each state on the requisition of Congress.

Question put for reconsidering.

Passed in the negative: 3 Ayes, 7 Noes.

A third motion was made to reconsider the sixth section of the 9th Article so far as it makes the assent of nine states necessary to exercise the powers with which Congress are thereby invested.

Question put for reconsidering.

Passed in the negative.

1. *A Journal of the Honorable House of Representatives of the State of Massachusetts-Bay* . . . [28 May 1777–1 May 1778] (Boston, 1777 [–1778]), 143. The House had received a copy of the Articles of Confederation earlier in the day.

2. Ibid., 158.

3. (LT), *Resolves of the General Assembly of the State of Massachusetts-Bay* . . . [28 May 1777–1 May 1778] ([Boston, 1778]), 48-49. These instructions were drawn up by a joint committee of the House of Representatives and the Council which had been appointed on 19 February. On 11 March, the day after it adopted the instructions, the legislature empowered the President of the Council to sign them and ordered that each delegate receive an attested copy.

4. PCC, Item 1, Rough Journals of Congress, DNA.

D. RHODE ISLAND, 23 June 1778

Instructions to the Delegates in Congress, 16 February 1778[1]

IT is Voted and Resolved, That the following instructions be, and they are hereby, given to the Delegates appointed to represent this State in Congress, *to wit:*

INSTRUCTIONS to the Honorable *Stephen Hopkins, William Ellery,* and *Henry Marchant,* Esqrs; Delegates from this State in Congress, respecting the proposed Articles of Confederation and perpetual Union between the *Thirteen United States.*

First. BY the fifth Article, no State can be represented by less than two Members. As it will be inconvenient and burthensome for the small States to keep in Congress more than two or three Members, it may happen from Sickness, Death, or some other unavoidable Accident, that such State may have not more than one Member present in Congress; and thereby be deprived of a Voice, which may be highly prejudicial. You are therefore instructed to move in Congress for an Alteration in that Article; so that in Case by Sickness, Death, or any other unavoidable Accident, but one of the Members of a State can attend Congress, such State may be represented in Congress by one Member for such reasonable Space of Time as shall be agreed upon by Congress, and ascertained by the Articles of Confederation.

Secondly. TAXES ought to be assessed equally; and nothing will have a greater Tendency to induce Freemen to submit to heavy Burthens, than an Opinion that they are justly proportioned: And as very material Alterations may happen in the Abilities of the different States to pay Taxes in the Course of a few Years; You are instructed to move in Congress for the following Addition to the eighth Article, "That such Estimate be taken and made once in every five Years at least."

Thirdly. THE King of *Great-Britain*, before the present War, was vested with the Property of great Quantities of Land; and enjoyed large Revenues arising from Quit-Rents within the *United States.*—By commencing and carrying on this unnatural War, with the avowed Design of reducing the *United States* to the most debasing and ignominious Servitude, that Crown hath justly forfeited such Lands and Revenues. If the Forfeiture takes Place, it will be in Consequence of the Exertions of all the *United States,* by whom the War is supported.—Consequently all the *United States* ought to be proportionably benefited by the Forfeiture.—But should the several States in which such Lands lie, and Revenues are raised, appropriate them to their seperate Use, they will at the End of the War be possessed of great Funds to reimburse themselves their Expences; while those States which are not in that Situation, although at a proportionable Expence of Blood and Treasure in recovering such Forfeiture, not receiving any Benefit therefrom, will be left to struggle with an immense Debt, which is unequal and unjust.—The Claim of the Crown of *Great-Britain* to such Lands and Revenues was uncontested before the present War, none of the States having formed any Pretensions thereto, which is another cogent Argument why the Forfeiture ought to be vested in all the *United States.* Omitting many Things which your Attention to this *important* Object will suggest to You, it is proper to observe that Congress have promised Lands to the Army; and that, unless they be provided out of such Forfeiture, several of the States, and this in particular, will be in a very unhappy Predicament: You are therefore instructed to move in Congress that it be inserted in the Articles of Confederation, that all such Lands and Revenues be forfeited to the *United States,* to be disposed of, and appropriated, by Congress, for the Benefit of the whole Confederacy.— It is not meant, by this Instruction, that Congress should claim the Jurisdiction of the forfeited Lands; but that the same should remain to the State in which it lies.

Fourthly. ALTHOUGH this Assembly deem the Amendments and Alterations herein proposed of very great Importance, yet the Completion of the UNION is so indispensibly necessary that You are instructed, after having used your utmost Influence to procure them to be made, in Case they should be rejected not to decline acceding, on the Part of this State, to the Articles of Confederation; taking Care that these proposed Amendments and Alterations be previously entered upon the Records of the Congress, that it may appear they were made before the signing of the Confederation; and that this State intends hereafter to renew the Motion for them.—This Assembly trusting that Congress, at some future Time, convinced of their Utility and Justice, will adopt them; and that they will be confirmed by all the States.

IT is further Voted and Resolved, That an Exemplification of this Act be made and transmitted by the Secretary, to the Delegates appointed to represent this State in Congress, who are indispensibly to observe and follow the said Instructions.

THIS Assembly having taken into Consideration the Articles of Confederation and perpetual Union between the States of *New-Hampshire, Massachusetts-Bay, Rhode-Island* and *Providence Plantations, Connecticut, New-York, New-Jersey, Pennsylvania, Delaware, Maryland, Virginia, North-Carolina, South-Carolina,* and *Georgia,* transmitted by Congress to this State; and having had them repeatedly read, and having maturely weighed, and most seriously deliberated upon them, as their Importance to this and the other States, and to Posterity, deserves; and considering also the pressing Necessity of completing the Union, as a Measure essential to the Preservation of the Independence and Safety of the said States, *Do Vote and Resolve,* and *It is Voted and Resolved,* That the Honorable *Stephen Hopkins,* Esq; *William Ellery,* Esq; and *Henry Marchant,* Esq; the Delegates to represent this State in Congress, or any one of them, be, and they are hereby, fully authorized and empowered, on the Part and Behalf of this State, to accede to and sign the said Articles of Confederation and perpetual Union, in such solemn Form and Manner as Congress shall think best adapted to a Transaction so important to the present and future Generations: Provided that the same be acceded to by Eight of the other States; And in Case any Alterations in, or Additions to, the said Articles of Confederation and perpetual Union, shall be made by Nine of the said States in Congress assembled, That the said Delegates, or any one of them, be, and they are hereby, authorized and empowered, in like Manner, to accede to and sign the said Articles of Confederation and perpetual Union, with the Alterations and Additions which shall be so made.

IT is further Voted and Resolved, That this Assembly will, and do hereby, in Behalf of the said State of *Rhode-Island* and *Providence Plantations,* in the most solemn Manner, pledge the Faith of the said State to hold and consider the Acts of the said Delegates, or any one of them, in so acceding to and signing the said Articles of Confederation and perpetual Union, as valid and binding upon the said State in all future Time.

AND it is further Voted and Resolved, That a fair Copy of this Act be made, and authenticated under the publick Seal of this State, with the Signature of his Excellency the Governor, and be transmitted to the said Delegates: And that the same shall be sufficient Warrant and Authority to the said Delegates, or any one of them, for the Purposes aforesaid.

IT is Voted and Resolved, That the Honorable *Henry Marchant,* Esq; be, and he is hereby, requested to give his Attendance on Congress by the twentieth of *March* next: That when a Report shall be made by the several Legislatures of the Articles of Confederation proposed to them by Congress, he may with our other Delegate procure such Alterations therein as are agreeable to the Instructions given them by this Assembly.

IT is further Voted and Resolved, That a Copy hereof, with an Exemplification of said Instructions, be transmitted to the said *Henry Marchant,* Esq; that he may proceed therewith accordingly.

Journals of Congress, 23 June 1778[2]

The delegates from Rhode Island, being called upon for the report of their constituents, produced instructions and thereupon moved,

1. In the 5th Article after the word "two" to insert "members unless by sickness, death or any other unavoidable accident but one of the members of a state can attend Congress, in which case such state may be represented in Congress by one member for the space of _____ Months."

Question put, to agree to the amendment.

Passed in the negative: one Aye and nine Noes.

2. In the 8th Article after the word "appoint" to add "such estimate to be taken and made once in every five years."

Question put.

Passed in the negative: 4 Ayes, 6 Noes.

3. In the 9th Article at the end of the 2nd paragraph after the words "for the benefit of the united states" to add, "provided nevertheless that all lands within these states, the property of which before the present war was vested in the crown of great Britain or out of

which revenues from quit rents arose, payable to the said crown shall be deemed, taken and considered as the property of these united states and be disposed of and appropriated by Congress for the benefit of the whole confederacy, reserving however to the states within whose limits such crown lands may be the entire and compleat jurisdiction thereof."

Question put.

Passed in the negative: 1 Aye, nine Noes.

1. (LT), *At the General Assembly of the Governor and Company of the State of Rhode-Island and Providence Plantations* . . . [Session Laws, 9–16 Feb. 1778] (Attleborough, Mass., [1778]), 24–28. On 20 December 1777 the legislature moved that the Articles of Confederation be considered during its next session. The legislature considered the Articles on 15 and 16 February 1778 and adopted instructions to the delegates. The Governor signed them on 18 February (JCC, XI, 663).

2. PCC, Item 1, Rough Journals of Congress, DNA.

E. CONNECTICUT, 23 June 1778

Governor and Council of Safety, 16 December 1777[1]

Advised, That His Excellency the Governor procure three hundred copies of the Articles of Confederation lately received from Congress, and order that the printer transmit one such copy to [the] selectmen of each town in this state as soon as possible, and the remainder to the General Assembly at their adjourned session at Hartford on the 8th day of January next.

Instructions to the Delegates in Congress, February 1778[2]

The Articles of Confederation and perpetual Union proposed by Congress to be entered into by the thirteen United States of America being laid before this Assembly by His Excellency the Governor were read and maturely considered. Whereupon,

Resolved, as the opinion of this Assembly, That said Articles in general appear to be well adapted to cement and preserve the union of said states, to secure their freedom and independence and promote their general welfare: but that with some amendments they may be rendered more perfect, equitable and satisfactory. Wherefore the delegates of this state are hereby instructed to propose to the consideration of Congress the following amendments, viz.:

1. That in the eighth Article, as a rule for determining each state's

proportion of the common expense, instead of the value of the lands, buildings, etc., as expressed in said Article, be inserted the number of inhabitants in each state; this being in the opinion of this Assembly a more certain, equitable and practicable rule than the other. Trade and manufactures, which employ and support great numbers of inhabitants, being sources of wealth to a state as well as the produce of lands; besides it will be very difficult, if not impossible, to obtain such an estimate of the value of the lands and buildings in the United States as would do justice or give satisfaction to the several states.

2. That next after the fifth paragraph in the 9th Article be inserted the following clause, viz.: Provided, That no land army shall be kept up by the United States in time of peace, nor any officers or pensioners kept in pay by them who are not in actual service, except such as are or may be rendered unable to support themselves by wounds received in battle in the service of said states, agreeable to the provision already made by a resolution of Congress.

The foregoing amendments being agreed to in substance may be made in such manner and form as Congress shall think proper.

And whereas .other amendments may be proposed by some of the other states, and it being highly expedient for the welfare and security of the said states that the Articles of Confederation be finally concluded and ratified as soon as possible, therefore,

Resolved, That the delegates of this state who shall be present in Congress be and they are hereby fully authorized and empowered in behalf of this state to agree to and ratify the said Articles of Confederation with such amendments, if any be, as by them in conjunction with the delegates of the other states in Congress shall be thought proper.

Journals of Congress, 23 June 1778[3]

The delegates from Connecticut being called upon for the report of their constituents produced instructions to move certain amendments. Whereupon, they moved in behalf of the state in the 8th Article to strike out what follows the words "in proportion to" to the end of the sentence, and in lieu thereof to insert "the number of inhabitants in each state."

Question put.

Passed in the negative: 3 Ayes, 9 Noes.

In the 9th Article, at the end of the 5 paragraph to add the words following: "Provided that no land army shall be kept up by the united states in time of peace, nor any officers or pensioners kept in pay by them, who are not in actual service except such as are or may be rendered unable to support themselves by wounds received in battle in the service of the said states agreeably to the provisions already made by a resolution of Congress."

Question put.

Passed in the negative: 1 Aye, 11 Noes.

1. Charles J. Hoadly, ed., *The Public Records of the State of Connecticut . . .* I (Hartford, Conn., 1894), 467. The Council met at Lebanon, home of Governor Jonathan Trumbull, Sr.

2. Ibid., I, 532–33. According to the Governor's message opening the February 1778 session at Hartford, the legislature had considered the Articles of Confederation in January (ibid., I, 521). The General Assembly met from 12 February 1778 until the first week or two in March, but the date the instructions were adopted cannot be determined.

3. PCC, Item 1, Rough Journals of Congress, DNA.

F. NEW YORK, 23 June 1778

Act of Ratification, 6 February 1778[1]

An act of Accession to, and Approbation of certain proposed Articles of Confederation and perpetual Union, between the United States of America, and to authorize the Delegates, of the State of New-York, *to ratify the same on the Part and Behalf of this State, in the Congress of the said United States.* Passed the 6th of February, 1778.

Whereas the Freedom, Sovereignty and Independence of the said States, which, with a Magnanimity, Fortitude, Constancy and Love of Liberty, hitherto unparalelled, they have asserted and maintained, against their cruel and unrelenting Enemies, the King and Parliament of the Realm of *Great-Britain,* will, for their lasting and unshaken Security, in a great Measure depend, under God, on a wise, well concerted, intimate and equal Confederation of the said United States. *And whereas* the Honorable Congress of the said United States, have transmitted, for the Consideration of the Legislature of this State; and for their Ratification in Case they shall approve of the same, the following Articles of confederation, *viz.*

[Text of Articles of Confederation]

And whereas the Senate and Assembly of this State of *New-York,* in Legislature, convened, have separately taken the said several Articles of Confederation into their respective most deliberate and mature

Consideration; and by their several and respective Resolutions, deliberately made and entered into for the Purpose, have fully and entirely approved of the same;

In Order therefore, That such Approval may be published and made known to the whole World, with all the Solemnities of Law; and that all the Subjects of this State, and others inhabiting and residing therein, from Time to Time, and at all Times thereafter, as long as the said Confederation shall subsist and endure, may be bound by and held to the due Observance of the said Articles of Confederation, as a Law of this State, if the same shall be duly ratified by all the said United States in Congress assembled.

Be it enacted, and declared by the People of the State of New-York, *represented in Senate and Assembly, and it is hereby enacted and declared by the Authority of the same,* That the said several above recited Articles of Confederation and all and singular the Clauses, Matters and Things in the same contained, be, and the same are hereby fully accepted, received and approved of, for and in Behalf of the People of this State.

And to the End that the same may, with all due Form and Solemnity, be ratified and confirmed by this State in Congress;

Be it further enacted by the Authority aforesaid, That the Delegates of this State, in the said Congress of the United States of *America,* or any two of the said Delegates, shall be, and hereby are fully authorised, impowered and required, wholly, intirely and absolutely, for and in Behalf of the People of this State, and in such Manner and under such Formalities, as shall be determined in Congress, to ratify and confirm, all and every of the said above recited Articles of Confederation, and all and singular the Clauses, Matters and Things in the same contained; and that on Exemplification of this Act, tested by his Excellency the Governor, or the Lieutenant Governor or President of the Senate of this State, for the Time being, administring the Government, and authenticated with the Great Seal of this State, shall be full and conclusive Evidence of this Act. *Provided always,* That nothing in this Act, or the said above recited Articles of Confederation contained, nor any Act, Matter or Thing, to be done and transacted by the Delegates of this State, in Congress, in and concerning the Premises or any Part thereof, shall bind or oblige, or be construed, deemed or esteemed to bind or oblige the Government, Legislature, People, Subjects, Inhabitants or Residents, of this State, until the said above recited Articles of Confederation, shall have been duly ratified, and confirmed by, or in Behalf of, all the said United States in Congress assembled; any Thing herein, or in the said above recited Articles of Confederation contained to the contrary thereof, in anywise notwithstanding.

Journals of Congress, 23 June 1778[2]

The delegates of New York being called upon for the report of their constituents respecting the Articles of Confederation, produced under the Great Seal of their state an exemplification of the act of the legislature thereof ratifying the said Articles as passed by Congress, with a proviso that the same shall not be binding on the state until all the other states in the Union ratify the same.

1. (LT), *Laws of the State of New-York . . .* [6 Feb. 1778–27 March 1783] (Poughkeepsie, 1782 [–1783]), 3–6. Governor George Clinton submitted the Articles of Confederation to the legislature on 16 January 1778. Both houses were virtually unanimous in support of the Articles, and only two members objected to the 11th Article. The Assembly also proposed to delete the words "on the Part and Behalf of this State" from the title of the act, but the Senate refused to agree. The act was sent to the Council of Revision on 5 February. The Council approved the act the next day, and Governor Clinton signed it on 16 February (JCC, XI, 667–68).

2. PCC, Item 1, Rough Journals of Congress, DNA.

G. NEW JERSEY, 23, 25 June 1778

New Jersey Representation to Congress, 15–16 June 1778[1]

To the UNITED STATES in CONGRESS Assembled. *The* Representation *of the* LEGISLATIVE-COUNCIL *and* GENERAL ASSEMBLY *of the State of* New-Jersey.

Sheweth,

That the Articles of Confederation and perpetual Union, between the States of *New-Hampshire, Massachusetts-Bay, Rhode-Island* and *Providence Plantations, Connecticut, New-York, New-Jersey, Pennsylvania, Delaware, Maryland, Virginia, North-Carolina, South-Carolina,* and *Georgia,* proposed by the Honourable the Congress, to the said States severally, for their Confirmation, have been by us fully and attentively considered, upon which we beg Leave to make the following remarks:

1st. In the fifth Article, where, among other Things, the Qualifications of the Delegates from the several States are described, there is no Mention of any Oath, Test, or Declaration to be taken or made by them, previous to their Admission to Seats in Congress.—It is indeed to be presumed, the respective States will be careful that the Delegates they send to assist in managing the general Interest of the Union, take the Oaths to the Government from which they derive their Authority; but as the United States collectively considered, have

Interests as well as each particular State, we are of Opinion, that some Test or Obligation binding each Delegate while he continues in the Trust, to consult and pursue the former as well as the latter, and particularly to assent to no Vote or Proceeding which may violate the general Confederation, is necessary. The Laws and Usages of all civilized Nations evince the Propriety of an Oath on such Occasions; and the more solemn and important the Deposite, the more strong and explicit ought the Obligation to be.

2d. By the sixth and ninth Articles, the Regulation of Trade seems to be committed to the several States within their separate Jurisdictions, in such a Degree as may involve many Difficulties and Embarrassments, and be attended with injustice to some States in the Union:—We are of Opinion, that the sole and exclusive Power of regulating the Trade of the United States with foreign Nations, ought to be clearly vested in the Congress, and that the Revenue arising from all Duties and Customs imposed thereon, ought to be appropriated to the building, equipping and manning of a Navy, for the Protection of the Trade, and Defence of the Coasts, and to such other publick and general Purposes, as to the Congress shall seem proper, and for the common Benefit of the States. This Principle appears to us to be just, and it may be added, that great Security will by this Means be derived to the Union from the Establishment of a common and mutual Interest.

3d. It is wisely provided in the sixth Article, that no Body of Forces shall be kept up by any State in Time of Peace, except such Number only as, in the Judgment of the United States in Congress assembled, shall be deemed requisite to garrison the Forts necessary for the Defence of such State: We think it ought also to be provided, and clearly expressed, that no Body of Troops be kept up by the United States, in Time of Peace, except such Number only as shall be allowed by the Assent of nine States. A standing Army, a Military Establishment and every Appendage thereof in Time of Peace, is totally abhorrent from the Ideas and Principles of this State.—In the memorable Act of Congress, declaring the United Colonies free and independent States, it is emphatically mentioned, as one of the Causes of Separation from *Great-Britain,* that the Sovereign thereof had kept up among us in Time of Peace, standing Armies without the Consent of the Legislatures—It is to be wished the Liberties and Happiness of the People may, by the Confederation, be carefully and explicitly guarded in this Respect.

4th. On the eighth Article we observe, that as frequent Settlements of the Quotas for Supplies and Aids to be furnished by the several States, in Support of the general Treasury, will be requisite, so they ought to be secured. It cannot be thought improper or unnecessary to have them struck once at least in every five Years, and oftener if Circumstances will allow; the Quantity or Value of Real Property in some States may increase much more rapidly than in others, and therefore the Quota which is at one Time just, will at another be disproportionate.

5th. The Boundaries and Limits of each State ought to be fully and finally fixed and made known; this we apprehend would be attended with very salutary Effects, by preventing Jealousies as well as Controversies, and promoting Harmony and Confidence among the States: If the Circumstances of the Times would not admit of this, previous to the Proposal of the Confederation to the several States, the Establishment of the Principles upon which, and the Rule and Mode by which the Determination may be conducted, at a Time more convenient and favourable, and a Provision for dispatching the same at an early Period not exceeding five Years from the final Ratification of the Confederation, would be satisfactory.

6th. The ninth Article provides, that no State shall be deprived of Territory for the Benefit of the United States:—Whether we are to understand that by Territory, is intended any Lands, the Property of which was heretofore vested in the Crown of *Great-Britain;* or that no Mention of such Lands is made in the Confederation; we are constrained to observe, that the present War, as we always apprehended, was undertaken for the general Defence and Interest of the confederating Colonies, now the United States. It was ever the confident Expectation of this State, that the Benefits derived from a successful Contest were to be general and proportionate, and that the Property of the common Enemy, falling in Consequence of a prosperous Issue of the War, would belong to the United States, and be appropriated to their Use: We are therefore greatly disappointed in finding no Provision made in the Confederation for empowering the Congress to dispose of such Property, but especially the vacant and unpatented Lands, commonly called the Crown Lands, for defraying the Expences of the War, and for other such publick and general Purposes.—The Jurisdiction ought in every Instance to belong to the respective States within the Charter or determined Limits of which such Lands may be seated; but Reason and Justice must decide, that the Property which existed in the Crown of *Great-Britain,* previous to the present Revolution, ought now to belong to the Congress, in Trust for the Use and Benefit of the United States: They have fought and bled for it in Proportion to their respective Abilities, and therefore the Reward ought not to be predilectionally distributed. Shall such States as are shut out by Situation from availing themselves of the least Advantage from this Quarter, be left to sink under an enormous Debt, whilst others are enabled in a short Period to replace all their Expenditures from the hard Earnings of the whole Confederacy?

7th. The ninth Article also provides, that the Requisitions for Land-Forces to be furnished by the several States, shall be proportioned to the Number of *white* Inhabitants in each.—In the Act of Independence we find the following Declaration: 'We hold these Truths to be self-evident, that all Men are created equal; that they are endowed by their Creator with certain unalienable Rights, among which are Life, Liberty, and the Pursuit of Happiness;' of this Doctrine it is not a very remote Consequence that all the Inhabitants of every Society, be the Colour of their Complexion what it may, are bound to promote the Interest thereof, according to their respective Abilities: They ought therefore to be brought into the Account on this Occasion. But admitting Necessity or Expediency to justify the Refusal of Liberty in certain Circumstances, to Persons of a particular Colour; we think it unequal to reckon Nothing upon such in this Case.—If the whole Number of Inhabitants in a State, whose Inhabitants are all Whites, both those who are called into the Field, and those who remain to till the Ground, and labour in Mechanick Arts and otherwise, are reckoned in the Estimate for striking the Proportion of Forces to be furnished by that State, ought even a Part of the latter Description to be left out in another? Should it be improper for special local Reasons to admit them in Arms, for the Defence of the Nation, yet we conceive that the Proportion of Forces to be embodied, ought to be fixed according to the whole Number of Inhabitants in the State, from whatever Class they may be raised. As it is of indispensible Necessity in every War, that a Part of the Inhabitants be employed for the Uses of Husbandry and otherwise at Home, while others are called into the Field, there must be the same Propriety that Persons of a different Colour who are employed for this Purpose in one State, while Whites are employed for the same Purpose in another, be reckoned in the Amount of the Inhabitants in the present Instance.

8th. In order that the Quota of Troops to be furnished in each State on Occasion of a War, may be equitably ascertained, we are of Opinion that the Inhabitants of the Several States ought to be numbered as frequently as the Nature of the Case will admit, and once at least every five Years, the disproportionate Increase in the Population of different States may render such Provision absolutely necessary.

9th. It is provided in the ninth Article, that the Assent of nine States out of thirteen shall be necessary to determine in sundry

Cases of the highest Concern. If this Proportion be proper and just, it ought to be kept up, should the States increase in Number, and a Declaration thereof made for the Satisfaction of the Union.

We think it our indispensable Duty to solicit the Attention of Congress to these Considerations and Remarks, and to request the Purport and Meaning of them may be adopted as Part of the general Confederation, by which Means we apprehend the mutual Interest of all the States will be better secured and promoted, and the Legislature of this State will then be justified in ratifying the same.

Ordered,

That the President do sign a Copy of the foregoing Representation, and transmit the same to the Delegates of this State, to be presented to Congress.

Journals of Congress, 23 June 1778[2]

The delegates from New Jersey being called upon for the report of their constituents respecting the Articles of Confederation laid before Congress a representation of the Legislative Council and General Assembly of their state.

Adjourned to 10 o'clock tomorrow.

Journals of Congress, 25 June 1778[3]

Congress took into consideration the representation from New Jersey which was read as follows:

[Text of the New Jersey Representation]

Whereupon, a motion was made, That the several articles in the Confederation referred to in the representation of the State of New Jersey be so far reconsidered at this time, as to admit the purport and meaning of the additions, alterations and amendments proposed in the said representation.

Question put.

Passed in the negative: 3 Ayes, 6 Noes, one divided.

1. (LT), *Journal of the Proceedings of the Legislative-Council of the State of New-Jersey* . . . [28 Oct. 1777–8 Oct. 1778] (Trenton, 1779), 77–79. Governor William Livingston submitted the Articles of Confederation to the General Assembly on 4 December 1777. The Assembly read them on 26 February 1778, but took no action. Livingston reminded the Assembly on 23 March and 29 May that it had not acted on the Articles. On 25 March a joint committee of the Assembly and Council began to consider the Articles, but after a few sessions it

118

accomplished little. On 2 June the joint committee began meeting again, and on 15 June it reported nine amendments to the Articles. On the same day another joint committee drafted a representation to accompany the report. The Council approved the report and the representation on 15 June, and the Assembly approved them on 15 and 16 June, respectively.

2. PCC, Item 1, Rough Journals of Congress, DNA.

3. Ibid.

H. PENNSYLVANIA, 25 June 1778

Act of Ratification, 5 March 1778[1]

The REPRESENTATIVES *of the Freemen of the Common-Wealth of* Pennsylvania, *in General Assembly met,*

To the Honourable Benjamin Franklin, *Doctor of Laws,* Robert Morris, *Esquire,* Daniel Roberdeau, *Esquire,* Jonathan B. Smith, *Esquire,* James Smith, *Esquire, of York Town,* William Clingan, *Esquire,* and Joseph Reed, *Esquire, Delegates for the said Common-Wealth in the Congress of the United States of America,* send Greeting.

KNOW YE, That We the said Representatives, having taken into our most serious and weighty consideration and deliberation, the Articles of Confederation between the States of New-Hampshire, Massachusetts-Bay, Rhode-Island and Providence Plantations, Connecticut, New-York, New-Jersey, Pennsylvania, Delaware, Maryland, Virginia, North-Carolina, South-Carolina and Georgia, lately transmitted to us by the Honourable HENRY LAURENS, Esquire, President of the said Congress, Do, by this present instrument, signed by our Speaker and sealed with the seal of the Laws of this Common-Wealth, accede to, ratify, confirm, and agree to the said Articles; which said articles are as follows, to wit.

[Text of Articles of Confederation]

And We the said Representatives do hereby authorise, impower, require and enjoin You the said *Benjamin Franklin, Robert Morris, Daniel Roberdeau, Jonathan B. Smith, James Smith, William Clingan,* and *Joseph Reed,* or any [two] of you, in the name of the said Common-Wealth of Pennsylvania to accede to, ratify, confirm and agree to the said Articles of Confederation. IN TESTIMONY whereof We have caused the Seal of the Laws of Pennsylvania to be hereunto affixed in General Assembly at Lancaster, the [5th] day of [March], in the year of our Lord One Thousand Seven Hundred and Seventy-eight.

Supreme Executive Council to the Delegates in Congress, Lancaster, 30 April 1778[2]

The Supreme Executive Council of Pennsylvania, thoroughly persuaded that the complete establishment of the Confederation of said states must greatly consolidate the Union, and invigorate the negotiations of Congress at this important conjuncture, do hereby add their concurrence in the Articles of Confederation, now under public consideration, to the acceptance and consent of the legislature of this state; and do recommend to you, gentlemen, to use your best endeavors and influence in forwarding the said business, which Council consider as of the highest importance to the honor, advantage and safety of the United Body of North America.

Journals of Congress, 25 June 1778[3]

The delegates of Pennsylvania were then called on for the report of their constituents relative to the Articles of Confederation, whereupon,

They moved in behalf of their state,

1. In the first paragraph of 5th Article to expunge the words "for the remainder of the year."

Question put.

Passed in the negative: 2 Ayes, 8 Noes, 1 divided.

2. That such part of the 9th Article as respects the post office be altered or amended so as that Congress be obliged to lay the accounts annually before the legislature[s] of the several states.

Question put.

Passed in the negative: 2 Ayes, 9 Noes.

3. In the 5th paragraph of the 9 Article to expunge the word "White."

Question put.

Passed in the negative: 3 Ayes, 7 Noes, one divided.

4. In the last section of the 9th Article after the word "delegates" add "respectively."

Question put.

Passed in the negative: 1 Aye, 10 Noes.

1. (LT), *Minutes of the Second General Assembly of the Common-Wealth of Pennsylvania* . . . [27 Oct. 1777–11 Sept. 1778] (Lancaster, 1778), 53–58. The Articles of Confederation were read on 8 December 1777. They were considered on 16–17 December, and then dropped until 25 February 1778. On 3 March a committee, consisting of John Read, James McLene, and Robert Whitehill, drafted

the resolutions which the Assembly adopted on 5 March.

2. Samuel Hazard, ed., *Pennsylvania Archives,* VI [1st series] (Philadelphia, Pa., 1853), 455. The letter was addressed to all of the delegates mentioned in the resolutions, save Benjamin Franklin, who was in Europe.

3. PCC, Item 1, Rough Journals of Congress, DNA.

I. VIRGINIA, 25 June 1778

Resolutions of Ratification, 16 December 1777[1]

Resolved, *nemine contra dicente,* That a speedy ratification of the Articles of Confederation between the United States of America will confound the devices of their foreign and frustrate the machinations of their domestic enemies, encourage their firm friends and fix the wavering, contribute much to the support of their public credit and the restoration of the value of their paper money, produce unanimity in their councils at home, and add weight to their negotiations abroad, and completing the independence of their country establish the best foundation for its prosperity.

Resolved, *nemine contra dicente,* That the Articles of Confederation and perpetual Union proposed by Congress the 17th of November last, between the States of New Hampshire, Massachusetts Bay, Rhode Island and Providence Plantations, Connecticut, New York, New Jersey, Pennsylvania, Delaware, Maryland, Virginia, North Carolina, South Carolina and Georgia, and referred for approbation to the consideration of the several legislatures of the said states, ought to be approved and ratified on the part of this commonwealth; and that our delegates in Congress be accordingly authorized and instructed to ratify the same, in the name and on the behalf of this commonwealth; and that they attend for that purpose on or before the 10th day of March next.

Journals of Congress, 25 June 1778[2]

The delegates from Virginia being called on for the report of their constituents relative to the Articles of Confederation informed Congress,

That they are empowered to ratify the same as they now stand.

1. *Journal of the House of Delegates of the Commonwealth of Virginia . . .* [20 Oct. 1777–24 Jan. 1778] (Richmond, Va., 1827), 80. The House read the Articles on 9 December and adopted the resolutions of ratification on 15 December. The Senate agreed to the resolutions the next day.

2. PCC, Item 1, Rough Journals of Congress, DNA.

J. SOUTH CAROLINA, 25 June 1778

Instructions to Delegates in Congress, 5 February 1778[1]

Resolved, *nemine contradicente,* That the delegates of this state in the Continental Congress, or any three of them, be, and they are hereby authorized, on the part of this state, to agree to, and ratify Articles of Confederation between the United States of America.

Journals of Congress, 25 June 1778[2]

The delegates from South Carolina, being called upon for the report of their constituents upon the Confederation, moved in behalf of their state:

1. In Article 4th between the words "free inhabitants," to insert, "White."

Passed in the negative: 2 Ayes, 8 Noes, 1 divided.

2. In the next line after "these states" insert "those who refuse to take up arms in defence of the confederacy."

Passed in the negative: 3 Ayes, 8 Noes.

3. After the words "the several states" insert "according to the law of such states respectively for the government of their own free white inhabitants."

Passed in the negative: 2 Ayes, 8 Noes, 1 divided.

4. After the words "of which the owner is an inhabitant" insert "except in cases of embargo."

Passed in the negative: 2 Ayes, 9 Noes.

5. In the 1 paragraph of 5 Article, strike out "first Monday in November" and insert "nineteenth day of April."

Passed in the negative: 1 Aye, 9 Noes, 1 divided.

6. In the 2 paragraph of 5 Article, substitute "three" in place of "two," and "two" in place of "three," and "four" in place of "six."

Passed in the negative: 2 Ayes, 9 Noes.

7. In 3 paragraph of 5 Article, for "committee" read "grand Council."

Passed in the negative: 1 Aye, 9 Noes, 1 divided.

8. In the first paragraph of 6 Article, for "prince or state" read "Prince or foreign state, except the same be upon the subject of commerce, nor then so as to interfere with any treaty or alliance of the united states made or treaty proposed by Congress."

Passed in the negative: 2 Ayes, 9 Noes.

9. In 2d paragraph of 6 Article, strike out "by some nation of Indians" and after the words "to invade such state" insert "or upon requisition to assist a sister state actually invaded or threatened with an invasion."

Passed in the negative: 3 Ayes, 8 Noes.

10. In 1 paragraph of 7 Article, strike out the words "of or under the rank of colonel" and after "shall be appointed" insert "and commissioned."

Passed in the negative: 2 Ayes, 8 Noes, 1 divided.

11. At the end of the 7 Article, add: "The troops to be raised shall be deemed the troops of that state by which they are raised. The congress or grand council of the states may when they think proper make requisition to any states for two thirds of the troops to be raised; which requisition shall be binding upon the said states respectively: but the remaining third shall not be liable to be drawn out of the state in which they are raised, without the consent of the executive authority of the same. When any forces are raised, they shall be under the command of the executive authority of the state, in which they are so raised, unless they be joined by troops from any other state, in which case the Congress or grand council of the states may appoint a general Officer to take the command of the whole: And until the same can be done the command shall be in the senior Officer present, who shall be amenable for his conduct to the executive authority of the state in which the troops are, and shall be liable to be suspended thereby. The expences of the troops so to be raised shall be defrayed by the state, to which they belong; but when called into service by the united states they shall be fed and paid at the expence of the United States."

Passed in the negative: two Ayes, nine Noes.

12. In the 1st line of 8 Article, strike out the words "charges of war and all other."

Passed in the negative: 2 Ayes, 8 Noes, 1 divided.

13. In the same Article, strike out the words "according to such mode as the united states in Congress assembled shall from time to time direct and appoint" and instead of "and improvements thereon shall be estimated" read "And improvements thereon shall by periods of years not exceeding ten, as often as may be required by Congress, be generally estimated by persons to be appointed by the legislatures of the respective states to value the same upon oath."

Passed in the negative: 2 Ayes, 9 Noes.

14. In first paragraph of 9th Article, strike out "appointing courts for the trial of piracies and felonies committed on the high seas." In

lieu thereof insert, "declaring what acts committed on the high seas shall be deemed piracies or felonies."

Passed in the negative: 2 Ayes, 9 Noes.

15. In the second paragraph of 9 Article, for "be the last resort on Appeal" read "decide and determine," and strike out all that relates to the mode of settling differences between states, and controversies concerning the private right of soil.[3]

Passed in the negative: 2 Ayes, 9 Noes.

16. In the 5 paragraph of 9 Article, after the words "in any term of" strike out "three" and insert "two."

Passed in the negative: 3 Ayes, 7 Noes, 1 divided.

17. In the 6 paragraph of 9 Article for "unless nine states" read "unless eleven states."

Passed in the negative: 2 Ayes, 9 Noes.

18. At the end of the same paragraph strike out the words "in Congress assembled."

Passed in the negative: 1 Aye, 10 Noes.

19. In the last paragraph of the 9th Article, after the words "and the yeas and nay of the delegates of each state on" for "any" read "every" and strike out the words "when it is desired by any delegate."

Passed in the negative: 2 Ayes, 9 Noes.

20. In the same sentence strike out the words "a state or" and the words "at his or their request," and after the words "and the" insert "respective states or the," and after "shall" insert "upon requisition."

Passed in the negative: 1 Aye, 10 Noes.

21. In the last sentence of the 13 Article, amend the last clause so as to read "unless such alteration be agreed to by eleven of the united states in Congress assembled and be afterwards confirmed by the legislatures of eleven of the united states."

Passed in the negative: 3 Ayes, 6 Noes, 2 divided.

1. PCC, Item 2, Transcript Journals of Congress, DNA. The General Assembly passed the resolution on 4 February, and the Legislative Council concurred the next day. No journals exist for either house. However, the nature of the debates in the Assembly is probably reflected in a forty-six page pamphlet entitled: *The Speech of the Hon. William Henry Drayton, Esquire, Chief-Justice of South-Carolina . . .* [20 Jan. 1778] (Charleston, 1778).

2. PCC, Item 1, Rough Journals of Congress, DNA. The instructions to the South Carolina delegates incorporating the amendments have not been located.

3. The clause beginning "all that relates . . ." was not placed in quotation marks by the Secretary of Congress because there is no such phrase in the Articles. The phrase was intended to strike out the entire second paragraph of the 9th Article (with the exception of the principal clause of the first sentence), and the entire third paragraph of the 9th Article.

K. EIGHT STATES SIGN THE ARTICLES OF CONFEDERATION, 9 July 1778[1]

The ratification of the Articles of Confederation, engrossed on a roll of parchment being laid before Congress, was examined and the blanks in the third line from the bottom being filled up at the table with the words "ninth" and "July," and the blank in the last line with the word "third," the same was signed on the part and in behalf of their respective states by the delegates of New Hampshire, Massachusetts Bay, Rhode Island and Providence Plantations, Connecticut, New York, Pennsylvania, Virginia and South Carolina agreeably to the powers vested in them.

The delegates of the states of New Jersey, Delaware and Maryland informed Congress that they have not yet received powers to ratify and sign.

North Carolina, whose legislature has ratified the Articles of Confederation, and the State of Georgia were not at this time represented in Congress.

1. PCC, Item 2, Transcript Journals of Congress, DNA. The entries in the rough Journals are essentially the same, but several deletions and insertions render them unclear in places. (For a collation of the rough and transcript journals, see JCC, XI, 677.)

L. NORTH CAROLINA SIGNS, 21 July 1778

Report of a Joint Committee of the Senate and the House of Commons, 19 December 1777[1]

That the first, second, third, eighth, and twelfth articles, the second and third sections of the fourth and the last section of the ninth articles of the Confederation recommended by Congress ought to be immediately ratified; and the delegates for this state ought to be instructed and empowered accordingly, and that the remaining clauses, articles, and sections thereof containing matters highly important and interesting to the future people of this state, and involving what may very materially affect the internal interests and sovereign independence thereof, and not immediately essential to the success of the present war, ought not to be ratified until there shall be full time and leisure for maturely and deliberately considering the same, and until upon such mature and deliberate consideration the same shall be approved.

The Senate, 22 December 1777[2]

On motion, Resolved, That James Davis, Esquire, be authorized to print the Articles of Confederation of the United States proposed to be laid before the legislatures of the respective states, and that he be obliged to send twelve copies thereof to each county in this state, and one copy to every member of this present General Assembly, and that for printing and sending the Confederation, and for printing and sending the Acts and Journals of the last session of this General Assembly to the justices and representatives of the several counties, be allowed the sum of five hundred and fifty pounds, and that the said Articles, Journals, and Acts, and the Acts and Journals of this session be delivered to the several county court clerks within three months after [the] expiration of this session of the General Assembly.

House of Commons, 24 December 1777[3]

We propose that those sections of the Articles of the Confederation that were agreed to be ratified in Congress, should be fairly transcribed and signed by the speakers of both houses of this Assembly and transmitted to Congress by Mr. [Thomas] Burke to be there ratified.

House of Commons, 24 April 1778[4]

Resolved unanimously, That the delegates of this state in Congress be empowered on behalf thereof to ratify and confirm the said Confederation of the United States.

The General Assembly to Governor Richard Caswell, New Bern, 25 April 1778[5]

The two houses of the General Assembly have taken into consideration the Confederacy proposed to the United States by the Continental Congress, and have unanimously acceded thereto, and request Your Excellency will be pleased to inform the President of the Continental Congress thereof, by the earliest opportunity.

Governor Richard Caswell to Henry Laurens, President of Congress, New Bern, 26 April 1778 (excerpt)[6]

I have the honor to enclose a message from the General Assembly to me, informing me that they have acceded to the Articles of Confederation, proposed to the United States by Congress—to which I beg leave to refer. . . .

Journals of Congress, 25 June 1778[7]

Delaware and North Carolina not having delegates present in Congress, no report was received from them saving what is contained in Governor Caswell's letter informing that the legislature of North Carolina have agreed to the Articles of Confederation.

Journals of Congress, 21 July 1778[8]

Pursuant to the powers in them vested, the delegates of North Carolina signed the ratification of the Articles of Confederation in behalf of their state.

1. MS, Journals of the Senate, Nc-Ar. The legislature received copies of the Articles of Confederation and other resolves and papers of Congress from Governor Richard Caswell on 15 December 1777. The documents were referred to a joint committee of both houses on 18 December, and the committee's report was adopted the next day.
2. Ibid.
3. MS, Journals of the House of Commons, Nc-Ar. The Senate concurred on the same day.
4. Ibid. The Senate concurred on the same day.
5. MS, Journals of the Senate, Nc-Ar. The House of Commons concurred on the same day.
6. FC, MS, Governor's Letter Books, I, 326–27, Nc-Ar.
7. PCC, Item 2, Transcript Journals of Congress, DNA. The rough Journals of Congress state only: "Delaware and North Carolina absent." Caswell's letter was read in Congress on 13 May 1778 (PCC, Item 9, History of the Confederation, DNA).
8. PCC, Item 1, Rough Journals of Congress, DNA.

M. GEORGIA SIGNS, 24 July 1778

House of Assembly, 26 February 1778[1]

The House resolved itself into a committee of the whole house to take into consideration the Articles of Confederation and perpetual Union, and after sometime spent therein, Mr. Speaker resumed the chair and Mr. Whitefield from the committee of the whole reported they had taken the said Articles into consideration and gone through the same and made several amendments thereto which were read and agreed to.

Extract from the Minutes, George Cuthbert, Clerk.

Report of the Amendments to the Articles of Confederation and perpetual Union.

4th. Article, 4 page 4th line, add the words "white inhabitants." 6th line, between the words "vagabonds and," add "all persons who refuse to bear arms in defense of the state to which they belong and all persons who have been or shall be attainted and adjudged guilty of high treason in any of the United States." 9 Article, 20th page 20 line, between the words "emitted to," add "and the expenditure of the same." 11 Article, page 25, between the words "Canada acceding," add "and the colonies of East and West Florida."

A true copy from the original taken the 24 May and examined by George Cuthbert, C.H.A.

Resolved, That the delegates for this state be authorized and required to lay before the general Congress of the United States the several alterations proposed and agreed upon by this House this day in the Articles of Confederation and that they do use their exertions to have such alterations agreed to and confirmed in Congress.

Resolved, That in case all or none of such alterations shall be agreed to and confirmed in Congress, that then and notwithstanding, they be empowered and required in behalf of this state to sign, ratify, and confirm the several Articles of the Confederation recommended to the respective legislatures of the United States by Congress or any other plan of a general confederation which shall be agreed upon by nine of the United States.

Extract from the Minutes, George Cuthbert, Clerk.

Journals of Congress, 25 June 1778[2]

The delegate from Georgia being called upon for the report of his constituents on the Confederation, informed Congress that he has not yet received any instructions or orders respecting the same; but that, his state having shown so much readiness to ratify the Articles of Confederation even in an imperfect state, and it being so much for their interest that the Confederation should be ratified, he had no doubt of their agreeing to it as it now stands.

Journals of Congress, 23 July 1778[3]

The delegates from Georgia laid before Congress the proceedings of the House of Assembly of that state respecting the Articles of Confederation, which were read.

Journals of Congress, 24 July 1778[4]

Pursuant to the powers in them vested, the delegates of Georgia signed the ratification of the Articles of Confederation.

1. PCC, Item 2, Transcript Journals of Congress, DNA. The journals of the Georgia House of Assembly for 1778 do not exist. This item was transcribed from a section of the Transcript Journals of Congress for 27 June 1778 entitled: "Powers of the states to their delegates to ratify the articles of Confederation." There is no evidence that the Georgia amendments were submitted to Congress for consideration.
2. PCC, Item 1, Rough Journals of Congress, DNA.
3. Ibid.
4. Ibid.

N. NEW JERSEY SIGNS, 26 November 1778

Act of Ratification, 20 November 1778[1]

An ACT to authorize and empower the Delegates of the State of New-Jersey, in Congress, to subscribe and ratify the Articles of Confederation and Perpetual Union between the several States.

Whereas Articles of Confederation and Perpetual Union between the States of *New-Hampshire, Massachusetts-Bay, Rhode-Island and Providence Plantations, Connecticut, New-York, New-Jersey, Pennsylvania, Delaware, Maryland, Virginia, North-Carolina, South-Carolina* and *Georgia,* signed in the General Congress of the said States by the Honourable *Henry Laurens,* Esquire, their President, have been laid before the Legislature of this State to be ratified by the same, if approved: And whereas, notwithstanding the Terms of the said Articles of Confederation and Perpetual Union are considered as in divers Respects unequal and disadvantageous to this State, and the Objections to several of the said Articles lately stated and sent to the General Congress aforesaid, on the Part of this State, are still viewed as just and reasonable, and sundry of them as of the most essential Moment to the Welfare and Happiness of the good People thereof, yet under the full Conviction of the present Necessity of acceding to the Confederacy proposed, and that every separate and detached State-Interest ought to be postponed to the general Good of the Union; and moreover, in firm Reliance that the Candour and Justice of the several States will, in due Time, remove, as far as possible, the Inequality which now subsists;

Sect. 1. Be it Enacted *by the Council and General Assembly of this State, and it is hereby Enacted by the Authority of the same,* That the Honourable *John Witherspoon, Abraham Clark, Nathaniel Scudder* and *Elias Boudinot,* Esquires, Delegates representing this State in the Congress of the United States, or any one or more of them be, and they hereby are authorized, empowered and directed on Behalf of this State, to subscribe and ratify the said Articles of Confederation and Perpetual Union between the several States aforesaid.

2. And be it further Enacted *by the Authority aforesaid,* That the said Articles of Confederation and Perpetual Union so as aforesaid subscribed and ratified, shall thenceforth become conclusive as to this State and obligatory thereon.

Passed at Trenton, November 20, 1778.

Journals of Congress, 25 November 1778[2]

Mr. Witherspoon, a delegate for the state of New Jersey, attended and laid before Congress powers to the delegates of that state to ratify the Articles of Confederation which were read as follows:

[Text of New Jersey Act of Ratification]

Journals of Congress, 26 November 1778[3]

In pursuance to the powers to them granted the delegates of New Jersey signed the Articles of Confederation and perpetual Union.

1. (LT), *Acts of the General Assembly of New Jersey* . . . [27 Oct.–12 Dec. 1778] (Trenton, 1779), 3–4. Congress's letter of 10 July 1778 urging the states which had not yet ratified the Articles of Confederation to do so as soon as possible was sent to the Assembly on 14 September by Governor William Livingston. A joint committee of the two houses, appointed on 21 September, reported four days later that it was "not expedient" to instruct the state's delegates in Congress. The same day another joint committee was appointed to draft a representation to Congress. The committee resubmitted the amendments originally adopted on 20 June 1778, with the exception of the last part of the 7th Article and the 8th

and 9th articles (III:G above). The Council adopted the representation, but the Assembly took no action at that session.

At the next session, on 7 November, the two houses appointed a joint committee which reported on 14 November that the state should put aside its objections and instruct its delegates to sign the Articles. Both houses adopted the report, and the act of ratification was adopted on 20 November.

2. PCC, Item 1, Rough Journals of Congress, DNA.

3. Ibid.

O. DELAWARE SIGNS, 22 February 1779

Journals of Congress, 25 June 1778[1]

Delaware and North Carolina not having delegates present in Congress, no report was received from them saving what is contained in Governor Caswell's letter informing that the legislature of North Carolina have agreed to the Articles of Confederation.

The Council, 28 January 1779[2]

The Council having resumed the consideration of the committee's report on the Articles of Confederation and perpetual Union, etc., came to the following resolutions thereon:

Resolved, That this state think it necessary, for the peace and safety of the states to be included in the Union, that a moderate extent of limits should be assigned for such of those states as claim to the Mississippi or South Sea, and that the United States in Congress assembled, should and ought to have the power of fixing their western limits.

Resolved also, That this state consider themselves justly entitled to a right, in common with the other members of the Union, to that extensive tract of country which lies to the westward of the frontiers of the United States, the property of which was not vested in or granted to individuals at the commencement of the present war; that the same hath been or may hereafter be gained from the king of Great Britain or the native Indians by the blood and treasure of all, and ought therefore to be a common estate, to be granted out on terms beneficial to the United States.

Resolved also, That the courts of law established within this state are competent for the purpose of determining all controversies concerning the private right of soil claimed within the same, and that they now, and at all times hereafter, ought to have cognizance of all such controversies; that the indeterminate provision, proposed in the 9th Article of the Confederation, for deciding upon controversies that may arise about some of those private rights of soil, tends to take away such cognizance and is contrary to the Declaration of Rights of this state, and therefore ought to receive an alteration.

The Council then, taking into consideration the strong and earnest recommendations of Congress forthwith to accede to the present plan of Confederacy, and the probable disadvantages that may attend the further delaying a ratification thereof,

Resolved, That, notwithstanding the terms of the Articles of Confederation aforesaid are considered as in divers respects unequal and disadvantageous to this state, and the objections in the report of the committee of this House and the resolves made thereon are viewed as just and reasonable and of great moment to the welfare and happiness of the good people thereof; yet, under the full conviction of the present necessity of acceding to the Confederacy proposed, and in firm reliance that the candor and justice of the several states will in due time remove, as far as possible, the objectionable parts thereof, the delegates appointed to represent this state in Congress, or any one or more of them, be authorized, empowered and directed, on behalf of this state, to subscribe and ratify the said Articles of Confederation and perpetual Union between the several states of New Hampshire, Massachusetts Bay, Rhode Island and Providence Plantations, Connecticut, New York, New Jersey, Pennsylvania, Delaware, Maryland, Virginia, North Carolina, South Carolina, and Georgia, and that the said Articles, when so subscribed and ratified, shall become obligatory on this state.

Act of Ratification, 1 February 1779[3]

An ACT *to authorise and impower the Delegates of the Delaware State to subscribe and ratify the articles of Confederation and perpetual union between the several states.*

WHEREAS articles of confederation and perpetual union between the states of New-Hampshire, Massachusett's Bay, Rhode Island and Providence Plantations, Connecticut, New York, New Jersey, Pennsylvania, Delaware, Maryland, Virginia, North Carolina, South Carolina, and Georgia, signed in the General Congress of the said states, by the honorable Henry Laurens, esquire, their then President, have been laid before the Legislature of this state to be ratified by the same, if approved. *And whereas* notwithstanding the terms of the articles of confederation and perpetual union are considered as in divers respects unequal and disadvantageous to this state, and the objections stated on the part of this state, are viewed as just and reasonable, and of great moment to the welfare and happiness of the good people thereof; yet under the full conviction of the present necessity of acceding to the confederacy proposed, and that the interest of particular states ought to be postponed to the general good of the union: And moreover, in firm reliance that the candour and justice of the several states, will, in due time, remove as far as possible the objectionable parts thereof,

Section 2. BE *it enacted by the General Assembly of Delaware, and it is hereby enacted by the authority of the same,* That the honorable John Dickinson, Nicholas Vandyke, and Thomas M'Kean, esquires, delegates appointed to represent this state in Congress, or any one, or more of them, be, and they hereby are, authorised, impowered and directed, on behalf of this state, to subscribe and ratify the said articles of confederation and perpetual union between the several states aforesaid.

Sect. 3. *And be it further enacted by the authority aforesaid,* That the said articles of confederation and perpetual union, so as aforesaid subscribed and ratified, shall thenceforth become obligatory on this state.

Passed February 1, 1779.

House of Assembly, 3 February 1779[4]

Whereas the Honorable John Dickinson, Nicholas Vandyke, and Thomas McKean, esquires have been chosen, by the joint ballot of both houses in the General Assembly, to represent the Delaware State in the Congress of the United States of America this present year,

Resolved, That they, or any of them, are hereby fully authorized and empowered, for and in behalf of this state, to concert, agree to, and execute any measure which they, or any two of them, together with a majority of the said Congress, shall judge necessary for the defense, security, interest and welfare of this state in particular, and the United States in general; and generally to exercise, in concert with other of the United States in Congress assembled, the respective powers prescribed in the Articles of Confederation and perpetual Union of the said states.

President Caesar Rodney to John Jay, President of Congress, Dover, 4 February 1779[5]

I have the pleasure to inform Your Excellency, that, I this day fixed the Great Seal to an act of the General Assembly empowering the delegates to ratify the Confederation, on the part of this state; and the delegates shall be furnished with a certified copy of the act, as soon as possible, for that purpose.

Journals of Congress, 8 February 1779[6]

A letter of 4 [February] from Cr. Rodney, President of the State of Delaware, was read informing that the legislature of that state have passed a law empowering their delegates to ratify the Confederation in behalf of that state.

Journals of Congress, 16 February 1779[7]

Mr. M'Kean, a delegate for Delaware, laid before Congress the following instrument empowering the delegates of that state or any of them to ratify and sign the Articles of Confederation.

[Text of the Delaware Act of Ratification]

Journals of Congress, 22 February 1779[8]

In pursuance of the powers in him vested Mr. M'Kean, a delegate of the state of Delaware, signed and ratified the Articles of Confederation in behalf of that state.

Journals of Congress, 23 February 1779[9]

The delegate of Delaware laid before Congress sundry resolutions passed by the Council of that state January 23, 1779 respecting the Articles of Confederation and perpetual Union, and concurred in by the House of Assembly January 28, 1779 previous to their passing a law to empower their delegates to sign and ratify the said Articles of Confederation and perpetual Union.

On which it was moved, "That the same be filed," to which it was moved in amendment to add, "Provided, That it shall never be considered as admitting any claim by the same set up or intended to be set up." On this amendment the yeas and nays being required by Mr. Ellery.

New Hampshire			Massachusetts		
Whipple	ay	ay	S. Adams	ay	ay
Frost	ay		Lovell	ay	
			Holton	ay	

Rhode Island			Delaware		
Ellery	ay ⎫ ay		M'Kean	no { no	
Collins	ay ⎭		Maryland		
Connecticut			Paca	no ⎫ no	
Root	ay { ay		Henry	no ⎭	
New York			Virginia		
Jay	no ⎫		T. Adams	ay ⎫	
G. Morris	no ⎬ divided		F.L. Lee	ay ⎪	
Floyd	ay ⎪		M. Smith	ay ⎪ ay	
Lewis	ay ⎭		Griffin	ay ⎬	
New Jersey			R.H. Lee	ay ⎪	
Witherspoon	no ⎫ no		Nelson	ay ⎭	
Frelinghuyson	no ⎭		North Carolina		
Pennsylvania			Penn	ay ⎫ ay	
Clingan	ay ⎫		Burke	ay ⎭	
Shippen	ay ⎪ ay				
Attlee	no ⎪		South Carolina		
Searle	ay ⎭		Drayton	ay { ay	

So it passed in the affirmative.

On the question.

Resolved, That the paper laid before Congress by the delegate from Delaware, and read, be filed, provided that it shall never be considered as admitting any claim by the same set up or intended to be set up.

1. PCC, Item 2, Transcript Journals of Congress, DNA. The rough Journals of Congress state only: "Delaware and North Carolina absent."

2. "Minutes of the Council of Delaware State, from 1776 to 1792," *Papers* of the Historical Society of Delaware, VI (Wilmington, Del., 1887), 371–73. On 15 May 1778 the Council read and considered a privately printed copy of the Articles of Confederation, "as there is little prospect of obtaining a certified copy of the same from Congress during the present sitting of the General Assembly." On 3 December 1778 the Council considered an attested copy of the Articles, and the next day it appointed a committee of three to report on them. The committee reported on 21 January 1779. Two days later the Council adopted the report, and on 28 January the House of Assembly concurred. The copy of these resolutions which was received by Congress is in PCC, Item 70, Maryland and Delaware State Papers, 1775–89, pp. 699-704, DNA.

3. (LT), *Laws of the State of Delaware* . . . [14 Oct. 1700–18 Aug. 1797] (2 vols., Newcastle, 1797), II, 645–46. On 23 January 1779, immediately after it adopted the report of the committee of three, the Council moved that a bill empowering the state's delegates to Congress to ratify the Articles be drafted. The House of Assembly approved the bill on 28 January, and the bill was engrossed on 1 February. The President signed the bill on 6 February (JCC, XIII, 188).

4. "Minutes of the Council," *Papers* of the Historical Society of Delaware, VI, 404. On 3 February 1779, the last day of the session, the House of Assembly re-

solved that the delegates to Congress be sent attested copies of the acts of ratification, and the Council concurred.

5. RC, PCC, Item 70, Maryland and Delaware State Papers, 1775–89, p. 695, DNA.
6. PCC, Item 1, Rough Journals of Congress, DNA.
7. Ibid.
8. Ibid.
9. Ibid.

P. MARYLAND SIGNS, 1 March 1781

Act of Ratification, 2 February 1781[1]

An ACT to empower the delegates of this state in congress to subscribe and ratify the articles of confederation.

Whereas it hath been said, that the common enemy is encouraged, by this state not acceding to the confederation, to hope that the union of the sister states may be dissolved, and therefore prosecutes the war in expectation of an event so disgraceful to America, and our friends and illustrious ally are impressed with an idea, that the common cause would be promoted by our formally acceding to the confederation: This general assembly, conscious that this state hath from the commencement of the war strenuously exerted herself in the common cause, and fully satisfied, that if no formal confederation was to take place, it is the fixed determination of this state to continue her exertions to the utmost, agreeable to the faith pledged in the union, from an earnest desire to conciliate the affection of the sister states, to convince all the world of our unalterable resolution to support the independence of the United States, and the alliance with His Most Christian Majesty, and to destroy for ever any apprehension of our friends or hope in our enemies of this state being again united to Great-Britain:

II. Be it enacted, *by the General Assembly of Maryland,* That the delegates of this state in congress, or any two or three of them, shall be and are hereby empowered and required, on behalf of this state, to subscribe the articles of confederation and perpetual union between the states of New-Hampshire, Massachusetts-bay, Rhode-island and Providence plantations, Connecticut, New-York, New-Jersey, Pennsylvania, Delaware, Maryland, Virginia, North-Carolina, South-Carolina, and Georgia, signed in the general congress of the said States by the honourable Henry Laurens, Esquire, their then president, and laid before the legislature of this state to be ratified, if approved; and that the said articles of confederation and perpetual union, so as aforesaid subscribed, shall thenceforth be ratified and become conclusive as to

this state, and obligatory thereon: And it is hereby declared, That
by acceding to the said confederation, this state doth not relinquish,
or intend to relinquish, any right or interest she hath with the other
United or Confederated States to the back country, but claims the
same as fully as was done by the legislature of this state in their
declaration which stands entered on the journals of congress, this
state relying on the justice of the several states hereafter, as to the
said claim made by this state: And it is further declared, That no
article in the said confederation can or ought to bind this or any
other state to guarantee any exclusive claim of any particular state
to the soil of the said back lands, or any such claim of jurisdiction
over the said lands, or the inhabitants thereof.

Journals of Congress, 12 February 1781[2]

The delegate for Maryland [Daniel Carroll] laid before Congress
a certified copy of an act of the legislature of that state which was read
as follows.

[Text of the Maryland Act of Ratification]

Journals of Congress, 1 March 1781[3]

According to the order of the day the Honorable John Hanson and
Daniel Carrol, two of the delegates for the State of Maryland, in pursuance of the act of the legislature of that state entitled: "An Act
to empower the delegates of this State in Congress to subscribe and
ratify the Articles of Confederation" which was read in Congress the
12 of February last and a copy thereof entered on the minutes, did
in behalf of the said State of Maryland sign and ratify the said Articles, by which act the Confederation of the United States of America
was completed, each and every of the Thirteen United States from
New Hampshire to Georgia, both included, having adopted and confirmed and by their delegates in Congress ratified the same.

1. (LT), *Laws of Maryland* . . . [23 March–16 May 1780] (Annapolis, [1780]),
Chap. XL. After 1778 the Maryland legislature refused to ratify the Articles of
Confederation for the reasons given in its instructions of 22 December 1777 and 20
June 1778 to the state's delegates in Congress (III:A above). On 15 December 1778
the legislature amplified those reasons in "A Declaration" (PCC, Item 70, Maryland
and Delaware State Papers, 1775–89, pp. 293–300, DNA) and in new instructions
to its delegates in Congress (JCC, XIV, 619–22).

The "Declaration" was read to Congress on 6 January 1779, and the new instructions to the delegates were entered on the Journals of Congress on 21 May 1779.

The deadlock between Maryland, which refused to ratify the Articles until Congress got control of western lands, and Virginia, which insisted that those lands belonged to Virginia, lasted until the end of 1780. By then, the threat of invasion by the British and pressure from the French led Maryland to reconsider.

The legislature appointed a joint committee of the two houses on 29 November 1780 to draft instructions to the delegates in Congress. Two months later, on 27 January 1781, the House passed a bill empowering the delegates to ratify, but the Senate rejected it the next day. On 29 January the House told the Senate that Maryland's refusal to ratify was no longer of any help in securing a share in western lands, and that the demand for a share might be improved by ratification. The Senate then agreed to the act of ratification on 2 February 1781. The legislature also adopted instructions to the state's delegates explaining that it had accepted ratification in order to preserve the Union and to guarantee French military aid against the British in the Chesapeake area.

2. PCC, Item 1, Rough Journals of Congress, DNA.

3. Ibid.

IV

Amendments to the Articles of Confederation, Grants of Power to Congress, and Ordinances for the Western Territory

3 February 1781–13 July 1787

A. GRANT OF POWER TO COLLECT IMPORT DUTIES, 3 February 1781[1]

Congress did not have the power to tax or collect revenue of any kind, either before or after the adoption of the Articles of Confederation on 1 March 1781, but it did have financial independence during the first five years of the War for Independence. Beginning in 1775, Congress issued paper money (as did the states) to pay much of the cost of fighting the war. By 1780 the paper currency had depreciated so much that Congress abandoned its use. Thereafter, Congress was dependent on the states to comply with its requisitions.

However, there were members of Congress who believed that Congress should have an income of its own. On 7 November 1780, Congress appointed a committee "to prepare and lay before Congress a plan for arranging the finances, paying the debts and economizing the revenue of the United States" (JCC, XVIII, 1028). The committee reported on 18 December that Congress should be vested with the "exclusive right to duties arising on certain imported articles," and that the states should be requested to pass laws granting Congress power to levy duties upon imported goods after 1 May 1781 (JCC, XVIII, 1157–64). Congress debated this and other reports on finance until it passed the impost proposal on 3 February 1781 after striking out a provision for the appointment of collectors by Congress.

The proposal was sent to the states on 8 February accompanied by a resolution of 7 February. The resolution provided that if hostilities prevented any legislature from meeting, the grant would go into effect as soon as the other states ratified, and that the money collected would be applied to the credit of the ratifying states (JCC, XIX, 124–25; LMCC, V, 563–64).

The ratification of the Articles of Confederation, less than a month after the grant was requested, transformed the grant into an amendment to the Articles requiring unanimous ratification by the thirteen states. By the fall of 1782, all the states except Rhode Island had ratified. Attempts to persuade Rhode Island failed, and the Virginia legislature defeated the amendment permanently when it rescinded Virginia's ratification in December.

Resolved That it be recommended to the several States as indispensibly necessary, that they vest a power in Congress to levy for the use of the United States a duty of five percent advalorem at the time and place of importation upon all goods wares and merchandizes of foreign growth & manufactures which may be imported into any of the said States from any foreign port Island or plantation after the first day of May 1781 except arms ammunition cloathing & other articles imported on account of the United States or any of them; and except wool cards & cotton cards & wire for making them and also except salt during the war.

Also a like duty of five percent on all prizes and prize goods condemned in the Court of Admiralty of any of these States as lawful prize.

That the monies arising from the said duties be appropriated to the discharge of the principal & interest of the debts already contracted or which may be contracted on the faith of the United States for supporting the present war.

That the said duties be continued until the said debts shall be fully & finally discharged.

1. (LT), PCC, Item 1, Rough Journals of Congress, DNA. No printed broadside of the proposal has been located.

B. AMENDMENT TO GIVE CONGRESS COERCIVE POWER OVER THE STATES AND THEIR CITIZENS, 16 March 1781[1]

A group of men dedicated to increasing the power of the central government was becoming influential in Congress by the time the Articles of Confederation were ratified on 1 March 1781. Consequently, on 6 March, James M. Varnum, James Madison, and James Duane were appointed "to prepare a plan to invest the United States in Congress assembled with full and explicit powers for effectually carrying into execution in the several states all acts or resolutions passed agreeably to the Articles of Confederation" (JCC, XIX, 236). The committee's report, largely in the handwriting of James Madison, was laid before Congress on 16 March. (For an analysis of the evolution of the report before it was submitted to Congress, see Hutchinson, III, 19–20.)

The report, which proposed an amendment to the Articles to give Congress coercive authority, was referred to a "grand committee" on 2 May. This committee delivered a much milder report on 20 July. It suggested "That it be recommended to the several states to pass laws empowering the United States in Congress assembled to have use and exercise the right of laying embargoes in time of war, provided that such embargoes extend to all the states in the Union, and be laid for a term not exceeding sixty days, at any one time.

"And also

"That the quotas of monies called for by the United States in Congress assembled when voted by the respective states, be appropriated and vested specifically by the legislatures of the respective states for the use of the United States in Congress assembled. And that the taxes so appropriated be paid by the collectors in the first instance, to such person or persons as the United States in Congress assembled shall appoint for receiving the same" (JCC, XX, 773).

Congress responded by turning this report over to a three-man committee which issued a report on 22 August (IV:C below).

Whereas it is stipulated and declared in the 13th. Article of the Confederation "that every State shall abide by the determinations of the United States in Congress assembled on all questions which by this Confederation are submitted to them. And that the Articles of this Confederation shall be inviolably observed by every State": by which Arti[c]le a general and implied power is vested in the United States in Congress assembled to enforce and carry into effect all the Articles of the said Confederation against any of the States which shall refuse or neglect to abide by such their determinations, or shall otherwise violate any of the said Articles, but no determinate and particular provision is made for that purpose: And Whereas the want of such provision may be made a pretext to call into Question the Legality of measures which may be necessary for preserving the authority of the Confederation & for doing justice to the States which shall duly fulfill their foederal engagements, and it is moreover most consonant to the spirit of a free constitution that on the one hand all exercise of power should be explicitly and precisely warranted, and on the other that the penal consequences of a violation of duty should be clearly promulged and understood: and Whereas it is further declared by the said 13th. Article of the Confederation that no addition shall be made to the Articles thereof, Unless the same shall be agreed to in a Congress of the United States and be afterwards confirmed by the Legislatures of every State: The United States in Congress assembled having seriously & maturely deliberated on these considerations, and being desirous as far as possible to cement & invigorate the federal Union, that it may be both established on the most immutable basis, and be the more effectual for securing the immediate object of it, do hereby agree to, and recommend to the Legislatures of every State to confirm & to authorise their Delegates in Congress to subscribe, the following clause as an Additional Article to the 13 Articles of Confederation & perpetual Union:

It is understood & hereby declared that in case any one or more of the Confederated States shall refuse or neglect to abide by the determinations of the United States in Congress assembled or to observe all the Articles of the Confederation as required in the 13th. Article, the said United States in Congress assembled are fully authorised to employ the force of the United States as well by sea as by land to compel such State or States to fulfill their federal engagements, and particularly to make distraint on any of the effects Vessels and Merchandizes of such State or States or of any of the Citizens thereof wherever found, and to prohibit and prevent their trade and intercourse as well with any other of the United States and the Citizens thereof, as with any foreign State, and as well by land as by sea, untill full compensation or compliance be obtained with respect to all Requisitions made by the United States in Congress assembled in pursuance of the Articles of Confederation.

And it is to be understood, and is hereby agreed and conceded that this Article shall be fully and absolutely binding and conclusive when all the States not actually in the Possession of the Enemy, shall enact the same

1. (LT), PCC, Item 24, Reports of Committees of Congress on the Relations between Congress and the States, 1775–86, pp. 25–26, DNA.

C. COMMITTEE REPORT ON CARRYING THE CONFEDERATION INTO EFFECT AND ON ADDITIONAL POWERS NEEDED BY CONGRESS, 22 August 1781[1]

The campaign to give Congress more power under the Articles of Confederation began on 16 March 1781, when a committee of Congress proposed that the Articles be amended to give Congress coercive authority over the states and their citizens (IV:B above). A second report on 20 July by another committee suggested that Congress be given power to lay temporary embargoes and that the states grant money to Congress. This report was turned over to a third committee on the same day. This committee, consisting of Edmund Randolph (chairman), Oliver Ellsworth, and James M. Varnum, was instructed "to prepare an exposition of the Confederation, a plan for its complete execution, and supplemental articles" (JCC, XX, 773; PCC, Item 24, Reports of Committees of Congress, 52). The report, in the handwriting of Varnum, was submitted to Congress on 22 August and was made the order of the day for 23 August (JCC, XXI, 893–96). There is no evidence that Congress ever considered the report.

The Committee appointed to prepare an exposition of the Confederation, a plan for its compleat execution & Supplimental Articles Report

That they ought to be discharged from the exposition of the Confederation because such a comment would be voluminous if co-extensive with the subject the omission to enumerate any congressional powers become an argument against their existence, & it will be early enough to insist upon them, when they shall be exercised & disputed—

They farther report that the Confederation requires execution in the following manner

1. By adjusting the mode & proportions of the Militia Aid to be furnish[ed] to a sister State labouring under Invasion—
2 by discribing the priviliges & immunities to which the Citizens of one State are intitled in another
3. by setting forth the conditions upon which a Criminal is to be delivd. up by one State upon the demand of the executive of another—
4. by declaring the method of exemplifying records & the operation of the Acts [&] Judicial Proceedings of the Courts of one States, contravening thos[e] of the States in which they are asserted—
5. by a form to be observed in the notification of the appointment [or?] suspension of Delegates—
6 By an oath to be taken by every delegate against secret trusts of salaries—
7. by Specifying the priviliges of delegates from Arrests, Imprisonment questioning for free Speech & debates in Congress saving as well their Answerability to their Constituents, as protesting against the [authority?] of Individual legislatures to absolve them from obligations to Secrecy—
8. By instituting an Oath to be taken by the Officers of the U S. or any of [them] against presents, Emoluments Office or title of any kind from a [King?] Prince or foreign State
9. By one universal plan of equipping training & governing the Militia—
10. By a scheme for estimating the value of all land within each State gran[ted] to or surveyed for any person or persons together with the buildings and improvements thereon: & the appointment of certain periods at which payment shall be made.
11. By establishing rules for captures on land & the distribution of the Sales.
12. by ascertaing. the jurisdiction of Congress in territorial questions—
13. by erecting a mint—
14. by fixing a standard of weights & measures throughout the U S.
15. by appointing a Comee. for Indian Affairs—
16. by regulating the post Office—
17. by establishing a census of white Inhabitants in each State—
18. by publishing the Journal of Congress monthly—
19. by registering seamen—
20. by liquidation of Old accounts against the U. S: &
21. by providing means of animadverting on delinquent States—
Resolved, That of the preceeding articles the 9th. be referred to the Bd. of War the 13th. 14th. & 16th. to the Supt. of Finance & the

others to a Comee. in order that the Subject matter thereof may be
extended in detail for the consideration of Congress—
    And your Committee further report
That as America became a Confederate Republic to crush the pr[esent]
& future foes of her Independence—
As of this Republic a general Council is a necessary Organ—
And without the extension of its power in the cases herein after
enumerated War may receive a fatal inclination & peace be exposed
to daily convulsions—
    It be resold. to recomd. to the sevl. States to authorise ye. U S. in
Congress Assemd.
1. To lay embargoes in time of war without any limitation—
2. to prescribe rules for impressing property into the service of the
   U S. during the present War—
3. to appoint the Collectors of & direct the mode of accounting for
   taxes imposed according to the requisitions of Congress—
4. to recognise the Independence of & admit into the foederal Union
   any part of one or more of the U S. with the Consent of the
   dismembered State
5. to stipulate in treaties With foreign nations for the establishment
   of [consular?] power, without referrence to the States individually
6. to destrain the property of a State delinquent in its assigned proportion of Men & Money
7. To vary the rules of suffrage in Congress, taking care that in
   questions for
       Waging War
       Granting letters of Marque & Reprisal in time of peace
       concluding or giving instructions for any Alliance
       Coining money
       regulating the value of Coin
       determining the total number of land & Sea forces & allotting
         to ea[ch] [state?] its quota of Men or Money—
       Emitting bills of Credit—
       Borrowing money—
       Fixing the number & force of Vessels of War, & appointing a
         Commander in Chief of the Army & Navy—
         At least two thirds of the U S shall agree [therein?]
       Resolved,
            That a comee. be appointed to prepare a representation
to the several States of the necessity of these Suplimental powers & of
pursuing in the modification thereof, one uniform plan—

    1. (LT), PCC, Item 24, Reports of Committees of Congress on the Relations
between Congress and the States, 1775–86, pp. 49–52, DNA.

D. GRANT OF TEMPORARY POWER TO COLLECT IMPORT DUTIES AND REQUEST FOR SUPPLEMENTARY FUNDS, 18 April 1783[1]

The request of Congress on 3 February 1781 for a grant of power to collect import duties to pay the debts of the United States was finally defeated in December 1782. Shortly thereafter, Congress began a long debate on the subject of finance and the means of securing an independent income. On 21 February 1783, Congress appointed a "special committee" consisting of Nathaniel Gorham (chairman), Alexander Hamilton, James Madison, Thomas FitzSimons, and John Rutledge (JCC, XXIV, 144). The committee reported on 6 March that a five percent import duty should be levied on all but a specified list of foreign goods. Congress ordered the report printed and distributed to the members (JCC, XXIV, 170-74; Hutchinson, VI, 311–16). A few days later Congress referred parts of the report back to the committee, which delivered a second report on 18 March (JCC, XXIV, 188–92). During the debates, Alexander Hamilton and James Wilson moved that land and house taxes be proposed, but they were defeated (JCC, XXIV, 191–92, 200–2). The modified report was adopted on 18 April by the vote of nine states to one (Rhode Island) (JCC, XXIV, 261).

The printed document submitted to the states included, in addition to the request for power to collect import duties for twenty-five years, an earlier request that the states value their lands for the purpose of sharing expenses (omitted here) and an amendment to the Articles of Confederation proposing that expenses among the states be shared according to population (IV:E below).

RESOLVED by nine states, That it be recommended to the several states, as indispensibly necessary to the restoration of public credit, and to the punctual and honorable discharge of the public debts, to invest the United States in Congress assembled, with a power to levy for the use of the United States, the following duties upon goods imported into the said states, from any foreign port, island or plantation.

Upon all rum of Jamaica proof, per gallon,	4-90ths of a dollar.	
Upon all other spirituous liquors,	3-90ths	do.
Upon Madeira wine,	12-90ths	do.
Upon all other wines,	6-90ths	do.
Upon common bohea tea per lb.	6-90ths	do.
Upon all other teas.	24-90ths	do.
Upon pepper per lb.	3-90ths	do.
Upon brown sugar per lb.	½-90th	do.
Upon loaf sugar,	2-90ths	do.
Upon all other sugars,	1-90th	do.
Upon molasses per gallon,	1-90th	do.
Upon cocoa and coffee per lb.	1-90th	do.

Upon all other goods, a duty of five per cent. ad valorem at the time and place of importation.

Provided that none of the said duties shall be applied to any other purpose than the discharge of the interest or principal of the debts contracted on the faith of the United States for supporting the war, agreeably to the resolution of the 16th day of December last, nor be continued for a longer term than twenty-five years; and provided that the collectors of the said duties shall be appointed by the states within which their offices are to be respectively exercised; but when so appointed, shall be amenable to and removeable by the United States in Congress assembled, alone; and in case any state shall not make such appointment within one month after notice given for that purpose, the appointment may be made by the United States in Congress assembled.

That it be further recommended to the several states, to establish for a term limited to twenty five years, and to appropriate to the discharge of the interest and principal of the debts contracted on the faith of the United States for supporting the war, substantial and effectual revenues of such nature as they may judge most convenient, for supplying their respective proportions of one million five hundred thousand dollars annually, exclusive of the aforementioned duties, which proportion shall be fixed and equalized from time to time, according to the rule which is or may be prescribed by the articles of confederation; and in case the revenues established by any state, shall at any time yield a sum exceeding its actual proportion, the excess shall be refunded to it; and in case the revenues of any state shall be found to be deficient, the immediate deficiency shall be made up by such state with as little delay as possible, and a future deficiency guarded against by an enlargement of the revenues established: provided that until the rule of the confederation can be carried into practice, the proportions of the said 1,500,000 dollars shall be as follows, viz.

New-Hampshire,	52,708
Massachusetts,	224,427
Rhode-Island,	32,318
Connecticut,	132,091
New-York,	128,243
New-Jersey	83,358
Pennsylvania,	205,189
Delaware,	22,443
Maryland,	141,517
Virginia,	256,487
North Carolina,	109,006
South Carolina,	96,183
Georgia,	16,030

The said last mentioned revenues to be collected by persons appointed as aforesaid, but to be carried to the separate credit of the states within which they shall be collected.

That an annual account of the proceeds and application of all the aforementioned revenues, shall be made out and transmitted to the several states, distinguishing the proceeds of each of the specified articles, and the amount of the whole revenue received from each state, together with the allowances made to the several officers employed in the collection of the said revenues.

That none of the preceding resolutions shall take effect until all of them shall be acceded to by every state, after which unanimous accession, however, they shall be considered as forming a mutual compact among all the states, and shall be irrevocable by any one or more of them, without the concurrence of the whole, or of a majority of the United States in Congress assembled.

That as a further mean, as well of hastening the extinguishment of the debts, as of establishing the harmony of the United States, it be recommended to the states which have passed no acts towards complying with the resolutions of Congress of the 6th of September and 10th of October, 1780, relative to the cession of territorial claims, to make the liberal cessions therein recommended, and to the states which may have passed acts complying with the said resolutions in part only, to revise and compleat such compliance.

1. Broadside (LT), PCC, Miscellaneous Papers, DNA.

E. AMENDMENT TO SHARE EXPENSES ACCORDING TO POPULATION, 18 April 1783[1]

> The debate over the basis for sharing common expenses among the states, which began during the writing of the Articles of Confederation in 1776 and 1777, resumed in March 1783. The "special committee," appointed on 21 February 1783 to report on an independent income for Congress, recommended on 6 March that the Articles of Confederation be amended. It proposed that common expenses be shared according to the number of all inhabitants, excluding Indians not paying taxes (JCC, XXIV, 173–74), instead of the value of land granted to or surveyed for individuals. The amendment went through the following stages:
>
> (1) On 18 March the special committee reported that expenses should be shared according to all white and other free inhabitants, those bound to servitude for a period of years [indentured servants] and "three-fifths of all other persons" [slaves] except for Indians not paying taxes (JCC, XXIV, 191).
>
> (2) On 20 March the three-fifths clause was dropped (JCC, XXIV, 198).
>
> (3) A committee reported on 28 March that expenses should be shared

according to the whole number of free inhabitants and one-half of all others except for Indians not paying taxes (Hutchinson, VI, 406–7).

(4) In the debate on 28 March various proposals were made as to the number of slaves to be counted. Madison finally moved, "in order to give a proof of the sincerity of his professions of liberality," that three-fifths of the slaves should be counted. John Rutledge seconded the motion, and James Wilson said that he "would sacrifice his opinion to this compromise." Congress approved the amendment five states to three. Theodorick Bland and Arthur Lee of Virginia then moved that the amended clause be struck out, and Congress agreed six states to five (Madison, Notes of Debates, Hutchinson, VI, 407–8; JCC, XXIV, 214–16).

(5) On 1 April Alexander Hamilton moved to reconsider the three-fifths clause and Congress then voted, eight states to one (Rhode Island) with Massachusetts divided, to reinsert the clause in the amendment (JCC, XXIV, 222–24). Madison explained the final vote as follows: "Those who voted differently from their former votes were influenced by the conviction of the necessity of the change and despair on both sides of a more favorable rate of the slaves" (Notes of Debates, Hutchinson, VI, 425).

That as a more convenient and certain rule of ascertaining the proportions to be supplied by the states respectively to the common treasury, the following alteration in the articles of confederation and perpetual union, between these states, be, and the same is hereby agreed to in Congress; and the several states are advised to authorise their respective delegates to subscribe and ratify the same as part of the said instrument of union, in the words following, to wit.

So much of the 8th of the articles of confederation and perpetual union between the thirteen states of America, as is contained in the words following, to wit.

"All charges of war, and all other expences that shall be incurred for the common defence or general welfare, and allowed by the United States in Congress assembled, shall be defrayed out of a common treasury, which shall be supplied by the several states in proportion to the value of all land within each state granted to or surveyed for any person, as such land and the buildings and improvements thereon, shall be estimated according to such mode as the United States in Congress assembled shall from time to time direct and appoint," is hereby revoked and made void; and in place thereof it is declared and concluded, the same having been agreed to in a Congress of the United States, that all charges of war and all other expences that have been or shall be incurred for the common defence or general welfare, and allowed by the United States in Congress assembled, except so far as shall be otherwise provided for, shall be defrayed out of a common treasury, which shall be supplied by the several states in proportion to the whole number of white and other free citizens and inhabitants, of every age, sex and condition, including those bound to servitude for a term of years, and three fifths of all other persons not comprehended in the foregoing description, except Indians, not paying taxes, in each state; which number shall be triennially taken and transmitted to the United States in Congress assembled, in such mode as they shall direct and appoint.

1. Broadside (LT), PCC, Miscellaneous Papers, DNA.

F. ORDINANCE FOR THE GOVERNMENT OF WESTERN TERRITORY, 23 April 1784[1]

On 15 October 1783 Congress requested a new cession from Virginia. Congress then resolved that government should be created in the West as soon as possible, and that a committee should be appointed to prepare a plan "consistent with the principles of the Confederation, for connecting with the Union by a temporary government, the purchasers and inhabitants of the said district, until their number and circumstances shall entitle them to form a permanent constitution for themselves, and as citizens of a free, sovereign and independent state, to be admitted to a representation in the Union; provided always, that such constitution shall not be incompatible with the republican principles, which are the basis of the constitutions of the respective states in the Union."

James Duane, James Madison, and Samuel Huntington were appointed to prepare a plan on 15 October 1783, but they had left Congress by 4 November. On 3 February 1784, Congress appointed a new committee consisting of Thomas Jefferson, Jeremiah Townley Chase of Maryland, and David Howell of Rhode Island. In drafting an ordinance for the government of the national domain, the committee was bound by the resolutions of Congress of 10 October 1780 and of 15 October 1783, and by the Virginia act of cession of 20 December 1783. Both congressional resolutions, which were incorporated in the Virginia cession, required that the West be divided into states not less than 100 miles nor more than 150 miles square, and that the states be admitted to the Union on a basis of equality with the original states.

The land companies made a last minute attempt to block acceptance of the Virginia cession, but Congress accepted it on 1 March 1784. Immediately thereafter, the draft of a plan of government, in Jefferson's handwriting, was laid before Congress. Congress debated and altered the draft in minor ways and made one major deletion: the provision forbidding slavery and indentured servitude in the national domain after the year 1800 (Boyd, "Plan for Government of the Western Territory," *The Papers of Thomas Jefferson*, VI, 581–616).

The Ordinance was published in newspapers, but apparently Congress did not send it to the states officially in 1784. Congress seems to have looked upon the Ordinance as only the first part of the plan for the national domain, the other part being the provision for the sale of the land. Hence, it was not until after the adoption of the Ordinance for the Sale of Western Territory on 20 May 1785 that Congress sent an official printed broadside containing both ordinances to the executives of the states. The broadside, attested by Richard Henry Lee as President of Congress and Charles Thomson as Secretary, was sent to the executives on 28 May 1785.

By the UNITED STATES in CONGRESS Assembled. APRIL 23, 1784.

RESOLVED, That so much of the territory ceded, or to be ceded by individual states, to the United States, as is already purchased, or shall be purchased, of the Indian inhabitants, and offered for sale by Congress, shall be divided into distinct states in the following manner, as nearly as such cessions will admit; that is to say, by parallels of latitude, so that each state shall comprehend from north to south two degrees of latitude, begining to count from the completion of forty-five degrees north of the equator; and by meridians of longitude, one of which shall pass through the lowest point of the rapids of Ohio, and the other through the western cape of the mouth of the great Kanhaway: but the territory eastward of this last meridian, between the Ohio, lake Erie, and Pennsylvania, shall be one state, whatsoever may be its comprehension of latitude. That which may lie beyond the completion of the forty-fifth degree between the said meridians shall make part of the state adjoining it on the south; and that part of the Ohio, which is between the same meridians coinciding nearly with the parallel of thirty-nine degrees, shall be substituted so far in lieu of that parallel as a boundary line.

That the settlers on any territory so purchased and offered for sale, shall, either on their own petition, or on the order of Congress, receive authority from them, with appointments of time and place, for their free males of full age, within the limits of their state, to meet together, for the purpose of establishing a temporary government, to adopt the constitution and laws of any one of the original states; so that such laws nevertheless shall be subject to alteration by their ordinary legislature; and to erect, subject to a like alteration, counties, townships, or other divisions, for the election of members for their legislature.

That when any such state shall have acquired twenty thousand free inhabitants, on giving due proof thereof to Congress, they shall receive from them authority, with appointments of time and place, to call a convention of representatives, to establish a permanent constitution and government for themselves. Provided that both the temporary and permanent governments be established on these principles as their basis.

First. That they shall for ever remain a part of this confederacy of the United States of America.

Second. That they shall be subject to the articles of confederation in all those cases, in which the original states shall be so subject; and to all the acts and ordinances of the United States in Congress assembled, conformable thereto.

Third. That they in no case shall interfere with the primary disposal of the soil by the United States in Congress assembled; nor with the ordinances and regulations which Congress may find necessary for securing the title in such soil to the bona fide purchasers.

Fourth. That they shall be subject to pay a part of the federal debts, contracted or to be contracted; to be apportioned on them by Congress, according to the same common rule and measure by which apportionments thereof shall be made on the other states.

Fifth. That no tax shall be imposed on lands the property of the United States.

Sixth. That their respective governments shall be republican.

Seventh. That the lands of non-resident proprietors shall in no case be taxed higher than those of residents within any new state, before the admission thereof to a vote by its delegates in Congress.

That whensoever any of the said states shall have of free inhabitants, as many as shall then be in any one, the least numerous, of the thirteen original states, such state shall be admitted by its delegates into the Congress of the United States, on an equal footing with the said original states; provided the consent of so many states in Congress is first obtained as may at the time be competent to such admission. And in order to adapt the said articles of confederation to the state of Congress, when its number shall be thus encreased, it shall be proposed to the legislatures of the states, originally parties thereto, to require the assent of two thirds of the United States in Congress assembled, in all those cases, wherein by the said articles, the assent of nine states is now required; which being agreed to by them, shall be binding on the new states. Until such admission by their delegates into Congress, any of the said states after the establishment of their temporary government shall have authority to keep a member in Congress, with a right of debating, but not of voting.

That measures not inconsistent with the principles of the confederation, and necessary for the preservation of peace and good order among the settlers, in any of the said new states, until they shall assume a temporary government as aforesaid, may from time to time be taken by the United States in Congress assembled.

That the preceding articles shall be formed into a charter of compact; shall be duly executed by the president of the United States in Congress assembled, under his hand, and the seal of the United States; shall be promulgated; and shall stand as fundamental constitutions between the thirteen original states, and each of the several states now newly described, unalterable from and after the sale of any part of the territory of such state, pursuant to this resolve, but by the joint consent of the United States in Congress assembled, and of the particular state within which such alteration is proposed to be made.

1. Broadside (LT) ([New York, 1785]).

G. GRANT OF TEMPORARY POWER TO REGULATE COMMERCE, 30 April 1784[1]

The British Order in Council of 2 July 1783 closing British West Indian ports to American ships (although not to American goods) created a widespread demand for retaliation. Congress responded on 26 January 1784 by appointing a committee consisting of Arthur Lee, Elbridge Gerry, and Jacob Read. The committee was instructed to consider a proposed address to the states concerning commerce (9 October 1783, JCC, XXV, 661–64; XXVI, 50); a Virginia act empowering Congress to retaliate against Great Britain for its restrictions on American trade; and, later, a Pennsylvania request that Congress be granted commercial powers. On 6 February Arthur Lee was dropped from the committee, and Hugh Williamson and Jeremiah Townley Chase were added. Thomas Jefferson became a fifth member on 14 April. The committee reported on 22 April. Congress discussed the report, adopted it on 30 April, and sent it to the states for approval (JCC, XXVI, 50, 70–71, 269–71, 317–22).

The trust reposed in Congress, renders it their duty to be attentive to the conduct of foreign nations, and to prevent or restrain as far may be, all such proceedings as might prove injurious to the United States. The situation of commerce at this time claims the attention of the several states, and few objects of greater importance can present themselves to their notice. The fortune of every citizen is interested in the success thereof; for it is the constant source of wealth and incentive to industry; and the value of our produce and our land must ever rise or fall in proportion to the prosperous or adverse state of trade.

Already has Great Britain adopted regulations destructive of our commerce with her West India Islands. There was reason to expect that measures so unequal and so little calculated to promote mercantile intercourse, would not be persevered in by an enlightened nation. But these measures are growing into system. It would be the duty of Congress, as it is their wish, to meet the attempts of Great-Britain with similar restrictions on her commerce; but their powers on this head are not explicit, and the propositions made by the legislatures of the several states, render it necessary to take the general sense of the union on this subject.

Unless the United States in Congress assembled shall be vested with powers competent to the protection of commerce, they can never command reciprocal advantages in trade; and without these, our foreign commerce must decline and eventually be annihilated. Hence it is necessary that the states should be explicit, and fix on some effectual mode by which foreign commerce not founded on principles of equality may be restrained.

That the United States may be enabled to secure such terms, they have

Resolved, That it be, and it hereby is recommended to the legislatures of the several states, to vest the United States in Congress assembled, for the term of fifteen years, with power to prohibit any goods, wares or merchandize from being imported into or exported from any of the states, in vessels belonging to or navigated by the subjects of any power with whom these states shall not have formed treaties of commerce.

Resolved, That it be, and it hereby is recommended to the legislatures of the several states, to vest the United States in Congress assembled, for the term of fifteen years, with the power of prohibiting the subjects of any foreign state, kingdom or empire, unless authorised by treaty, from importing into the United States, any goods wares or merchandize, which are not the produce or manufacture of the dominions of the sovereign whose subjects they are.

Provided, That to all acts of the United States in Congress assembled, in pursuance of the above powers, the assent of nine states shall be necessary.

1. Broadside (LT), PCC, Item 49, Letters and Papers of Charles Thomson, 1781–89, f. 481, DNA.

H. AMENDMENT TO GRANT COMMERCIAL POWERS TO CONGRESS, 28 March 1785[1]

As the post-war commercial depression deepened, many merchants, mostly in the Northern States, were convinced that the request of Congress of 30 April 1784 for temporary commercial powers (IV:G above) would be inadequate even if the states ratified it. Merchants demanded an amendment to the Articles of Confederation giving Congress wider and permanent power over commerce.

Congress responded on 6 December 1784 by appointing a committee consisting of John Jay, Elbridge Gerry, James Monroe, Richard Dobbs Spaight, and William Houstoun to consider investing Congress with the power to regulate trade. The committee was renewed on 24 January 1785. Jay, who had become Secretary for Foreign Affairs, was replaced by William Samuel Johnson, and sometime later Rufus King replaced Gerry (JCC, XXVIII, 17, 70, 148).

On 16 February the committee reported an amendment to the Articles of Confederation, but consideration was delayed until 28 March. Meanwhile, on 11 March, Congress instructed the committee "to report a circular letter to accompany the recommendation proposed in the report." Congress considered the amendment on 28 March and debated it again on 13 and 14 July, but there was so much opposition that the amendment was never sent to the states (JCC, XXVIII, 70, 148, 201–5; XXIX, 533, 539).

The proposed amendment revived the antagonism between the "carrying states" of the North and the "planting states" of the South over the issue of trade regulation, an issue which had surfaced during the writing of the Articles of Confederation. It aroused, too, those who feared a powerful central government. James Monroe, a member of Congress, summarized the arguments of the opponents of the amendment as follows: "1. That it was dangerous to concentrate power, since it might be turned to mischievous purposes; that independent of the immediate danger of intoxication in those entrusted with it, and their attempts on the government, it put us more in the power of other nations. 2. That the interests of the different parts of the Union were different from each other, and that the regulations which suited the one would not the other part. That 8 states [i.e., the Northern States] were of a particular interest whose business it would be to combine to shackle and fetter the others [i.e., the Southern States]. 3. That all attacks upon the Confederation were dangerous and calculated, even if they did not succeed, to weaken it" (to James Madison, 26 July 1785, LMCC, VIII, 172).

That the first paragraph of the 9th of the Articles of Confederation be altered so as to read thus—viz

"The United States in Congress Assembled shall have the sole and exclusive right and power of determining, on peace and war, except in the cases mentioned in the sixth Article—of sending and receiving Ambassadors—entering into treaties and alliances—of regulating the trade of the States as well with foreign Nations, as with each other, and of laying such imposts and duties, upon imports and exports, as may be necessary for the purpose; provided that the Citizens of the States, shall in no instance be subjected to pay higher imposts and duties, than those imposed on the subjects of foreign powers; provided also that the Legislative power of the several States shall not be restrained from prohibiting the importation or exportation of any species of goods or commodities whatsoever, provided also that all such duties as may be imposed, shall be collected under the authority and accrue to the use of the State in which the same shall be payable. And provided lastly that every Act of Congress for the above purpose shall have the assent of nine States in Congress assembled—of establishing rules for deciding in all cases, what Captures on Land or Water, shall be legal, and in what manner prizes taken by Land or Naval forces in the service of the United States shall be divided or appropriated of granting Letters of Marque & reprisal in time of peace—appointing Courts for the trial of piracies and felonies, committed on the high seas, and establishing Courts for receiving and determining finally appeals in all cases of Captures, provided that no Member of Congress shall be appointed Judge of any of the said Courts"—

1. (LT), PCC, Item 24, Reports of Committees of Congress on the Relations between Congress and the States, 1775–86, pp. 125–26, DNA.

I. ORDINANCE FOR THE SALE OF WESTERN LANDS, 20 May 1785[1]

Congress accepted the Virginia cession of the Northwest Territory on 1 March 1784. The next day Congress appointed Thomas Jefferson, Hugh Williamson, David Howell, Elbridge Gerry, and Jacob Read to prepare a report on "the most eligible means of disposing of such part of the western lands as may be obtained of the Indians by the proposed treaty of peace and for opening a land office" (Boyd, VII, 147). On 4 March, five commissioners were appointed to negotiate with the Indians for their lands in the territory northwest of the Ohio River.

The report on the sale of western lands, written by Thomas Jefferson, was laid before Congress on 30 April and read on 28 May. Only four delegates voted to consider it. Congress resumed discussion of the ordinance in the spring of 1785 after receiving favorable reports from the commissioners negotiating with the Indians. After heated debates, a grand committee was appointed to draft a new ordinance. On one side were those, mostly Northerners, who feared that the sale of western lands would hinder the sale of vacant lands in the East, and who feared as well the political impact of new western states. On the other side were those, mostly Southerners, who looked forward to the rapid settlement of the West and the political advantage which they assumed agrarian states in the West would give the South.

The debate centered around the size of the tracts to be sold. New Englanders insisted that the land should be sold in lots so large that only a few large investors or groups of investors could afford to purchase them, while the Virginians insisted that the lots be small enough for individuals to buy. William Grayson of Virginia, who drafted the Ordinance, declared that if it had not been for the pressure of public creditors, who hoped to be paid by funds derived from the sale of the land, no ordinance making possible the settlement of the West would have been adopted.

The Ordinance was a compromise which provided that part of the territory would be sold in township lots and part in sections of a square mile each. However, the sale of lands would not begin until seven ranges of townships had been surveyed. This resulted, in effect, in a victory for those opposed to rapid settlement, because only four of the seven ranges had been surveyed by 1787.

The Ordinance was adopted on 20 May 1785 and published as a broadside, the first part of which contained the Ordinance for the Government of the Western Territory adopted on 23 April 1784. Charles Thomson, Secretary of Congress, sent the official broadside to the executives of the states on 28 May.

An ORDINANCE for ascertaining the Mode of disposing of LANDS in the WESTERN TERRITORY.

BE it ORDAINED by the UNITED STATES in CONGRESS assembled, That the territory ceded by individual states, to the United States, which has been purchased of the Indian inhabitants, shall be disposed of in the following manner.

A surveyor from each state shall be appointed by Congress or a Committee of the States, who shall take an oath for the faithful discharge of his duty, before the geographer of the United States, who is hereby empowered and directed to administer the same; and the like oath shall be administered to each chain carrier, by the surveyor under whom he acts.

The geographer, under whose direction the surveyors shall act, shall occasionally form such regulations for their conduct, as he shall deem necessary; and shall have authority to suspend them for misconduct in office, and shall make report of the same to Congress or to the Committee of the States; and he shall make report in case of sickness, death, or resignation of any surveyor.

The surveyors, as they are respectively qualified, shall proceed to divide the said territory into townships of six miles square, by lines running due north and south, and others crossing these at right angles, as near as may be, unless where the boundaries of the late Indian purchases may render the same impracticable, and then they shall depart from this rule no farther than such particular circumstances may require. And each surveyor shall be allowed and paid at the rate of two dollars for every mile in length he shall run, including the wages of chain carriers, markers, and every other expence attending the same.

The first line running north and south as aforesaid, shall begin on
the river Ohio, at a point that shall be found to be due north from
the western termination of a line which has been run as the southern
boundary of the state of Pennsylvania: and the first line running
east and west, shall begin at the same point, and shall extend throughout the whole territory; provided that nothing herein shall be construed, as fixing the western boundary of the state of Pennsylvania.
The geographer shall designate the townships or fractional parts of
townships, by numbers progressively from south to north; always
beginning each range with No. 1; and the ranges shall be distinguished
by their progressive numbers to the westward. The first range extending from the Ohio to the lake Erie, being marked No. 1. The
geographer shall personally attend to the running of the first east
and west line; and shall take the latitude of the extremes of the first
north and south line, and of the mouths of the principal rivers.

The lines shall be measured with a chain; shall be plainly marked
by chaps on the trees, and exactly described on a plat; whereon
shall be noted by the surveyor, at their proper distances, all mines,
salt springs, salt licks and mill seats, that shall come to his knowledge;
and all water-courses, mountains and other remarkable and permanent things over or near which such lines shall pass, and also the
quality of the lands.

The plats of the townships respectively, shall be marked by sub-
divisions into lots of one mile square, or 640 acres, in the same direction as the external lines, and numbered from 1 to 36; always beginning the succeeding range of the lots with the number next to
that with which the preceding one concluded. And where from the
causes before mentioned, only a fractional part of a township shall be
surveyed, the lots protracted thereon, shall bear the same numbers as
if the township had been entire. And the surveyors in running the
external lines of the townships, shall at the interval of every mile,
mark corners for the lots which are adjacent, always designating the
same in a different manner from those of the townships.

The geographer and surveyors, shall pay the utmost attention to
the variation of the magnetic needle; and shall run and note all lines
by the true meridian, certifying with every plat what was the variation at the times of running the lines thereon noted.

As soon as seven ranges of townships, and fractional parts of townships, in the direction from south to north, shall have been surveyed,
the geographer shall transmit plats thereof to the board of treasury,
who shall record the same with the report, in well bound books to
be kept for that purpose. And the geographer shall make similar
returns from time to time of every seven ranges as they may be sur-

veyed. The secretary at war shall have recourse thereto, and shall take by lot therefrom, a number of townships and fractional parts of townships, as well from those to be sold entire, as from those to be sold in lots, as will be equal to one seventh part of the whole of such seven ranges, as nearly as may be, for the use of the late continental army; and he shall make a similar draught from time to time, until a sufficient quantity is drawn to satisfy the same, to be applied in manner hereinafter directed. The board of treasury shall from time to time, cause the remaining numbers, as well those to be sold entire, as those to be sold in lots, to be drawn for, in the name of the thirteen states respectively, according to the quotas in the last preceding requisition on all the states: provided that in case more land than its proportion is allotted for sale in any state at any distribution, a deduction be made therefor at the next.

The board of treasury shall transmit a copy of the original plats, previously noting thereon, the townships and fractional parts of townships, which shall have fallen to the several states by the distribution aforesaid, to the commissioners of the loan-office of the several states, who, after giving notice of not less than two nor more than six months, by causing advertisements to be posted up at the court-houses or other noted places in every county, and to be inserted in one newspaper published in the states of their residence respectively, shall proceed to sell the townships or fractional parts of townships, at public vendue, in the following manner, viz. The township or fractional part of a township No. 1, in the first range, shall be sold entire; and No. 2, in the same range, by lots; and thus in alternate order through the whole of the first range. The township or fractional part of a township No. 1, in the second range, shall be sold by lots; and No. 2 in the same range, entire; and so in alternate order through the whole of the second range; and the third range shall be sold in the same manner as the first, and the fourth in the same manner as the second, and thus alternately throughout all the ranges: provided that none of the lands within the said territory, be sold under the price of one dollar the acre, to be paid in specie or loan-office certificates, reduced to specie value by the scale of depreciation, or certificates of liquidated debts of the United States, including interest, besides the expence of the survey and other charges thereon, which are hereby rated at thirty-six dollars the township, in specie or certificates as aforesaid, and so in the same proportion for a fractional part of a township or of a lot, to be paid at the time of sales, on failure of which payment, the said lands shall again be offered for sale.

There shall be reserved for the United States out of every township, the four lots, being numbered 8, 11, 26, 29, and out of every fractional part of a township, so many lots of the same numbers as shall be found thereon, for future sale. There shall be reserved the lot No. 16, of every township, for the maintainance of public schools within the said township; also one third part of all gold, silver, lead and copper mines, to be sold, or otherwise disposed of, as Congress shall hereafter direct.

When any township or fractional part of a township shall have been sold as aforesaid, and the money or certificates received therefor, the loan officer shall deliver a deed in the following terms.

The UNITED STATES of AMERICA, to all to whom these presents shall come greeting.

Know ye, that for the consideration of _____dollars, we have granted, and hereby do grant and confirm unto_____ the township (or fractional part of the township, as the case may be) numbered_____ in the_____range, excepting therefrom, and reserving one third part of all gold, silver, lead and copper mines within the same; and the lots No. 8, 11, 26, and 29, for future sale or disposition; and the lot No. 16, for the maintainance of public schools. To have to the said_____ his heirs and assigns forever; (or if more than one purchaser, to the said _____ and their heirs and assigns forever as tenants in common.) In witness whereof, A.B. commissioner of the loan-office in the state of _____ hath, in conformity to the ordinance passed by the United States in Congress assembled, the [20th] day of [May] in the year of our Lord [1785], hereunto set his hand, and affixed his seal, this _____day of _____in the year of our Lord_____and of the independence of the United States of America

And when any township or fractional part of a township shall be sold by lots as aforesaid, the commissioner of the loan-office shall deliver a deed therefor in the following form.

The UNITED STATES of AMERICA, to all to whom these presents shall come greeting.

Know ye, That for the consideration of_____dollars, we have granted, and hereby do grant and confirm unto_____the lot (or lots as the case may be) numbered_____ in the township (or fractional part of the township, as the case may be) numbered _____ in the range,_____excepting and reserving one third part of all gold, silver, lead and copper mines within the same, for future sale or disposition. To have to the said _____ his heirs and assigns forever; (or if more than one purchaser, to the said _____their heirs and assigns forever as tenants in common.) In witness whereof, A.B. commissioner of the loan-office in the state of_____hath, in conformity to the ordinance passed by the United States in Congress assembled, the [20th] day of [May] in the year of our Lord [*1785*], hereunto set his hand, and affixed his seal, this_____ day of_____in the year of our Lord_____ and of the independence of the United States of America_____

Which deeds shall be recorded in proper books, by the commissioners of the loan-office, and shall be certified to have been recorded, previous to their being delivered to the purchaser, and shall be good and valid to convey the lands in the same described.

The commissioners of the loan-offices respectively, shall transmit to the board of treasury every three months, an account of the townships, fractional parts of townships, and lots committed to their charge; specifying therein the names of the persons to whom sold; and the sums of money or certificates received for the same. And shall cause all certificates by them received, to be struck through with a circular punch; and they shall be duly charged in the books of the treasury, with the amount of the monies or certificates, distinguishing the same, by them received as aforesaid.

If any township or fractional part of a township or lot, remains unsold for eighteen months, after the plat shall have been received by the commissioners of the loan office, the same shall be returned to the board of treasury, and shall be sold in such manner as Congress may hereafter direct.

And whereas Congress by their resolutions of September 16th and 18th, in the year 1776, and the 12th of August 1780, stipulated grants of land to certain officers and soldiers of the late continental army, and by the resolution of 22d September 1780, stipulated grants of land to certain officers in the hospital department of the late continental army; for complying therefore with such engagements, Be it ordained, That the secretary at war, from the returns in his office, or such other sufficient evidence as the nature of the case may admit, determine who are the objects of the above resolutions and engagements, and the quantity of land to which such persons or their representatives are respectively entitled, and cause the townships or fractional parts of townships herein before reserved for the use of the late continental army, to be drawn for in such manner as he shall deem expedient, to answer the purpose of an impartial distribution. He shall from time to time transmit certificates, to the commissioners of the loan offices of the different states, to the lines of which the military claimants have respectively belonged, specifying the name and rank of the party, the terms of his engagement, and time of his service, and the division, brigade, regiment or company to which he belonged, the quantity of land he is entitled to, and the township or fractional part of a township and range out of which his portion is to be taken.

The commissioners of the loan offices shall execute deeds for such undivided proportions in manner and form herein before mentioned, varying only in such a degree as to make the same conformable to the certificate from the secretary at war.

Where any military claimants of bounty in lands shall not have belonged to the line of any particular state, similar certificates shall be sent to the board of treasury, who shall execute deeds to the parties for the same.

The secretary at war, from the proper returns, shall transmit to the board of treasury, a certificate, specifying the name and rank of the several claimants of the hospital department of the late continental army, together with the quantity of land each claimant is entitled to, and the township or fractional part of a township and range out of which his portion is to be taken; and thereupon the board of treasury shall proceed to execute deeds to such claimants.

The board of treasury, and the commissioners of the loan-offices in the states, shall within eighteen months, return receipts to the secretary at war, for all deeds which have been delivered, as also all the original deeds which remain in their hands for want of applicants, having been first recorded; which deeds so returned, shall be preserved in the office, until the parties or their representatives require the same.

And be it further ordained, That three townships adjacent to lake Erie, be reserved to be hereafter disposed of by Congress, for the use of the officers, men, and others, refugees from Canada, and the refugees from Nova-Scotia, who are or may be entitled to grants of land under resolutions of Congress now existing, or which may hereafter be made respecting them, and for such other purposes as Congress may hereafter direct.

And be it further ordained, That the towns of Gnadenhutten, Schoenbrun and Salem, on the Muskingum, and so much of the lands adjoining to the said towns, with the buildings and improvements thereon, shall be reserved for the sole use of the Christian Indians, who were formerly settled there, or the remains of that society, as may, in the judgment of the geographer, be sufficient for them to cultivate.

Saving and reserving always, to all officers and soldiers entitled to lands on the northwest side of the Ohio, by donation or bounty from the commonwealth of Virginia, and to all persons claiming under them, all rights to which they are so entitled, under the deed of cession executed by the delegates for the state of Virginia, on the first day of March, 1784, and the act of Congress, accepting the same; and to the end that the said rights may be fully and effectually secured, according to the true intent and meaning of the said deed of cession and act aforesaid: Be it ordained, that no part of the land included between the rivers called little Miami and Scioto, on the northwest side of the river Ohio, be sold, or in any manner alienated, until there shall first have been laid off and appropriated for the said officers and soldiers, and persons claiming under them, the lands they are entitled to, agreeably to the said deed of cession and act of Congress accepting the same.

> DONE by the United States in Congress Assembled, the Twentieth Day of May, in the Year of our Lord One Thousand Seven Hundred and Eighty-five, and of our Sovereignty and Independence the Ninth.
> RICHARD HENRY LEE, P.

CHARLES THOMSON, Secretary.

1. Broadside (LT) ([New York, 1785]). For the manuscript version retained by Congress and attested by Secretary Charles Thomson and President Richard Henry Lee, see PCC, Item 175, Copies of Ordinances of the Congress, 1781–88, pp. 88–100, DNA.

J. AMENDMENTS TO THE ARTICLES OF CONFEDERATION PROPOSED BY A GRAND COMMITTEE OF CONGRESS, 7 August 1786[1]

The widespread public debate over the issue of more power for the central government led to extended debates in Congress during the spring of 1786. Some members argued that a convention should be called, but the majority insisted that the proper method was for Congress to propose amendments to the Articles of Confederation.

On 3 May 1786 Congress, upon a motion of Charles Pinckney, agreed to sit as a "committee of the whole" in order "to take into consideration the state of public affairs" (JCC, XXX, 230). After sitting as a commitee from time to time, Congress appointed a "grand committee" on 3 July "to report such amendments to the Confederation and a draft of such resolutions as it may be necessary to recommend to the several states for the purpose of obtaining from them such powers as will render the federal government adequate to the ends for which it was instituted." The grand committee consisted of Samuel Livermore, Nathan Dane, James Manning, William Samuel Johnson, Melancton Smith, John Cleves Symmes, Charles Pettit, John Henry, Henry Lee, Timothy Bloodworth, Charles Pinckney, and William Houstoun. The grand committee appointed a sub-committee of three, Pinckney, Dane, and Johnson, to draft its report.

The grand committee reported seven amendments on 7 August, and Congress set 14 August for consideration of the amendments (JCC, XXX, 494–98). There is no record that Congress discussed the amendments on the 14th or any other day. The adoption of the amendments was blocked by the quarrel between the North and the South over the treaty with Spain which Secretary for Foreign Affairs John Jay proposed to negotiate with the Spanish minister, Don Diego de Gardoqui (see, for example, Timothy Bloodworth to Governor Richard Caswell of North Carolina, 4 September, LMCC, VIII, 462).

The Grand Committee consisting of Mr: Livermore, Mr: Dane Mr: Manning, Mr: Johnson Mr: Smith Mr: Symmes, Mr Pettit, Mr: Henry Mr: Lee, Mr: Bloodworth, Mr: Pinckney and Mr: Houstoun appointed to report such amendments to the confederation and such resolutions as it may be necessary to recommend to the several states for the purpose of obtaining from them such powers as will render the federal government adequate to the ends for which it was instituted

Beg leave to submit the following Report to the consideration of Congress.

Resolved That it be recommended to the Legislatures of the several States to adopt the following Articles as Articles of the Confederation, and to authorise their Delegates in Congress to sign and Ratify the same Severally as they shall be adopted, to wit—
Art. 14.
The United States in Congress Assembled shall have the sole and exclusive power of Regulating the trade of the States as well with foreign Nations as with each other and of laying such prohibitions, and such Imposts and duties upon imports, and exports, as may be Necessary for the purpose; provided the Citizens of the States shall in no instance be subjected to pay higher duties and Imposts than those imposed on the subjects of foreign powers, provided also, that all such duties as may be imposed shall be collected under such Regulations as the United States in Congress Assembled shall establish consistent with the Constitutions of the States Respectively and to accrue to the use of the State in which the same Shall be payable; provided also that the Legislative power of the several States shall not be restrained from laying embargoes in times of Scarcity— And provided lastly that every Act of Congress for the above purpose shall have the assent of Nine States in Congress Assembled, and in that proportion when there shall be more than thirteen in the Union.
Art. 15.
That the respective States may be induced to perform the several duties mutually and solemnly agreed to be performed by their federal Compact, and to prevent unreasonable delays in any State in furnishing her just proportion of the common Charges of the Union when called upon, and those essential evils which have heretofore often arisen to the Confederacy from Such delays, it is agreed that

whenever a Requisition Shall be made by Congress upon the several States on the principles of the Confederation for their quotas of the common charges or land forces of the Union Congress shall fix the proper periods when the States Shall pass Legislative Acts comply ing therewith and give full and compleat effect to the same; and if any State shall Neglect, seasonably to pass such Acts such State shall be charged with an additional sum to her quota called for from the time She may be required to pay or furnish the same, which additional sum or charge shall be at the rate of ten per Cent P[er] annum on her said Quota, and if the Requisition shall be for Land forces, and any State shall Neglect to furnish her quota in time the average expence of such quota shall be ascertained by Congress and such State shall be charged therewith, or with the average expence of what she may be deficient and in addition thereto from the time her forces were Required to be ready to act in the field with a farther sum which sum shall be at the rate of twelve per Cent per Annum on the amount of such expence.

Art. 16.

And that the Resources of any State which may be negligent in furnishing her just proportion of the Common expence of the Union may in a reasonable time be applied, it is further agreed that if any State shall so Neglect as aforesaid to pass laws in compliance with the said Requisition and to adopt Measures to give the same full effect for the space of Ten months, and it shall then or afterwards be found that a Majority of the States have passed such Laws and adopted such measures the United States in Congress Assembled shall have full power and authority to levy, assess and collect all sums and duties with which any such State so neglecting to comply with the Requisition may Stand charged on the same by the Laws and Rules by which the last State tax next preceeding such Requisition in such State was levied assessed and Collected—to apportion the sum so required on the Towns or Counties in such State to order the sums so apportioned to be assessed by the Assessors of such last State tax and the said assessments to be committed to the Collectors of the same last State tax to collect and to make Return of such Assessments and Commitments to the Treasurer of the United States who by himself or his deputy when directed by Congress Shall have power to recover the monies of such Collectors for the use of the United States in the same manner and under the same penalties as State taxes are recovered and collected by the Treasurers of the re- spective States, and the several Towns or Counties Respectively shall be responsible for the conduct of said Assessors and Collectors, and in case there shall be any Vacancy in any of said Offices of Assessors or

Collectors by death removal, refusal to serve, Resignation or otherwise, then other fit persons shall be chosen to fill such Vacancies in
the usual manner in such Town or Country within Twenty days after
Notice of the assessment, and in case any Towns or Counties, any
Assessors, Collectors or Sheriffs shall Neglect or refuse to do their
duty Congress shall have the Same rights and powers to compel
them to do the same, that the State may have in Assessing and collecting State Taxes.

And if any State by any Legislative Act shall prevent or delay the
due Collection of said sums as aforesaid, Congress shall have full
power and authority to appoint Assessors and Collectors thereof and
Sheriffs to enforce the Collections under the warrants of distress issued
by the Treasurer of the United States, and if any further Opposition
shall be made to such Collections by the State or the Citizens thereof,
and their conduct not disapproved of by the State, such conduct on the
part of the State Shall be considered as an open Violation of the
federal compact.

Art 17.

And any State which from time to time Shall be found in her
payments on any Requisition in advance on an average of the payments made by the States shall be allowed an interest of _____
per Cent P[er] annum on her said advanced sums or expences and
the State which from time to time shall be found in arrear on the
principles aforesaid shall be charged with an Interest of _____
P[er] Cent per Annum on the sums in which she may be so in arrear.

Art 18.

In case it shall hereafter be found Necessary by Congress to establish
any new Systems of Revenue and to make any New Regulations in
the finances of the U S for a limited term not exceeding fifteen years
in their operation for supplying the common Treasury with monies
for defraying all charges of war, and all other expences that shall
be incurred for the common defence, or general welfare, and such
new Systems or Regulations shall be agreed to and adopted by the
United States in Congress Assembled and afterwards be confirmed
by the Legislatures of eleven States, and in that proportion when there
shall be more than thirteen States in the Union, the same Shall become binding on all the States as fully as if the Legislatures of all
the States should confirm the same

Art 19.

The United States in Congress Assembled shall have the Sole and
exclusive power of declaring what offences against the United States
shall be deemed treason and what Offences against the same Mis-

prision of treason, and what Offences shall be deemed piracy or felonies on the high Seas, and to annex suitable punishments to all the Offences aforesaid respectively and power to institute a federal Judicial Court for trying and punishing all Officers appointed by Congress for all crimes, offences and Misbehaviour in their Offices, and to which Court an Appeal Shall be allowed from the Judicial Courts of the several States, in all Causes wherein questions Shall arise on the meaning and construction of Treaties entered into by the United States with any foreign power, or on the Law of Nations, or wherein any question shall arise respecting any Regulations that may hereafter be made by Congress Relative to trade and Commerce, or the Collection of federal Revenues pursuant to powers that shall be vested in that body, or wherein questions of importance may arise, and the United States shall be a party—provided that the trial of the fact by Jury shall ever be held sacred, and also the benefits of the writ of *Habeas Corpus;* provided also that no member of Congress or Officer holding any other Office under the United States shall be a Judge of said Court, and the said Court shall consist of Seven Judges, to be appointed from the different parts of the Union to wit, one from New Hampshire, Rhodeisland and Connecticut, one from Massachusetts, one from New-York and New Jersey, one from Pensylvania, one from Delaware and Maryland, one from Virginia, and one from North Carolina South Carolina and Georgia, and four of whom shall be a quorum to do business.

Art 20.

That due attention may be given to the Affairs of the Union early in the federal year, and the sessions of Congress made as short as conveniently may be each State shall elect her Delegates annually before the first of July, and make it their duty to give an Answer before the first of September in every year whither they accept their appointments or not, and make effectual provision for filling the places of those who may decline, before the first of October yearly, and to transmit to Congress by the tenth of the same month the Names of the Delegates who shall be appointed and accept their appointments, and it shall be the indispensable duty of Delegates to make a Representation of their State in Congress on the first monday in November Annually, and if any Delegate or Delegates when required by Congress to attend so far as may be Necessary to keep up a Representation of each State in Congress, or having taken his or their Seat, shall withdraw without leave of Congress unless recalled by the State he or they shall be proceeded against as Congress shall direct, provided no punishment Shall be further extended than to disqualifications any longer to be members of Congress, or to hold any Office of trust or profit under the United States, or any individual State, and the several States shall adopt regulations effectual to the attainment of the ends of this Article.

1. (LT), PCC, Item 24, Reports of Committees of Congress on the Relations between Congress and the States, 1775–86, pp. 179–94, DNA. The manuscript, in the handwriting of Henry Remsen, a clerk of Congress, is endorsed: "Report of the Grand committee on federal powers—vizt Mr. Pinckney.—Mr. Dane.—Mr. Johnson.—Entd. Read 7 Aug 1786 Order for Monday 14." The report was printed as a broadside for the use of the members of Congress.

K. ORDINANCE FOR THE GOVERNMENT OF THE TERRITORY OF THE UNITED STATES NORTH-WEST OF THE RIVER OHIO, 13 July 1787[1]

The events which led to the adoption of the Ordinance of 1787 began early in 1786, when Congress appointed committees to reconsider the government Ordinance of 1784 and the land Ordinance of 1785. A committee reported on 24 March that the division of the territory northwest of the Ohio River into ten future states should be changed to provide for a smaller number. Another committee declared on 10 May that government over the territory should be created before any land was sold and that the government should be by officials appointed by Congress, not government created by the inhabitants of the territory.

The proposed plan of government presented on 10 May 1786 was debated in July and again in September 1786. Congress resumed debate on the plan in April 1787 shortly before it received the offer of the Ohio Company for the purchase of lands beyond the seven ranges of townships provided for by the land Ordinance of 1785. Negotiations for the sale of the land and the drafting of the new government ordinance went hand in hand. Congress adopted the Ordinance on 13 July, and on 23 July it authorized the Board of Treasury to make a contract with the Ohio Company for the sale of the land. The contract with the agents of the Ohio Company was signed on 27 October 1787.

An Ordinance for the Government of the Territory of the United States, North-West of the River Ohio.

Be it Ordained by the United States in Congress assembled, That the said territory, for the purposes of temporary government, be one district; subject, however, to be divided into two districts, as future circumstances may, in the opinion of Congress, make it expedient.

Be it ordained by the authority aforesaid, That the estates both of resident and non-resident proprietors in the said territory, dying intestate, shall descend to, and be distributed among their children, and the descendants of a deceased child in equal parts; the descendants of a deceased child or grandchild to take the share of their deceased parent in equal parts among them: And where there shall be no children or descendants, then in equal parts to the next of kin, in equal degree; and among collaterals the children of a deceased brother or sister of the intestate, shall have in equal parts among them their deceased parents share; and there shall in no case be a distinction between kindred of the whole, and half blood; saving in all cases to the widow of the intestate her third part of the real estate for life, and one third part of the personal estate; and this law relative to descents and dower, shall remain in full force until altered by the Legislature of the district. And until the governor and judges shall adopt laws as herein after mentioned, estates in the said territory may be devised or bequeathed by wills in writing, signed and Sealed by him or her, in whom the estate may be, (being of full age) and attested by three witnesses;—and real estates may be conveyed by lease and release, or bargain and sale, signed sealed, and delivered by the person, being of full age, in whom the estate may be, and attested by two witnesses, provided such wills be duly proved, and such conveyances be acknowledged or the execution thereof duly proved, and be recorded, within one year after proper magistrates, courts, and registers shall be appointed for that purpose; and personal property may be transferred by delivery, saving however, to the French and Canadian inhabitants and other settlers of the Kaskaskies, Saint Vincents and the Neighbouring Villages who have heretofore professed themselves Citizens of Virginia, their laws and customs now in force among them, relative to the descent and conveyance of property.

Be it ordained by the authority aforesaid, That there shall be appointed from time to time, by Congress, a governor, whose Commission shall continue in force for the term of three years, unless sooner revoked by Congress; he shall reside in the district, and have a freehold estate therein, in one thousand acres of land, while in the exercise of his Office.

There shall be appointed from time to time, by Congress, a secretary, whose Commission shall continue in force for four years, unless sooner revoked, he shall reside in the district, and have a freehold estate therein, in five hundred Acres of land, while in the exercise of his Office; it shall be his duty to keep and preserve the acts and laws passed by the Legislature, and the public records of the district, and the proceedings of the governor in his executive department; and transmit authentic copies of such acts and proceedings every six months, to the Secretary of Congress: There shall also be appointed a court to consist of three judges, any two of whom to form a Court, who shall have a common law jurisdiction, and reside in the district, and have each therein a freehold estate in five hundred acres of land while in the exercise of their Offices; and their Commissions shall continue in force during good behaviour.

The governor and judges or a majority of them shall adopt and publish in the district, such laws of the original States, criminal and civil, as may be necessary, and best suited to the circumstances of the district, and report them to Congress, from time to time, which laws shall be in force in the district until the organization of the general Assembly therein, unless disapproved of by Congress; but afterwards the legislature shall have authority to alter them as they shall think fit.

The governor for the time being, shall be commander in chief of the militia, appoint and Commission all Officers in the same, below the rank of general Officers; all general Officers shall be appointed and Commissioned by Congress.

Previous to the organization of the general assembly the governor shall appoint such Magistrates and other civil officers, in each County or Township as he shall find Necessary for the preservation of the peace and good order in the same: After the general Assembly shall be organized, the powers and duties of Magistrates and other Civil Officers shall be regulated and defined by the said assembly, but all magistrates and other civil Officers, not herein otherwise directed, shall during the continuance of this temporary government be appointed by the governor.

For the prevention of crimes and injuries, the laws to be adopted or made shall have force in all parts of the district, and for the execution of process, criminal and Civil, the governor shall make proper divisions thereof—and he shall proceed from time to time as circumstances may require to lay out the parts of the district in which the Indian titles shall have been extinguished, into Counties and townships, subject however, to such alterations, as may thereafter be made by the Legislature.

So soon as there shall be five thousand free male inhabitants, of full age, in the district, upon giving proof thereof to the governor, they shall receive authority, with time and place to elect representatives from their Counties or Townships, to represent them in the general assembly; provided that for every five hundred free male inhabitants there shall be one representative, and so on progressively with the number of free male inhabitants, shall the right of representation increase, until the number of representatives shall amount to twenty five, after which the number and proportion of representatives shall be regulated by the legislature; provided that no person be eligible or qualified to act as a representative, unless he shall have been a Citizen of one of the United States three years and be a resident in the district, or unless he shall have resided in the district three years, and in either case shall likewise hold in his own right, in fee simple two hundred acres of land within the same: Provided also, that a freehold in fifty acres of land in the district, having been a Citizen of one of the states, and being resident in the district; or the like freehold and two years residence in the district shall be necessary to qualify a man as an elector of a representative.

The representatives thus elected, shall serve for the term of two years, and in case of the death of a representative or removal from Office, the governor shall issue a writ to the County or Township for which he was a member, to elect another in his stead to serve for the residue of the term.

The general assembly, or Legislature, shall consist of the governor, legislative Council, and a house of representatives. The legislative Council, shall consist of five members, to continue in Office five years unless sooner removed by Congress, any three of whom to be a quorum, and the members of the Council shall be nominated and appointed in the following manner, to wit: As soon as representatives shall be elected, the governor shall appoint a time and place for them to meet together, and when met, they shall nominate ten persons residents in the district, and each possessed of a freehold in five hundred acres of land, and return their names to Congress; five of whom Congress shall appoint and Commission to serve as aforesaid; and whenever a vacancy shall happen in the Council, by death, or removal from Office, the house of representatives shall nominate two persons qualified as aforesaid, for each vacancy and return their names to Congress; one of whom Congress shall appoint and Commission for the residue of the term; and every five years, four months at least before the expiration of the time of service of the members of Council, the said house shall nominate ten persons qualified as aforesaid, and return their names to Congress, five of whom Congress shall appoint and Commission to serve as members of the Council five years, unless sooner removed. And the governor, legislative Council, and house of representatives shall have authority to make laws in all cases for the good government of the district not repugnant to the principles and articles in this Ordinance established and declared. And all bills having passed by a majority in the house, and by a majority in the Council, shall be referred to the governor for his assent; but no bill or legislative Act whatever, shall be of any force without his assent. The governor shall have a power to convene prorogue and dissolve the general assembly, when in his opinion it shall be expedient.

The governor, judges, legislative Council, secretary and such other Officers as Congress shall appoint in the district, shall take an oath or affirmation of fidelity, and of Office, the governor before the President of Congress, and all other Officers before the governor. As soon a legislature shall be formed in the district, the Council and house assembled in one room, shall have authority by joint ballot to elect a delegate to Congress, who shall have a seat in Congress, with a right of debating, but not of voting during this temporary government.

And for extending the fundamental principles of civil and religious liberty, which form the basis whereon these republics, their laws, and constitutions are erected; to fix and establish those principles as the basis of all laws, constitutions, and governments, which forever hereafter shall be formed in the said territory;—to provide also for the establishment of states and permanent government therein, and for their admission to a share in the federal Councils on an equal footing with the original states, at as early periods as may be consistent with the general interest.

It is hereby Ordained and declared by the authority aforesaid, That the following articles shall be considered as Articles of compact between the original States and the people and states in the said territory, and forever remain unalterable, unless by common consent, to wit.

Article the First. No person demeaning himself in a peaceable and orderly manner shall ever be molested on account of his mode of worship or religious sentiments in the said territory.

Article the Second. The inhabitants of the said territory shall always be entitled to the benefits of the writ of habeas corpus, and of the trial by jury; of a proportionate representation of the people in the legislature, and of judicial proceedings according to the course of the common law; all persons shall be bailable unless for Capital Offences, where the proof shall be evident, or the presumption great; all fines shall be moderate, and no cruel or unusual punishments shall be inflicted; no man shall be deprived of his liberty or property but by the judgment of his peers, or the law of the land; and should the public exigencies make it Necessary for the common preservation to take any persons property, or to demand his particular services, full compensation shall be made for the same; and in the just preservation of rights and property it is understood and declared, that no law ought ever to be made, or have force in the said territory, that shall in any manner whatever interfere with, or affect private contracts or engagements bona fide and without fraud, previously formed.

Article the Third. Religion, morality and knowledge being necessary to good government and the happiness of mankind, schools, and the means of education shall forever be encouraged. The utmost good faith shall always be observed towards the Indians; their lands and property shall never be taken from them without their consent; and in their property, rights and liberty, they never shall be invaded or disturbed, unless in just and lawful wars authorised by Congress; but laws founded in justice and humanity shall from time to time be made, for preventing wrongs being done to them, and for preserving peace and friendship with them.

Article the Fourth. The said territory and the States which may be formed therein shall forever remain a part of this confederacy of the United States of America, subject to the articles of Confederation and to such alterations therein as shall be constitutionally made; and to all the acts and ordinances of the United States in Congress assembled, conformable thereto. The inhabitants and settlers in the said territory, shall be subject to pay a part of the federal debts contracted or to be contracted, and a proportional part of the expences of government, to be apportioned on them by Congress, according to the same common rule and measure by which apportionments thereof shall be made on the other states; and the taxes for paying their proportion, shall be laid and levied by the authority and direction of the legislatures of the district or districts or new states, as in the original states, within the time agreed upon by the United States in Congress assembled. The legislatures of those districts or new states shall never interfere with the primary disposal of the soil by the United states in Congress assembled, nor with any regulations Congress may find necessary for securing the title in such soil to the bona fide purchasers. No tax shall be imposed on lands the property of the United states; and in no case shall non-resident proprietors be taxed higher than residents. The navigable waters leading into the Missisippi and St. Lawrence, and the carrying places between the same shall be common highways, and forever free, as well to the inhabitants of the said territory, as to the Citizens of the United States, and those of any other states that may be admitted into the confederacy, without any tax, impost, or duty therefor.

Article the Fifth. There shall be formed in the said territory not less than three, nor more than five states; and the boundaries of the states, as soon as Virginia shall alter her act of cession, and consent to the same, shall become fixed and established as follows to wit; The western state in the said territory shall be bounded by the Missisippi, the Ohio and Wabash rivers; a direct line drawn from the Wabash and Post Vincents due north to the territorial lines between the United States and Canada, and by the said territorial line to the lake of the Woods and Missisippi. The middle state shall be bounded by the said direct line, the Wabash from Post Vincents to the Ohio; by the Ohio, by a direct line drawn due north from the mouth of the Great Miami to the said territorial line, and by the said territorial line. The eastern state shall be bounded by the last mentioned direct line, the Ohio, Pennsylvania, and the said territorial line; provided however, and it is further understood and declared that the boundaries of these three states, shall be subject so far to be altered, that if Congress shall hereafter find it expedient, they shall have authority to form one or two states in that part of the said territory which lies north of an east and west line drawn through the southerly bend or extreme of lake Michigan: and whenever any of the said states shall have sixty thousand free inhabitants therein, such state shall be admitted by its delegates into the Congress of the United states on an equal footing with the original states in all respects whatever; and shall be at liberty to form a permanent constitution and state government; provided the constitution and government so to be formed, shall be republican, and in conformity to the principles contained in these articles; and so far as it can be consistent with the general interest of the confederacy, such admission shall be allowed at an earlier period, and when there may be a less number of free inhabitants in the state than sixty thousand.

Article the Sixth. There shall be neither slavery nor involuntary servitude in the said territory otherwise than in punishment of crimes whereof the party shall have been duly convicted: provided always that any person escaping into the same from whom labor or service is lawfully claimed in any one of the original states, such fugitive may be lawfully reclaimed and conveyed to the person claiming his, or her labor, or service as aforesaid.

Be it ordained by the authority aforesaid, That the resolutions of the twenty third day of April, one thousand seven hundred and eighty four relative to the subject of this ordinance be, and the same are hereby repealed and declared null and void.

> Done by the United States in Congress assembled, the thirteenth day of July, in the year of our Lord one thousand seven hundred and eighty seven, and of their Sovereignty and Independence the twelfth.

CHAS THOMSON secy   WILLM. GRAYSON Chairman

1. DS (LT), PCC, Item 175, Copies of Ordinances of the Congress, 1781–88, pp. 121–34, DNA. For the broadside version attested by Secretary Charles Thomson, see PCC, Miscellaneous Papers, DNA.

V

The Calling of the Constitutional Convention

21 January 1786–21 February 1787

Introduction

The idea of a constitutional convention stemmed from the debate over the creation of state governments in 1776. In several states citizens argued that the revolutionary bodies that had taken the place of the colonial governments could not write constitutions. They insisted that only conventions elected for the purpose could do so and that the constitutions could not go into effect until they had been approved by the people. As a result, the first constitutions of some of the states, including Pennsylvania, Maryland, and Massachusetts, were written by constitutional conventions.

The idea that a constitutional convention should be the means of creating a central government for the United States was widespread by 1780. Military defeats, economic stress, and the refusal of Maryland to ratify the Articles of Confederation led some men to propose military dictatorship, while others, including General Nathanael Greene, General John Sullivan, and Thomas Paine, suggested that a "general" or "continental" convention be called. The most comprehensive proposal for a convention to create a strong central government, one backed by military power and public creditors, was made by Alexander Hamilton on 3 September of that year.

For a time after the ratification of the Articles of Confederation in March 1781, the proponents of a powerful central government tried to increase the power of Congress under the Articles, but the idea of a convention was not abandoned. In the summer of 1782 both houses of the New York legislature adopted resolutions on the deplorable "state of the nation," particularly in financial matters, and requested Congress to call "a general convention of the states, specially authorized to revise and amend the Confederation, reserving a right to the respective [state] legislatures, to ratify their determinations."

Congress submitted the proposal to various committees between August 1782 and the middle of 1783, but by then the opponents of a strong central government were regaining control of Congress. The final result was a committee report on 2 September 1783 which recommended that further consideration of a convention be dropped until the states had responded to Congress's request of 18 April 1783 for the power to collect import duties.

By the end of 1783 the supporters of a strong central government —a "national" government—were becoming convinced that they could never achieve their goal under the rules prescribed by the Articles of Confederation. Therefore they turned increasingly to the idea of a constitutional convention, an idea expressed in newspapers, pamphlets, and private letters.

Proposals for a convention came to naught until 21 January 1786 when the Virginia legislature elected eight commissioners to meet with delegates from other states to consider the problems of trade and to consider the preparation of an act to give Congress power to regulate trade. On 19 February, Edmund Randolph, the chairman of the Virginia delegation, sent the resolution to the executives of each of the states and informed them that the proposed convention would meet at Annapolis, Maryland on the first Monday in September 1786.

Some men, particularly New Englanders, suspected the motives behind the call. Rufus King commented that it did not come from those who favored a common commercial system for the United States. Stephen Higginson, a Boston merchant, declared that the men elected to the convention wanted to combine "political objects" with "commercial" ones. They were all "esteemed great aristocrats . . . few of them have been in the commercial line, nor is it probable they know or care much about commercial objects."

Nine states elected delegates, but delegates from four states—Massachusetts, New Hampshire, Rhode Island, and North Carolina—did not attend. The delegates who did attend were Alexander Hamilton and Egbert Benson from New York; Abraham Clark, William C. Houston, and James Schureman from New Jersey; Tench Coxe from Pennsylvania; George Read, John Dickinson, and Richard Bassett from Delaware; and Edmund Randolph, James Madison, and St. George Tucker from Virginia. All but four of the delegates—Benson, Schureman, Coxe, and Tucker—were later elected to the Constitutional Convention of 1787, although Clark refused to attend.

The delegates met on 11 September, elected John Dickinson chairman, wrote a report, and adjourned on 14 September. The report was addressed to the legislatures of the five states represented at Annapolis, and copies were sent to Congress and to the executives of the other states.

The report called upon the states to elect delegates to meet in convention at Philadelphia on the second Monday in May "to devise such further provisions as shall appear to them necessary to render the constitution of the Foederal Government adequate to the exigencies of the Union. . . ." The report raised grave doubts in the minds of some supporters of a strong central government such as John Jay.

They believed that a convention could have no legal or constitutional standing unless it were called by the Confederation Congress. There were others who believed that the only legal method of proposing changes was that prescribed by the constitution-in-being: the Articles of Confederation. Therefore, the action of Congress on the report of the Annapolis Convention would be of crucial importance; and, for a time, it was uncertain what Congress would do, if anything at all.

By 20 September Congress received the report of the Annapolis Convention, and on 11 October it appointed a grand committee of ten members (three states being absent) to consider the report. New England delegates, and particularly those from Massachusetts, opposed the appointment of the committee. Rufus King, a Massachusetts delegate, then at home, told the Massachusetts House of Representatives on 11 October 1786: "The Confederation was the act of the people. No part could be altered but by consent of Congress and confirmation of the several legislatures. Congress therefore ought to make the examination first, because if it was done by a convention, no legislature could have a right to confirm it." Nathan Dane, another Massachusetts delegate and a member of the grand committee, told the Massachusetts House that he suspected the Annapolis Convention wanted to discard the federal system and replace it with another. As a result of the opposition, and of the poor attendance common at the end of the federal year, Congress took no further action in the fall of 1786.

According to the Articles of Confederation, the federal year began on the first Monday in November, but in practice it began after the first of January. Congress did not have a quorum for the new federal year until 12 February 1787. By then, several states, including Virginia, had elected delegates to the proposed convention.

Even more important was the fact that by February 1787 the political climate had changed radically as a result of agrarian outbursts throughout the United States. In April 1786 a paper money party, whose members were looked upon as "Levellers" in other states, captured control of the government of Rhode Island. By February 1787, it was widely reported that the Rhode Island legislature was considering a bill for the equal distribution of all property every thirteen years. In September 1786 New Hampshire farmers surrounded the legislature at Exeter, and some of them shouted for the abolition of debts and taxes and for the equal distribution of property. Sheriffs in Pennsylvania, Virginia, and South Carolina found it difficult and often impossible to collect taxes, and some of them in Pennsylvania were beaten up by irate farmers. The violence culminated dramati-

cally in Massachusetts with the armed uprising known as Shays's
Rebellion.

It was against this background of mounting tension that the Confederation Congress considered the report of the Annapolis Convention, although many members of Congress still remained skeptical
of a constitutional convention. On 13 February 1787 Congress added
two delegates to the grand committee which had been appointed in
October 1786. Six days later the committee, by a one-vote majority,
endorsed the report of the Annapolis Convention without qualification by recommending that the states send delegates to the proposed
convention on the second Monday in May, and that the convention
devise provisions to render the federal government "adequate to the
exigencies of the Union. . . ."

When Congress took up the committee report on 21 February, the
New York delegates moved to postpone the report in order to consider a motion based on instructions they had received from their
legislature. The instructions directed the delegates to propose that
a convention be called "for the purpose of revising the Articles of
Confederation . . . to render them adequate to the preservation and
support of the Union." The New York instructions and motion thus
ignored the report of the Annapolis Convention; and proposed that
Congress take the lead by calling a convention at an unspecified time
and place. They also ignored the actions of the states that had already
elected delegates to a convention. The New York motion to postpone
the report was rejected.

The Massachusetts delegates then moved that the committee report
be postponed to consider a Massachusetts motion, and Congress agreed.
The motion proposed that Congress call a convention "for the sole
and express purpose of revising the Articles of Confederation," with
the "alterations and provisions" to go into effect when approved by
Congress and by the states. However, the motion implicitly acknowledged the call of the Annapolis Convention by providing that the
"delegates who shall have been appointed by the several states" should
meet in Philadelphia on the second Monday in May.

The Massachusetts motion based the call on quite different grounds
than the report from Annapolis, since it sharply and specifically
limited the purpose of the Convention. Furthermore, the preamble
based the call on the grounds that the Articles of Confederation
contained provision for altering them, that experience had revealed
defects in them, and that several states, particularly New York, had
suggested a convention. The Massachusetts motion passed by a vote
of eight states to one. The "no" vote came from the Connecticut
delegates, who consistently opposed a convention.

A. VIRGINIA CALLS MEETING TO CONSIDER GRANTING CONGRESS POWER TO REGULATE TRADE, 21 January–23 February 1786

Resolution of the Virginia Legislature, 21 January[1]

Resolved, That Edmund Randolph, James Madison, jun. Walter Jones, Saint George Tucker, and Meriwether Smith, Esquires, be appointed Commissioners, who, or any three of whom, shall meet such Commissioners as may be appointed by the other States in the Union at a time and place to be agreed on, to take into consideration the trade of the United States; to examine the relative situations and trade of the said States; to consider how far a uniform system in their commercial regulations may be necessary to their common interest and their permanent harmony; and to report to the several States such an act relative to this great object, as, when unanimously ratified by them, will enable the United States in Congress effectually to provide for the same.

That the said Commissioners shall immediately transmit to the several States copies of the preceding resolution, with a circular letter requesting their concurrence therein, and proposing a time and place for the meeting aforesaid.

Edmund Randolph to the Executives of the States, Richmond, 19 February[2]

I do myself the honor of transmitting to Your Excellency the enclosed resolution. The commissioners thereby appointed have instructed me to open the communication, which it directs with the several states. It is impossible for me to decide how far the uniform system in commercial regulations, which is the subject of that resolution, may or may not be attainable. I can only venture to declare that the desire of such an arrangement arose from a regard to the federal interest.

The commissioners of Virginia have therefore only to request the concurrence of your state, and to propose the first Monday in September next as the time, and the city of Annapolis as the place for the meeting of the different deputies.

Governor Patrick Henry to the Executives of the States, Richmond, 23 February[3]

The General Assembly have appointed Edmund Randolph, James Madison, Junr., Walter Jones, St. George Tucker, Meriwether Smith, David Ross, William Ronald, and George Mason, esquires commissioners to meet others from the different states in the Union at a time and place to be agreed on for the purpose of framing such regulations of trade as may be judged necessary to promote the general interest.

I have to request Your Excellency's attention to this subject, and that you will be pleased to make such communication of it as may be necessary to forward the views of this legislature.

1. (LT), *Journal of the House of Delegates of the Commonwealth of Virginia . . .* [17 Oct. 1785-21 Jan. 1786] (Richmond, Va., 1828), 151. The original resolution proposed only Randolph, Jones, and Madison as delegates. The House of Delegates added Tucker and Smith and the Senate, in an amendment to the House resolution, added George Mason, David Ross, and William Ronald (James Madison to Thomas Jefferson, Richmond, 22 January 1786, Boyd, IX, 199; James Madison to James Monroe, Richmond, 22 January 1786, Madison Papers, DLC). The Senate also proposed a second, unknown amendment, which it receded from after the House of Delegates rejected it (*Journal of the Senate of the Commonwealth of Virginia . . .* [17 Oct. 1785-21 Jan. 1786] [Richmond, Va., 1827], 102-3). For background on and the authorship of this resolution, see Boyd, IX, 204-8.

2. Copy, Governor's Letter Books, VIII, 200, Nc-Ar. No recipient's copy of Randolph's letter has been located.

3. RC, John Work Garrett Library, Johns Hopkins University. There is no indication on the letter as to which state executive the letter was sent.

B. PROCEEDINGS AND REPORT OF THE COMMISSIONERS AT ANNAPOLIS, MARYLAND, 11-14 September 1786[1]

Annapolis in the State of Maryland September 11th. 1786.

At a meeting of Commissioners from the States of New York, New Jersey Pennsylvania, Delaware and Virginia—

Present

Alexander Hamilton Egbert Benson	New York
Abraham Clarke William C. Houston James Schuarman	New Jersey
Tench Coxe	Pennsylvania

George Read   ⎫   Edmund Randolph   ⎫
John Dickinson   ⎬ Delaware   James Madison, Junior   ⎬ Virginia
Richard Bassett ⎭   Saint George Tucker   ⎭

Mr. Dickinson was unanimously elected Chairman.

The Commissioners produced their Credentials from their respective States: which were read.

After a full communication of Sentiments, and deliberate consideration of what would be proper to be done by the Commissioners now assembled it was unanimously agreed, that a Committee be appointed to prepare a draft of a Report to be made to the States having Commissioners—attending at this meeting—Adjourned 'till Wednesday Morning.

Wednesday September 13th 1786.

Met agreeable to Adjournment.

The Committee, appointed for that purpose, reported the draft of the report, which being read, the meeting proceeded to the consideration thereof, and after some time spent therein. Adjourned 'till tomorrow Morning

Thursday Septr. 14th. 1786

Met agreeable to Adjournment.

The meeting resumed the Consideration of the draft of the Report and after some time spent therein, and amendments made, the same was unanimously agreed to, and is as follows, to wit.

To the Honorable, the Legislatures of Virginia, Delaware Pennsylvania, New Jersey, and New York—

The Commissioners from the said States, respectively assembled at Annapolis, humbly beg leave to report.

That, pursuant to their several appointments, they met at Annapolis in the State of Maryland, on the eleventh day of September Instant, and having proceeded to a Communication of their powers; they found that the States of New York, Pennsylvania, and Virginia, had, in substance, and nearly in the same terms, authorised their respective Commissioners "to meet such Commissioners as were, or might be, appointed by the other States in the Union, at such time and place, as should be agreed upon by the said Commissioners to take into consideration the trade and Commerce of the United States, to consider how far an uniform system in their commercial intercourse and regulations might be necessary to their common interest and permanent harmony, and to report to the several States, such an Act, relative to this great object, as when unanimously ratified by them would enable the United States in Congress assembled effectually to provide for the same"

That the State of Delaware, had given similar powers to their Commissioners, with this difference only that the Act to be framed, in virtue of those powers, is required to be reported "to the United States in Congress Assembled, to be agreed to by them, and confirmed by the Legislatures of every State."

That the State of New Jersey had enlarged the object of their Appointment, empowering their Commissioners, "to consider how far an uniform system in their commercial regulations and *other important matters,* might be necessary to the common interest and permanent harmony of the several States." and to report such an Act on the subject, as when ratified by them "would enable the United States in Congress—Assembled, effectually to provide for the exigencies of the Union."

That appointments of Commissioners have also been made by the States of New Hampshire, Massachusetts, Rhode Island, and North Carolina, none of whom however have attended; but that no information has been received by your Commissioners of any appointment having been made by the States of Connecticut, Maryland, South Carolina or Georgia.

That the express terms of the powers to your Commissioners supposing a deputation from all the States, and having for object the Trade and commerce of the United States, Your Commissioners did not conceive it advisable to proceed on the business of their mission, under the Circumstance of so partial and defective a representation.

Deeply impressed however with the magnitude and importance of the object confided to them on this occasion, Your Commissioners cannot forbear to indulge an expression of their earnest and unanimous wish. that speedy measures may be taken, to effect a general meeting, of the States, in a future Convention, for the same, and such other purposes, as the situation of public affairs, may be found to require.

If in expressing this wish or in intimating any other sentiment, Your Commissioners should seem to exceed the strict bounds of their appointment, they entertain a full confidence, that a conduct, dictated by an anxiety for the welfare, of the United States, will not fail to receive an indulgent construction.

In this persuasion, Your Commissioners submit an opinion, that the Idea of extending the powers of their Deputies, to other objects than those of Commerce which has been adopted by the State of New Jersey, was an improvement on the original plan, and will deserve to be incorporated into that of a future Convention, they are the

more naturally led to this conclusion, as in the course of their re-
flections on the subject, they have been induced to think, that the
power of regulating trade is of such comprehensive extent, and will
enter so far into the general System of the foederal government, that
to give it efficacy, and to obviate questions and doubts concerning
its precise nature and limits may require a correspondent adjustment
of other parts of the Foederal System.

That there are important defects in the system of the Foederal
Government is acknowledged by the Acts of all those States, which
have concurred in the present Meeting; That the defects, upon a
closer examination, may be found greater and more numerous, than
even these acts imply, is at least so far probable, from the embarrassments which characterise the present State of our national affairs—
foreign and domestic, as may reasonably be supposed to merit a deliberate and candid discussion, in some mode, which will unite the
Sentiments and Councils of all the States. In the choice of the
mode your Commissioners are of opinion,—that a Convention of
Deputies from the different States, for the special and sole purpose of
entering into this investigation and digesting a plan for supplying
such defects as may be discovered to exist, will be entitled to a
preference from considerations which will occur, without being par-
ticularised.

Your Commissioners decline an enumeration of those national circumstances on which their opinion respecting the propriety of a future Convention with more enlarged powers, is founded; as it would
be an useless intrusion of facts and observations, most of which have
been frequently the subject of public discussion, and none of which
can have escaped the penetration of those to whom they would in
this instance be addressed. They are however of a nature so serious,
as, in the view of your Commissioners to render the situation of the
United States delicate and critical, calling for an exertion of the
united virtue and wisdom of all the members of the Confederacy.

Under this impression, Your Commissioners, with the most respectful deference, beg leave to suggest their unanimous conviction, that
it may essentially tend to advance the interests of the union, if the
States, by whom they have been respectively delegated, would themselves concur, and use their endeavours to procure the concurrence of
the other States, in the appointment of Commissioners, to meet at
Philadelphia on the second Monday in May next, to-take into consideration the situation of the United States, to devise such further
provisions as shall appear to them necessary to render the constitut-
tion of the Foederal Government adequate to the exigencies of the
Union; and to report such an Act for that purpose to the United

States in Congress Assembled, as when agreed to, by them, and afterwards confirmed by the Legislatures of every State will effectually provide for the same.

Though your Commissioners could not with propriety—address these observations and sentiments to any but the states they have the honor to Represent, they have nevertheless concluded from motives of respect, to transmit Copies of this report to the United States in Congress assembled, and to the executives of the other States.

By order of the Commissioners

Dated at Annapolis
September 14th. 1786

Resolved, that the Chairman sign the aforegoing Report in behalf of the Commissioners
Then adjourned without day —

Egbt. Benson Alexander Hamilton	} New York	Geo: Read John Dickinson Richard Bassett	} Delaware
Abra. Clark Wm Chll Houston Js. Schureman	} New Jersey	Edmund Randolph Js. Madison Jr	} Virginia
Tench Coxe	} Pennsylvania	St. George Tucker	

1. DS (LT), PCC, DNA. This document, in the handwriting of Alexander Hamilton, was signed by all the delegates present. According to James Madison, "Hamilton was certainly the member who drafted the address" (Syrett, III, 686, n. 1). Copies of the report, but not of the proceedings, were signed by John Dickinson and sent with covering letters from Dickinson to Congress and to the executives of the states. The copy of the report sent to Congress differs only slightly from the text of the report in Hamilton's handwriting. For the copy sent to Congress, see PCC, Item 78, Letters Addressed to Congress, 1775–89, VIII, 187–94, DNA.

C. CONFEDERATION CONGRESS CALLS THE CONSTITUTIONAL CONVENTION, 21 February 1787[1]

Congress assembled as before.

The report of a grand committee[2] consisting of Mr. [Nathan] Dane, Mr. [James M.] Varnum, Mr. S[tephen] M[ix] Mitchell, Mr. [Melancton] Smith, Mr. [Lambert] Cadwallader, Mr. [William] Irwine, Mr. N[athaniel] Mitchell, Mr. [Uriah] Forrest, Mr. [William] Grayson, Mr. [William] Blount, Mr. [John] Bull, and Mr. [William] Few to whom was referred a letter of 14 September 1786 from J[ohn] Dickinson written at the request of commissioners from the states of Virginia, Delaware, Pennsylvania, New Jersey, and New York assembled at the city of Annapolis together with a copy of the report of the said commissioners to the legislatures of the states by whom they were appointed, being an order of the day was called up and which is contained in the following resolution, viz:

"Congress having had under consideration the letter of John Dickinson, Esquire, chairman of the commissioners who assembled at Annapolis during the last year, also the proceedings of the said commissioners and entirely coinciding with them as to the inefficiency of the federal government and the necessity of devising such farther provisions as shall render the same adequate to the exigencies of the Union do strongly recommend to the different legislatures to send forward delegates to meet the proposed convention on the second Monday in May next at the city of Philadelphia."

The delegates for the state of New York thereupon laid before Congress instructions[3] which they had received from their constituents and in pursuance of the said instructions moved to postpone the farther consideration of the report in order to take up the following proposition, to wit:

"That it be recommended to the states composing the Union that a convention of representatives from the said states respectively be held at _____ on _____for the purpose of revising the Articles of Confederation and perpetual Union between the United States of America and reporting to the United States in Congress assembled and to the states respectively such alterations and amendments of the said Articles of Confederation as the representatives met in such convention shall judge proper and necessary to render them adequate to the preservation and support of the Union."[4]

On the question to postpone for the purpose above mentioned the yeas and nays being required by the delegates for New York.

Massachusetts			Pennsylvania		
King	ay)	ay	Irwine	no)	
Dane	ay)		Meredith	ay }	no
			Bingham	no)	
Connecticut					
Johnson	ay)	d[5]	Delaware		
S. M. Mitchell	no)		N.Mitchell	no {	6
New York					
Smith	ay)	ay	Maryland		
Benson	ay)		Forrest	no {	
New Jersey					
Cadwallader	ay)		Virginia		
Clarke	no }	no	Grayson	ay)	ay
Schurman	no)		Madison	ay)	

North Carolina			Georgia		
Blount	no ⎤ no		Few	ay ⎤ d	
Hawkins	no ⎦		Pierce	no ⎦	

South Carolina		
Bull	no ⎤	
Kean	no ⎟ no	
Huger	no ⎟	
Parker	no ⎦	

So the question was lost.

A motion was then made by the delegates for Massachusetts to postpone the farther consideration of the report in order to take into consideration a motion which they read in their place. This being agreed to, the motion of the delegates for Massachusetts was taken up and, being amended, was agreed to as follows:

"Whereas there is provision in the Articles of Confederation and perpetual Union for making alterations therein by the assent of a Congress of the United States and of the legislatures of the several states; and whereas experience hath evinced that there are defects in the present Confederation, as a mean to remedy which several of the states and particularly the state of New York by express instructions to their delegates in Congress have suggested a convention for the purposes expressed in the following resolution and such convention appearing to be the most probable mean of establishing in these states a firm national government.[7]

"Resolved that in the opinion of Congress it is expedient that on the second Monday in May next a convention of delegates who shall have been appointed by the several states be held at Philadelphia for the sole and express purpose of revising the Articles of Confederation and reporting to Congress and the several legislatures such alterations and provisions therein as shall when agreed to in Congress and confirmed by the states render the federal constitution adequate to the exigencies of government and the preservation of the Union."[8]

1. PCC, Item 1, Rough Journals of Congress, DNA.

2. The grand committee was renewed on 12 February 1787 and two new members, representing Rhode Island and Maryland, were added the next day. Because of changes in membership, some of the original ten members were also replaced.

3. The New York Assembly adopted the instructions on 17 February, and the Senate concurred three days later (PCC, Item 67, New York State Papers, 1775–88, II, 555–56, DNA). For Alexander Hamilton's supposed authorship, see Syrett, IV, 93.

4. The wording of the original motion, in the handwriting of Egbert Benson, is identical with that printed in the Journals (PCC, Item 36, Motions Made in Congress, 1777–88, III, 323, DNA).

5. When the votes of delegates from a state were equally divided, the vote of the state was not counted and was marked "d" in the Journals.

6. Under the Articles of Confederation, two delegates had to be in attendance for a state to be represented. A single delegate might vote but the vote was not counted.

7. The preamble and the resolution in the handwriting of Nathan Dane are in ibid, III, 330–31. The only significant difference between Dane's manuscript and the version in the Journals is in the first sentence of the preamble. Dane's manuscript motion reads: "Whereas by the federal Constitution of the United States provision is made for making alterations in it by the consent of a Congress of the United States and the legislatures of all the States. . . ."

8. The resolution was sent to the states by Charles Thomson the day it was adopted (PCC, Item 18, Letter Books of the Secretary of Congress, Letter Book B, 114, DNA). The act was printed in the newspapers at least three dozen times between 24 February and 15 March. On 5 May the New York *Daily Advertiser* also printed the complete Journal entry for 21 February.

For the official copy of the resolution sent to the states, see CC:1.

D. JAMES MADISON, NOTES OF DEBATES IN CONGRESS, 21 February[1]

The report of the Convention at Annapolis in September 1786 had been long under consideration of a committee of the Congress for the last year; and was referred over to a grand committee of the present year. The latter committee after considerable difficulty and discussion, agreed on a report by a majority of *one* only (see the Journals) which was made a few days ago to Congress and set down as the order for this day. The report coincided with the opinion held at Annapolis that the Confederation needed amendments and that the proposed convention was the most eligible means of effecting them. The objections which seemed to prevail against the recommendation of the convention by Congress, were with some: (1) that it tended to weaken the federal authority by lending its sanction to an extra-constitutional mode of proceeding—with others (2) that the interposition of Congress would be considered by the jealous as betraying an ambitious wish to get power into their hands by any plan whatever that might present itself. Subsequent to the report, the delegates from New York received instructions from its legislature to move in Congress for a recommendation of a convention; and those from Massachusetts had, it appeared, received information which led them to suppose it was becoming the disposition of the legislature of that state to send deputies to the proposed convention in case Congress should give their sanction to it.[2] There was reason to believe however from the language of the instruction from New York that her object was to obtain a new convention, under the sanction of Congress rather than to accede to the one on foot, or perhaps by dividing the plans of the states in their appointments to frustrate all of them.

The latter suspicion is in some degree countenanced by their refusal of the Impost a few days before the instruction passed, and by their other marks of an unfederal disposition.[3] The delegates from New York in consequence of their instructions made the motion on the Journal to postpone the report of the committee in order to substitute their own proposition. Those who voted against it considered it as liable to the objection abovementioned. Some who voted for it, particularly Mr. Madison, considered it susceptible of amendment when brought before Congress, and that if Congress interposed in the matter at all it would be well for them to do it at the instance of a state, rather than spontaneously. This motion being lost, Mr. [Nathan] Dane from Massachusetts, who was at bottom unfriendly to the plan of a convention, and had dissuaded his state from coming into it, brought forward a proposition, in a different form, but liable to the same objection with that from New York. After some little discussions, it was agreed on all sides, except by Connecticut who opposed the measure in every form, that the resolution should pass as it stands on the Journal, sanctioning the proceedings and appointments already made by the states as well as recommending farther appointments from other states, but in such terms as do not point directly to the former appointments.

It appeared from the debates and still more from the conversation among the members that many of them considered this resolution as a deadly blow to the existing Confederation. Doctor [William Samuel] Johnson, who voted against it, particularly declared himself to that effect. Others viewed it in the same light, but were pleased with it as the harbinger of a better Confederation.

The reserve of many of the members made it difficult to decide their real wishes and expectations from the present crisis of our affairs. All agreed and owned that the federal government in its existing shape was inefficient and could not last long. The members from the Southern and Middle states seemed generally anxious for some republican organization of the system which would preserve the Union and give due energy to the government of it. Mr. [William] Bingham alone avowed his wishes that the Confederacy might be divided into several distinct confederacies, its great extent and various interests being incompatible with a single government. The Eastern members were suspected by some of leaning towards some antirepublican establishment (the effect of their late confusions), or of being less desirous or hopeful of preserving the unity of the empire. For the first time the idea of separate confederacies had got into the newspapers. It appeared today under the Boston head.[4] Whatever the views of leading men in the Eastern States may be, it would seem that the great body of the people, particularly in Connecticut, are equally indisposed either to dissolve or divide the Confederacy or to submit to any anti-republican innovations.

1. MS, Madison Papers, DLC. It is evident from the contents of Madison's notes that they cover more than the debates on 21 February and that they were probably written sometime later. For other accounts of events on 21 February, see Madison's letters to George Washington, 21 February; to Edmund Pendleton, 24 February; and to Edmund Randolph, 25 February, LMCC, VIII, 545–46, 547–48, 549n.

2. For the shift of opinion in Massachusetts, see Robert A. East, "The Massachusetts Conservatives in the Critical Period," in Richard B. Morris, ed., *The Era of the American Revolution* (New York, N.Y., 1939).

3. The New York legislature had ratified the Impost of 1783 in May 1786 but had refused to grant Congress the power to remove collectors appointed by the states. In August 1786 Congress requested New York to alter its ratification to allow removal, but the legislature categorically refused to do so on 15 February 1787.

4. Madison probably refers to an item which first appeared in the Boston *Independent Chronicle,* 15 February, which was reprinted in the New York *Daily Advertiser,* 23 February; New York *Independent Journal,* 24 February; and *New York Gazetteer,* 26 February. This is further evidence that Madison wrote his notes of the debates sometime after 21 February. The article is as follows:

"How long, asks a correspondent, are we to continue in our present inglorious acquiescence in the shameful resistance that some of the states persist in, against federal and national measures? How long is Massachusetts to suffer the paltry politics, weak jealousy, or local interests of New York and Pennsylvania, to distract our own government, and keep us holden to those wretched measures which has so long made America the pity or contempt of Europe? How long are we to distress our own numerous citizens with the weight of continental taxes, and support our delegation in an assembly, which has no powers to maintain the reputation, or advance the real interest of our commonwealth? This state has made reiterated and strenuous exertions to restore that firmness, confidence, and greatness, which distinguished united America from 1774 to 1782, but to little purpose. It is therefore now time to form a new and stronger union. The five states of New England, closely confederated, can have nothing to fear. Let then our General Assembly immediately recall their delegates from the shadowy meeting which still bears the name of Congress, as being a useless and expensive establishment. Send proposals for instituting a new congress, as the representative of the nation of New England, and leave the rest of the continent to pursue their own imbecile and disjointed plans, until they have experimentally learned the folly, danger and disgrace of them, and acquired magnanimity and wisdom sufficient to join a confederation that may rescue them from destruction."

VI

Appointments of Delegates to the Constitutional Convention

23 November 1786–15 September 1787

Introduction

Members of Congress agreed early in 1786 that the central government needed more power, but the question, as James Monroe explained to James Madison, "is whether it will be better to correct the vices of the Confederation by recommendation gradually as it moves along, or by a Convention."

By March 1786 some members of Congress were ready to propose a "general convention." Charles Pinckney told Congress in May that the federal government would fall unless Congress acquired more power and that the states must be told that it was necessary to call a convention for the purpose, or that they must grant the power to Congress. James Monroe spoke for those opposed to a convention when he replied that Congress had the right to compel the states to comply when it acted according to the powers given it by the Articles of Confederation and that therefore "he saw no occasion of a convention."

The outcome of the debate was that Congress decided to draft amendments to the Articles of Confederation rather than to call a convention. Shortly thereafter, the delegates who had met at Annapolis to consider a grant of commercial power to Congress called upon the states to send delegates to a convention in May 1787 to consider measures "to render the constitution of the Foederal Government adequate to the exigencies of the Union; and to report such an Act for that purpose to the United States in Congress Assembled, as when agreed to, by them, and afterwards confirmed by the Legislatures of every State will effectually provide for the same."

The report was laid before Congress in October, but the Massachusetts and certain other delegates blocked congressional approval. They argued that the Articles of Confederation provided that amendments should originate in Congress and be approved by the states, and that it would derogate from the dignity and weight of Congress "to take a secondary position in the business."

The question of the legality of a convention also concerned men who favored more power for Congress. In January 1787 Rufus King reported that John Jay and others were opposed to a convention "not alone because it is unauthorized, but from an opinion that the result will prove inefficacious." Jay, who ardently supported the creation of a powerful central government, explained his doubts to George Washington in a letter of 7 January. "To me the policy of *such* a convention appears questionable; their authority is to be derived from acts of state legislatures. Are the state legislatures authorized, either by themselves or others, to alter constitutions? I think not. . . ." Jay asked if it would not be better for Congress to declare the present government inadequate and suggest that the people in each state elect conventions for the sole and express purpose of appointing delegates to a general convention for the purpose of amending the Articles of Confederation. He declared that no alterations in the government should be made, or would easily take place, "unless deducible from the only source of just authority—*the People.*"

Washington replied that he favored the proposed convention, although he said that "in strict propriety a convention so holden may not be legal. . . ." He thought that Congress might "give it a coloring by recommendation, which would fit it more to the taste" but that "however constitutionally it might be done," it would not be expedient "for delicacy on the one hand, and jealousy on the other, would produce a mere nihil."

On 23 November the Virginia legislature adopted an act authorizing the appointment of delegates to a convention. The act specifically approved of the Annapolis Convention's call for a convention and declared that a convention was "preferable to the discussion of the subject in Congress. . . ." The act, an eloquent political document, was circulated throughout the United States by Governor Edmund Randolph. On 24 November New Jersey empowered its delegates in the language of the Annapolis Convention, except that it omitted the reference to approval by Congress and the states. The Pennsylvania Assembly cited the Virginia authorization act and quoted the report of the Annapolis Convention in electing and empowering its delegates on 30 December. North Carolina elected and empowered delegates on 6 January, Delaware on 3 February, and Georgia on 10 February 1787. Each of the states quoted or paraphrased the report of the Annapolis Convention, although Delaware forbade one change in the Articles of Confederation: the states were not to be deprived of equal votes in Congress.

Four of the six states—Virginia, Pennsylvania, Delaware, and Georgia—required approval by Congress of any changes proposed. New Hampshire went further in its resolution of 17 January 1787 electing delegates. The House used the language of the Annapolis Convention, but the Senate offered an amendment which the House accepted: the New Hampshire delegates were to attend only if Congress signified that it approved the convention "as advantageous to the Union, and not an infringement of the powers granted to Congress by the Confederation."

New York and Massachusetts took the lead in limiting the powers of the proposed convention. The New York legislature instructed its delegates in Congress to move that Congress call a convention, a motion that ignored the call from Annapolis. The delegates did so on 21 February. The next day the Massachusetts legislature adopted resolutions authorizing the election of delegates and defining their power. The delegates were instructed not to interfere with those parts of the Articles of Confederation which provided for the annual election of delegates, their recall at any time, their serving in Congress more than three years in any six, or holding any office of profit under the United States. Furthermore, any proposed changes must be laid before Congress which, if it judged them, or any part of them proper, would lay them before the states, and if approved by them, would become part of the Articles of Confederation.

Congress' call of a convention "for the sole and express purpose of revising the Articles of Confederation" was followed by the election of delegates by Massachusetts, New York, South Carolina, Connecticut, Maryland, and a second election by New Hampshire. After electing delegates on 3 March, the Massachusetts legislature repealed its instructions of 22 February and replaced them with new instructions based solely upon the congressional resolution of 21 February. The New York legislature also agreed that its delegates would attend the Convention "for the sole and express purpose of revising the Articles of Confederation," and so did Connecticut. The South Carolina act authorizing the election of delegates stated that the Articles of Confederation should be revised, and that the revisions should be approved by Congress and by the "several states." The Maryland act cited the call of the Annapolis Convention rather than the call of Congress, and required approval of any proposals by Congress and by the "several states."

Rhode Island alone refused to elect delegates. The majority of the legislature insisted that constitutional changes should be made only in accordance with Article XIII of the Articles of Confederation. Furthermore, the majority declared that the legislature could not elect delegates "for the express purpose of altering a Constitution, which the people at large are only capable of appointing the Members." The minority of the legislature scorned the interpretation and agreed that the power to elect delegates lay with the legislature.

The opposing positions concerning the constitutionality and legality of the Constitutional Convention set forth in debates before the Convention met; in the instructions to the delegates elected; and in the debates in the Convention, in Congress, and in the state conventions which followed have been reflected in studies of the period from time to time since then.

Upon their arrival in Philadelphia, the delegates presented their credentials, but Secretary William Jackson did not record them in the Convention Journals, and the originals have disappeared. Before their disappearance, however, Benjamin Bankson, a clerk of Congress, recorded them in a manuscript volume labelled "Ratifications of the Constitution" (RCC, DNA). Bankson's "Journal" has been used as the standard source for the instructions of the delegates ever since.

The Journal is a hodgepodge of acts, resolutions, commissions, and legislative proceedings, with much duplication. Furthermore, some of the documents Bankson transcribed were copies or copies of copies. Moreover, the authorization acts of North Carolina, South Carolina, and Massachusetts, as well as Rhode Island's reasons for not sending delegates are not included.

It seems fitting, therefore, to transcribe the documents below from the contemporary session laws and legislative journals of the states rather than to provide yet another copy of material in Bankson's Journal. The documents below consist of legislative acts and resolutions authorizing the election of delegates and acts appointing delegates if they are not named in the authorization acts. The states have been arranged in chronological order according to the dates on which the delegates were elected.

Of the seventy-four men chosen, fourteen resigned or refused appointments, five never attended, and thirteen left the Convention before 5 September. Those who resigned or refused appointments were Erastus Wolcott (Connecticut); John Neilson and Abraham Clark (New Jersey); Robert Hanson Harrison, Charles Carroll of Carrollton, Thomas Sim Lee, Thomas Stone, and Gabriel Duvall (Maryland); Patrick Henry, Thomas Nelson, and Richard Henry Lee (Virginia); Richard Caswell and Willie Jones (North Carolina); and Henry Laurens (South Carolina). The delegates who did not resign but did not attend were John Pickering and Benjamin West (New Hampshire); Francis Dana (Massachusetts); and George Walton and Nathaniel Pendleton (Georgia).

Following the documents for the appointment of delegates is a list of the fifty-five men who attended the Convention.

A. NEW JERSEY, 23 November 1786

House and Council Elect Delegates, 23 November[1]

David Brearley, William Paterson, William C. Houston, John Neilson, esquires were elected commissioners to meet the commissioners of the other states at Philadelphia, in May next, on commercial and other matters.

Resolution Authorizing and Empowering the Delegates, 24 November[2]

Resolved, That the Honorable David Brearley, William C. Houston, William Paterson and John Neilson, esquires, commissioners appointed on the part of this state, or any three of them, be, and they hereby are authorized and empowered to meet such commissioners as have been or may be appointed by the other states in the Union at the city of Philadelphia, in the commonwealth of Pennsylvania, on the second Monday in May next, for the purpose of taking into consideration the state of the Union as to trade and other important objects, and of devising such further provisions as shall appear necessary to render the Constitution of the federal government adequate to the exigencies thereof.

1. *Minutes and Proceedings of the Joint Meeting* [31 Oct.–24 Nov. 1786] (Trenton, 1786), 36.

2. *Votes and Proceedings of the Eleventh General Assembly of the State of New-Jersey* . . . [24 Oct.–24 Nov. 1786] (Trenton, 1786), 73–74. The Assembly and the Council adopted this resolution on 24 November.

John Neilson resigned from the delegation before the Convention met, and the legislature appointed Abraham Clark and Governor William Livingston on 18 May. Clark declined the appointment on the ground that it was inconsistent with his duties as a member of Congress. Jonathan Dayton was appointed to replace Clark on 5 June 1787.

B. VIRGINIA, 4 December 1786

Act Authorizing the Election of Delegates, 23 November[1]

An ACT *for appointing* DEPUTIES *from this Commonwealth to a* CONVENTION *proposed to be held in the City of* Philadelphia *in* May *next, for the purpose of revising the* FEDERAL CONSTITUTION.

Section I. Whereas the Commissioners who assembled at Annapolis, on the fourteenth day of September last, for the purpose of devising and reporting the means of enabling Congress to provide effectually for the Commercial Interests of the United States, have represented the necessity of extending the revision of the Federal System to all its defects; and have recommended that Deputies for that purpose be appointed by the several Legislatures, to meet in Convention in the City of Philadelphia, on the second day of May next; a provision which seems preferable to a discussion of the subject in Congress, where it might be too much interrupted by the ordinary business before them, and where it would besides be deprived of the valuable counsels of sundry individuals, who are disqualified by the Constitution or Laws of particular States, or restrained by peculiar circumstances from a seat in that Assembly: And whereas the General Assembly of this Commonwealth, taking into view the actual situation of the Confederacy, as well as reflecting on the alarming representations made from time to time by the United States in Congress, particularly in their Act of the fifteenth day of February last,[2] can no longer doubt that the crisis is arrived at which the good people of America are to decide the solemn question, whether they will by wise and magnanimous efforts reap the just fruits of that Independence, which they have so gloriously acquired, and of that Union which they have cemented with so much of their common blood; or whether by giving way to unmanly jealousies and prejudices, or to partial and transitory interests, they will renounce the auspicious blessings prepared for them by the Revolution, and furnish to its enemies an eventual triumph over those by whose virtue and valour it has been accomplished: And whereas the same noble and extended policy, and the same fraternal and affectionate sentiments, which originally determined the Citizens of this Commonwealth to unite with their brethren of the other States in establishing a Federal Government, cannot but be felt with equal force now, as motives to lay aside every inferior consideration, and to concur in such further concessions and provisions, as may be necessary to secure the great objects for which that Government was instituted, and to render the United States as happy in peace, as they have been glorious in war:

Sect. II. *BE it therefore enacted by the General Assembly of the Commonwealth of Virginia,* That seven Commissioners be appointed by joint ballot of both Houses of Assembly, who, or any three of them, are hereby authorized as Deputies from this Commonwealth, to meet such Deputies as may be appointed and authorised by other States, to assemble in Convention at Philadelphia, as above recommended, and to join with them in devising and discussing all such alterations and further provisions, as may be necessary to render the Federal Constitution adequate to the exigencies of the Union; and in reporting such an Act for that purpose, to the United States in Congress, as, when agreed to by them, and duly confirmed by the several States, will effectually provide for the same.

Sect. III. *AND be it further enacted,* That in case of the death of any of the said Deputies, or of their declining their appointments, the Executive are hereby authorised to supply such vacancies. And the Governor is requested to transmit forthwith a copy of this Act to the United States in Congress, and to the Executives of each of the States in the Union.

House and Senate Elect Delegates, 4 December[3]

The House, according to the order of the day, proceeded by joint ballot with the Senate, to the appointment of seven deputies from this commonwealth, to a convention proposed to be held in the city of Philadelphia in May next, for the purpose of revising the federal constitution, and the members having prepared tickets with the names of the persons to be appointed, and deposited the same in the ballot boxes, Mr. Corbin, Mr. Matthews, Mr. David Stuart, Mr. George Nicholas, Mr. Richard Lee, Mr. Wills, Mr. Thomas Smith, Mr. Goodall, and Mr. Turberville were nominated in committee to meet a committee from the Senate in the conference chamber, and jointly with them to examine the ballot boxes, and report to the House on whom the majority of votes should fall.

The committee then withdrew, and after some time returned into the House and reported that the committee had, according to order, met a committee from the Senate in the conference chamber, and jointly with them examined the ballot boxes and found a majority of votes in favor of George Washington, Patrick Henry, Edmund Randolph, John Blair, James Madison, George Mason, and George Wythe, esquires.

1. (LT), *Acts Passed at a General Assembly of the Commonwealth of Virginia* . . . [16 Oct. 1786–11 Jan. 1787] (Richmond, [1787]), 11. The act was introduced in the House on 3 November, and final action was completed when the Senate adopted the bill on 23 November.

2. On 15 February 1786 a committee of Congress reported on the state of the Impost of 1783 (IV:D above). Congress then resolved to resubmit the Impost to those states that "have not fully compiled with the same," and warned them "that the most fatal evils will inevitably flow from a breach of public faith, pledged by solemn contract, and a violation of those principles of justice, which are the only solid basis of the honor and prosperity of nations" (JCC, XXX, 70–76).

3. *Journal of the House of Delegates of the Commonwealth of Virginia* . . . [16 Oct. 1786–11 Jan. 1787] (Richmond, [1787]), 86. Patrick Henry declined to serve, and on 22 February 1787 the Executive Council appointed Thomas Nelson to fill the vacancy. Nelson declined, and Richard Henry Lee was appointed by the Council on 20 March. Lee also declined, and James McClurg was appointed unanimously by the Council on 5 April.

C. PENNSYLVANIA, 30 December 1786

Act Electing and Empowering Delegates, 30 December[1]

An ACT *appointing Deputies to the Convention, intended to be held in the City of* Philadelphia, *for the purpose of revising the Foederal Constitution.*

Sect. I. Whereas the General Assembly of this Commonwealth, taking into their serious consideration the representations heretofore made to the Legislatures of the several States in the Union, by the United States in Congress assembled; and also weighing the difficulties under which the Confoederated States now labour, are fully convinced of the necessity of revising the Foederal Constitution, for the purpose of making such alterations and amendments as the exigencies of our public affairs require: *And whereas* the Legislature of the state of Virginia have already passed an act of that Commonwealth, impowering certain commissioners to meet at the city of Philadelphia, in May next, a convention of commissioners, or deputies, from the different states; and the Legislature of this state are fully sensible of the important advantages which may be derived to the United States, and every of them, from co-operating with the commonwealth of Virginia, and the other states of the confederation, in the said design.

Sect. II. *Be it enacted, and it is hereby enacted by the Representatives of the Freemen of the Commonwealth of Pennsylvania in General Assembly met, and by the authority of the same,* That Thomas Mifflin, Robert Morris, George Clymer, Jared Ingersoll, Thomas Fitzsimons, James Wilson and Governeur Morris, Esquires, are hereby appointed deputies from this state to meet in the convention of the deputies of the respective states of North-America, to be held at the city of Philadelphia, on the second day of the month of May next. And the said Thomas Mifflin, Robert Morris, George Clymer, Jared Ingersoll, Thomas Fitzsimons, James Wilson and Governeur Morris, Esquires, or any four of them are hereby constituted and appointed deputies from this state, with powers to meet such deputies as may be appointed and authorised by the other states to assemble in the said convention at the city aforesaid, and to join with them in devising, deliberating on, and discussing all such alterations and further provisions as may be necessary to render the foederal constitution fully adequate to the exigencies of the Union; and in reporting such act or acts for that purpose, to the United States in Congress assembled, as when agreed to by them, and duly confirmed by the several states, will effectually provide for the same.

Sect. 3. *And be it further enacted by the authority aforesaid,* That in case any of the said deputies, hereby nominated, shall happen to die, or to resign his or their said appointment or appointments, the Supreme Executive Council shall be and hereby are empowered and required to nominate and appoint other person or persons in lieu of him or them so deceased, or who has or have so resigned; which person or persons, from and after such nomination and appointment, shall be, and hereby are declared to be vested with the same powers respectively, as any of the deputies nominated and appointed by this act, is vested with by the same. *Provided always,* that the Council are not hereby authorised, nor shall they make any such nomination or appointment, except in vacation, and during the recess of the General Assembly of this state.

Signed by Order of the House,

THOMAS MIFFLIN, Speaker:

Enacted into a Law at Philadelphia,
on Saturday, December, *the thirtieth, in
the year of our Lord, one thousand seven
hundred and eighty six.*

PETER ZACHARY LLOYD,
Clerk of the General Assembly.

1. (LT), *Laws Enacted in the First Sitting of the Eleventh General Assembly of the Commonwealth of Pennsylvania* . . . [23 Oct.–30 Dec. 1786] ([Philadelphia, 1787]), 193–94. On 28 March 1787 the Assembly passed a supplemental act appointing Benjamin Franklin a delegate.

D. NORTH CAROLINA, 6 January 1787

Act Authorizing the Election of Delegates, 6 January[1]

An Act *for appointing Deputies from this state, to a convention proposed to be held in the city of Philadelphia in May next, for the purpose of revising the foederal constitution.*

Whereas in the formation of the foederal compact which frames the bond of union of the American states, it was not possible in the infant state of our republics to devise a system which in the course of time and experience would not manifest imperfections that it would be necessary to reform. And whereas the limited powers which by the articles of confederation are vested in the Congress of the United States, have been found far inadequate to the enlarged purposes which they were intended to produce. And whereas Congress hath by repeated and most urgent representations, endeavoured to awaken this and the other states of the union, to a sense of the truly critical and alarming situation into which they must be unavoidably cast, unless measures are forthwith taken to enlarge the powers of Congress, that they may thereby be enabled to avert the dangers which threaten our existence as a free and independent people. And whereas this state hath been ever desirous to act upon the enlarged system of the general good of the United States, without bounding its views to the narrow and selfish object of partial convenience, and has been at all times ready to make every concession to the safety and happiness of the whole, which justice and sound policy could vindicate:

I. *Be it therefore enacted by the General Assembly of the state of* North-Carolina, *and by the authority of the same,* That five Commissioners be appointed by joint ballot of both Houses of Assembly, who, or any three of them, are hereby authorised as Deputies from this state, to meet at Philadelphia on the first day of May next, then and there to meet and confer with such Deputies as may be appointed by the other states for similar purposes, and with them to discuss and decide upon the most effectual means to remove the defects of our foederal union, and to procure the enlarged purposes which it was intended to effect, and that they report such an act to the General Assembly of this state, as when agreed to by them, will effectually provide for the same.

II. *And be it further enacted,* That in case of the death or resignation of any of the said Deputies, or of their declining their appointments, his Excellency the Governor for the time being, is hereby authorised to supply such vacancies, and the Governor is required to transmit forthwith a copy of this act to the United States in Congress assembled, and to the executives of each of the states in the union.

House and Senate Elect Delegates, 6 January

THE SENATE[2]

Ordered, That the following message be sent to the House of Commons:

Mr. Speaker and Gentlemen, We propose that the deputies from this state to assist in revising the federal constitution be immediately balloted for. Mr. Herritage and Mr. Wynns will superintend the balloting.

THE HOUSE[3]

Ordered, That the following message be sent to the Senate:

Mr. Speaker and Gentlemen, We agree to ballot for persons to assist in an alteration of the federal constitution as by you proposed. We nominate Governor Caswell, Alexander Martin, Esquire, Richard Dobbs Spaight, Hugh Williamson, William R. Davie, Willie Jones and Samuel Johnston, esquires.

Ordered, That Mr. Willis and Mr. Winslow be appointed to superintend the balloting.

. . . .

Mr. Willis from the joint balloting for members to attend a meeting proposed to be held at Philadelphia in May next, for the purpose of revising the federal constitution, reported, That His Excellency Richard Caswell, Esquire, Alexander Martin, William R. Davie, Richard Dobbs Spaight and Willie Jones, esquires were elected for the purpose aforesaid.

The House taking this report into consideration concurred therewith.

THE SENATE[4]

The General Assembly now proceeded to ballot for deputies to represent this state in convention, as before agreed on; which being ended, Mr. Herritage and Mr. Wynns, appointed on the part of this house to superintend the same, reported, That having pursuant to the order of the house attended the balloting aforesaid, on closing the poll it appeared, that His Excellency Richard Caswell, Alexander Martin, William R. Davie, Richard D. Spaight and Willie Jones, esquires were elected deputies as aforesaid.

The house taking this report into consideration,

Resolved, That they do concur therewith.

1. (LT), *The Laws of North-Carolina* . . . [18 Nov. 1786–6 Jan. 1787] (Fayetteville, [1787]), 6. After considering Virginia's act authorizing the appointment of delegates, a Senate committee, on 5 January, recommended that North Carolina send delegates to the proposed convention. On the same day, a bill for this purpose was read and passed three times in both the Senate and the House. The House ordered the bill engrossed, and the next day it was signed into law.

2. *The Journal of the Senate* . . . [20 Nov. 1786–6 Jan. 1787] ([New Bern, 1787]), 74.

3. MS [Journal of the House of Commons, 18 Nov. 1786–6 Jan. 1787], 550–52, Nc-Ar. Caswell and Jones declined the appointments. On the recommendation of the Governor, the Council filled the vacancies by appointing Hugh Williamson on 14 March and William Blount on 16 April.

4. *Senate Journal,* 74.

E. DELAWARE, 3 February 1787

Act Electing and Empowering Delegates, 3 February[1]

An ACT *appointing Deputies from this State to the Convention, proposed to be held in the City of Philadelphia, for the Purpose of revising the Foederal Constitution.*

Whereas the General Assembly of this State are fully convinced of the Necessity of revising the Foederal Constitution, and adding thereto such further Provisions as may render the same more adequate to the Exigencies of the Union; and whereas the Legislature of *Virginia* have already passed an Act of that Commonwealth, appointing and authorizing certain Commissioners to meet, at the City of Philadelphia, in *May* next, a Convention of Commissioners or Deputies from the different States: And this State being willing and desirous of co-operating with the Commonwealth of *Virginia,* and the other States in the Confederation, in so useful a Design;

Sect. 1. BE IT THEREFORE ENACTED by the General Assembly of *Delaware,* That *George Read, Gunning Bedford, John Dickinson, Richard Bassett,* and *Jacob Broom,* Esquires, are hereby appointed Deputies from this State to meet in the Convention of the Deputies of other States, to be held at the City of *Philadelphia* on the Second Day of *May* next. And the said *George Read, Gunning Bedford, John Dickinson, Richard Bassett,* and *Jacob Broom,* Esquires, or any Three of them, are hereby constituted and appointed Deputies from this State, with Powers to meet such Deputies as may be appointed and authorized by the other States to assemble in the said Convention at the City aforesaid, and to join with them in devising, deliberating on, and discussing, such Alterations and further Provisions, as may be necessary to render the Foederal Constitution adequate to the Exigencies of the Union; and in reporting such Act or Acts for that Purpose to the United States in Congress assembled, as when agreed to by them, and duly confirmed by the several States, may effectually provide for the same: So always and provided, that such Alterations, or further Provisions, or any of them, do not extend to that Part of the Fifth Article of the Confederation of the said States, finally ratified on the first Day of *March,* in the Year One Thousand Seven Hundred and Eighty-one, which declares, that "in determining Questions in the United States in Congress assembled, each State shall have one Vote."

Sect. 2. AND BE IT ENACTED, That in case any of the said

Deputies, hereby nominated, shall happen to die, or to resign his or their Appointment, the President or Commander in Chief, with the Advice of the Privy-Council, in the Recess of the General Assembly, is hereby authorized to supply such Vacancies.

Signed, by Order of the House of Assembly,
JOHN COOK, Speaker.
Signed, by Order of the Council,
GEORGE CRAGHEAD, Speaker.

Passed, at *Dover, February* 3, 1787.

1. (LT), *Laws of the General Assembly of the Delaware State* . . . [20 Oct. 1786–6 Feb. 1787] (Wilmington, 1787), 22–23.

F. GEORGIA, 10 February 1787

Act Electing and Empowering Delegates, 10 February[1]

AN ORDINANCE For the Appointment of Deputies from this State for the Purpose of revising the Federal Constitution.

Be it ordained by the Representatives of the Freemen of the State of Georgia, in General Assembly met, and by the authority of the same, That William Few, Abraham Baldwin, William Pierce, George Walton, William Houstoun, and Nathaniel Pendleton, Esquires, be, and they are hereby appointed commissioners, who, or any two or more of them, are hereby authorised as deputies from this state to meet such deputies as may be appointed and authorised by other states, to assemble in convention at Philadelphia, and to join with them in devising and discussing all such alterations and farther provisions, as may be necessary to render the federal constitution adequate to the exigencies of the union, and in reporting such an Act for that purpose to the United States in Congress assembled, as when agreed to by them, and duly confirmed by the several states, will effectually provide for the same. In case of the death of any of the said deputies, or of their declining their appointments, the Executive are hereby authorised to supply such vacancies.

By Order of the House,
WILLIAM GIBBONS, *Speaker.*

Augusta, February 10, 1787.

1. (LT), [*Georgia Session Laws,* 2 Jan.–11 Feb. 1787] ([Augusta, 1787]), 21. Walton and Pendleton did not attend.

G. MASSACHUSETTS, 3 March 1787

Resolution Authorizing the Appointment of Delegates and Providing Instructions for Them, 22 February[1]

Resolved that five Commissioners be appointed, by the General Assembly, who, or any three of whom, are hereby empowered, to meet such Commissioners, as are or may be appointed by the Legislatures of the other States in the Union, at Philadelphia, on the second day of may next, & with them to consider the trade & commerce of the United States; & how far an uniform system in their commercial intercourse & regulation, may be necessary for their common interest & permanent harmony;

And also to consider, how far it may be necessary to alter any of the articles of the present Confederation, so as to render the Constitution of the federal Government, more adequate to the exigences of the Union; & what further powers may be necessary to be vested in Congress for the common welfare & security, & with them to form a report for that purpose;—Such alterations & additions as may be made, to be however consistent with the true republican spirit & genius of the present articles of Confederation.

Provided, that the said Commissioners on the part of this Commonwealth, are hereby particularly instructed, by no means to interfere with the fifth of the articles of the Confederation, which provides, "for the annual election of Delegates in Congress, with a power reserved to each State, to recall its Delegates or any of them, within the Year, and to send others in their stead for the remainder of the Year— And which also provides, that no person shall be capable of being a Delegate, for more than three years in any term of six years, or being a Delegate, shall be capable of holding any Office under the United States, for which he, or any other for his benefit, receives any salary, fees, or emolument of any kind."

The report of the said Commissioners, from the several Legislatures, to be laid before the United States in Congress assembled, to the intent, that if they shall judge it proper, they may recommend the said report or any part of it to the Legislatures of the several States for their consideration; and if agreed to by them, that the same may become a part of the Confederation of the United States.

And if any of the Commissioners who shall be appointed by the General Assembly, shall resign, or by death, or otherwise, be prevented from attending the said Convention, it shall be in the power of the Governor with the advice of Council to supply any vacancy that may take place as aforesaid, and he is requested to supply such vacancy accordingly.

House and Senate Elect Delegates, 3 March

THE HOUSE[2]

Mr. Jones was charged with a message to acquaint the Honorable Senate that the House were ready to proceed to the choice of five delegates to represent this commonwealth in convention at Philadelphia in May next.

The Honorable T. Dalton, Esquire came down and said that the Senate were also ready.

Mr. Otis, Mr. Vans, Mr. Davis, Mr. Frothingham, and Mr. Dawes were then appointed a committee to collect, count and sort the votes of the House. A return of the House being made, there appeared to be 105 members present. The committee having attended the service assigned and compared the votes with those of the Honorable Senate reported that,

The Honorable Francis Dana, Esquire was the only person chosen. Whereupon the House again proceeded to the choice and the committee having proceeded to collect and compare the votes as aforementioned reported that the Honorable Elbridge Gerry, Esquire, the Honorable Nathaniel Gorham, Esquire, the Honorable Rufus King, Esquire, and the Honorable Caleb Strong, Esquire were chosen.

THE SENATE[3]

The committee of each branch of the legislature appointed to collect, count and sort the votes in their respective houses, for five delegates to represent this commonwealth in a convention to be held at Philadelphia, in May next, having met and compared their lists, it appeared that the two houses were united in the choice of the Honorable Francis Dana, Nathl. Gorham, Elbridge Gerry, Rufus King, and Caleb Strong, esquires.

House Resolution of 7 March Repealing the Resolution of 22 February[4]

Whereas on the 22d day of February 1787, it was, by the Legislature of this Commonwealth, Resolved, that five Commissioners be appointed by the General Assembly, who, or any three of whom, were empowered to meet such Commissioners as are or may be appointed by the Legislatures of the other States in the Union at Philadelphia on the second day of May next for purposes mentioned in said resolution—

Resolved, that the said resolve, & every part thereof be, & it is hereby repealed—

Resolved, that the Secretary be, & he is hereby directed not to publish or print this, or the first mentioned resolve, any resolve or order to the contrary notwithstanding—

House Substitute of 7 March for the Resolution of 22 February[5]

Whereas Congress did on the 21st day of February 1787 Resolve, "that in the opinion of Congress it is expedient that on the second monday in May next a Convention of Delegates who shall have been appointed by the several States to be held at Philadelphia, for the sole & express purpose of revising the articles of Confederation, and reporting to Congress & the several Legislatures, such alterations & provisions therein, as shall when agreed to in Congress, and confirmed by the States, render the federal Constitution adequate to the exigences of Government; & the preservation of the Union"—

And Whereas the Legislature of this Commonwealth did on the third day of this present month elect the honorable Francis Dana, Elbridge Gerry, Nathaniel Gorham, Rufus King, and Caleb Strong esquires, Delegates, or any three of them to attend and represent this Commonwealth at the aforesaid Convention, for the sole & express purpose mentioned in the aforerecited resolve of Congress—

Resolved that his excellency the Governour be, & he hereby is requested to grant to the said Francis Dana, Elbridge Gerry, Nathaniel Gorham, Rufus King & Caleb Strong esqrs a commission agreably to said resolution of Congress

Senate Amendment to the House Substitute, 9 March[6]

And it is further Resolved, that the Said Delegates on the part of this Commonwealth be, and they are hereby instructed not to acceed to any alterations or additions that may be proposed to be made in the present Articles of Confederation, which may appear to them, not to consist with the true republican Spirit and Genius of the Said Confederation: and particularly that they by no means interfere with the fifth of the Said Articles which provides, "for the annual election of Delegates in Congress, with a power reserved to each State to recal its Delegates, or any of them within the Year & to send others in their stead for the remainder of the year—

And which also provides, that no person shall be capable of being a Delegate for more than three years in any term of six years, or being a Delegate shall be capable of holding any Office under the United States for which he or any other for his benefit, receives any salary, fees, or emolument of any kind"—

Ordered that the Secretary serve the aforenamed Delegates, severally, and such others as may hereafter be appointed in their stead with an attested copy of the last foregoing resolve—

House Proceedings, 10 March[7]

[Senate amendment] read and nonconcurred.

Senate Proceedings, 10 March[8]

[House resolution] read again in Senate and reconsidered, and the Senate concur with the Honorable House.[9]

[House] resolve repealing a resolve of the 22d. February 1787 respecting the commissioners who are to meet at Philadelphia. Read and concurred.

1. MS (LT), Resolves, 1786, Chap. 43A, M-Ar. This resolution was proposed by the Senate on 21 February and adopted by the House the next day.

Governor James Bowdoin laid the report of the Annapolis Convention and other papers before the legislature on 2 October 1786. On 11 October, Rufus King, and on 9 November, Nathan Dane, Massachusetts delegates to Congress, addressed the House and reported the arguments in Congress for and against a convention. The legislature did not act on the report of the Annapolis Convention during the fall session. Nor did it act after it reconvened on 31 January 1787 until Governor Bowdoin, on 19 February, laid before it the Virginia and North Carolina acts appointing delegates to the Convention and urged that "The subject is important and merits an attentive consideration."

2. MS, A Journal of the Honourable House of Representatives . . . [31 May 1786–10 March 1787], 475, M-Ar. On 22 February the Senate had proposed and the House had agreed that the choice of delegates might originate in either house. The House proposed on 1 March that the delegates be elected at the same time by the two houses acting separately. The next day, after the Governor delivered the resolution of Congress of 21 February calling the Convention, the House proposed and the Senate agreed to elect delegates at eleven o'clock A.M. on 3 March.

3. MS [Journal of the Senate, 31 Jan.–10 March 1787], 59–60, M-Ar.

4. MS (LT), Resolves, 1786 [Chap. 147], M-Ar. This document is endorsed: "Resolve/Repealing a Resolve/appointg Delegates to/Convention in Philadelphia/May next/Mr. Adams/Mr. Cranch/March 10th. 1787/Ordered not to be published/copied for Delegates/ p. 399."

5. MS (LT), Resolves, 1786, Chap. 147, M-Ar.

6. MS (LT), ibid.

7. MS, House Journal, 501.

8. MS, Senate Journal, 70.

9. The House resolution of 7 March, which copied the congressional resolution of 21 February, was approved by the Senate on 10 March and was embodied in the commission Governor Bowdoin issued each delegate on 9 April (RCC, Ratifications of the Constitution, 4–5, DNA).

H. NEW YORK, 6 March 1787

Assembly and Senate Authorize Election of Delegates, 26–28 February

THE ASSEMBLY, 26 February[1]

Resolved (if the honorable the Senate concur herein), That five delegates be appointed on the part of this state, to meet such delegates as may be appointed on the part of the other states respectively, on the second Monday in May next, at Philadelphia, for the sole and express purpose of revising the Articles of Confederation and reporting to Congress, and to the several legislatures, such alterations and provisions therein, as shall, when agreed to in Congress, and confirmed by the several states, render the federal constitution adequate to the exigencies of government and the preservation of the Union; and that in case of such concurrence, the two houses of the legislature will meet, on Thursday next, at such place as the honorable the Senate shall think proper, for the purpose of electing the said delegates, by joint ballot.

Ordered, That Mr. John Livingston deliver a copy of the last preceding resolution to the honorable the Senate.

THE SENATE, 26 February[2]

Ordered, That the consideration of the said resolution be postponed until tomorrow.

THE SENATE, 27 February[3]

Resolved, That the Senate do not concur with the honorable the Assembly in their said resolution.

Ordered, That Mr. Williams deliver a copy of the preceding resolution of nonconcurrence to the honorable the Assembly.

THE SENATE, 28 February[4]

[A resolution was offered which copied the House resolution of 26 February, except for two changes: (1) the election was to be held on the following Tuesday instead of Thursday and (2) the delegates were to be elected in the manner provided by the state constitution for the election of delegates to Congress; that is by the two houses balloting separately rather than jointly.]

Which resolution having been read, Mr. Haring moved that instead of *five,* that *three* delegates be appointed for the purposes set forth in the said resolution. Debates arose, and the question being put thereon, it was carried in the affirmative, in manner following, viz.:

For the affirmative. Mr. Yates, Mr. Tredwell, Mr. Haring, Mr. Ward, Mr. Russell, Mr. Hopkins, Mr. Swartwout, Mr. Hathorn, Mr. Humfrey, Mr. Parks, Mr. Williams.

For the negative. Mr. Stoutenburgh, Mr. Vanderbilt, Mr. Townsend, Mr. Morris, Mr. Peter Schuyler, Mr. L'Hommedieu, Mr. Philip Schuyler.

Mr. Haring then moved to expunge, after the words "Tuesday next" to the end of the resolution, and to substitute the following, viz.: "Meet at such place as the honorable the Assembly shall think proper for the purpose of electing the said delegates by joint ballot." Debates arose, and the question being put thereon, it was carried in the negative, in manner following viz.:

For the negative. Mr. Stoutenburgh, Mr. Tredwell, Mr. Vanderbilt, Mr. Townsend, Mr. Morris, Mr. Peter Schuyler, Mr. Swartwout, Mr. L'Hommedieu, Mr. Humfrey, Mr. Parks, Mr. Williams, Mr. Philip Schuyler.

For the affirmative. Mr. Yates, Mr. Haring, Mr. Ward, Mr. Russell, Mr. Hopkins, Mr. Hathorn.

Mr. Yates then moved to insert in the said resolution, after the words "and provisions therein," the following, viz.: "not repugnant to or inconsistent with the constitution of this state." Debates arose, and the question being put thereon, it was carried in the negative, in manner following, viz.:

For the negative. Mr. Stoutenburgh, Mr. Tredwell, Mr. Vanderbilt, Mr. Townsend, Mr. Morris, Mr. Peter Schuyler, Mr. L'Hommedieu, Mr. Williams, Mr. Philip Schuyler.

For the affirmative. Mr. Yates, Mr. Haring, Mr. Ward, Mr. Russell, Mr. Hopkins, Mr. Swartwout, Mr. Hathorn, Mr. Humfrey, Mr. Parks.

The Senate being equally divided upon the question, His Honor the President [Pierre Van Cortlandt] voted in the negative. Thereupon,

Resolved (if the honorable the Assembly concur herein), That three delegates be appointed on the part of this state, to meet such delegates as may be appointed on the part of the other states respectively, on the second Monday in May next at Philadelphia for the sole and express purpose of revising the Articles of Confederation, and reporting to Congress and to the several legislatures such alterations and provisions therein as shall when agreed to in Congress and confirmed by the several states, render the federal constitution adequate to the exigencies of government and the preservation of the Union; and that in case of such concurrence the two houses of the legislature will on Tuesday next, proceed to nominate and appoint the said delegates in like manner as is directed by the constitution of this state, for nominating and appointing delegates to Congress.

Ordered, That Mr. Williams deliver a copy of the preceding resolution to the honorable the Assembly.

THE ASSEMBLY, 28 February[5]

Resolved, That the House do concur with the honorable the Senate, in the said resolution.

Ordered, That Mr. Dongan deliver a copy of the last preceding resolution of concurrence, to the honorable the Senate.

Assembly and Senate Elect Delegates, 6 March

THE ASSEMBLY[6]

The order for the day, for the nomination and appointment of three delegates on the part of this state, to meet such delegates as may be appointed on the part of the other states respectively, on the second Monday in May next, at Philadelphia, for the sole and express purpose of revising the Articles of Confederation, pursuant to concurrent resolutions of both houses of the legislature, on the 28th ultimo, having been read; the House proceeded openly to nominate three delegates for that purpose; and each of the members present nominated three persons, as follows, viz.:

	Robert Yates	James Duane	Alexander Hamilton	Robert R. Livingston	John Lansing, Jr.	Melancton Smith	John Tayler
Vrooman	1	1	1				
C. Livingston	1	1	1				
Malcom	1	1	1				
Hamilton	1	1		1			
Bayard	1	1	1				
Ray	1	1			1		
Bancker	1	1	1				
Denning	1	1	1				
Brooks	1	1	1				
Doughty	1		1		1		
Clark	1		1	1			
Harper	1		1		1		
Parker	1		1		1		
Jones	1					1	1
Wyckoff	1		1	1			
Thorne	1		1		1		
Schenck	1	1	1				
Taulman	1		1		1		
Frost	1	1	1				
C. Smith	1	1	1				
Patterson	1				1	1	
Hedges	1		1			1	
Sickles	1	1	1				
Duboys	1		1	1			
Cooper	1	1	1				
Townsend	1		1		1		
Havens	1	1	1				
Dongan	1	1	1				
D'Witt	1		1		1		
Batcheller	1		1		1		
N. Smith	1		1		1		

	Robert Yates	James Duane	Alexander Hamilton	Robert R. Livingston	John Lansing, Jr.	Melancton Smith	John Tayler
E. Clark	1	1	1				
Strang	1		1				1
Paine	1		1				1
Frey	1		1				1
Crane	1	1	1				
Savage	1	1	1				
Martin	1		1				1
Griffen	1		1				1
Lockwood	1		1				1
Purdy	1		1				1
James Livingston	1	1	1				

	Robert Yates	James Duane	Alexander Hamilton	Robert R. Livingston	John Lansing, Jr.	Melancton Smith	John Tayler
Snyder	1		1		1		
Tierce	1		1				1
Tayler	1	1	1				
Glen	1	1	1				
John Livingston	1	1	1				
Osborn	1		1		1		
Ludenton	1		1		1		
Brinckerhoff	1		1		1		
Bronck	1	1	1				
Tompkins	1		1		1		

[Three separate resolutions nominating Yates, Hamilton, and Lansing appear at this point.]

Resolved, That the Honorable Robert Yates, Esquire, and Alexander Hamilton, and John Lansing, Junior, esquires be, and they are hereby nominated by this House, delegates on the part of this state to meet such delegates as may be appointed on the part of the other states respectively, on the second Monday in May next, at Philadelphia, pursuant to concurrent resolutions of both houses of the legislature, on the 28th ultimo.

Resolved, That this House will meet the honorable the Senate immediately, at such place as they shall appoint, to compare the lists of persons nominated by the Senate and Assembly respectively, as delegates on the part of this state to meet such delegates as may be appointed on the part of the other states respectively, on the second Monday in May next, at Philadelphia, pursuant to concurrent resolutions of both houses of the legislature, on the 28th ultimo.

Ordered, That Mr. N. Smith deliver a copy of the last preceding resolution, to the honorable the Senate.

THE SENATE[7]

The Senate proceeded pursuant to the concurrent resolutions of the Senate and Assembly of the 28th of February last past, to nominate three delegates on the part of this state to meet such delegates as may be appointed on the part of the other states respectively, on the second Monday in May next, at Philadelphia, when the Honorable Robert Yates, Esquire, John Lansing, Junior, and Alexander Hamilton, esquires were openly nominated. Thereupon,

Resolved, That the Honorable Robert Yates, Esquire, John Lansing, Junior, and Alexander Hamilton, esquires are nominated delegates on the part of this state to meet such delegates as may be appointed on the part of the other states respectively, on the second Monday in

May next, at Philadelphia, pursuant to the concurrent resolutions of both houses of the legislature of the 28th of February last past.

. . . .

Resolved, That the Senate will immediately meet the honorable the Assembly in the Assembly chamber to compare the lists of persons nominated by the Senate and Assembly respectively, as delegates on the part of this state to meet such delegates as may be appointed on the part of the other states respectively, on the second Monday in May next, at Philadelphia, pursuant to the concurrent resolutions of both houses of the legislature of the 28th of February last past.

Ordered, That Mr. Vanderbilt deliver a copy of the preceding resolution to the honorable the Assembly.

The Senate accordingly met the honorable the Assembly in the Assembly chamber, and being returned, the President reassumed the chair and informed the Senate that on comparing the respective lists of the Senate and Assembly, they were found to agree in the nomination of the Honorable Robert Yates, Esquire, John Lansing Junior, and Alexander Hamilton, esquires. Thereupon,

Resolved, That the Honorable Robert Yates, John Lansing, Junior, and Alexander Hamilton, esquires are duly nominated and appointed delegates on the part of this state to meet such delegates as may be appointed on the part of the other states respectively on the second Monday in May next at Philadelphia, for the sole and express purpose of revising the Articles of Confederation, and reporting to Congress and the several legislatures such alterations and provisions therein, as shall, when agreed to in Congress and confirmed by the several states, render the federal constitution adequate to the exigencies of government and the preservation of the Union.

1. *Journal of the Assembly of the State of New-York* . . . [12 Jan.–21 April 1787] (New York, 1787), 68. On 13 January Governor George Clinton delivered the report of the Annapolis Convention to the legislature.

2. *Journal of the Senate of the State of New-York* . . . [12 Jan.–21 April 1787] (New York, 1787), 43.

3. Ibid.

4. Ibid., 44–45.

5. *Assembly Journal,* 71.

6. Ibid., 82–84.

7. *Senate Journal,* 50–51.

I. SOUTH CAROLINA, 8 March 1787

Act Authorizing the Election of Delegates, 8 March[1]

AN ACT For appointing deputies from the state of South-Carolina to a convention of the united states of America, proposed to be held in the city of Philadelphia in the month of May. one thousand seven hundred and eighty-seven for the purpose of revising the foederal constitution.

WHEREAS the powers at present vested in the united states in congress assembled, by the articles of confederation and perpetual union of the said states, are found by experience greatly inadequate to the weighty purposes they were originally intended to answer, and it is become absolutely necessary to the welfare of the confederate states that other and more ample powers in certain cases should be vested in and exercised by the said united states in congress assembled, and also that the articles of confederation and perpetual union of the united states should be revised, in order to remedy defects, which at their original formation in the time of war and general tumult could not be foreseen nor sufficiently provided against: AND WHEREAS this state is and ever hath been ready and willing to co-operate with the other states in union, in devising and adopting such measures as will most effectually ensure the peace and general welfare of the confederacy:

Be it enacted by the honorable the senate and house of representatives now met and sitting in general assembly, and by the authority of the same, THAT five commissioners be forthwith appointed by joint ballot of the senate and house of representatives, who or any three or more of them, being first duly commissioned by his excellency the governor for the time being, under his hand and the great seal of the state, by virtue of this act. shall be and are hereby authorised as deputies from this state. to meet such deputies or commissioners as may be appointed and authorised by other of the united states, to assemble in convention at the city of Philadelphia in the month of May next after passing this act. or as soon thereafter as may be, and to join with such deputies or commissioners. they being duly authorised and impowered in devising and discussing all such alterations, clauses, articles and provisions as may be thought necessary to render the foederal constitution entirely adequate to the actual situation and future good government of the confederated states, and that the said deputies or commissioners, or a majority of those who shall be present, provided the state be not represented by less than two, do join in reporting such an act to the united states in congress assembled, as when approved and agreed to by them, and duly ratified and confirmed by the several states, will effectually provide for the exigencies of the union.

In the Senate house, the eighth day of March, in the year of Lord

*one thousand seven hundred and eighty-seven, and in the eleventh
year of the independence of the united states of America.*
    JOHN LLOYD, President of the Senate.
    JOHN JULIUS PRINGLE, Speaker of the house of representatives.

House and Senate Elect Delegates, 8 March[2]

A message was sent to the Senate desiring their attendance in this
House to proceed to the election of five deputies to represent this
state in a convention of the United States proposed to be held at
the city of Philadelphia in the month of May 1787 for the purpose
of revising the federal constitution.
    The Senate accordingly attended and voted with this House for
five deputies. Upon casting up the ballots it appeared that the
Honorable John Rutledge, Charles Cotesworth Pinckney, Henry
Laurens, Charles Pinckney and Pierce Butler, esquires had a majority
of the votes of the members present.
    Mr. Speaker thereupon declared the Honorable John Rutledge,
Charles Cotesworth Pinckney, Henry Laurens, Charles Pinckney and
Pierce Butler, esquires to be duly elected deputies for the purpose
of revising the federal constitution.

    1. (LT), *Acts, Ordinances, and Resolves, of the General Assembly of the State of
South-Carolina: Passed in March, 1787* [1 Jan.–28 March 1787] (Charleston, 1787),
71–72.
    2. MS, Journals of the House of Representatives of the State of South Carolina,
245, Sc-Ar. Laurens declined.

J. CONNECTICUT, 17 May 1787

Act Electing and Empowering Delegates, 17 May[1]

An Act for appointing Delegates to meet in a Convention of the
States, to be held at the City of Philadelphia, on the 2d. Monday of
May instant.
    Whereas the Congress of the United States, by their Act of the 21st
of February 1787, have recommended that on the 2d Monday of May
instant, a Convention of Delegates, who shall have been appointed
by the several States, be held at Philadelphia, for the sole & express
Purpose of revising the Articles of Confederation.
    Be it enacted by the Governor Council & Representatives in Gen-
eral Court assembled, and by Authority of the same—

That the Honble William S. Johnson, Roger Sherman & Oliver Ellsworth Esqrs be, and they hereby are, appointed Delegates to attend the sd Convention, and are requested to proceed to the City of Philadelphia for that Purpose, without Delay, and the said Delegates, and in Case of Sickness or Accident, such one or more of them, as shall actually attend the said Convention, is and are hereby authorized and impowered to represent this State therein, & to confer with such Delegates appointed by the several States, for the Purposes mentioned in the sd Act of Congress, that may be present and duly empowered to act in said Convention, and to discuss upon such Alterations and Provisions, agreeable to the general Principles of Republican Government, as they shall think proper, to render the foederal Constitution adequate to the Exigencies of Government, and the Preservation of the Union; and they are further directed, pursuant to the said Act of Congress, to report such Alterations and Provisions, as may be agreed to, by a Majority of the united States represented in Convention, to the Congress of the United States, and to the General Assembly of this State.

passd. in the upper House

Test. George Wyllys Secrety

Concurred, in the lower House

Test. Jed Huntington Clerk

1. DS (LT), Connecticut Archives Revolutionary War, 1st Series, XXXVII, document 276, Ct. Volume XXXVII is labelled "Slaves 1764–1789." The document is endorsed "Bill appointing Delegates to attend Convention &c—May 1787 p[assed] u[pper] H[ouse] p[assed] l[ower] H[ouse] X To Delegates Seal."

On Saturday, 12 May, after a lengthy debate, the Assembly passed a bill appointing William Samuel Johnson, Erastus Wolcott, and Oliver Ellsworth deputies to the proposed convention. The Council concurred but proposed an amendment striking out the clause "'or any two of them' in the 2d and 3d line of the bill." The Assembly accepted the amendment on 14 May. The next day Wolcott resigned, and Roger Sherman was appointed to fill the vacancy. The act printed here was passed on 17 May. For a report of the debate in the Assembly, see CC:25.

K. MARYLAND, 26 May 1787

Report of Joint Legislative Conference, 28 December 1786 (excerpt)[1]

Thomas Stone, Esquire, from the conference appointed to consider and determine the nature and extent of the powers to be given to the deputies to meet in convention upon the subject of revising the federal constitution, brings in and delivers to the president the following report:

At a meeting of the conferrees of the Senate and House of Delegates, present, from the Senate, Thomas Stone, Charles Carroll, of Carrollton, William Hemsley, esquires; from the House of Delegates, Thomas Johnson, Samuel Chase, William Paca, John H. Stone, Robert Wright, esquires.

It is agreed, that the deputies appointed by this state, or any three or more of them, be authorized on behalf of this state to meet such deputies as may be appointed and authorized by the other states to assemble in convention at Philadelphia, for the purpose of revising the federal system, and to join with them in considering such alterations and further provisions as may be necessary to render the federal constitution adequate to the exigencies of the Union, and in reporting such an act for that purpose to the United States in Congress, as when agreed to by them, and duly confirmed by the several states, will effectually provide for the same.

That the proceedings of the deputies, and any act agreed to in said convention, be reported by the deputies to the next session of Assembly.

House Notifies Senate It Intends to Adjourn, 5 January 1787[2]

We have determined, when we adjourn, to adjourn to Tuesday the 20th day of March next, and hope the material and necessary business now under consideration may be finished in a few days; and we request your honors to dispatch the bills now before your House.

Senate Message to House Objecting to Adjournment, 20 January (excerpt)[3]

With inexpressible regret we perceive, by your message of the sixth of January by Mr. Bowie, that you have determined to adjourn to the 20th of March, and leave the material business of the session unfinished, after sitting upwards of eight weeks at a heavy charge to the public.

Although we have been officially informed, that the continental treasury is empty, and the necessity of raising troops has been urged by Congress, you have not passed an assessment bill to bring any money into the state or continental treasury, nor have you taken any measures to comply with the requisition of Congress for raising a troop of horse.

An act of the Commonwealth of Virginia for appointing deputies to meet at Philadelphia in May next for revising the federal government, and correcting its defects, was early communicated to this legislature. In consequence thereof your House proposed to appoint deputies, which we acceded to, and a conference took place to ascertain the powers to be given to the deputies. A report was made by the conferrees, which has been agreed to by the Senate.

As this proposition originated with you, and the measure is confessedly necessary and important, we are not a little surprised that you have resolved to adjourn, without making this appointment. Although it may be urged, that this deputation may be made at the session proposed by your House to be held in March next, time enough for the deputies to meet at Philadelphia in May, yet it must be obvious, that the other states, perceiving that the legislature of this state has adjourned without making the appointment, may conclude that the measure has not met their approbation. This inference may create suspicions destructive of that unanimity which is admitted, by the wisest and best men in the United States, to be absolutely necessary to preserve the federal Union.

The neighboring states of Virginia and Pennsylvania have discovered their sense of the importance of this meeting, and their expectations of its effects, by appointing some of their first characters to assist in the deliberations.

We cannot account for your postponing the consideration of these great and interesting subjects, and your adjournment to the 20th of March, unless it be to appeal to the people upon the bill for an emission of paper money, which we rejected. This appeal tends to weaken the powers of government, and to disseminate divisions and discord among the citizens of this state, at a crisis, when the energy of the one, and the union of the other, are more than ever necessary. Appeals to the people, upon a diversity of opinion arising between the two branches of the legislature upon any public measure, are unprecedented. The framers of our government have nowhere intimated the propriety of one branch appealing to the people from the proceedings of the other. Every man of reflection will readily perceive, if this practice should prevail, that the public business will no longer be conducted by a select legislature, consisting of two branches, equally free and independent, calmly deliberating and determining on the propriety of public measures; but that the state will be convulsed upon every difference of opinion between those branches, respecting any question which either may think important. Thus the checks wisely established by the constitution will in time be destroyed, force instead of reason will govern, and liberty must finally yield to despotism; for the same causes, all circumstances being similar, will produce here the same effects which they produced in the ancient republics of Greece and Rome. It must also be obvious, that the members of your House being more numerous and more dispersed throughout the state than the members of the Senate, they will have greater opportunities of influencing the people, whose sense is to be collected, in so short a time, and before the merits of the question can be freely and fully discussed. Hence it is probable, that in most cases of difference between the two houses, the majority of the people will be induced to adopt the sentiments of the delegates; in consequence therefore of such appeals to the people, the Senate will be deprived of that freedom of debate and decision, which the constitution meant to secure to that branch, and every benefit which might result to the state from that freedom will be precluded. In such a situation, the powers of the Senate would be annihilated, and although its name and semblance might remain, its real utility would cease.

We consider ourselves bound by the most sacred and solemn engagements to preserve inviolate every part of our constitution, and will not remain silent under measures which may tend to subvert our free and happy government.

If appeals are to be made, where is the line to be drawn? The present is a case of policy, blended with justice, but if appeals are proper in such case, why not in a case of justice only? And if so, and the sense of a majority, however collected, is in all cases to govern, then there are no rights in this state which are secured against the opinion of such a majority, full as well qualified to decide upon questions of justice and right, as upon political regulations. The bill which we have rejected declares, that the bills of credit shall not be a tender, we presume, upon the principle, that it would have been unjust. Suppose the people, upon the present appeal made to them by your House, should instruct the General Assembly to make the bills of credit to be emitted a tender in all cases; this instruction, however unjust the object of it might be, even in your opinion, would be conclusive, according to your doctrine, and the General Assembly would be obliged to comply with it, notwithstanding both branches might be fully satisfied that a clause to that effect would be impolitic, as well as iniquitous.

To some perhaps, who do not look forward to consequences, these appeals may appear flattering; but others, not unacquainted with the history of free governments, will recollect, that measures calculated to obtain the favor of the people very often produced tumult and confusion, which generally terminated in the destruction of equal law and liberty. We are confident our fellow citizens are

warmly attached to this government, that they will view with equal
concern and distrust, all acts in any degree tending to weaken and
endanger it, and cautiously avoid engagements calculated to fetter
the free deliberations of the legislature. Printed anonymous instructions, stating that the Senate have appealed to the people upon the
emission of paper money, are now circulating, when in truth no act
or proceeding of this House, in the least countenances a supposition
that we wish to disturb the public tranquility by a measure so likely
to produce heat and division. It would be well for you to consider,
that although the rejected bill may be such a favorite as to induce
the majority of your House to hazard dangerous consequences to
force it upon the Senate, yet when once fair argument is declined,
and an appeal is made from the dictates of judgment to the voice of
numbers, freedom of discussion and decision will be taken away, and
that some of the present majority of your House, by a similar practice on some future occasion, may be reduced to the same situation
in which they are now endeavoring to place the Senate.

These observations are not dictated by any apprehension in this
House, that there is a majority of the citizens of this state in favor
of an emission of bills of credit upon loan, on the terms, and for the
purposes, contained in your bill. We are satisfied, that the objections to the bill are unanswerable; and that if the sense of the
people could be fairly collected, the majority would be against the
measure. We are also convinced, that the majority would increase,
if time were given to discuss, understand, and form a right judgment
on the subject. Without venturing to combat our reasoning in a
constitutional manner, you propose to adjourn to a time so very
short, that it is impossible a deliberate consideration of the question, and a free interchange of sentiments between the citizens, can
take place. To decide justly, the judgment should be free from all
bias. The passions are too apt to mingle with the decisions of large
collected bodies of people; when so assembled, even the most moderate are liable to be inflamed by declamation and hurried into
measures inconsistent with their real welfare.

. . . .

We have truly stated the reasons which induced us to reject the
bills herein mentioned. We humbly hope the rectitude of our intentions will justify us before God, and we doubt not the reasons assigned will fully vindicate our conduct to those of our fellow citizens
who will examine them carefully and with temper. Our characters
ought to exempt us from the reproach of duplicity; no part of our
conduct can warrant the imputation, or justly subject us to the
suspicion of having an interest separate from that of the people, or

of being impatient of equal liberty. Some of us have been in the Senate for ten years. A new election has lately been made, and a majority of the old compose the present Senate. From this reelection and continuance of the same persons in the same trust, we may, without vanity, infer, that the conduct of the late Senate has been generally approved, and that no suspicions are entertained against the present. We therefore flatter ourselves, that we possess the confidence of the people. If, for a steady adherence to principles we conceive intimately connected with the prosperity of the state, that confidence should be withdrawn, we shall regret this unmerited change of sentiment, but we should certainly deserve to forfeit the esteem of our fellow citizens, if, accommodating our conduct to the opinions of others, we betray a want of sufficient fortitude, even to risk temporary disapprobation to secure permanent happiness to this country. We cannot consent to close the session without pressing upon your candid and serious attention the important subjects referred to in this message, and expressing our opinion, that the legislature is bound to attend to these subjects, and to adopt the proper means for carrying them into execution. A spring session will be attended with great inconvenience to individuals, and an unnecessary expense to the public; to defray this expense, additional taxes must be laid upon the people, who are represented by you as unable to pay those taxes which cannot be dispensed with, but at the hazard of all order and government. We are ready and willing to accede to any measures which shall appear to us calculated to promote the public welfare, give strength to the Confederacy, and stability to our government; and we exceedingly lament, that the harmony of the two branches of the legislature, so necessary to promote these important purposes, should be interrupted; but, gentlemen, if you are determined to adjourn without finishing the public business, we shall have the several matters before us dispatched, so that an end may be put to the session this evening, and we shall hold ourselves acquitted before our country and the world, of the evils which may result from a measure we can neither prevent or approve.

House Reply to Senate Message, 20 January[4]

The length of your message, and the communication of it within a few hours only of the proposed time for closing the session, prevents us from making full observations upon it. We shall only say in reply, that we have paid every possible attention to the public affairs of the Union, and the interest and happiness of our people. You have thought proper to overrule every material system proposed by us for these purposes, and have brought forward nothing essential in their stead.

The people must decide upon our conduct and yours as to the utility, policy and rectitude of the systems respectively proposed; and we trust we can meet our God and our country with consciences quiet and undisturbed as your own.

We repeat our request to close this session this evening.

Act Electing and Empowering Delegates, 26 May[5]

An ACT for the appointment of, and conferring powers in, deputies from this state to the federal convention.

Be it enacted, *by the general assembly of Maryland,* That the honourable James McHenry, Daniel of Saint Thomas Jenifer, Daniel Carroll, John Francis Mercer, and Luther Martin, Esquires, be appointed and authorised, on behalf of this state, to meet such deputies as may be appointed and authorised by any other of the United States to assemble in convention at Philadelphia, for the purpose of revising the federal system, and to join with them in considering such alterations, and further provisions, as may be necessary to render the federal constitution adequate to the exigencies of the union, and in reporting such an act for that purpose to the United States in congress assembled, as, when agreed to by them, and duly confirmed by the several states, will effectually provide for the same; and the said deputies, or such of them as shall attend the said convention, shall have full power to represent this state for the purposes aforesaid; and the said deputies are hereby directed to report the proceedings of the said convention, and any act agreed to therein, to the next session of the general assembly of this state.

1. *Votes and Proceedings of the Senate of the State of Maryland* [7 Nov. 1786–20 Jan. 1787] ([Annapolis, 1787]), 15–16.

On 16 December 1786 the Senate received Governor Edmund Randolph's letter of 1 December enclosing Virginia's act of 23 November authorizing the appointment of convention delegates. The Senate read the documents and referred them to the House, which appointed a five-man committee on 19 December to consider them. The committee reported the same day that the legislature should appoint by joint ballot seven delegates to the proposed convention. The House accepted the report two days later and the Senate "cheerfully" agreed, suggesting, however, that before any delegates were appointed a joint legislative conference should determine "the nature and extent" of the delegates' powers. The House accepted the Senate's recommendation on 22 December and appointed Thomas Johnson, John H. Stone, Samuel Chase, William Paca, and Robert Wright. The Senate appointed Thomas Stone, Charles Carroll of Carrollton, and William Hemsley. The conference report was read in the Senate on 28 December and in the House on 1 January, but neither house seems to have adopted it.

2. *Votes and Proceedings of the House of Delegates of the State of Maryland* [7 Nov. 1786–20 Jan. 1787] ([Annapolis, 1787]), 60. This message "was sent to the Senate by Mr. R. Bowie" on 6 January.

3. *Senate Proceedings,* 37–39. The portions of the message omitted concern the Senate's defense of its refusal to pass certain bills unrelated to the election of delegates.

4. *House Proceedings,* 102–3. The legislature then adjourned on 20 January.

5. (LT), *Laws of Maryland* . . . [10 April–26 May 1787] (Annapolis, [1787]), 6–7. On 20 April the House proposed that each house, acting separately, should elect five delegates. The Senate agreed the next day. The House nominated John Henry, Charles Carroll of Carrollton, Governor William Smallwood, Robert Hanson Harrison, James McHenry, Thomas Sim Lee, Daniel of St. Thomas Jenifer, George Gale, Alexander C. Hanson, and Robert Goldsborough. The Senate nominated Thomas Johnson, William Paca, Samuel Chase, and Thomas Stone. Henry, Gale, Paca, Johnson, and Chase did not wish to serve and "their names were struck out." The legislature then elected Harrison, Carroll, Stone, McHenry, and Lee on 23 April.

On 26 April Stone declined to serve. The House proposed another election and nominated Daniel of St. Thomas Jenifer, Gabriel Duvall, and Alexander C. Hanson. Duvall and Jenifer received the same number of votes in the Senate, and eventually both men were added to the delegation.

Charles Carroll resigned on 10 May, Harrison on 12 May, and Duvall on 14 May. The House then informed the Senate on 22 May that it was nominating Luther Martin, John Francis Mercer, and Daniel Carroll to fill the vacancies. On 24 May Thomas Sim Lee resigned. The Senate then voted that the three men nominated by the House should be added to the delegation without holding an official election, and the House agreed and adopted an act authorizing the appointment of delegates. The Senate agreed the same day. The engrossed act was signed into law on 26 May.

L. NEW HAMPSHIRE, 27 June 1787

Resolution Electing and Empowering Delegates, 17 January[1]

Resolved, That any two of the delegates[2] of this state to the Congress of the United States, be, and hereby are appointed and authorized as deputies from this state to meet such deputies as may be appointed and authorized by other states in the Union, to assemble in convention at Philadelphia on the second day of May next, and to join with them in devising and discussing all such alterations and further provisions as to render the federal constitution adequate to the exigencies of the Union, and in reporting such an act to the United States in Congress, as when agreed to by them and duly confirmed by the several states, will effectually provide for the same; but in case of the death of any of said deputies, or their declining their appointments, the executive is hereby authorized to supply such vacancies, and the president is requested to transmit forthwith a copy of this resolve to the United States in Congress, and to the executive of each of the states in the Union.

The foregoing resolve was returned from the Senate for the following amendment: "that the said delegates shall proceed to join the convention aforesaid in case Congress shall signify to them that they approve of the said convention as advantageous to the Union, and not an infringement of the powers granted to Congress by the Confederation." Which amendment was read and concurred.

Act Electing and Empowering Delegates, 27 June[3]

An Act for Appointing Deputies from This State to the Convention, Proposed to Be Holden in the City of Philadelphia in May 1787 for the Purpose of Revising the Federal Constitution

Whereas in the formation of the federal compact, which frames the bond of union of the amirican-states, it was not possible in the infant state of our republic to devise a system which in the course of time and experiance, would not manifest imperfections, that it would be necessary to reform.

And Whereas, the limited powers, which by the articles of confederation are vested in the Congress of the united states, have been found far inadequate to the enlarged purposes which they were intended to produce.

And whereas Congress hath, by repeated and most urgent representations, endeavoured to awaken this, and other states of the union, to a sense of the truly critical, and alarming situation, in which they may inevitably be involved, unless timely measures be taken to enlarge the powers of Congress, that they may thereby be enabled, to avert the dangers which threaten our existance, as a free and indepandant people. And whereas, this state hath been ever desireous to act upon the liberal system of the general good of the united states, without circumscribing its views to the narrow, and selfish objects, of partial convenience; and has been at all times ready to make every concession to the safety and happiness of the whole, which justice and sound policy could vindicate—

Be it therefore enacted by the Senate and House of Representatives in general court convened, that John Langdon, John Pickering, Nicholas Gilman, and Benjamin West Esqrs be, and hereby are, appointed Commissioners; they, or any two of them, are hereby authorized, and impowered, as Deputies from this State to meet at Philadelphia said Convention, or any other place to which the said Convention may be adjourned; for the purposes aforesaid, there to confer with such deputies, as are, or may be appointed by the other States for similar

purposes; and with them to discuss and decide upon the most effectual means to remedy the defects of our federal union; and to procure,
and secure, the enlarged purposes which it was intended to effect,
and to report such an act, to the United States in Congress, as when
agreed to by them, and duly confirmed by the several States, will
effectually provide for the same—

1. *A Journal of the Proceedings of the Honourable House of Representatives of
the State of New-Hampshire* . . . [13 Dec. 1786–18 Jan. 1787] (Portsmouth, 1787),
184.
2. In June 1786 the New Hampshire legislature appointed Nicholas Gilman, John
Langdon, Pierse Long, and John Sparhawk delegates to Congress, but none of them
attended Congress between 20 September 1786 and 25 September 1787. No evidence
has been found to indicate why the New Hampshire delegates did not attend,
although it was possibly because the state lacked money to pay their expenses.
After the passage of the second act appointing delegates to the Convention on 27
June, a widely circulated newspaper story reported that John Langdon had offered
to pay the expenses of the New Hampshire delegates to the Convention because
the state had no money (*New Hampshire Mercury*, 5 July). Whether he did or
not, he and Nicholas Gilman appeared in the Constitutional Convention for the
first time on 23 July.
3. (LT), Albert S. Batchellor, et al., eds., *Laws of New Hampshire* . . . [1679–
1835] (10 vols., Manchester, N.H., and elsewhere, 1904–1922), V, 264–65.

M. RHODE ISLAND'S REASONS FOR REFUSAL TO APPOINT DELEGATES, 15 September 1787

General Assembly to the President of Congress[1]

State of Rhode-Island & Providence Plantations. In General Assembly
September Session AD 1787.
Sir, Permit the Legislative of this State to address you on a Subject
Which has engaged the attention of the confederated Union; the
singularity of our not sending forward to the Convention at Philadelphia, Delegates to represent us there, agreeably to a Resolution
of Congress passed the 21st February AD 1787, for the purpose of
revising the Articles of Confederation. Our conduct has been repro-
bated by the illiberal, and many severe and unjust sarcasmes propa-
gated against us, but Sir, when we State to you the reason, and evince
the Cause the liberal mind will be convinced that we were actuated
by that great principle which hath ever been the Characteristic of
this State, the Love of true Constitutional liberty, and the fear we
have of making innovations on the Rights and Liberties of the Citizens at large.
Our conduct during the late trying contest, has shewn forth con-

spicuous, that it was not from sinister motives but to pervade over the whole. And we presume Sir, that we shall be enabled to fix the same sentiments now.

Your Hon. Body informed us that the Powers invested in Congress for the Regulation of Trade were not sufficient for the purpose of the great national Regulations requisite, we granted you by an Act of our State the whole and sole power of making such Laws as would be effectual for that purpose, other States not passing similar laws it had no effect.

An impost was like wise granted but other States in the Union not acceding thereto that measure has proved abortive,—The Requisition of the 21st Feby last hath not been acceded too, because, we conceived that as a Legislative Body, we could not appoint Delegates, to do that which only the People at large are intitled to do; by a Law of our State the Delegates in Congress are chosen by the Suffrages of all the Freemen therein and are appointed to represent them in Congress; and for the Legislative body to have appointed Delegates to represent them in Convention, when they cannot appoint Delegates in Congress, (unless upon the Death or other incident matter) must be absurd; as that Delegation in Convention is for the express purpose of altering a Constitution, which the people at large are only capable of appointing the Members.

By the 13th. Article in the Confederation "every State shall abide by the determinations of the United States in Congress assembled, on all questions which by this Confederation are submitted to them. And the Articles of Confederation shall be inviolably observed by every State and the Union shall be perpetual; nor shall any alteration at any time be made in any of them unless such alteration be agreed to in a Congress of the United States and be afterwards confirmed by the Legislatures of every State."—As the Freemen at large here have the Power of electing Delegates to represent them in Congress, we could not consistantly appoint Delegates in a Convention, which might be the means of dissolving the Congress of the Union and having a Congress without a Confederation.—You will impute it Sir, to our being diffident of power and an apprehension of dissolving a compact, which was framed by the Wisdom of Men who gloried in being instrumental in preserving the Religious and Civil rights of a Multitude of people, and an almost unbounded territory, that said Requisition hath not been complied with, and fearing when the Compact should once be broken we must all be lost in a Common ruin.

We shall ever esteem it a pleasure to join with our Sister States in being instrumental in what ever may be advantageous to the Union,

and to add strength and permanance thereto, upon Constitutional
principles.

We are Sir, with every sentiment of respect and Esteem,

Your very obedt. Servts

Signed at the request of the General Assembly

John Collins Go

Protest of the Newport and Providence Deputies[2]

State of Rhode Island & Providence Plantations In General Assembly September Session AD 1787.

We the Subscribers beg leave to protest against the Report of a
Letter to the President of Congress, assigning the reasons for the
Legislature of this State's refusing to send Members to the Convention at Philadelphia for revising the Articles of Confederation &c.
For the following Reasons. 1st. For that it has never been thought
heretofore by the Legislature of this State, or while it was a Colony,
inconsistent with or any Innovation upon the Rights and Liberties
of the Citizens of this State to concur with the Sister States or Colonies in appointing Members or Delegates to any Convention proposed
for the General Benefit, but with the highest approbation of the
good people of this State and while a Colony, the Legislature have at
various times agreed to Conventions with the Sister States and
Colonies and found their Interests greatly served thereby. That to the
Congress appointed in the begining of the late arduous struggle
with Great Britain, the Members sent from this then Colony were
appointed with the fullest power for carrying on a Defensive War with
and finally for declaring these States Independant of Great Britain,
and for forming Articles of Confederation, both which Glorious events
were received and confirmed by the Legislature of this State with
the loudest Acclamations of the people at large.

2dly. That the Powers mentioned in said Letter to have been invested in Congress, for the regulating Trade were granted by the
Legislature of this State, as also finally granting the Impost, which
is inconsistant with the Ideas contained in said Letter, That all such
powers are not in the Legislature, but in the people at large.

3dly. That by the Articles of Confederation which hath become part
of the Constitution of the State it is expressly provided, That when
any Alteration is made in the Articles of Confederation it shall be
agreed to in a Congress of the United States and be afterwards con-

firmed by the Legislatures of every State. Which is plainly expressive, that, this Power is in the Legislature only.

4thly. By the Articles of Confederation, the appointment of Delegates in Congress is declared to be by the Legislatures of the several States in such manner as the Legislatures of each State shall direct.— That therefore as the power of appointing Delegates did begin and was continued in the Legislature of this State for several Years, and until by Act of the same Legislature the Election of Delegates to Congress was committed to the people at large; and as the General Assembly still on the Death or Resignation of any of the Delegates of this State, or on the recall of any Delegate or Delegates, do exercise the power of appointing others in their Stead, and do by a Law they have enacted prevent their Delegates from proceeding to Congress until special Order or Direction from the Legislature; so it is certain The Legislature had Constitutionally the power of sending Delegates to Congress,—and to presume they have not Power to send Members to a proposed Convention, recommended by Congress, and under the Invitations of their Sister States, must be inconsistant with those powers which all Legislatures must be presumed to possess for the preservation of the Rights Liberties and Privilidges of the People,—Inconsistant with the most common Apprehension; and that a Contrary supposition is most absurd.

5thly. As it would have been our highest Honor and Interest, to have complied with the tender Invitations of our Sister States, and of Congress,—So our Non-compliance hath been our highest Imprudence, And therefore it would have been more Consistant with our Honor and dignity to have lamented our mistake, and decently appollogised for our Errors, than to have endeavoured to support them on ill founded reasons and indefensible principles.—For these and other reasons which might have been added had we not been expressly limited to one Hour for making our protest, We disscent from the Reasons suggested in said Letter.

Hy Marchant Geo: Champlin John Topham Daniel Mason Wm Tripp	} Members for the Town of Newport	John Brown Welcome Arnold Benja Bourne Joseph Nightingale	} Members for the Town of Providence

A True Copy,
Witness
Hy Sherburne Dy Secry

1. RC (LT), PCC, Item 64, State Papers of New Hampshire and of Rhode Island and Providence Plantations, 1775–88, pp. 600–3, DNA. This document, addressed "His Excellency the President of Congress," was endorsed by Secretary Charles Thomson, "Sept Session 1787 Reasons of Rhodeisland &c for not sending delegates to Convention. read, 24 Sept 1787."

The Rhode Island legislature had rejected proposals to elect delegates on three separate occasions: 14 March, 5 May, and 16 June 1787. On 15 September the majority of the legislature adopted a letter to the President of Congress giving the state's official position. This letter and an official protest by the Newport and Providence Assembly deputies were forwarded to Congress by Governor John Collins on 17 September. The letter was read in Congress on 24 September, four days after Congress received the Constitution from the Convention.

2. RC (LT), ibid, 592–94. This manuscript was endorsed by Secretary Thomson, "Protest of members agt reasons of legislature of Rhodeisland for not sending delegates to Convention."

Delegates Who Attended the Constitutional Convention[1]

NEW HAMPSHIRE
John Langdon
Nicholas Gilman
MASSACHUSETTS
Nathaniel Gorham
Rufus King
Elbridge Gerry
Caleb Strong
CONNECTICUT
William Samuel Johnson
Roger Sherman
Oliver Ellsworth
NEW YORK
Alexander Hamilton
John Lansing, Jr.
Robert Yates
NEW JERSEY
William Livingston
David Brearley
William Paterson
Jonathan Dayton
William C. Houston
PENNSYLVANIA
Benjamin Franklin
Thomas Mifflin
Robert Morris
George Clymer
Thomas FitzSimons
Jared Ingersoll
James Wilson
Gouverneur Morris
DELAWARE
George Read
Gunning Bedford, Jr.

John Dickinson
Richard Bassett
Jacob Broom
MARYLAND
James McHenry
Daniel of St. Thomas Jenifer
Daniel Carroll
Luther Martin
John Francis Mercer
VIRGINIA
George Washington
John Blair
James Madison
Edmund Randolph
George Mason
George Wythe
James McClurg
NORTH CAROLINA
William Blount
Richard Dobbs Spaight
Hugh Williamson
Alexander Martin
William R. Davie
SOUTH CAROLINA
John Rutledge
Charles Pinckney
Charles Cotesworth Pinckney
Pierce Butler
GEORGIA
William Few
Abraham Baldwin
William Pierce
William Houstoun

---

1. The names of the men who left the Convention before its conclusion are set in italic type.

VII

The Resolutions
and Draft Constitutions of the
Constitutional Convention

29 May–17 September 1787

Introduction

On 21 February 1787 the Confederation Congress called the Constitutional Convention to meet in Philadelphia on Monday, 14 May, but a quorum of seven states was not present until 25 May when George Washington of Virginia was elected president and William Jackson of Pennsylvania, a non-delegate, secretary. Thereafter, the Convention met five or six hours a day, six days a week, until 17 September. The only exception was when the Convention adjourned between 26 July and 6 August to give the Committee of Detail time to prepare the first draft of the Constitution.

Seventy-four delegates were elected to the Convention but only fifty-five attended, and only forty-one of the fifty-five were present when the Convention adjourned *sine die* on 17 September. Rhode Island did not elect delegates, and those from New Hampshire did not arrive until 23 July. Robert Yates and John Lansing, Jr. left the Convention on 10 July, and thereafter New York did not have a vote because it was represented by only one delegate, Alexander Hamilton. As a result, no more than eleven states ever voted on any issue in the Convention.

Planning for the Convention began during the winter of 1786–1787. Men such as George Washington, Henry Knox, Stephen Higginson, James Madison, Edmund Randolph, and John Jay wrote to one another about the changes that should be made in the central government. They agreed that the single-house Congress of the Articles of Confederation should be replaced by a government with three branches consisting of a congress with two houses, an executive, and a judiciary; that the central government should be given power over the states and their citizens; and that the equal representation of the states in Congress should be replaced by representation according to population in both houses of Congress.

The Virginia delegates arrived in Philadelphia early, talked with other delegates as they arrived, met regularly with one another, and drafted resolutions setting forth the broad principles upon which a new constitution should be based. Not all of the Virginia delegates agreed with the principles, as the debates in the Convention were to reveal, but the fifteen resolutions were presented to the Convention on 29 May by the Governor of Virginia, Edmund Randolph.

232

The rules adopted by the Convention were similar to those of the Confederation Congress. Each state had one vote which was determined by a majority of its delegates. If a state's delegates were equally divided, the state's vote was recorded as "divided." If a state was represented by only one delegate, its vote was not counted. The Convention also imposed a rule of secrecy upon its members, a rule not always observed. One of the most important rules adopted was that no vote was to be taken as final and that any question could be reopened for further debates and votes at any time. The rule meant endless repetition of arguments, but more importantly, the rule made it possible for men to change their minds and to compromise issues in the course of the debates.

*   *   *   *

At the very outset the Convention faced the issue of whether or not to work within the existing constitutional framework of the United States. Should it abide by the resolution of the Confederation Congress calling the Convention for the "sole and exclusive" purpose of revising and amending the Articles of Confederation? If the Convention decided to do so, any amendments to the Articles would have to be approved by Congress and ratified unanimously by the legislatures of the thirteen states. The Convention decided instead to work outside the constitutional framework by (1) creating a new constitution rather than proposing amendments to the Articles of Confederation; (2) providing for ratification by state conventions rather than by state legislatures; and (3) by rejecting the congressional resolution of 21 February calling the Convention (and most of the state acts electing delegates) which provided that the work of the Convention should be "agreed to" by Congress before transmittal to the states.

Governor Edmund Randolph proposed this constitutional revolution on 29 May in his speech presenting the Virginia Resolutions. He told the Convention that "our chief danger arises from the democratic parts of our [state] constitutions. It is a maxim which I hold incontrovertible, that the powers of government exercised by the people swallows up the other branches. None of the constitutions have provided sufficient checks against the democracy." At the end of his speech he "candidly confessed" that the Virginia Resolutions "were not intended for a federal government—he meant a strong *consolidated* union, in which the idea of states should be nearly annihilated." Another reporter recorded that Randolph "pointed out the various defects of the federal system, the necessity of transforming it into a national efficient government. . . ."

The next day Randolph moved the adoption of the first Virginia Resolution, which stated that the Articles of Confederation ought to be revised and enlarged. Gouverneur Morris of Pennsylvania pointed out that the remaining Virginia Resolutions contradicted the first one. Randolph then withdrew the first resolution and offered three new ones in its place: (1) that a federal government would not accomplish the objects of the Articles of Confederation; (2) that no treaty among sovereign states could accomplish or secure their common defense, liberty and welfare; and (3) that "a *national* government ought to be established consisting of a *supreme* legislative, executive and judiciary."

General Charles Cotesworth Pinckney of South Carolina and Elbridge Gerry of Massachusetts responded by arguing that if the new resolutions were adopted, the Convention would have no legal foundation because it had been called to revise the Articles of Confederation, not to abandon them. As a result, the first two resolutions were dropped, and the Convention turned to the third calling for the creation of a national government with a "supreme" legislature, executive, and judiciary. When a delegate asked what the word "supreme" meant, Gouverneur Morris replied, according to one reporter, that there was "no such thing" as a federal government. According to another reporter, Morris declared that the distinction between a "federal" and a "national" government was that the former was a "mere compact" among states, and that the latter had "a complete and compulsive operation." The Convention then adopted the third resolution and thus agreed to the abandonment of the existing federal government and the creation of a national government. This fundamental decision was not challenged directly until 13 June when the revised Virginia Resolutions were submitted to the Convention for approval. At that point, William Paterson of New Jersey asked that consideration of the plan be delayed and that time be given "to digest one purely federal. . . ."

Opposition to the Virginia Resolutions had been mounting steadily. Delegates from the small states united with other delegates who were opposed to an all-powerful central government and who wanted to retain the federal structure of the Articles of Confederation. Although they had won the Convention's approval for a motion that the Senate be elected by state legislatures, they were alarmed by the proposals of those who argued for the complete subordination of the states to the central government. Consequently, they drafted amendments to the Articles of Confederation which were presented by William Paterson on 15 June.

John Lansing of New York told the Convention that "the two systems are fairly contrasted. The one now offered is on the basis of amending the federal government, and the other to be reported as a national government, on propositions which exclude the propriety of amendment." Lansing and others again denied that the Convention had the legal right to create a national government.

The Convention debated the New Jersey Amendments on the 15th, 16th, and 18th of June. On the 19th the Convention rejected the Amendments and voted to accept the revised Virginia Resolutions by a vote of seven states to three, with one state divided. However, the next day the Convention made a concession to the opponents of a national government. At the end of the debate on the first Amended Virginia Resolution, which read "that a national government ought to be established," the Convention voted to drop the words "national government" wherever they appeared in the resolutions, and to substitute the words "the government of the United States. . . ." However, in the debates that followed, delegates continued to use the words "national government."

The second fundamental decision in abandoning the existing constitution concerned the method of ratification. The Articles of Confederation required that amendments be proposed by Congress and ratified by all the states before they could become a part of the constitution. The fifteenth Virginia Resolution of 29 May provided that after Congress approved the amendments to be offered by the Convention, that they be submitted to "an assembly or assemblies of Representatives" recommended by the state legislatures and "expressly chosen by the people, to consider & decide thereon." Some delegates argued that the state legislatures must approve amendments as provided for in the Articles of Confederation, but they were overridden. Furthermore, the Convention voted that ratification by only nine state conventions would be sufficient to establish the Constitution as the instrument of government among the ratifying states.

The third basic decision in abandoning the old government concerned the approval of Congress. The fifteenth Virginia Resolution of 29 May required that approval, but this resolution was challenged on 31 August when Gouverneur Morris and Charles Pinckney moved that the requirement be struck out. The Convention agreed, eight states to three.

*   *   *   *

The decision to replace the Articles of Confederation with a new constitution was fundamental, but once that decision was made, the Convention concentrated upon the character of the constitution to be created. The issues involved were many and resulted in protracted debates. The major issues concerned the distribution of power between the central government and the state governments, the distribution of power among the branches of the central government, the balance of power between the large and the small states, and the balance of power between the North and the South.

Most of the issues were debated again and again. The Convention debated the Virginia Resolutions of 29 May item by item until 19 June when the revised Resolutions were agreed to. Then the Convention debated and amended the revised Resolutions until 24 July when it turned over the results to the Committee of Detail, which presented a draft constitution to the Convention on 6 August. Once more the Convention started at the beginning and debated the issues it had previously debated until 10 September, when the results of its decisions were turned over to the Committee of Style to write the final draft of the Constitution. The Committee of Style reported on 12 September. The debates began again, as the Convention made some changes and rejected others, until it agreed to the Constitution on 17 September.

Some of the issues were rooted in the colonial past; others had been raised and debated repeatedly on the state and national levels in the years between 1774 and 1786. Sometimes the debates were so heated that delegates threatened to break up the Convention, but eventually they agreed to compromises, even though they often declared that they would never do so.

Most members of the Convention agreed that the central government needed coercive power over the states and their citizens, but they disagreed as to the extent of that power. A minority of extreme nationalists argued that the states had to be subordinated absolutely to the will of the central government, and a few even argued that the states should be abolished except as mere administrative districts.

The Virginia Resolutions proposed that Congress should have the power to veto state laws contrary to the Constitution, and, at first, the Convention added the power to veto all state legislation. James Madison of Virginia argued that such a veto was "absolutely necessary to a perfect system" and James Wilson of Pennsylvania described it as "the keystone wanted to complete the wide arch of government we are raising." In August, the Convention finally abolished the congressional veto, the majority agreeing with John Rutledge that "if nothing else, this alone would damn and ought to damn the Constitution."

Another means of controlling the states was by armed force. The Virginia Resolutions of 29 May proposed that Congress should have the power to "call forth the force of the Union" against a state not meeting its obligations. The Constitution gave Congress power to call forth militia "to execute the Laws of the Union," and the guarantee of republican governments and protection against domestic violence, the delegates were told, meant power to suppress domestic rebellions.

The draft constitution of 6 August revived the issue by giving Congress specific power to subdue rebellions in the states. However, the draft limited the power by providing that Congress could act only when called upon to do so by a state legislature. The nationalists sought to remove the restriction, but the opposition was overwhelming.

In its final form, the Constitution guarantees a republican form of government to each state and protection against invasion, and against "domestic violence" when called upon by a state legislature, or by the executive when the legislature is not in session. However, the Constitution is ambiguous as to what agency of the "United States" should respond to the call from a state: the Congress or the President.

The Constitution contains no ambiguity whatever in placing restraints upon the economic power of the states. The delegates were almost as one in agreeing that the states should be forbidden to issue paper money or to make anything but gold and silver legal tender in the payment of debts, and forbidden to pass bills of attainder, ex post facto laws, or laws impairing the obligation of contracts. The importance the Convention attached to those provisions is indicated by James Wilson's statement to the Pennsylvania Convention that if the Constitution contained only those lines, "I think it would be worth our adoption."

The ultimate supremacy of the central government over the states, potentially if not actually, was guaranteed by providing that the Constitution and the laws and treaties of the United States were the "supreme Law of the Land" and that the judges in every state were bound thereby "any Thing in the Constitution or Laws of any State to the Contrary notwithstanding."

At the same time that the Virginia Resolutions of 29 May proposed the creation of a congress with sweeping power over the states, they also proposed that Congress should be all-powerful within the central government. Congress would elect an executive who would be ineligible for a second term, and judges of the "national judiciary," who would serve during good behavior. The executive and the judges, acting as a "council of revision," would have the power to veto laws enacted by Congress, but Congress could override the vetoes.

Many members of the Convention, and especially those whose careers as legislators began before 1776, were devoted to the principle of legislative supremacy in government. Roger Sherman of Connecticut expressed their views when he told the Convention that the presidency was "nothing more than an institution for carrying the will of the legislature into effect," for the legislature was "the depository of the supreme will of the society." Therefore, the President should be elected by and be dependent upon Congress; and that if he were not dependent, it would be "the very essence of tyranny, if there was any such thing."

Nationalists such as James Madison, Gouverneur Morris, James Wilson, and Charles Pinckney, whose political careers began with independence, had no more faith in Congress as a legislature than they had in state legislatures. They proposed drastic changes in the Virginia Resolutions. They argued that Congress should not elect the President, that he should appoint judges of the national judiciary, and that with the judges he should have an absolute veto over the acts of Congress. The Convention rejected all such proposals during the debate on the Virginia Resolutions between 28 May and 13 June.

The nationalists resumed the struggle in July when they reiterated their arguments about the danger of unchecked legislative power. Gouverneur Morris declared that public liberty was in greater danger from "legislative usurpations" than from any other source. James Madison argued that the judges must share the veto power because the executive and judicial branches acting together would be too weak to withstand the assaults of Congress. Madison warned the Convention of the danger that had arisen from the unchecked state legislatures. He said that the "legislatures of the states had betrayed a strong propensity to a variety of pernicious measures. One object of the national legislature was to control this propensity. One object of the national executive, so far as it would have a negative on the laws, was to control the national legislature, so far as it might be infected with a similar propensity."

The method of electing the President and the extent of the President's power were debated throughout the Convention with as much intensity as any other issue. Supporters of presidential power were able to substitute election of the President by the Electoral College for election by Congress, and then removed the limitation on the number of terms a President might serve. But they were defeated in their attempts to give the President an absolute veto over acts of Congress.

The majority of the Convention believed that the President should have specific powers and duties, and these are stated in the Constitution. At the same time, however, the Constitution made possible a potentially more powerful office by making the President commander in chief of the army and navy and by providing an oath for the President to "execute the Office of President" and to "preserve, protect and defend the Constitution."

The debates over the distribution of power between the central government and the states, and over the distribution of power among the three branches of the central government were long and intense. But they were no more intense than the debates between the large and the small states and the Northern and the Southern states over the power they should exercise within the central government.

The controversy between the large and the small states began at the First Continental Congress in 1774. The delegates from Virginia, which had twenty percent of the population of the colonies, demanded that voting in Congress be according to population. The smaller colonies insisted upon their integrity and equality and they won their point when Congress agreed that each colony should have one vote. The dispute revived in 1776 during the debates over the Articles of Confederation. The delegates from Virginia, Pennsylvania, and Massachusetts, the three largest states, argued that voting should be by population, but again they were defeated. They did not give up. The Virginia Resolutions of 29 May 1787 proposed that representation in both houses of Congress be by population with the House of Representatives elected by the people and the Senate elected by the House from nominations by the state legislatures. The nationalists from the large states, in order to free the central government from any state control, argued that the state governments should have no power over the election of delegates to either house.

The nationalists were opposed by the delegates from the smaller states and by "federalists" who believed that any new government must be partly federal in structure. Early in June, the Convention voted that the state legislatures should elect Senators, a decision that was never reversed despite continued opposition from the extreme nationalists. The delegates from the small states and the federalists then proposed that each state have one vote in the Senate. "Otherwise," declared Roger Sherman, "a few large states will rule."

Sherman's compromise was rejected on 11 June and the debate continued. James Madison predicted that if the states were given equality in the Senate the result would be incessant war, dictatorship, and foreign intervention. The Convention finally agreed on 29 June that representation in the House of Representatives should be according to population. Oliver Ellsworth of Connecticut then moved, as Sherman had earlier, that the states should have equal votes in the Senate. Ellsworth declared that "We were partly national; partly federal" and that equality in the Senate was a reasonable compromise. Rufus King of Massachusetts responded that he was ready for any event rather than to submit to a government "founded on a vicious principle of representation" and on 2 July the Convention deadlocked five states to five.

The debate continued until 16 July, when the Convention voted five states to four, with Massachusetts divided, for equal representation in the Senate. Some of the delegates from the large states proposed to withdraw from the Convention and write a constitution of their own, but the majority was on the side of political realism. The Constitution thus provided for the retention of part of the federal structure of the Articles of Confederation and guaranteed the preservation of equal representation by including at the end of Article V the provision that no state could be deprived of its equality in the Senate without its consent.

Another divisive issue, deeply rooted in the colonial past, was the conflict between the Northern and the Southern states. By 1776 Northerners (particularly New Englanders) and Southerners were convinced that the social, political, and economic differences between them were real and substantial. Those differences emerged in the writing of the Articles of Confederation when Northerners insisted that slaves should be counted if the expenses of the central government were shared among the states according to population. Southerners won in 1776 when Congress voted that expenses would be shared according to the value of settled lands. The debate resumed in 1783 when Congress proposed to amend the Articles of Confederation by providing, as the first draft of the Articles had in 1776, for sharing expenses according to population. This time Southerners were ready to compromise. James Madison and John Rutledge proposed that three-fifths of the slaves should be counted. Congress agreed and sent the amendment to the states for ratification.

Four years later James Wilson used the wording of the amendment of 1783 but in a different context. In a bid for Southern support for representation by population in both houses of Congress, he proposed that each state be represented in the House of Representatives according to the number of white and other free citizens, indentured servants, and "three-fifths of all other persons . . . except Indians not paying taxes. . . .:" The Convention agreed despite some opposition, but the dispute did not begin in earnest until 2 July when the Convention deadlocked on the issue of equality of the states in the Senate. Various compromises, including apportionment in the House of Representatives, were offered with Northerners and Southerners alike trying to increase the number of Representatives assigned to their states.

In the debate on 10 July on a report assigning Representatives, Rufus

King declared that the four New England States had more people and fewer Representatives than the Southern States, and that "no principle would justify giving them [the Southern States] a majority." Charles Cotesworth Pinckney replied that he did not expect the Southern States to have a majority "but wished them to have something like an equality," for if Congress had the power to regulate trade, the Southern States "will be nothing more than overseers for the Northern States." Pinckney thus reflected the fear of a fellow South Carolinian, Edward Rutledge, who had opposed the first draft of the Articles of Confederation in 1776 because he feared New England would dominate Congress, and that it might exploit Southern exporters of farm produce by granting a monopoly of the carrying trade to Northern shipowners.

The debate over the granting of commercial powers to Congress during the 1780s and the proposed Jay-Gardoqui treaty in 1786 had convinced Southerners that centralized power to regulate trade must be limited to protect their interests. Meanwhile, Northern merchants were equally convinced that Congress must have unlimited power to regulate trade.

Northerners and Southerners alike knew that control of the House of Representatives would be crucial in such matters as the regulation of trade. They knew too that the estimated population of the United States in 1787 would give control of the House to the Northern States. Delegates from all sections also knew that the area southwest of the Ohio River was growing dramatically and that Kentucky was asking for statehood. New western states, as men saw the future in 1787, would be "Southern" and "agrarian" states, and their interests would be opposed to the interests of the "commercial" states of the North.

Gouverneur Morris of Pennsylvania led Northern delegates in arguing that new western states should never be given enough Representatives to outvote the "Atlantic states." Most Southerners insisted that new states should be represented according to population, and Edmund Randolph of Virginia counterattacked by proposing that the first Congress under the Constitution should be required to take a census within a year, and every ten years thereafter, and that the House of Representatives should be reapportioned every ten years. Southerners were convinced that unless such a provision were added to the Constitution, the Northern States would never voluntarily surrender their control of the House of Representatives.

Most Northern delegates opposed the required census, and in the course of the debates upon it, they attacked the representation allotted to the South for three-fifths of the slaves. James Wilson, who had proposed the "bargain" in June, denounced it and the slave trade in

July. Gouverneur Morris predicted that the South and the new western states would join in an agrarian persecution of Northern commerce, and declared that he would vote for the "vicious principle" of equality in the Senate to protect the commercial North from such persecution. One Southerner replied that if the Convention tried to eliminate the representation earlier granted for three-fifths of the slaves, the Convention would come to an end.

Edmund Randolph of Virginia and John Rutledge of South Carolina were key members of the committee which wrote the first draft of the Constitution which was presented to the Convention on 6 August. The draft protected Southern interests by (1) requiring a two-thirds majority of each house to enact laws regulating trade; (2) forbidding Congress to levy export duties; and (3) forbidding Congress to levy import duties on or prohibit the importation of "such persons" as the states might think proper.

Northern delegates objected violently. Nathaniel Gorham of Massachusetts declared that the "Eastern states had no motive to union but a commercial one." Gouverneur Morris declared that if export taxes were forbidden, Northern freemen would be exploited to pay the expenses of government. He denounced the "slaves states" for their misery and poverty and moved that representation be based on free inhabitants only. George Mason of Virginia denounced the slave trade and so too did delegates from the Northern States. John Rutledge replied that the South would leave the Union if the slave trade were prohibited.

Yet the men who took unalterable stands indicated that they were willing to compromise. Gouverneur Morris, for example, suggested that the issues of trade regulation, export taxes, and the slave trade be sent to a committee so that "they may form a bargain between the Northern and Southern states." Various delegates declared that they would never bargain, but the committee proposed a compromise which the Convention accepted: (1) a simple majority of both houses of Congress would be enough to enact laws regulating trade and (2) the migration or importation of slaves could not be prohibited until 1808. The three New England states, Maryland, and the three southernmost states voted for the bargain. Virginia, Pennsylvania, New Jersey, and Delaware opposed it. This compromise of the power struggle between the North and the South at the end of August made possible the completion of the work of the Convention.

The successive and changing decisions of the Convention upon the issues outlined above are embodied in the documents printed below. The formal evolution of the Constitution can be followed step by step in those documents, although that evolution cannot be fully understood without a careful analysis of the notes of debates taken by James Madison, Robert Yates, James McHenry, Rufus King, and others. And that evolution cannot be understood without recognizing the fact that those debates took place within the context of the debates among American leaders over the nature of government that had begun long before independence was declared in 1776.

A. THE VIRGINIA RESOLUTIONS, 29 May[1]

> The resolutions presented by Edmund Randolph were prepared by the Virginia delegates before the Convention assembled. No evidence exists as to who wrote the resolutions Randolph read to the Convention, and the original manuscript has never been located. Since the delegates were not presented with printed copies of documents until they received the draft constitution of 6 August, they made copies for their own use during the debates. Several copies exist, but Max Farrand, the editor of *The Records of the Federal Convention,* concluded that the copy in Madison's Notes of Debates "is an accurate copy of the original" (III, 593–94).

1. Resolved that the articles of Confederation ought to be so corrected & enlarged as to accomplish the objects proposed by their institution; namely, "common defence, security of liberty and general welfare."

2. Resd. therefore that the rights of suffrage in the National Legislature ought to be proportioned to the Quotas of contribution, or to the number of free inhabitants, as the one or the other rule may seem best in different cases.

3. Resd. that the National Legislature ought to consist of two branches.

4. Resd. that the members of the first branch of the National Legislature ought to be elected by the people of the several States every_____for the term of_____; to be of the age of_____ years at least, to receive liberal stipends by which they may be compensated for the devotion of their time to public service; to be ineligible to any office established by a particular State, or under the authority of the United States, except those peculiarly belonging to the functions of the first branch, during the term of service, and for the space of_____after its expiration; to be incapable of re-election for the space of_____after the expiration of their term of service, and to be subject to recall.

5. Resold. that the members of the second branch of the National Legislature ought to be elected by those of the first, out of a proper number of persons nominated by the individual Legislatures, to be of

the age of _____ years at least; to hold their offices for a term sufficient to ensure their independency, to receive liberal stipends, by which they may be compensated for the devotion of their time to public service; and to be ineligible to any office established by a particular State, or under the authority of the United States, except those peculiarly belonging to the functions of the second branch, during the term of service, and for the space of _____ after the expiration thereof.

6. Resolved that each branch ought to possess the right of originating Acts; that the National Legislature ought to be impowered to enjoy the Legislative Rights vested in Congress by the Confederation & moreover to legislate in all cases to which the separate States are incompetent, or in which the harmony of the United States may be interrupted by the exercise of individual Legislation; to negative all laws passed by the several States contravening in the opinion of the National Legislature the articles of Union; and to call forth the force of the Union agst. any member of the Union failing to fulfill its duty under the articles thereof.

7. Resd. that a National Executive be instituted, to be chosen by the National Legislature for the term of _____ years, to receive punctually at stated times, a fixed compensation for the services rendered, in which no increase or diminution shall be made so as to affect the Magistracy, existing at the time of increase or diminution, and to be ineligible a second time; and that besides a general authority to execute the National laws, it ought to enjoy the Executive rights vested in Congress by the Confederation.

8. Resd. that the Executive and a convenient number of the National Judiciary, ought to compose a Council of revision with authority to examine every act of the National Legislature before it shall operate, & every act of a particular Legislature before a Negative thereon shall be final; and that the dissent of the said Council shall amount to a rejection, unless the Act of the National Legislature be again passed, or that of a particular Legislature be again negatived by _____ of the members of each branch.

9. Resd. that a National Judiciary be established to consist of one or more supreme tribunals, and of inferior tribunals to be chosen by the National Legislature, to hold their offices during good behaviour; and to receive punctually at stated times fixed compensation for their services, in which no increase or diminution shall be made so as to affect the persons actually in office, at the time of such increase or diminution. that the jurisdiction of the inferior tribunals shall be to hear & determine in the first instance, and of the supreme tribunal to hear and determine in the dernier resort, all piracies &

felonies on the high seas, captures from an enemy; cases in which foreigners or citizens of other States applying to such jurisdictions may be interested, or which respect the collection of the National revenue; impeachments of any National officers, and questions which may involve the national peace and harmony.

10. Resolvd. that provision ought to be made for the admission of States lawfully arising within the limits of the United States, whether from a voluntary junction of Government & Territory or otherwise, with the consent of a number of voices in the National legislature less than the whole.

11. Resd. that a Republican Government & the territory of each State, except in the instance of a voluntary junction of Government & territory, ought to be guaranteed by the United States to each State

12. Resd. that provision ought to be made for the continuance of Congress and their authorities and privileges, until a given day after the reform of the articles of Union shall be adopted, and for the completion of all their engagements.

13. Resd. that provision ought to be made for the amendment of the Articles of Union whensoever it shall seem necessary, and that the assent of the National Legislature ought not to be required thereto.

14. Resd. that the Legislative Executive & Judiciary powers within the several States ought to be bound by oath to support the articles of Union

15. Resd. that the amendments which shall be offered to the Confederation, by the Convention ought at a proper time, or times, after the approbation of Congress to be submitted to an assembly or assemblies of Representatives, recommended by the several Legislatures to be expressly chosen by the people, to consider & decide thereon.

1. MS (LT), James Madison, Notes of Debates, Madison Papers, DLC.

B. CHARLES PINCKNEY'S PLAN, 29 May[1]

On 29 May the Journals of the Convention record that Charles Pinckney "laid before the House . . . the draft of a federal government to be agreed upon between the free and independent states of America." The plan was not discussed by the Convention but was turned over to the Committee of Detail on 24 July.

The document written by Pinckney has never been found, but a document in James Wilson's handwriting has been identified as a synopsis. This document is printed below. For a discussion of the Pinckney Plan, see J. Franklin Jameson, "Studies in the History of the Federal Convention of 1787," American Historical Association Annual Report . . . 1902 (2 vols., Washington, D.C., 1903), I, 111–32;

[Andrew C. McLaughlin], "Sketch of Pinckney's Plan for a Constitution, 1787," *American Historical Review*, IX (1903–1904), 735–47; and Farrand, III, 595–609.

1. A Confederation between the free and independent States of N.H. &c is hereby solemnly made uniting them together under one general superintending Government for their common Benefit and for their Defense and Security against all Designs and Leagues that may be injurious to their Interests and against all [Foes?] and Attacks offered to or made upon them or any of them

2. The Stile

3. Mutual Intercourse—Community of Privileges—Surrender of Criminals—Faith to Proceedings &c.

4. Two Branches of the Legislature—Senate—House of Delegates—together the U.S. in Congress assembled

H.D. to consist of one Member for every ____ thousand Inhabitants 3/5 of Blacks included Senate to be elected from four Districts—to serve by Rotation of four Years—to be elected by the H.D. either from among themselves or the People at large

5. The Senate and H.D. shall by joint Ballot annually chuse the Presidt. U.S. from among themselves or the People at large.—In the Presidt. the executive Authority of the U.S. shall be vested.—His Powers and Duties He shall have a Right to advise with the Heads of the different Departments as his Council

6. Council of Revision, consisting of the Presidt. S. for for. Affairs, S. of War, Heads of the Departmts of Treasury and Admiralty or any two of them togr. wt the Presidt.

7. The Members of S. & H.D. shall each have one Vote, and shall be paid out of the common Treasury.

8. The Time of the Election of the Members of the H.D. and of the Meeting of U.S. in C. assembled.

9. No State to make Treaties—lay interfering Duties—keep a naval or land Force (Militia excepted) to be disciplined &c according to the Regulations of the U.S:

10. Each State retains its Rights not expressly delegated—But no Bill of the Legislature of any State shall become a Law till it shall have been laid before S. & H.D. in C. assembled and received their Approbation:

11. The exclusive Powers of S. & H.D. in C. assembled.

12. The S. & H.D. in C. ass. shall have the exclusive Power of regulating Trade and levying Imposts—Each State may lay Embargoes in Times of Scarcity

13. _____ of establishing Post Offices

14. S. & H.D. in C. ass. shall be the last Resort on Appeal in Dis-

putes between two or more States; which Authority shall be exercised in the following Manner &c.

15. S. & H.D. in C. ass. shall institute Offices and appoint officers for the Departments of for. Affairs, War, Treasury and Admiralty—

They shall have the exclusive Power of declaring what shall be Treason & Misp. of Treason agt. U.S.—and of instituting a federal judicial Court, to which an Appeal shall be allowed from the judicial Courts of the several States in all Causes wherein Questions shall arise on the Construction of Treaties made by U.S: or on the Law of Nations—or on the Regulations of U.S. concerning Trade & Revenue— or wherein U.S. shall be a Party. The Court shall consist of _____ Judges to be appointed during good Behaviour—S. & H.D. in C. ass. shall have the exclusive Right of instituting in each State a Court of Admiralty, and appointing the Judges &c. of the same for all maritime Causes which may arise therein respectively.

16. S. & H.D. in C. ass. shall have the exclusive Right of coining Money—regulating its Alloy & Value—fixing the Standard of Weights and Measures throughout U.S.

17. Points in which the Assent of more than a bare Majority shall be necessary.

18. Impeachments shall be by the H.D. before the Senate and the Judges of the federal judicial Court.

19. S. & H.D. in C. ass. shall regulate the Militia thro' the U.S.

20. Means of enforcing and compelling the Payment of the Quota of each State.

21. Manner and Conditions of admiting new States.

22. Power of dividing annexing and consolidating States on the Consent and Petition of such States.

23. The Assent of the Legislature of _____ States shall be suffi- cient to invest future additional Powers in U.S. in C. ass. and shall bind the whole Confederacy.

24. The Articles of Confederation shall be inviolably observed un- less altered as before directed, and the Union shall be perpetual.

25. The said States of N.H. &c. guarrantee mutually each other and their Rights against all other Powers and against all Rebellions &c.

1. MS (LT), James Wilson Papers, PHi. The document is in an unnumbered folio volume entitled "Second Draft of Constitution."

C. THE AMENDED VIRGINIA RESOLUTIONS, 13–19 June[1]

> The Convention revised and amended the Virginia Resolutions from
> 29 May to 13 June in the committee of the whole. They were then

presented to the delegates sitting as the Convention on 13 June. Adoption of the Resolutions was delayed until 19 June while the Convention debated the amendments to the Articles of Confederation proposed by William Paterson of New Jersey (VII:D below). On 19 June, in a single vote, the Convention accepted the amended Virginia Resolutions and rejected the New Jersey Amendments. Massachusetts, Connecticut, Pennsylvania, Virginia, North Carolina, South Carolina, and Georgia voted "aye." New York, New Jersey, and Delaware voted "no." The vote of Maryland was divided.

State of the resolutions submitted to the consideration of the House by the honorable Mr. Randolph, as altered, amended, and agreed to in a Committee of the whole House.

1. Resolved that it is the opinion of this Committee that a national government ought to be established consisting of a Supreme Legislative, Judiciary, and Executive.

2. Resolved that the national Legislature ought to consist of Two Branches.

3. Resolved that the Members of the first branch of the national Legislature ought to be elected by the People of the several States for the term of Three years.

To receive fixed stipends, by which they may be compensated for the devotion of their time to public service to be paid out of the National-Treasury.

To be ineligible to any Office established by a particular State or under the authority of the United-States (except those peculiarly belonging to the functions of the first branch) during the term of service, and under the national government for the space of one year after it's expiration.

4. Resolved that the Members of the second Branch of the national Legislature ought to be chosen by the individual Legislatures.

To be of the age of thirty years at least.

To hold their offices for a term sufficient to ensure their independency, namely seven years.

To receive fixed stipends, by which they may be compensated for the devotion of their time to public service—to be paid out of the national Treasury.

To be ineligible to any Office established by a particular State, or under the authority of the United States (except those peculiarly belonging to the functions of the second branch) during the term of service; and under the national government, for the space of One year after it's expiration.

5. Resolved that each branch ought to possess the right of originating acts.

6. Resolved that the national Legislature ought to be empowered to enjoy the legislative rights vested in Congress by the confederation—and moreover to legislate in all cases to which the separate States are incompetent: or in which the harmony of the United States may be interrupted by the exercise of individual legislation.

To negative all laws passed by the several States contravening, in the opinion of the national legislature the articles of union, or any treaties subsisting under the authority of the union.

7. Resolved that the right of suffrage in the first branch of the national Legislature ought not to be according to the rule established in the articles of confederation: but according to some equitable ratio of representation—namely in proportion to the whole number of white and other free citizens and inhabitants of every age, sex, and condition including those bound to servitude for a term of years, and three fifths of all other persons not comprehended in the foregoing description, except Indians, not paying taxes in each State.

8. Resolved that the right of suffrage in the second branch of the national Legislature ought to be according to the rule established for the first.

9. Resolved that a national Executive be instituted to consist of a Single Person.

To be chosen by the National legislature for the term of Seven years.

With power to carry into execution the National Laws.

To appoint to Offices in cases not otherwise provided for.

To be ineligible a second time, and to be removable on impeachment and conviction of mal practice or neglect of duty.

To receive a fixed stipend, by which he may be compensated for the devotion of his time to public service to be paid out of the national Treasury.

10. Resolved that the national executive shall have a right to negative any legislative act: which shall not be afterwards passed unless by two third parts of each branch of the national Legislature.

11. Resolved that a national Judiciary be established to consist of One supreme Tribunal. The Judges of which to be appointed by the second Branch of the National Legislature.

To hold their offices during good behaviour.

To receive, punctually, at stated times, a fixed compensation for their services: in which no encrease or diminution shall be made so as to affect the persons actually in office at the time of such encrease or diminution.

12. Resolved that the national Legislature be empowered to appoint inferior Tribunals.

13. Resolved that the jurisdiction of the national Judiciary shall

extend to cases which respect the collection of the national revenue: impeachments of any national Officers: and questions which involve the national peace and harmony.

14. Resolved that provision ought to be made for the admission of States, lawfully arising within the limits of the United States, whether from a voluntary junction of government and territory, or otherwise, with the consent of a number of voices in the national Legislature less than the whole.

15. Resolved that provision ought to be made for the continuance of Congress and their authorities until a given day after the reform of the articles of Union shall be adopted; and for the completion of all their engagements.

16. Resolved that a republican constitution, and it's existing laws, ought to be guaranteed to each State by the United States.

17. Resolved that provision ought to be made for the amendment of the articles of Union, whensoever it shall seem necessary.

18. Resolved that the Legislative, Executive, and Judiciary powers within the several States ought to be bound by oath to support the articles of Union.

19. Resolved that the amendments which shall be offered to the confederation by the Convention, ought at a proper time or times, after the approbation of Congress to be submitted to an assembly or assemblies of representatives, recommended by the several Legislatures, to be expressly chosen by the People to consider and decide thereon.

1. MS (LT), RCC, DNA. These resolutions, in William Jackson's handwriting, were presented to the Convention on 13 June and adopted on 19 June. The document is a literal transcript, but the related parts of each clause are placed in paragraph form and punctuation and capitalization altered accordingly.

D. THE NEW JERSEY AMENDMENTS TO THE ARTICLES OF CONFEDERATION, 15 June[1]

The amendments proposed by William Paterson of New Jersey were far more than "New Jersey amendments." They represented the views of the delegates from the small states and of those delegates who were opposed to a national government or who at least insisted that the central government must retain some of the federal character of the Articles of Confederation. Nevertheless, they agreed that the central government needed more power and the proposed amendments provided for such power. Among the delegates probably involved in drafting the amendments, in addition to Paterson, were Roger Sherman and Oliver Ellsworth of Connecticut; John Lansing, Jr. and Robert Yates of New York; the Delaware delegates, including John Dickinson; and possibly Luther Martin of Maryland.

On 19 June the Convention approved a motion to reject the New

Jersey Amendments and accept the amended Virginia Resolutions. Massachusetts, Connecticut, Pennsylvania, Virginia, North Carolina, South Carolina, and Georgia voted for the motion. New York, New Jersey, and Delaware voted against it. The vote of Maryland was divided.

1. Resd. that the articles of Confederation ought to be so revised, corrected & enlarged, as to render the federal Constitution adequate to the exigencies of Government, & the preservation of the Union.

2. Resd. that in addition to the powers vested in the U. States in Congress, by the present existing articles of Confederation, they be authorized to pass acts for raising a revenue, by levying a duty or duties on all goods or merchandizes of foreign growth or manufacture imported into any part of the U. States, by Stamps on paper, vellum or parchment, and by a postage on all letters or packages passing through the general post-office, to be applied to such federal purposes as they shall deem proper & expedient, to make rules & regulations for the collection thereof, and the same from time to time, to alter & amend in such manner as they shall think proper: to pass Acts for the regulation of trade & commerce as well with foreign nations as with each other: provided that all punishments, fines, forfeitures & penalties to be incurred for contravening such acts rules and regulations shall be adjudged by the Common law Judiciarys of the State in which any offence contrary to the true intent & meaning of such Acts rules & regulations shall have been committed or perpetrated, with liberty of commencing in the first instance all suits & prosecutions for that purpose in the superior common law Judiciary in such State, subject nevertheless, for the correction of all errors, both in law & fact in rendering Judgment, to an appeal to the Judiciary of the U. States

3. Resd. that whenever requisitions shall be necessary, instead of the rule for making requisitions mentioned in the articles of Confederation, the United States in Congs. be authorized to make such requisitions in proportion to the whole number of white & other free citizens & inhabitants of every age sex and condition including those bound to servitude for a term of years & three fifths of all other persons not comprehended in the foregoing description, except Indians not paying taxes; that if such requisitions be not complied with, in the time specified therein, to direct the collection thereof in the non complying States & for that purpose to devise and pass acts directing & authorizing the same; provided that none of the powers hereby vested in the U. States in Congs. shall be exercised without the consent of at least _____ States, and in that proportion if the number of Confederated States should hereafter be increased or diminished.

4. Resd. that the U. States in Congs. be authorized to elect a federal Executive to consist of _____ persons, to continue in office for the term of _____ years, to receive punctually at stated times a fixed compensation for their services, in which no increase or diminution shall be made so as to affect the persons composing the Executive at the time of such increase or diminution, to be paid out of the federal treasury; to be incapable of holding any other office or appointment during their time of service and for _____ years thereafter; to be ineligible a second time, & removeable by Congs. on application by a majority of the Executives of the several States; that the Executives besides their general authority to execute the federal acts ought to appoint all federal officers not otherwise provided for, & to direct all military Operations; provided that none of the persons composing the federal Executive shall on any occasion take command of any troops, so as personally to conduct any enterprise as General, or in other capacity.

5. Resd. that a federal Judiciary be established to consist of a supreme Tribunal the Judges of which to be appointed by the Executive, & to hold their offices during good behaviour, to receive punctually at stated times a fixed compensation for their services in which no increase or diminution shall be made, so as to affect the persons actually in office at the time of such increase or diminution; that the Judiciary so established shall have authority to hear & determine in the first instance on all impeachments of federal officers, & by way of appeal in the dernier resort in all cases touching the rights of Ambassadors, in all cases of captures from an enemy, in all cases of piracies & felonies on the high seas, in all cases in which foreigners may be interested, in the construction of any treaty or treaties, or which may arise on any of the Acts for regulation of trade, or the collection of the federal Revenue: that none of the Judiciary shall during the time they remain in office be capable of receiving or holding any other office or appointment during their time of service, or for _____ thereafter.

6. Resd. that all acts of the U. States in Congs. made by virtue & in pursuance of the powers hereby & by the articles of Confederation vested in them, and all Treaties made & ratified under the authority of the U. States shall be the supreme law of the respective States, so far forth as those Acts or Treaties shall relate to the said States or their Citizens, and that the Judiciary of the several States shall be bound thereby in their decisions, any thing in the respective laws of the Individual States to the contrary notwithstanding; and that if any State, or any body of men in any State shall oppose or prevent ye. carrying into execution such acts or treaties, the federal Executive

shall be authorized to call forth ye power of the Confederated States, or so much thereof as may be necessary to enforce and compel an obedience to such Acts, or an Observance of such Treaties.

7. Resd. that provision be made for the admission of new States into the Union.

8. Resd. the rule for naturalization ought to be the same in every State

9. Resd. that a Citizen of one State committing an offence in another State of the Union, shall be deemed guilty of the same offence as if it had been committed by a Citizen of the State in which the offence was committed.

1. MS (LT), James Madison, Notes of Debates, Madison Papers, DLC.

E. ALEXANDER HAMILTON'S PLAN, 18 June[1]

During the debate over the amended Virginia Resolutions and the New Jersey Amendments to the Articles of Confederation on 18 June, Alexander Hamilton made a long speech which was reported in varying detail by five members of the Convention: Hamilton's own notes for the speech, and the notes of James Madison, Robert Yates, John Lansing, Jr., and Rufus King. Hamilton's notes and the reports of his speech are annotated and printed in Syrett, IV, 178–207.

Hamilton believed that both the amended Virginia Resolutions and the New Jersey Amendments were inadequate, particularly the latter. Toward the end of his speech, Hamilton read his plan. According to Madison, Hamilton said that "he did not mean to offer the paper he had sketched as a proposition to the committee [of the whole]. It was meant only to give a more correct view of his ideas and to suggest the amendments which he would probably propose to the plan of Mr. R[andolph]. . . ."

The plan printed below is in Hamilton's handwriting. Evidently someone later added Roman numerals at the beginning of each paragraph and capital letters in the margins, and underlined certain words in the text. Syrett (IV, 207–9) prints the plan with these additions. They have been deleted in the text printed below since they do not appear to have been added by Hamilton.

The Supreme Legislative Power of the United States of America to be vested in two distinct bodies of men—the one to be called the Assembly the other the senate; who together shall form the Legislature of the United States, with power to pass all laws whatsoever, subject to the negative hereafter mentioned.

The Assembly to consist of persons elected by the People to serve for three years.

The Senate to consist of persons elected to serve during good behaviour. Their election to be made by Electors chosen for that purpose by the People. In order to this The States to be divided into election districts. On the death, removal or resignation of any senator his place to be filled out of the district from which he came.

The Supreme Executive authority of the United States to be vested in a governor to be elected to serve during good behaviour. His election to be made by Electors chosen by electors chosen by the people in the election districts aforesaid. or by ~~persons~~ electors chosen for that purpose by the respective legislatures—provided that [if] an election be not made within a [limited time?] the President of the Senate shall [then?] be the Governor—The Governor to have a negative upon all laws about to be passed—and to have the execution of all laws passed—to be the Commander in Chief of the land and naval forces and of the Militia of the United States—to have the direction of war, when authorised or began—to have with the advice and approbation of the Senate the power of making all treaties—to have the appointment of the heads or chief officers of the departments of finance war and foreign affairs—to have the nomination of all other officers (ambassadors to foreign nations included) subject to the approbation or rejection of the Senate—to have the power of pardonning all offences but treason, which he shall not pardon without the approbation of the Senate—

On the death resignation or removal of the Governor his authorities to be exercised by the President of the Senate.

The Senate to have the sole power of declaring war—the power of advising and approving all treaties—the power of approving or rejecting all appointments of officers except ~~such as~~ the heads or chiefs ~~officers~~ of the departments of finance war and foreign affairs.

The Supreme Judicial authority of the United States to be vested in ~~not less than six nor more than~~ twelve Judges, to hold their offices during good behaviour with adequate and permanent salaries. This Court to have original jurisdiction in all causes of capture and an appellative jurisdiction (from the Courts of the several states) in all causes in which the revenues of the general government or the citizens of foreign nations are concerned.

The Legislature of the United States to have power to institute Courts in each state for the determination of all causes of capture and of all matters relating to their revenues, or in which the Citizens of foreign nations are concerned.

The Governor Senators and all Officers of the United States to be liable to impeachment for mal and corrupt conduct, and upon conviction to be removed from office and disqualified for holding any ~~office~~ place of trust or profit. ~~The Governor to be impeachable by consent of the national legislature or by the legislative bodies of~~

~~any~~ _____ ~~states. The Senators and all officers by either branch of the national legislature or by the legislative bodies of any~~ _____ ~~states.~~ All impeachments to be tried by a Court to consist of the Judges of the Supreme Court [and] Chief or Senior Judge of the superior Court of law of each state—provided that such judge hold his place during good behaviour and have a permanent salary. ~~After removal from office either of the foregoing characters (The Governor) may be prosecuted in the ordinary course of law for any crime committed while in office.~~

All laws of the particular states contrary to the constitution or laws of the United States to be utterly void. And the better to prevent such laws being passed the Governor or President of each state shall be appointed by the general government and shall have a negative upon the laws about to be passed in the state of which he is governor or President.

No state to have any forces land or naval—and the Militia of all the states to be under the sole and exclusive direction of the United States the officers of which to be appointed and commissioned by them.

1. MS (LT), Hamilton Papers, DLC. The words lined out in the document were apparently deleted by Hamilton.

F. RESOLUTIONS SUBMITTED TO THE COMMITTEE OF DETAIL, 24, 26 July

The Convention debated the revised Virginia Resolutions from 19 June until 23 July, when it voted unanimously to submit "the proceedings of the Convention for the establishment of a national government" to a committee "for the purpose of reporting a Constitution. . . ." The next day the Convention elected the Committee of Detail consisting of John Rutledge of South Carolina (chairman), Edmund Randolph of Virginia, James Wilson of Pennsylvania, Oliver Ellsworth of Connecticut, and Nathaniel Gorham of Massachusetts.

On 24 July the Convention turned over to the Committee the results of its decisions since the 19th of June, the New Jersey Amendments to the Articles of Confederation, and the plan presented by Charles Pinckney on 29 May. The Convention continued to debate the presidency and property qualifications for members of Congress and other officials on the 25th and 26th. It turned these resolutions over to the Committee on 26 July and adjourned to meet again on 6 August.

The text printed below is reconstructed from: (1) the amended Virginia Resolutions (VII:C above); (2) the Journals of the Convention; (3) James Madison's Notes of Debates; and (4) a document in the James Wilson papers in the Historical Society of Pennsylvania which Farrand states "evidently represents the proceedings referred to the Committee of Detail" (II, 129–32). The material from these sources is transcribed literally.

The procedure used in compiling the following document is similar to the technique used by John Quincy Adams in his 1819 edition of the *Journals*. Adams, however, had only the Journals to trace the evolution of the resolutions.

To show how the amended Virginia Resolutions were altered and expanded between 19 June and 26 July, the document below is set as follows: (1) the parts of the amended Virginia Resolutions retained are set in roman type; (2) the parts of the amended Virginia Resolutions deleted are set in lined-out type; and (3) the new matter added by the Convention is set in italic type.

Resolutions Submitted on 24 July

1. Resolved that ~~it is the opinion of this Committee that a national~~ *the* government *of the United States* ought to ~~be established consisting~~ *consist* of a Supreme Legislative, Judiciary, and Executive.

2. Resolved that the ~~national~~ Legislature ~~ought to~~ consist of Two Branches.

3. Resolved that the Members of the first branch of the ~~national~~ Legislature ought to be elected by the People of the several States for the term of ~~Three~~ *two* years.

~~To receive fixed stipends, by which they may be compensated for the devotion of their time to public service to be paid out of the National Treasury.~~

To be of the age of 25 years at least.

To be ineligible to *and incapable of holding* any Office ~~established by a particular State~~ or under the authority of the United-States (except those peculiarly belonging to the functions of the first branch) during the term of service, ~~and under the national government for the space of one year after it's expiration~~ *of the first branch.*

4. Resolved that the Members of the second Branch of the ~~national~~ *United States* Legislature ought to be chosen by the individual Legislatures.

To be of the age of thirty years at least.

To hold their offices ~~for a term sufficient to ensure their independency, namely~~ *for* ~~seven~~ *six* years, *one third to go out biennially.*

To receive ~~fixed stipends, by which they may be compensated~~ *a compensation* for the devotion of their time to public service. ~~to be paid out of the National Treasury.~~

To be ineligible to, *and incapable of holding* any office ~~established by a particular State, or~~ under the authority of the United States (except those peculiarly belonging to the functions of the second branch) during the term ~~of service, and under the national government, for the space of~~ *for which they are elected, and for* one year ~~after it's expiration~~ *thereafter.*

5. Resolved that each Branch ought to possess the right of originating acts.

6. Resolved that the national Legislature ought to ~~be empowered to enjoy~~ *possess* the legislative rights vested in Congress by the confederation—and moreover to legislate in all cases *for the general interests of the Union, and also in those* to which the ~~separate~~ States are *separately* incompetent, or in which the harmony of the United States may be interrupted by the exercise of individual legislation. ~~To negative all laws passed by the several States contravening, in the opinion of the national legislature, the articles of union, or any treaties subsisting under the authority of the union.~~ *Resolved that the legislative acts of the United States made by virtue and in pursuance of the articles of Union and all Treaties made and ratified under the authority of the United States shall be the supreme law of the respective States as far as those acts or Treaties shall relate to the said States, or their Citizens and Inhabitants—and that the Judiciaries of the several states shall be bound thereby in their decisions, any thing in the respective laws of the individual States to the contrary notwithstanding.*

7. Resolved that the right of suffrage in the first branch of the ~~national~~ Legislature *of the United States* ought not to be according to the rule established in the articles of confederation but according to some equitable ratio of representation– ~~namely.~~ ~~In proportion to the whole number of white and other free citizens and inhabitants of every age, sex, and condition including those bound to servitude for a term of years, and three fifths of all other persons not comprehended in the foregoing description, except Indians, not paying taxes in each State.~~ *Resolved that in the original formation of the Legislature of the United States the first Branch thereof shall consist of Sixty five members—of which number*

New Hampshire shall send	*Three*
Massachusetts	*Eight*
Rhode Island	*One*
Connecticut	*Five*
New York	*Six*
New Jersey	*Four*
Pennsylvania	*Eight*
Delaware	*One*
Maryland	*Six*
Virginia	*Ten*
North Carolina	*Five*
South Carolina	*Five*
Georgia	*Three.*

But as the present situation of the States may probably alter in the number of their inhabitants the Legislature of the United States shall be authorized from time to time to apportion the number of representatives: and in case any of the States shall hereafter be divided, or enlarged by addition of territory, or any two or more States united, or any New States created within the limits of the United States the Legislature of the United States shall possess authority to regulate the number of representatives: in any of the foregoing cases upon the principle of their number of inhabitants, according to the provisions hereafter mentioned, namely,

Provided always that representation ought to be proportioned according to direct Taxation; and in order to ascertain the alteration in the direct Taxation, which may be required from time to time by the changes in the relative circumstances of the States.

Resolved that a Census be taken within six years from the first Meeting of the Legislature of the United States, and once within the term of every Ten years afterwards of all the inhabitants of the United States in the manner and according to the ratio recommended by Congress in their resolution of April 18. 1783—and that the Legislature of the United States shall proportion the direct Taxation accordingly.

Resolved that all Bills for raising or appropriating money, and for fixing the salaries of the Officers of the Government of the United States shall originate in the first Branch of the Legislature of the United States, and shall not be altered or amended by the second Branch—and that no money shall be drawn from the Public Treasury but in pursuance of appropriations to be originated by the first Branch.

That from the first meeting of the Legislature of the United States until a Census shall be taken, all monies for supplying the public Treasury by direct Taxation shall be raised from the several States according to the number of their representatives respectively in the first Branch.

8. Resolved that ~~the right of suffrage~~ in the second Branch of the ~~national~~ Legislature *of the United States* ~~ought to be according to the rule established for the first~~ each State shall have an equal vote.

9. Resolved that a national Executive be instituted to consist of a Single Person.

To be chosen by the national Legislature for the term of seven years. *To be ineligible a second time.*

With power to carry into execution the national Laws.

To appoint to Offices in cases not otherwise provided for.

~~To be ineligible a second time, and~~ To be removable on impeachment and conviction of malpractice or neglect of duty.

To receive a fixed ~~stipend,~~ *compensation* ~~by which he may be compensated~~ for the devotion of his time to public service.

To be paid out of the ~~national~~ *public* Treasury.

10. Resolved that the national Executive shall have a right to negative any legislative act, which shall not be afterwards passed unless by two third parts of each Branch of the national Legislature.

11. Resolved that a national Judiciary be established To consist of One supreme Tribunal. The Judges of which to *shall* be appointed by the second Branch of the national Legislature.

To hold their Offices during good behaviour.

To receive, punctually, at stated times a fixed compensation for their services in which no ~~encrease or~~ diminution shall be made so as to affect the Persons actually in Office at the time of such ~~encrease or~~ diminution.

12. Resolved that the national Legislature be empowered to appoint inferior Tribunals.

13. Resolved that the jurisdiction of the national Judiciary shall extend to cases ~~which respect the collection of the national revenue: impeachments of any national Officers:~~ *arising under laws passed by the general Legislature,* and *to such other* questions ~~which~~ *as* involve the National peace and harmony.

14. Resolved that provision ought to be made for the admission of States lawfully arising within the limits of the United States, whether from a voluntary junction of government and territory, or otherwise with the consent of a number of voices in the national Legislature less than the whole.

~~15. Resolved that provision ought to be made for the continuance of Congress and their authorities until a given day after the reform of the articles of Union shall be adopted; and for the completion of all their engagements.~~

16. Resolved that a republican ~~Constitution, and it's existing laws,~~ *form of Government* ~~ought to~~ *shall* be guaranteed to each State ~~by the United States.~~ *and that each State shall be protected against foreign and domestic violence.*

17. Resolved that provision ought to be made for the amendment of the articles of union, whensoever it shall seem necessary.

18. Resolved that the legislative, Executive, and Judiciary Powers within the several States, *and of the national Government,* ought to be bound by oath to support the articles of union.

19. Resolved that the amendments which shall be offered to the

confederation by the Convention ought at a proper time or times after the approbation of Congress to be submitted to an assembly or assemblies of representatives, recommended by the several Legislatures, to be expressly chosen by the People to consider and decide thereon.

Additional Resolutions Submitted on 26 July

Resolved that the representation in the second Branch of the Legislature of the United States consist of Two Members from each State, who shall vote per capita.

Resolved that it be an instruction to the Committee to whom were referred the proceedings of the Convention for the establishment of a national government, to receive a clause or clauses, requiring certain qualifications of ~~landed~~ property and citizenship in the United States for the Executive, the Judiciary, and the Members of both branches of the Legislature of the United States; ~~and for disqualifying all such persons as are indebted to, or have unsettled accounts with the United States from being Members of either Branch of the national Legislature.~~

G. DRAFT CONSTITUTION BY THE COMMITTEE OF DETAIL, 6 August[1]

> Despite the Convention's rule of secrecy, the election of the Committee of Detail on 24 July was soon public knowledge. On 28 July the *Pennsylvania Herald* reported that the Convention had adjourned to give a committee "time to arrange and systemize the materials which that honorable body have collected." On the same day the Philadelphia *Independent Gazetteer* listed the names of the committee members (see CC:55 for the circulation of these items).
>
> The Committee of Detail went considerably beyond the previous resolutions of the Convention in writing the first draft of the Constitution. The Committee incorporated provisions from the Articles of Confederation, from some of the state constitutions, and from plans submitted to but not accepted by the Convention. It even borrowed some of the phraseology of the Committee Report on Carrying the Confederation into Effect and on Additional Powers Needed by Congress of 22 August 1781 (IV:C above) which Edmund Randolph and Oliver Ellsworth had helped to write. Edmund Randolph, John Rutledge, and James Wilson wrote and annotated successive drafts, and then the Committee had the final draft set in type. After correcting the proof, the draft was printed in final form, the first printed document submitted to the Convention.

We the People of the States of New-Hampshire, Massachusetts, Rhode-Island and Providence Plantations, Connecticut, New-York,

New-Jersey, Pennsylvania, Delaware, Maryland, Virginia, North-Carolina, South-Carolina, and Georgia, do ordain, declare and establish the following Constitution for the Government of Ourselves and our Posterity.

ARTICLE I. The stile of this Government shall be, "The United States of America."

II. The Government shall consist of supreme legislative, executive and judicial powers.

III. The legislative power shall be vested in a Congress, to consist of two separate and distinct bodies of men, a House of Representatives, and a Senate; each of which shall, in all cases, have a negative on the other. The Legislature shall meet on the first Monday in December in every year.

IV. Sect. 1. The members of the House of Representatives shall be chosen every second year, by the people of the several States comprehended within this Union. The qualifications of the electors shall be the same, from time to time, as those of the electors in the several States, of the most numerous branch of their own legislatures.

Sect. 2. Every Member of the House of Representatives shall be of the age of twenty-five years at least; shall have been a citizen in the United States for at least three years before his election; and shall be, at the time of his election, a resident of the State in which he shall be chosen.

Sect. 3. The House of Representatives shall, at its first formation, and until the number of citizens and inhabitants shall be taken in the manner herein after described, consist of sixty-five Members, of whom three shall be chosen in New-Hampshire, eight in Massachusetts, one in Rhode-Island and Providence Plantations, five in Connecticut, six in New-York, four in New-Jersey, eight in Pennsylvania, one in Delaware, six in Maryland, ten in Virginia, five in North-Carolina, five in South-Carolina, and three in Georgia.

Sect. 4. As the proportions of numbers in the different States will alter from time to time; as some of the States may hereafter be divided; as others may be enlarged by addition of territory; as two or more States may be united; as new States will be erected within the limits of the United States, the Legislature shall, in each of these cases, regulate the number of representatives by the number of inhabitants, according to the provisions herein after made, at the rate of one for every forty thousand.

Sect. 5. All bills for raising or appropriating money, and for fixing the salaries of the officers of government, shall originate in the House of Representatives, and shall not be altered or amended by the Senate. No money shall be drawn from the public Treasury, but in pursuance of appropriations that shall originate in the House of Representatives.

Sect. 6. The House of Representatives shall have the sole power of impeachment. It shall choose its Speaker and other officers.

Sect. 7. Vacancies in the House of Representatives shall be supplied by writs of election from the executive authority of the State, in the representation from which they shall happen.

V. Sect. 1. The Senate of the United States shall be chosen by the Legislatures of the several States. Each Legislature shall chuse two members. Vacancies may be supplied by the Executive until the next meeting of the Legislature. Each member shall have one vote.

Sect. 2. The Senators shall be chosen for six years; but immediately after the first election they shall be divided, by lot, into three classes, as nearly as may be, numbered one, two and three. The seats of the members of the first class shall be vacated at the expiration of the second year, of the second class at the expiration of the fourth year, of the third class at the expiration of the sixth year, so that a third part of the members may be chosen every second year.

Sect. 3. Every member of the Senate shall be of the age of thirty years at least; shall have been a citizen in the United States for at least four years before his election; and shall be, at the time of his election, a resident of the State for which he shall be chosen.

Sect. 4. The Senate shall chuse its own President and other officers.

VI. Sect. 1. The times and places and the manner of holding the elections of the members of each House shall be prescribed by the Legislature of each State; but their provisions concerning them may, at any time, be altered by the Legislature of the United States.

Sect. 2. The Legislature of the United States shall have authority to establish such uniform qualifications of the members of each house, with regard to property, as to the said Legislature shall seem expedient.

Sect. 3. In each House a majority of the members shall constitute a quorum to do business; but a smaller number may adjourn from day to day.

Sect. 4. Each House shall be the judge of the elections, returns and qualifications of its own members.

Sect. 5. Freedom of speech and debate in the Legislature shall not be impeached or questioned in any court or place out of the Legislature; and the members of each House shall, in all cases, except treason, felony and breach of the peace, be privileged from arrest during their attendance at Congress, and in going to and returning from it.

Sect. 6. Each House may determine the rules of its proceedings; may punish its members for disorderly behaviour; and may expel a member.

Sect. 7. The House of Representatives, and the Senate, when it shall be acting in a legislative capacity, shall keep a journal of their proceedings, and shall, from time to time, publish them: and the yeas and nays of the members of each House, on any question, shall, at the desire of one-fifth part of the members present, be entered on the journal.

Sect. 8. Neither House, without the consent of the other, shall adjourn for more than three days nor to any other place than that at which the two Houses are sitting. But this regulation shall not extend to the Senate, when it shall exercise the powers mentioned in the _____ article.

Sect. 9. The members of each House shall be ineligible to, and incapable of holding any office under the authority of the United States, during the time for which they shall respectively be elected: and the members of the Senate shall be ineligible to, and incapable of holding any such office for one year afterwards.

Sect. 10. The members of each House shall receive a compensation for their services, to be ascertained and paid by the State, in which they shall be chosen.

Sect. 11. The enacting stile of the laws of the United States shall be. "Be it enacted, and it is hereby enacted by the House of Representatives, and by the Senate of the United States, in Congress assembled."

Sect. 12. Each House shall possess the right of originating bills, except in the cases beforementioned.

Sect. 13. Every bill, which shall have passed the House of Representatives and the Senate, shall, before it become a law, be presented to the President of the United States, for his revision. If, upon such revision, he approve of it, he shall signify his approbation by signing it. But if, upon such revision, it shall appear to him improper for being passed into a law, he shall return it, together with his objections against it, to that House in which it shall have originated, who shall enter the objections at large on their Journal, and proceed to reconsider the bill. But if, after such reconsideration, two thirds of that House shall, notwithstanding the objections of the President, agree to pass it, it shall, together with his objections, be sent to the other House, by which it shall likewise be reconsidered, and, if approved by two thirds of the other House also, it shall become a law. But, in all such cases, the votes of both Houses shall be determined by Yeas and Nays; and the names of the persons voting for or against the bill shall be entered in the Journal of each House respectively. If any bill shall not be returned by the President within seven days after it shall have been presented to him, it shall be a law, unless the Legislature, by their adjournment, prevent its return; in which case it shall not be a law.

VII. Sect. 1. The Legislature of the United States shall have the power to lay and collect taxes, duties, imposts and excises;

To regulate commerce with foreign nations, and among the several States;

To establish an uniform rule of naturalization throughout the United States;

To coin money;

To regulate the value of foreign coin;

To fix the standard of weights and measures;

To establish post-offices;

To borrow money, and emit bills on the credit of the United States;

To appoint a Treasurer by ballot;

To constitute tribunals inferior to the supreme court;

To make rules concerning captures on land and water;

To declare the law and punishment of piracies and felonies committed on the high seas, and the punishment of counterfeiting the coin of the United States, and of offences against the law of nations;

To subdue a rebellion in any State, on the application of its Legislature;

To make war;

To raise armies;

To build and equip fleets;

To call forth the aid of the militia, in order to execute the laws of the Union, enforce treaties, suppress insurrections, and repel invasions;

And to make all laws that shall be necessary and proper for carrying into execution the foregoing powers, and all other powers vested, by this Constitution, in the government of the United States, or in any department or officer thereof.

Sect. 2. Treason against the United States shall consist only in levying war against the United States, or any of them; and in adhering to the enemies of the United States, or any of them. The Legislature of the United States shall have power to declare the punishment of treason. No person shall be convicted of treason, unless on the testimony of two witnesses. No attainder of treason shall work corruption of blood, nor forfeiture, except during the life of the person attainted.

Sect. 3. The proportions of direct taxation shall be regulated by the whole number of white and other free citizens and inhabitants, of every age, sex and condition, including those bound to servitude for a term of years, and three fifths of all other persons not comprehended in the foregoing description, (except Indians not paying taxes) which number shall, within six years after the first meeting of the Legislature, and within the term of every ten years afterwards, be taken in such manner as the said Legislature shall direct.

Sect. 4. No tax or duty shall be laid by the Legislature on articles exported from any State; nor on the migration or importation of such persons as the several States shall think proper to admit; nor shall such migration or importation be prohibited.

Sect. 5. No capitation tax shall be laid, unless in proportion to the census herein before directed to be taken.

Sect. 6. No navigation act shall be passed without the assent of two-thirds of the members present in each House.

Sect. 7. The United States shall not grant any title of nobility.

VIII. The acts of the Legislature of the United States made in pursuance of this constitution, and all treaties made under the authority of the United States shall be the supreme law of the several States, and of their citizens and inhabitants; and the judges in the several States shall be bound thereby in their decisions; any thing in the constitutions or laws of the several States to the contrary notwithstanding.

IX. Sect. 1. The Senate of the United States shall have power to make treaties, and to appoint ambassadors, and judges of the supreme court.

Sect. 2. In all disputes and controversies now subsisting, or that may hereafter subsist between two or more States, respecting jurisdiction or territory, the Senate shall possess the following powers. Whenever the Legislature, or the Executive authority, or the lawful agent of any State, in controversy with another, shall, by memorial to the Senate, state the matter in question, and apply for a hearing; notice of such memorial and application shall be given, by order of the Senate, to the Legislature or the Executive Authority of the other State in controversy. The Senate shall also assign a day for the appearance of the parties, by their agents, before that House. The agents shall be directed to appoint, by joint consent, commissioners or judges to constitute a court for hearing and determining the matter in question. But if the agents cannot agree, the Senate shall name three persons out of each of the several States, and from the list of such persons each party shall alternately strike out one, until the number shall be reduced to thirteen; and from that number not less than seven nor more than nine names, as the Senate shall direct, shall, in their presence, be drawn out by lot; and the persons, whose names shall be so drawn, or any five of them shall be commissioners or judges to hear and finally determine the controversy; provided a majority of the judges, who shall hear the cause, agree in the determination. If either party shall neglect to attend at the day assigned, without shewing sufficient reasons for not attending, or, being present, shall refuse to strike, the Senate shall proceed to nominate three persons out of each State, and the clerk of the Senate shall strike in behalf of the party absent or refusing. If any of the parties shall refuse to submit to the authority of such court; or shall not appear to prosecute or defend their claim or cause, the court shall nevertheless proceed to pronounce judgment. The judgment shall be final and conclusive. The proceedings shall be transmitted to the President of the Senate, and shall be lodged among the public records for the security of the parties concerned. Every commissioner shall, before he sit in judgment, take an oath, to be administered by one of the judges of the supreme or superior court of the State where the cause shall be tried, "well and truly to hear and determine the matter in question, according to the best of his judgment, without favour, affection, or hope of reward."

Sect. 3. All controversies concerning lands claimed under different grants of two or more States, whose jurisdictions, as they respect such lands, shall have been decided or adjusted subsequent to such grants, or any of them, shall, on application to the Senate, be finally determined, as near as may be, in the same manner as is before prescribed for deciding controversies between different States.

X. Sect. 1. The Executive Power of the United States shall be vested in a single person. His stile shall be, "The President of the United States of America;" and his title shall be, "His Excellency." He shall be elected by ballot by the Legislature. He shall hold his office during the term of seven years; but shall not be elected a second time.

Sect. 2. He shall, from time to time, give information to the Legislature of the State of the Union. He may recommend to their consideration such measures as he shall judge necessary, and expedient. He may convene them on extraordinary occasions. In case of disagreement between the two Houses, with regard to the time of adjournment, he may adjourn them to such time as he think proper. He shall take care that the laws of the United States be duly and faithfully executed. He shall commission all the officers of the United States; and shall appoint officers in all cases not otherwise provided for by this constitution. He shall receive Ambassadors, and may corre-

spond with the Supreme Executives of the several States. He shall
have power to grant reprieves and pardons; but his pardon shall
not be pleadable in bar of an impeachment. He shall be Commander
in Chief of the Army and Navy of the United States, and of the
Militia of the several States. He shall, at stated times, receive for
his services, a compensation, which shall neither be encreased nor
diminished during his continuance in office. Before he shall enter
on the duties of his department, he shall take the following Oath
or Affirmation, "I _____ solemnly swear (or affirm)
that I will faithfully execute the Office of President of the United
States of America." He shall be removed from his office on impeachment by the House of Representatives, and conviction in the
Supreme Court, of treason, bribery, or corruption. In case of his
removal as aforesaid, death, resignation, or disability to discharge
the powers and duties of his office, the President of the Senate shall
exercise those powers and duties until another President of the
United States be chosen, or until the disability of the President be
removed.

XI. Sect. 1. The Judicial Power of the United States shall be vested
in one Supreme Court, and in such Inferior Courts as shall, when
necessary, from time to time, be constituted by the Legislature of
the United States.

Sect. 2. The Judges of the Supreme Court, and of the Inferior
courts, shall hold their offices during good behaviour. They shall,
at stated times, receive for their services, a compensation, which
shall not be diminished during their continuance in office.

Sect. 3. The Jurisdiction of the Supreme Court shall extend to all
cases arising under laws passed by the Legislature of the United
States; to all cases affecting Ambassadors, other Public Ministers
and Consuls; to the trial of impeachments of Officers of the United
States; to all cases of Admiralty and Maritime Jurisdiction; to Controversies between two or more States (except such as shall regard
Territory or Jurisdiction) between a State and citizens of another
State, between citizens of different States, and between a State or
the citizens thereof and foreign States; citizens or subjects. In cases
of Impeachment, cases affecting Ambassadors, other Public Ministers
and Consuls, and those in which a State shall be party, this Jurisdiction shall be original. In all the other cases beforementioned, it
shall be appellate, with such exceptions and under such regulations
as the Legislature shall make. The Legislature may assign any
part of the jurisdiction abovementioned (except the trial of the
President of the United States) in the manner and under the limita-

tions which it shall think proper, to such Inferior Courts as it shall constitute from time to time.

Sect. 4. The trial of all criminal offences (except in cases of impeachments) shall be in the State where they shall be committed; and shall be by jury.

Sect. 5. Judgment, in cases of Impeachment, shall not extend further than to removal from office, and disqualification to hold and enjoy any office of honour, trust or profit under the United States. But the party convicted shall nevertheless be liable and subject to indictment, trial, judgment and punishment, according to law.

XII. No State shall coin money; nor grant letters of marque and reprisals; nor enter into any treaty, alliance, or confederation; nor grant any title of nobility.

XIII. No State, without the consent of the Legislature of the United States, shall emit bills of credit, or make any thing but specie a tender in payment of debts; lay imposts or duties on imports; nor keep troops or ships of war in time of peace; nor enter into any agreement or compact with another State, or with any foreign power; nor engage in any war, unless it shall be actually invaded by enemies, or the danger of invasion be so imminent, as not to admit of a delay, until the Legislature of the United States can be consulted.

XIV. The citizens of each State shall be entitled to all privileges and immunities of citizens in the several States.

XV. Any person charged with treason, felony, or high misdemeanor in any State, who shall flee from justice, and shall be found in any other State, shall, on demand of the Executive Power of the State from which he fled, be delivered up and removed to the State having jurisdiction of the offence.

XVI. Full faith shall be given in each State to the acts of the Legislatures, and to the records and judicial proceedings of the courts and magistrates of every other State.

XVII. New States lawfully constituted or established within the limits of the United States may be admitted, by the Legislature, into this government; but to such admission the consent of two thirds of the Members present in each House shall be necessary. If a new State shall arise within the limits of any of the present States, the consent of the Legislatures of such States shall be also necessary to its admission. If the admission be consented to, the new States shall be admitted on the same terms with the original States. But the

Legislature may make conditions with the new States concerning the public debt, which shall be then subsisting.

XVIII. The United States shall guaranty to each State a Republican form of government; and shall protect each State against foreign invasions, and, on the application of its Legislature, against domestic violence.

XIX. On the application of the Legislatures of two thirds of the States in the Union, for an amendment of this Constitution, the Legislature of the United States shall call a Convention for that purpose.

XX. The Members of the Legislatures, and the executive and judicial officers of the United States, and of the several States, shall be bound by oath to support this Constitution.

XXI. The ratification of the Conventions of _____ States shall be sufficient for organising this Constitution.

XXII. This Constitution shall be laid before the United States in Congress assembled, for their approbation; and it is the opinion of this Convention that it should be afterwards submitted to a Convention chosen in each State, under the recommendation of its Legislature, in order to receive the ratification of such Convention.

XXIII. To introduce this government, it is the opinion of this Convention, that each assenting Convention should notify its assent and ratification to the United States in Congress assembled; that Congress, after receiving the assent and ratification of the Conventions of _____ States, should appoint and publish a day, as early as may be, and appoint a place for commencing proceedings under this Constitution; that after such publication, the Legislatures of the several States should elect Members of the Senate, and direct the election of Members of the House of Representatives; and that the Members of the Legislature should meet at the time and place assigned by Congress, and should, as soon as may be, after their meeting, choose the President of the United States, and proceed to execute this Constitution.

1. Broadside (LT). None of the surviving copies of the printed report of the Committee of Detail are entirely legible. This document was transcribed from George Washington's copy (RCC, DNA), Abraham Baldwin's copy (NNPM), and Charles Cotesworth Pinckney's copy (Pinckney Family Papers, DLC). This document has been transcribed literally with three exceptions: Roman numerals have been placed at the beginning of paragraphs instead of being centered on the page; the abbreviation "Sect." has not been set in italic type; and the printer's misnumbering of Roman numerals after VI has been corrected.

H. AMENDED DRAFT CONSTITUTION SUBMITTED TO THE COMMITTEE OF STYLE, 10 September

John Rutledge, chairman of the Committee of Detail, submitted the draft constitution to the Convention on 6 August. Two days later the *Pennsylvania Herald* reported that the Convention was debating the plan by paragraphs, and a week later it reported that the debate on 13 August lasted until five o'clock. Both reports were widely reprinted, and thereafter newspapers hinted that the people could expect a new constitution. On 22 August, for instance, the *Pennsylvania Gazette* asked the states to adopt "the new frame of federal government."

The Convention debated the twenty-three provisions of the draft constitution item by item from 7 to 31 August, but postponed some items for later consideration. On 31 August it submitted the postponed items and other matters to a committee of which David Brearley, Chief Justice of New Jersey, was chairman. The committee finished its report, much of which concerned the election and powers of the President, by 5 September. The Convention completed action on this report by 8 September, when it elected a committee "to revise the style of and arrange the articles agreed to by the house." The Committee of Style consisted of William Samuel Johnson of Connecticut (chairman), Alexander Hamilton of New York, Gouverneur Morris of Pennsylvania, James Madison of Virginia, and Rufus King of Massachusetts.

However, some delegates demanded further consideration; and on Monday, 10 September, the Convention adopted additional resolutions concerning the amending process and pardons in cases of treason. An effort by Edmund Randolph to restore the requirement of congressional approval of the Constitution was not acted upon, although he was supported by Benjamin Franklin, Elbridge Gerry, Roger Sherman, and Alexander Hamilton. The Convention's final action on 10 September was to instruct the Committee of Style "to prepare an address to the people to accompany the present constitution, and to be laid with the same before the United States in Congress."

The basic document given to the Committee of Style by the Convention was probably George Washington's copy of the printed draft constitution of 6 August (RCC, DNA), annotated with amendments and word changes in the handwriting of Washington and William Jackson, Secretary of the Convention. This copy was among the papers of the Convention which President Washington delivered to the Secretary of State in 1796. It is likely, therefore, that it was used by the Committee of Style as a record of the alterations made in the Committee of Detail report by the Convention.

The text printed below is reconstructed from: (1) the draft constitution of 6 August (VII:G above); (2) the Journals of the Convention; and (3) James Madison's Notes of Debates. The material from these sources is transcribed literally.

To show how the draft constitution was altered by the Convention between 7 August and 10 September, the document is set in type as follows: (1) the parts of the draft retained are set in roman type;

(2) the parts of the draft deleted are set in lined-out type; and (3) the additions made by the Convention are set in italic type.

There are some differences in punctuation and capitalization between the Committee of Detail Report and the revisions placed in the Journals. In such cases we have followed the usage of the Journals.

We the People of the States of New-Hampshire, Massachusetts, Rhode-Island and Providence Plantations, Connecticut, New-York, New-Jersey, Pennsylvania, Delaware, Maryland, Virginia, North-Carolina, South Carolina, and Georgia, do ordain, declare and establish the following Constitution for the Government of Ourselves and our Posterity.

ARTICLE I. The stile of this Government shall be, "The United States of America."

II. The Government shall consist of supreme legislative, executive and judicial powers.

III. The legislative power shall be vested in a Congress, to consist of two separate and distinct bodies of men, a House of Representatives, and a Senate. ~~each of which shall, in all cases, have a negative on the other.~~ The Legislature shall meet *at least once in every year; and such meeting shall be* on the first monday in December ~~in every year~~ *unless a different day shall be appointed by law.*

IV. Sect. 1. The members of the House of Representatives shall be chosen every second year, by the people of the several States comprehended within this Union. The qualifications of the electors shall be the same, from time to time, as those of the electors in the several States, of the most numerous branch of their own legislatures.

Sect. 2. Every Member of the House of Representatives shall be of the age of twenty-five years at least; shall have been a citizen ~~in~~ *of* the United States for at least ~~three~~ *seven* years before his election; and shall be, at the time of his election, ~~a resident~~ *an inhabitant* of the State in which he shall be chosen.

Sect. 3. The House of Representatives shall, at its first formation, and until the number of citizens and inhabitants shall be taken in the manner herein after described, consist of sixty-five Members, of whom three shall be chosen in New-Hampshire, eight in Massachusetts, one in Rhode-Island and Providence Plantations, five in Connecticut, six in New-York, four in New-Jersey, eight in Pennsylvania, one in Delaware, six in Maryland, ten in Virginia, five in North-Carolina, five in South-Carolina, and three in Georgia.

Sect. 4. As the proportions of numbers in the different States will alter from time to time; as some of the States may hereafter be divided;

as others may be enlarged by addition of territory; as two or more States may be united; as new States will be erected within the limits of the United States, the Legislature shall, in each of these cases, regulate the number of representatives by the number of inhabitants, according to the ~~provisions~~ *rule* herein after made ~~at~~ *for direct taxation not exceeding* the rate of One for every forty thousand. *Provided that every State shall have at least one representative.*

~~Sect. 5. All bills for raising or appropriating money, and for fixing the salaries of the officers of government, shall originate in the House of Representatives; and shall not be altered or amended by the Senate. No money shall be drawn from the public Treasury, but in pursuance of appropriations that shall originate in the House of Representatives.~~

Sect. 6. The House of Representatives shall have the sole power of impeachment. It shall choose its Speaker and other officers.

Sect. 7. Vacancies in the House of Representatives shall be supplied by writs of election from the executive authority of the State, in the representation from which they shall happen.

V. Sect. 1. The Senate of the United States shall be chosen by the Legislatures of the several States. Each Legislature shall chuse two members. vacancies *happening by refusals to accept resignations or otherwise* may be supplied by the *Legislature of the State in the representation of which such vacancies shall happen or* by the executive *thereof* until the next meeting of the Legislature. Each member shall have one vote.

Sect. 2. The Senators shall be chosen for six years; but immediately after *they shall be assembled in consequence of* the first election they shall be divided, by lot, into three classes, as nearly as may be, numbered one, two and three. The seats of the members of the first class shall be vacated at the expiration of the second year, of the second class at the expiration of the fourth year, of the third class at the expiration of the sixth year, so that a third part of the members may be chosen every second year.

Sect. 3. Every member of the Senate shall be of the age of thirty years at least; shall have been a citizen ~~in~~ *of* the United States for at least ~~four~~ *nine* years before his election; and shall be, at the time of his election, ~~a resident~~ *an inhabitant* of the State for which he shall be chosen.

Sect. 4. The Senate shall chuse its own President and other officers.

VI. Sect. 1. The times and places and the manner of holding the elections of the members of each House shall be prescribed by the Legislature of each State *respectively*; but ~~their provisions concerning them~~ *regulations in each of the foregoing cases* may, at any time, be *made or* altered by the Legislature of the United States.

~~Sect. 2. The Legislature of the United States shall have authority to establish such uniform qualifications of the members of each house, with regard to property, as to the said Legislature shall seem expedient.~~

Sect. 3. In each House a majority of the members shall constitute a quorum to do business; but a smaller number may adjourn from day to day *and may be authorised to compel the attendance of absent members in such manner and under such penalties as each House may provide.*

Sect. 4. Each House shall be the judge of the elections, returns and qualifications of its own members.

Sect. 5. Freedom of speech and debate in the Legislature shall not be impeached or questioned in any court or place out of the Legislature; and the members of each House shall, in all cases, except treason, felony and breach of the peace, be privileged from arrest during their attendance at Congress, and in going to and returning from it.

Sect. 6. Each House may determine the rules of its proceedings; may punish its members for disorderly behaviour; and may expel a member *with the concurrence of two thirds.*

Sect. 7. The House of Representatives, and the Senate, ~~when it shall be acting in a legislative capacity,~~ shall keep a journal of their proceedings, and shall, from time to time, publish them *except such parts thereof as in their judgment require secrecy* and the yeas and nays of the members of each House, on any question, shall, at the desire of one-fifth part of the members present, be entered on the journal.

Sect. 8. *During the session of the Legislature* neither House, without the consent of the other, shall adjourn for more than three days nor to any other place than that at which the two Houses are sitting. ~~But this regulation shall not extend to the Senate, when it shall exercise the powers mentioned in the_____article.~~

Sect. 9. The Members of each House shall be ineligible to ~~and incapable of holding~~ any *civil* office under the authority of the United States *created, or the emoluments whereof shall have been encreased* during the time for which they shall respectively be elected: ~~and the members of the Senate shall be ineligible to, and incapable of holding any such office for one year afterwards.~~ *and no person holding any office under the United States shall be a Member of either House during his continuance in Office.*

Sect. 10. The members of each House shall receive a compensation for the services, to be ~~ascertained and~~ paid ~~by the State, in which they shall be chosen~~ *out of the Treasury of the United States to be ascertained by law.*

Sect. 11. The enacting stile of the laws of the United States shall be. "Be it enacted, ~~and it is hereby enacted by the House of Representatives, and~~ by the Senate ~~of the United States,~~ *and Representatives in Congress assembled.*"

Sect. 12. ~~Each House shall possess the right of originating bills, except in the cases beforementioned.~~ *all Bills for raising revenue shall originate in the House of representatives: but the Senate may propose or concur with amendments as on other bills. no money shall be drawn from the Treasury but in consequence of appropriations made by law.*

Sect. 13. Every bill, which shall have passed the House of Representatives and the Senate, shall, before it become a law, be presented to the President of the United States, for his revision. If, upon such revision, he approve of it, he shall signify his approbation by signing it. But if, upon such revision, it shall appear to him improper for being passed into a law, he shall return it, together with his objections against it, to that House in which it shall have originated, who shall enter the objections at large on their Journal, and proceed to reconsider the bill. But if, after such reconsideration, ~~two thirds~~ *three fourths* of that House shall, notwithstanding the objections of the President, agree to pass it, it shall, together with his objections, be sent to the other House, by which it shall likewise be reconsidered, and, if approved by ~~two thirds~~ *three fourths* of the other House also, it shall become a law. But, in all such cases, the votes of both Houses shall be determined by Yeas and Nays; and the names of the persons voting for or against the bill shall be entered in the Journal of each House respectively. If any bill shall not be returned by the President within ~~seven~~ *ten* days (*sundays excepted*) after it shall have been presented to him, it shall be a law, unless the Legislature, by their adjournment, prevent its return; in which case it shall not be a law.

Sect. 14. every order, resolution or vote, to which the concurrence of the Senate and House of representatives may be necessary (except on a question of adjournment, and in the cases hereinafter mentioned) shall be presented to the President for his revision; and before the same shall have force, shall be approved by him, or, being disapproved by him, shall be repassed by the Senate and House of representatives, according to the rules and limitations prescribed in the case "of a bill."

VII. Sect. 1. The Legislature ~~of the United States~~ shall have ~~the~~ power to lay and collect taxes, duties, imposts, and excises, *to pay the debts and provide for the common defence and general welfare of the United States.*

To regulate commerce with foreign nations, and among the several States; *and with the Indian tribes.*

To establish an uniform rule of naturalization throughout the United States;

To coin money;

To regulate the value of foreign coin;

To fix the standard of weights and measures;

To establish post-offices; *and post roads;*

To borrow money, ~~and emit bills~~ on the credit of the United States;

To appoint a Treasurer by *joint* ballot;

To constitute tribunals inferior to the supreme court;

To make rules concerning captures on land and water;

To ~~declare the law and punishment of~~ *define and punish* piracies and felonies committed on the high seas ~~and the punishment of~~ *To punish the* counterfeiting *of* the *securities and current* coin of the United States, and ~~of~~ offences against the law of nations;

~~To subdue a rebellion in any State, on the application of its Legislature;~~

To ~~make~~ *declare* war; *and grant letters of marque and reprisal.*

To raise *and support* armies; *But no appropriation of money to that use shall be for a longer term than two years.*

~~To build and equip fleets;~~ *provide and maintain a navy;*

To make rules for the government and regulation of the land and naval forces.

To ~~call~~ *provide for calling* forth the ~~aid of~~ militia ~~in order~~ to execute the laws of the Union, ~~enforce treaties,~~ suppress insurrections, and repel invasions;

To make laws for organizing, arming, and disciplining the militia, and for governing such part of them as may be employed in the service of the United States, reserving to the States, respectively, the appointment of the Officers, and the authority of training the militia according to the discipline prescribed by the United States.

To establish uniform laws on the subject of bankruptcies.

To exercise exclusive legislation in all cases whatsoever over such district (not exceeding ten miles square) as may by cession of particular States and the acceptance of the Legislature become the seat of the Government of the United States, and to exercise like authority over all Places purchased by the consent of the Legislature of the State for the erection of Forts, Magazines, Arsenals, Dock Yards and other needful buildings.

To promote the progress of science and useful arts by securing for limited times to Authors and Inventors the exclusive right to their respective writings and discoveries.

And to make all laws that shall be necessary and proper for carrying into execution the foregoing powers, and all other powers vested, by this Constitution, in the government of the United States, or in any department or officer thereof.

all debts contracted and engagements entered into, by or under the authority of Congress shall be as valid against the United States under this constitution as under the confederation.

Sect. 2. Treason against the United States shall consist only in levying war against ~~the United States, or any of~~ them, ~~and~~ *or* in adhering to ~~the~~ *their* enemies ~~of the United States, or any of them.~~ *giving them aid and comfort.* The Legislature ~~of the United States~~ shall have power to declare the punishment of treason. No person shall be convicted of treason, unless on the testimony of two witnesses *to the same overt-act or on confession in open court.* No attainder of treason shall work corruption of blood, nor forfeiture, except during the life of the person attainted. *The Legislature shall pass no bill of attainder, nor any ex post facto laws.*

Sect. 3. The proportions of direct taxation shall be regulated by the whole number of ~~white and other~~ free citizens and inhabitants, of every age, sex and condition, including those bound to servitude for a term of years, and three fifths of all other persons not comprehended in the foregoing description, (except Indians not paying taxes) which number shall, within ~~six~~ *three* years after the first meeting of the Legislature, and within the term of every ten years afterwards, be taken in such manner as the said Legislature shall direct.

Sect. 4. No tax or duty shall be laid by the Legislature on articles exported from any State. ~~nor on~~ The migration or importation of such persons as the several States *now existing* shall think proper to admit ~~nor~~ shall ~~such migration or importation~~ *not* be prohibited *by the Legislature prior to the year 1808. but a tax or duty may be imposed on such importation not exceeding ten dollars for each person nor shall any regulation of commerce or revenue give preference to the ports of One State over those of another or oblige Vessels bound to or from any State to enter clear or pay duties in another.*

and all duties, imposts, and excises, laid by the Legislature, shall be uniform throughout the United States.

Sect. 5. No capitation tax shall be laid, unless in proportion to the census herein before directed to be taken.

~~Sect. 6. No navigation act shall be passed without the assent of two-thirds of the members present in each House.~~

Sect. 7. The United States shall not grant any title of nobility. *No person holding any office of profit or trust under the United States, shall without the consent of the Legislature accept of any present, emolument, office, or title of any kind whatever, from any king, prince or foreign State.*

VIII. ~~The acts of the Legislature~~ *This Constitution and the Laws* of the United States, *which shall be* made in pursuance ~~of this constitution,~~ *thereof* and all treaties made *or which shall be made* under the authority of the United-States shall be the supreme law of the several States, and of their citizens and inhabitants; and the Judges in the several States shall be bound thereby in their decisions; any thing in the constitutions or laws of the several States to the contrary notwithstanding.

IX. Sect. 1. The Senate of the United States shall have power to ~~make treaties, and to appoint ambassadors, and judges of the supreme court.~~ *try all impeachments: but no person shall be convicted without the concurrence of two thirds of the Members present: and every Member shall be on oath.*

~~Sect. 2. In all disputes and controversies now subsisting, or that may hereafter subsist between two or more States, respecting jurisdiction or territory, the Senate shall possess the following powers. Whenever the Legislature, or the Executive authority, or the lawful agent of any State, in controversy with another, shall, by memorial to the Senate, state the matter in question, and apply for a hearing; notice of such memorial and application shall be given, by order of the Senate, to the Legislature or the Executive Authority of the other State in controversy. The Senate shall also assign a day for the appearance of the parties, by their agents, before that House. The agents shall be directed to appoint, by joint consent, commissioners or judges to constitute a court for hearing and determining the matter in question. But if the agents cannot agree, the Senate shall name three persons out of each of the several States, and from the list of such persons each party shall alternately strike out one, until the number shall be reduced to thirteen; and from that number not less than seven nor more than nine names, as the Senate shall direct, shall, in their presence, be drawn out by lot; and the persons, whose names shall be so drawn, or any five of them shall be commissioners or judges to hear and finally determine the controversy; provided a majority of the judges, who shall hear the cause, agree in the determination. If either party shall neglect to attend at the day assigned, without shewing sufficient reasons for not attending, or, being present, shall refuse to strike, the Senate shall proceed to nominate three persons out of each State, and the clerk of the Senate shall strike in behalf of the party absent or refusing. If any of the parties shall refuse to submit to the authority of such court; or shall not appear to prosecute or defend their claim or cause, the court shall nevertheless proceed to pronounce judgment. The judgment shall be final and conclusive. The proceedings~~

~~shall be transmitted to the President of the Senate, and shall be lodged~~
~~among the public records for the security of the parties concerned.~~
~~Every commissioner shall, before he sit in judgment, take an oath,~~
~~to be administered by one of the judges of the supreme or superior~~
~~court of the State where the cause shall be tried, "well and truly to~~
~~hear and determine the matter in question, according to the best of~~
~~his judgment, without favour, affection, or hope of reward."~~

~~Sect. 3. All controversies concerning lands claimed under different~~
~~grants of two or more States, whose jurisdictions, as they respect such~~
~~lands, shall have been decided or adjusted subsequent to such grants,~~
~~or any of them, shall, on application to the Senate, be finally deter-~~
~~mined, as near as may be, in the same manner as is before prescribed~~
~~for deciding controversies between different States.~~

X. Sect. 1. The Executive Power of the United States shall be vested
in a single person. His stile shall be, "The President of the United
States of America;" and his title shall be, "His Excellency." ~~He shall~~
~~be elected by ballot by the Legislature.~~ He shall hold his office during
the term of ~~seven~~ *four* years, ~~but shall not be elected a second time.~~
and together with the Vice President, chosen for the same term, be
elected in the following manner.

Each State shall appoint, in such manner as it's legislature may
direct, a number of Electors equal to the whole number of Senators
and Members of the House of representatives to which the State may
be entitled in the Legislature. But no Person shall be appointed an
Elector who is a member of the Legislature of the United States, or
who holds any office of profit or trust under the United States.

The Electors shall meet in their respective States and vote by ballot
for two Persons of whom one at least shall not be an inhabitant of
the same State with themselves.—and they shall make a list of all the
Persons voted for, and of the number of votes for each, which list they
shall sign and certify, and transmit sealed to the seat of the general
Government, directed to the President of the Senate.

The President of the Senate shall in the presence of the Senate and
House of representatives open all the certificates and the votes shall
then be counted.

The Person having the greatest number of votes shall be the Presi-
dent (if such number be a majority of the whole number of the Electors
appointed) and if there be more than one who have such majority,
and have an equal number of votes, then the House of representatives
shall immediately choose by ballot one of them for President, the
representation from each State having one vote—But if no Person
have a majority, then from the five highest on the list, the House of

*representatives shall, in like manner, choose by ballot the President—
In the choice of a President by the House of representatives a quorum
shall consist of a Member or Members from two thirds of the States.
and the concurrence of a majority of all the States, shall be necessary
to such choice.—and, in every case after the choice of the President,
the Person having the greatest number of votes of the Electors shall
be the vice-President: But, if there should remain two or more who
have equal votes, the Senate shall choose from them the Vice President.
The Legislature may determine the time of chusing the Electors and
of their giving their votes: and the manner of certifying and transmitting their votes—But the election shall be on the same day throughout the United States.*

*The Legislature may declare by law what officer of the United
States shall act as President in case of the death, resignation, or disability of the President and Vice President; and such Officer shall act
accordingly, until such disability be removed, or a President shall be
elected.*

*Sect. 2. No person except a natural born Citizen, or a Citizen of the
U.S. at the time of the adoption of this Constitution shall be eligible
to the office of President: nor shall any Person be elected to that
office, who shall be under the age of 35 years, and who has not been
in the whole, at least 14 years a resident within the U. S.*

*Sect. 3. The Vice President shall be ex officio, President of the
Senate, except when they sit to try the impeachment of the President,
in which case the Chief Justice shall preside, and excepting also when
he shall exercise the powers and duties of President, in which case,
and in case of his absence, the Senate shall chuse a President pro
tempore—The Vice President when acting as President of the Senate
shall not have a vote unless the House be equally divided.*

*Sect. 4. The President by and with the advice and consent of the
Senate, shall have power to make treaties: and he shall nominate
and by and with the advice and consent of the Senate shall appoint
Ambassadors other public Ministers, and Consuls, Judges of the supreme Court, and all other officers of the U.S. whose appointments
are not otherwise herein provided for. But no Treaty shall be made
without the consent of two thirds of the Members present.*

*That the President shall have power to fill up all vacancies that
may happen during the recess of the Senate by granting commissions
which shall expire at the end of the next session of the Senate.*

Sect. 2. [5] He shall, from time to time, give ~~information~~ to the
Legislature *information* of the State of the Union. ~~He may~~ *and*
recommend to their consideration such measures as he shall judge
necessary, and expedient. He may convene ~~them~~ *both or either of*

the Houses on extraordinary occasions, *and* in case of disagreement between the two Houses, with regard to the time of adjournment, he may adjourn them to such time as he *shall* think proper. He shall take care that the laws of the United States be duly and faithfully executed. He shall commission all the officers of the United States; and shall appoint ~~officers in~~ *to* all ~~cases not~~ *offices established by this Constitution, except in cases herein* otherwise provided for ~~by this Constitution~~ *and to all offices which may here after be created by law.* He shall receive Ambassadors, ~~and may correspond with the Supreme Executives of the several States,~~ *and other public Ministers.* He shall have power to grant reprieves and pardons, ~~but his pardon shall not be pleadable in bar of an~~*except in cases of* impeachment. He shall be Commander in Chief of the Army and Navy of the United States, and of the militia of the several States *when called into the actual service of the United States; and may require the opinion in writing of the principal officer in each of the executive departments, upon any subject relating to the duties of their respective offices.* He shall, at stated times, receive for his services, a compensation, which shall neither be encreased nor diminished during his continuance in office. Before he shall enter on the duties of his department, he shall take the following Oath or Affirmation, "I _____ solemnly swear (or affirm) that I will faithfully execute the Office of President of the United States of America, *and will to the best of my judgment and power, preserve, protect and defend the Constitution of the United States.*" He shall be removed from his office on impeachment by the House of representatives, and conviction ~~in~~ *by* the ~~Supreme Court~~ *Senate,* ~~of~~ *for* treason *or* bribery, ~~or corruption~~ *or other high crimes and misdemeanors against the United States; the Vice President and other civil Officers of the United States shall be removed from Office on impeachment and conviction as aforesaid; and* in case of his removal as aforesaid, death, *absence,* resignation or ~~disability~~ *inability* to discharge the powers ~~and~~ *or* duties of his office ~~the President of the Senate~~ *the Vice President* shall exercise those powers and duties until another President ~~of the United States~~ be chosen, or until the ~~disability~~ *inability* of the President be removed.

XI. Sect. 1. The Judicial Power of the United States *both in Law and Equity* shall be vested in one Supreme Court, and in such Inferior Courts as shall, when necessary, from time to time, be constituted by the Legislature of the United States.

Sect. 2. The Judges of the Supreme Court, and of the Inferior courts, shall hold their offices during good behaviour. They shall, at stated times, receive for their services, a compensation, which shall not be diminished during their continuance in office.

Sect. 3. The ~~Jurisdiction of the Supreme Court~~ *Judicial Power* shall extend to all cases *both in law and equity* arising under *this constitution the* laws ~~passed by the Legislature~~ of the United States; *and treaties made or which shall be made under their authority*; to all cases affecting Ambassadors, other Public Ministers and Consuls; to the trial of impeachments of Officers of the United States; to all cases of Admiralty and Maritime Jurisdiction; to Controversies *to which the United States shall be a Party, controversies* between two or more States (except such as shall regard Territory or Jurisdiction) between a State and citizens of another State, between citizens of different States, *between Citizens of the same State claiming lands under grants of different States,* and between a State or the citizens thereof and foreign States; citizens or subjects. In cases of impeachment, cases affecting Ambassadors, other Public Ministers and Consuls, and those in which a State shall be Party, ~~this Jurisdiction~~ *the supreme Court* shall ~~be~~ *have* original *jurisdiction.* In all the other cases before mentioned, ~~it~~ *the Supreme Court* shall ~~be~~ *have* appellate *jurisdiction both as to law and fact* with such exceptions and under such regulations as the Legislature shall make. ~~The Legislature may assign any part of the jurisdiction abovementioned (except the trial of the President of the United States) in the manner and under the limitations which it shall think proper, to such Inferior Courts as it shall constitute from time to time.~~

Sect. 4. The trial of all ~~criminal offences~~ *crimes* (except in cases of impeachments) ~~shall be in the State where they shall be committed; and~~ shall be by Jury—*and such trial shall be held in the State where the said crimes shall have been committed; but when not committed within any State then the trial shall be at such place or places as the Legislature may direct.*

The privilege of the writ of Habeas Corpus shall not be suspended; unless where in cases of rebellion or invasion the public safety may require it.

Sect. 5. Judgment, in cases of Impeachment, shall not extend further than to removal from office, and disqualification to hold and enjoy any office of honour, trust or profit under the United States. But the party convicted shall nevertheless be liable and subject to indictment, trial, judgment and punishment, according to law.

XII. No State shall coin money *nor emit bills of credit nor make any thing but gold and silver coin a tender in payment of debts nor pass any bill of attainder or ex post facto laws* nor grant letters of marque and reprisals; nor enter into any treaty, alliance, or confederation; nor grant any title of nobility.

XIII. No State, without the consent of the Legislature of the United States, shall ~~emit bills of credit, or make any thing but specie a tender in payment of debts~~ lay imposts or duties on imports *or exports nor with such consent but for the use of the treasury of the United States;* nor keep troops or ships of war in time of peace; nor enter into any agreement or compact with another State, or with any foreign power; nor engage in any war, unless it shall be actually invaded by enemies, or the danger of invasion be so imminent, as not to admit of a delay, until the Legislature of the United States can be consulted.

XIV. The citizens of each State shall be entitled to all privileges and immunities of citizens in the several States.

XV. Any person charged with treason, felony, or ~~high misdemeanor~~ *other crime* in any State, who shall flee from justice, and shall be found in any other State, shall, on demand of the Executive Power of the State from which he fled, be delivered up and removed to the State having jurisdiction of the offence.
If any Person bound to service or labor in any of the United States shall escape into another State, He or She shall not be discharged from such service or labor in consequence of any regulations subsisting in the State to which they escape; but shall be delivered up to the person justly claiming their service or labor.

XVI. Full faith *and credit* shall be given in each State to the *public* Acts, ~~of the Legislatures,~~ and to the records, and judicial proceedings ~~of the courts and magistrates~~ of every other State, *and the Legislature may by general laws prescribe the manner in which such acts, records, and proceedings shall be proved and the effect thereof.*

XVII. New States ~~lawfully constituted or established within the limits of the United States~~ may be admitted by the Legislature into this ~~government~~ *Union*: ~~but to such admission the consent of two thirds of the Members present in each House shall be necessary. If a new State shall arise within the limits of any of the present States, the consent of the Legislatures of such States shall be also necessary to its admission. If the admission be consented to, the new States shall be admitted on the same terms with the original States. But the Legislature may make conditions with the new States concerning the public debt, which shall be then subsisting~~ *but no new State shall be hereafter formed or erected within the jurisdiction of any of the present States without the consent of the Legislature of such State as well as of the general Legislature. Nor shall any State be formed by the junction of two or more States or parts thereof without the consent of the Legislatures of such States as well as of the Legislature of the United States.*

The Legislature shall have power to dispose of and make all needful rules and regulations respecting the territory or other property belonging to the United States: and nothing in this Constitution contained shall be so construed as to prejudice any claims either of the United States or of any particular State.

XVIII. The United States shall guaranty to each State a Republican form of government; and shall protect each State against ~~foreign~~ invasions, and, on the application of its Legislature *or Executive,* against domestic violence.

XIX. ~~On the application of the Legislatures of two thirds of the States in the Union, for an amendment of this Constitution, the Legislature of the United States shall call a Convention for that purpose.~~
The Legislature of the United States, whenever two thirds of both Houses shall deem necessary, or on the application of two thirds of the Legislatures of the several States, shall propose amendments to this Constitution which shall be valid to all intents and purposes as part thereof, when the same shall have been ratified by three fourths at least of the Legislatures of the several States, or by Conventions in three fourths thereof, as one or the other mode of ratification may be proposed by the Legislatures of the United-States: Provided that no amendments which may be made prior to the year 1808. shall in any manner affect the 4th and 5th Sections of article the 7th.

XX. The Members of the Legislatures, and the executive and judicial officers of the United States, and of the several States, shall be bound by oath *or affirmation* to support this Constitution.
But no religious test shall ever be required as a qualification to any office or public trust under the authority of the United States.

XXI. The ratification of the Conventions of *nine* States shall be sufficient for organising this Constitution *between the said States.*

XXII. This Constitution shall be laid before the United States in Congress assembled, ~~for their approbation;~~ and it is the opinion of this Convention that it should be afterwards submitted to a Convention chosen in each State, under the recommendation of its Legislature, in order to receive the ratification of such Convention.

XXIII. To introduce this government, it is the opinion of this Convention, that each assenting Convention should notify its assent and ratification to the United States in Congress assembled; that Congress, after receiving the assent and ratification of the Conventions of *nine* States, should appoint and publish a day, as early as may be, and appoint a place for commencing proceedings under this Constitution; that after such publication, the Legislatures of the several States should elect Members of the Senate, and direct the election of Members of the House of Representatives; and that the Members of the Legislature should meet at the time and place assigned by Congress, and should, as soon as may be, after their meeting, ~~choose the President of the United States,~~ and proceed to execute this Constitution.

Additional Proceedings Referred to the Committee of Style, 10 September

That it be an instruction to the Committee to prepare an address to the People to accompany the present constitution, and to be laid with the same before the United States in Congress.[1]

Mr. Randolph moved to refer to the Committee also a motion relating to pardons in cases of Treason—which was agreed to nem: con:[2]

1. (LT), Farrand, II, 556–57. No address to the people was prepared, but a letter addressed to the President of Congress was drafted by the Committee and presented to the Convention on 12 September.

2. (LT), Farrand, II, 564. Randolph apparently wanted to deny the President the power to grant pardons in cases of treason. However, the committee draft provided that, except in cases of impeachment, the President had the power to grant pardons and reprieves for "offences against the United States." Randolph moved on 15 September that the President be denied the power to grant pardons in cases of treason, but the motion failed eight states to two, with one state divided (Farrand, II, 626–27).

I. DRAFT CONSTITUTION BY THE COMMITTEE OF STYLE, AS AMENDED BY THE CONVENTION, 12–17 September

William Samuel Johnson presented the report of the Committee of Style to the Convention on 12 September. Many years later, James Madison said that Gouverneur Morris put the *"finish"* on the report (to Jared Sparks, 8 April 1831, Farrand, III, 499). The document was read, ordered printed, and the four-page broadside was given to each delegate the following morning.

The Committee of Style reduced the twenty-three articles and forty sections of the revised report of the Committee of Detail to seven articles and twenty-one sections, and rearranged some clauses. The Committee made only a few substantive changes. Perhaps the most significant alteration was in the Preamble, which had not been discussed previously by the Convention. The Committee changed the phrase "We the People of the States of New-Hampshire, Massachusetts," etc., to read "WE, the People of the United States. . . ."

The Committee also submitted the draft of a letter to accompany the Constitution and two resolutions to replace articles XXII and XXIII of the revised report of the Committee of Detail. The letter, in the handwriting of Gouverneur Morris (RCC, DNA), was read and agreed to by paragraphs on 12 September. The next day the Convention postponed consideration of the two resolutions, and there is no indication that they were considered again. However, they were sent to the Confederation Congress with the Constitution and the letter.

The Convention made several changes in the report of the Committee of Style between 12 and 17 September. The Convention (1) restored the two-thirds rule for overriding presidential vetoes; (2) permitted states to levy export duties to execute their inspection laws, subject to the revision and control of Congress; (3) deleted the power of Congress to appoint a treasurer; (4) expanded the concept of direct taxes to include more than a capitation tax; (5) prohibited Congress from favoring the ports of one state over those of another; and (6) changed the apportionment of Representatives from one for forty thousand to one for thirty thousand according to the method prescribed in the Constitution. This last change was made on 17 September after the Constitution had been engrossed, but before the engrossed copy was agreed to and signed.

The Convention rejected other proposed alterations. Some of the defeated motions were (1) to appoint a committee to prepare a bill of rights; (2) to declare "that the liberty of the press should be inviolably observed;" (3) to require a two-thirds vote of Congress for the passage of navigation acts before 1808; (4) to give an additional Representative each to North Carolina and Rhode Island; (5) to give Congress the power to grant charters of incorporation to construct canals; (6) to give Congress the power to establish a nonsectarian national university; and (7) to appoint a committee to draft an address to the people of the United States to accompany the Constitution.

In the document printed below, the changes made by the Convention were determined by comparing the printed copy of the Committee of Style report (Rufus King's copy, photostat, DLC) with the engrossed Constitution. The material is transcribed literally. The document is set in type as follows: (1) the parts of the report left unchanged by the Convention are set in roman type; (2) the parts of the report deleted by the Convention are set in lined-out type; and (3) the additions and changes made by the Convention are set in italic type.

WE, the People of the United States, in order to form a more perfect union, to establish justice, insure domestic tranquility, provide for the common defence, promote the general welfare, and secure the blessings of liberty to ourselves and our posterity, do ordain and establish this Constitution for the United States of America.

ARTICLE I.

Sect. 1. ALL legislative powers herein granted shall be vested in a Congress of the United States, which shall consist of a Senate and House of Representatives.

Sect. 2. The House of Representatives shall be composed of members chosen every second year by the people of the several states, and the electors in each state shall have the qualifications requisite for electors of the most numerous branch of the state legislature.

No person shall be a representative who shall not have attained to the age of twenty-five years, and been seven years a citizen of the United States, and who shall not, when elected, be an inhabitant of that state in which he shall be chosen.

Representatives and direct taxes shall be apportioned among the several states which may be included within this Union, according to their respective numbers, which shall be determined by adding to the whole number of free persons, including those bound to ~~servitude~~ *Service* for a term of years, and excluding Indians not taxed, three-fifths of all other persons. The actual enumeration shall be made within three years after the first meeting of the Congress of the United States, and within every subsequent term of ten years, in such manner as they shall by law direct. The number of representatives shall not exceed one for every ~~forty~~ *thirty* thousand, but each state shall have at least one representative: and until such enumeration shall be made, the state of New-Hampshire shall be entitled to chuse three, Massachusetts eight, Rhode-Island and Providence Plantations one, Connecticut five, New-York six, New-Jersey four, Pennsylvania eight, Delaware one, Maryland six, Virginia ten, North-Carolina five, South-Carolina five, and Georgia three.

When vacancies happen in the representation from any state, the Executive authority thereof shall issue writs of election to fill such vacancies.

The House of Representatives shall choose their Speaker and other officers; and ~~they~~ shall have the sole power of impeachment.

Sect. 3. The Senate of the United States shall be composed of two senators from each state, chosen by the legislature thereof, for six years: and each senator shall have one vote.

Immediately after they shall be assembled in consequence of the first election, they shall be divided as equally as may be into three classes. The seats of the senators of the first class shall be vacated at the expiration of the second year, of the second class at the expiration of the fourth year, and of the third class at the expiration of the sixth year, so that one-third may be chosen every second year: and if vacancies happen by resignation, or otherwise, during the recess of the Legislature of any state, the Executive thereof may make temporary appointments until the next meeting of the Legislature, *which shall then fill such Vacancies.*

No person shall be a senator who shall not have attained to the age of thirty years, and been nine years a citizen of the United States, and who shall not, when elected, be an inhabitant of that state for which he shall be chosen.

The Vice-President of the United States shall be, ~~ex officio~~, President of the senate, but shall have no vote, unless they be equally divided.

The Senate shall choose their other officers, and also a President pro tempore, in the absence of the Vice-President, or when he shall exercise the office of President of the United States.

The Senate shall have the sole power to try all impeachments. When sitting for that purpose, they shall be on oath *or Affirmation*. When the President of the United States is tried, the Chief Justice shall preside: And no person shall be convicted without the concurrence of two-thirds of the members present.

Judgment in cases of impeachment shall not extend further than to removal from office, and disqualification to hold and enjoy any office of honor, trust or profit under the United States: but the party convicted shall nevertheless be liable and subject to indictment, trial, judgment and punishment, according to law.

Sect. 4. The times, places and manner of holding elections for senators and representatives, shall be prescribed in each state by the legislature thereof: but the Congress may at any time by law make or alter such regulations, *except as to the Places of chusing Senators.*

The Congress shall assemble at least once in every year, and such meeting shall be on the first Monday in December, unless they shall by law appoint a different day.

Sect. 5. Each house shall be the judge of the elections, returns and qualifications of its own members, and a majority of each shall constitute a quorum to do business: but a smaller number may adjourn from day to day, and may be authorised to compel the attendance of absent members, in such manner, and under such penalties as each house may provide.

Each house may determine the rules of its proceedings; punish its members for disorderly behaviour, and, with the concurrence of two-thirds, expel a member.

Each house shall keep a journal of its proceedings, and from time to time publish the same, excepting such parts as may in their judgment require secrecy; and the yeas and nays of the members of either house on any question shall, at the desire of one-fifth of those present, be entered on the journal.

Neither house, during the session of Congress, shall, without the consent of the other, adjourn for more than three days, nor to any other place than that in which the two houses shall be sitting.

Sect. 6. The senators and representatives shall receive a compensation for their services, to be ascertained by law, and paid out of the treasury of the United States. They shall in all cases, except treason, felony and breach of the peace, be privileged from arrest during their attendance at the session of their respective houses, and in going to and returning from the same; and for any speech or debate in either house, they shall not be questioned in any other place.

No senator or representative shall, during the time for which he was elected, be appointed to any civil office under the authority of the United States, which shall have been created, or the emoluments whereof shall have been encreased during such time; and no person holding any office under the United States, shall be a member of either house during his continuance in office.

Sect. 7. ~~The enacting stile of the laws shall be, "Be it enacted by the senators and representatives in Congress assembled."~~

All bills for raising revenue shall originate in the house of representatives: but the senate may propose or concur with amendments as on other bills.

Every bill which shall have passed the house of representatives and the senate, shall, before it become a law, be presented to the president of the United States. If he approve he shall sign it, but if not he shall return it, with his objections to that house in which it shall have originated, who shall enter the objections at large on their journal, and proceed to reconsider it. If after such reconsideration two-thirds of that house shall agree to pass the bill, it shall be sent, together with the objections, to the other house, by which it shall likewise be reconsidered, and if approved by two-thirds of that house, it shall become a law. But in all such cases the votes of both houses shall be determined by yeas and nays, and the names of the persons voting for and against the bill shall be entered on the journal of each house respectively. If any bill shall not be returned by the President within ten days (Sundays excepted) after it shall have been presented to him, the same shall be a law, in like manner as if he had signed it, unless the Congress by their adjournment prevent its return, in which case it shall not be a law.

Every order, resolution, or vote to which the concurrence of the Senate and House of Representatives may be necessary (except on a question of adjournment) shall be presented to the President of the United States; and before the same shall take effect, shall be approved by him, or, being disapproved by him, shall be repassed by ~~three-~~

~~fourths~~ *two thirds* of the Senate and House of Representatives, according to the rules and limitations prescribed in the case of a bill.

Sect. 8. The Congress ~~may by joint ballot appoint a treasurer. They~~ shall have power

To lay and collect taxes, duties, imposts and excises; to pay the debts and provide for the common defence and general welfare of the United States; *but all Duties, Imposts and Excises shall be uniform throughout the United States*;

To borrow money on the credit of the United States.

To regulate commerce with foreign nations, *and* among the several states, and with the Indian tribes.

To establish an uniform rule of naturalization, and uniform laws on the subject of bankruptcies throughout the United States.

To coin money, regulate the value thereof, and of foreign coin, and fix the standard of weights and measures.

To provide for the punishment of counterfeiting the securities and current coin of the United States.

To establish post offices and post roads.

To promote the progress of science and useful arts, by securing for limited times to authors and inventors the exclusive right to their respective writings and discoveries.

To constitute tribunals inferior to the supreme court.

To define and punish piracies and felonies committed on the high seas, and offences against the law of nations.

To declare war, grant letters of marque and reprisal, and make rules concerning captures on land and water.

To raise and support armies: but no appropriation of money to that use shall be for a longer term than two years.

To provide and maintain a navy.

To make rules for the government and regulation of the land and naval forces.

To provide for calling forth the militia to execute the laws of the union, suppress insurrections and repel invasions.

To provide for organizing, arming and disciplining the militia, and for governing such part of them as may be employed in the service of the United States, reserving to the States respectively, the appointment of the officers, and the authority of training the militia according to the discipline prescribed by Congress.

To exercise exclusive legislation in all cases whatsoever, over such district (not exceeding ten miles square) as may, by cession of particular States, and the acceptance of Congress, become the seat of the government of the United States, and to exercise like authority over all places purchased by the consent of the legislature of the state in which the same shall be, for the erection of forts, magazines, arsenals, dockyards, and other needful buildings—And

To make all laws which shall be necessary and proper for carrying into execution the foregoing powers, and all other powers vested by this constitution in the government of the United States, or in any department or officer thereof.

Sect. 9. The migration or importation of such persons as *any of* the ~~several~~ states now existing shall think proper to admit, shall not be prohibited by the Congress prior to the year one thousand eight hundred and eight, but a tax or duty may be imposed on such importation, not exceeding ten dollars for each person.

The privilege of the writ of habeas corpus shall not be suspended, unless when in cases of rebellion or invasion the public safety may require it.

No bill of attainder ~~shall be passed, nor any~~ *or* ex post facto law *shall be passed.*

No capitation, *or other direct,* tax shall be laid, unless in proportion to the census *or Enumeration* herein before directed to be taken.

No tax or duty shall be laid on articles exported from any state.

No Preference shall be given by any Regulation of Commerce or Revenue to the Ports of one State over those of another: nor shall Vessels bound to, or from, one State, be obliged to enter, clear, or pay Duties in another.

No money shall be drawn from the treasury, but in consequence of appropriations made by law; *and a regular Statement and Account of the Receipts and Expenditures of all public Money shall be published from time to time.*

No title of nobility shall be granted by the United States. And no person holding any office of profit or trust under them, shall, without the consent of the Congress, accept of any present, emolument, office, or title, of any kind whatever, from any king, prince, or foreign state.

Sect. 10. ~~No state shall coin money, nor emit bills of credit, nor make any thing but gold or silver coin a tender in payment of debts, nor pass any bill of attainder, nor ex post facto laws, nor laws altering or impairing the obligation of contracts; nor grant letters of marque and reprisal, nor enter into any treaty, alliance, or confederation, nor grant any title of nobility.~~

No State shall enter into any Treaty, Alliance, or Confederation; grant Letters of Marque and Reprisal; coin Money; emit Bills of Credit; make any Thing but gold and silver Coin a Tender in Pay-

ment of Debts; pass any Bill of Attainder, ex post facto Law, or Law impairing the Obligation of Contracts, or grant any Title of Nobility.

No state shall, without the consent of *the* Congress, lay *any* imposts or duties on imports or exports, ~~nor with such consent, but to the use of the treasury of the United States.~~ *except what may be absolutely necessary for executing it's inspection Laws: and the net Produce of all Duties and Imposts, laid by any State on Imports or Exports, shall be for the Use of the Treasury of the United States; and all such Laws shall be subject to the Revision and Controul of the Congress. No State shall, without the Consent of Congress, lay any Duty of Tonnage,* ~~Nor~~ keep troops, ~~nor~~ *or* ships of war in time of peace, ~~nor~~ enter into any agreement or compact with another state, ~~nor~~ *or* with any *a* foreign power, ~~Nor~~ *or* engage in ~~any~~ war, unless ~~it shall be~~ actually invaded ~~by enemies~~, or ~~the~~ *in such imminent* danger ~~of invasion be so imminent~~, as *will* not ~~to~~ admit of delay. ~~until the Congress can be consulted~~.

II.

Sect. 1. The executive power shall be vested in a president of the United States of America. He shall hold his office during the term of four years, and, together with the vice-president, chosen for the same term, be elected, ~~in the following manner:~~ *as follows*

Each state shall appoint, in such manner as the legislature thereof may direct, a number of electors, equal to the whole number of senators and representatives to which the state may be entitled in *the* Congress: but no senator or representative, ~~shall be appointed an elector, nor~~ *or* ~~any~~ person holding an office of trust or profit under the United States, *shall be appointed an Elector.*

The electors shall meet in their respective states, and vote by ballot for two persons, of whom one at least shall not be an inhabitant of the same state with themselves. And they shall make a list of all the persons voted for, and of the number of votes for each; which list they shall sign and certify, and transmit sealed to the seat of the ~~general~~ government *of the United States,* directed to the president of the senate. The president of the senate shall in the presence of the senate and house of representatives open all the certificates, and the votes shall then be counted. The person having the greatest number of votes shall be the president, if such number be a majority of the whole number of electors appointed; and if there be more than one who have such majority, and have an equal number of votes, then the house of representatives shall immediately chuse by ballot one of them for president; and if no person have a majority, then from the five highest on the list the said house shall in like manner choose the president. But in choosing the president, the votes shall be taken by states, and not per capita, the representation from each state having one vote. A quorum for this purpose shall consist of a member or members from two-thirds of the states, and a majority of all the states shall be necessary to a choice. In every case, after the choice of the president, by the representatives, the person having the greatest number of votes of the electors shall be the vice-president. But if there should remain two or more who have equal votes, the senate shall choose from them by ballot the vice-president.

The Congress may determine the time of chusing the electors, and the time in *day on* which they shall give their votes; but the election *which day* shall be on the same day throughout the United States.

No person except a natural born citizen, or a citizen of the United States, at the time of the adoption of this constitution, shall be eligible to the office of president; neither shall any person be eligible to that office who shall not have attained to the age of thirty-five years, and been fourteen years a resident within the United States.

In case of the removal of the president from office, or of his death, resignation, or inability to discharge the powers and duties of the said office, the same shall devolve on the vice-president, and the Congress may by law provide for the case of removal, death, resignation or inability, both of the president and vice-president, declaring what officer shall then act as president, and such officer shall act accordingly, until the disability be removed, or the period for chusing another *a* president arrive. *shall be elected.*

The president shall, at stated times, receive *for his services,* a fixed compensation, for his services which shall neither be encreased nor diminished during the period for which he shall have been elected, *and he shall not receive within that Period any other Emolument from the United States, or any of them.*

Before he enter on the execution of his office, he shall take the following oath or affirmation: "I_____, do solemnly swear (or affirm) that I will faithfully execute the office of president of the United States, and will to the best of my judgment and power, *Ability,* preserve, protect and defend the constitution of the United States."

Sect. 2. The president shall be commander in chief of the army and navy of the United States, and of the militia of the several States, *when called into the actual Service of the United States;* he may require the opinion, in writing, of the principal officer in each of the executive departments, upon any subject relating to the duties of their respective offices, ~~when called into the actual service of the United States~~, and he shall have power to grant reprieves and pardons for offences against the United States, except in cases of impeachment.

He shall have power, by and with the advice and consent of the senate, to make treaties, provided two-thirds of the senators present concur; and he shall nominate, and by and with the advice and consent of the senate, shall appoint ambassadors, other public ministers and consuls, judges of the supreme court, and all other officers of the United States, whose appointments are not herein otherwise provided for, *and which shall be established by Law: but the Congress may by Law vest the Appointment of such inferior Officers, as they think proper, in the President alone, in the Courts of Law, or in the Heads of Departments.*

The president shall have power to fill up all vacancies that may happen during the recess of the senate, by granting commissions which shall expire at the end of their next session.

Sect. 3. He shall from time to time give to the Congress information of the state of the union, and recommend to their consideration such measures as he shall judge necessary and expedient: he may, on extraordinary occasions, convene both houses, or either of them, and in case of disagreement between them, with respect to the time of adjournment, he may adjourn them to such time as he shall think proper: he shall receive ambassadors and other public ministers: he shall take care that the laws be faithfully executed, and shall commission all the officers of the United States.

Sect. 4. The president, vice-president and all civil officers of the United States, shall be removed from office on impeachment for, and conviction of treason, bribery, or other high crimes and misdemeanors.

III.

Sect. 1. The judicial power of the United States, ~~both in law and equity,~~ shall be vested in one supreme court, and in such inferior courts as the Congress may from time to time ordain and establish. The judges, both of the supreme and inferior courts, shall hold their offices during good behaviour, and shall, at stated times, receive for their services, a compensation, which shall not be diminished during their continuance in office.

Sect. 2. The judicial power shall extend to all cases, ~~both~~ in law and equity, arising under this constitution, the laws of the United States, and treaties made, or which shall be made, under their authority.

To all cases affecting ambassadors, other public ministers and consuls. To all cases of admiralty and maritime jurisdiction. To controversies to which the United States shall be a party. To controversies between two or more States; between a state and citizens of another state; between citizens of different States; between citizens of the same state claiming lands under grants of different States, and between a state, or the citizens thereof, and foreign States, citizens or subjects.

In *all* cases affecting ambassadors, other public ministers and consuls, and those in which a state shall be party, the supreme court shall have original jurisdiction. In all the other cases before mentioned, the supreme court shall have appellate jurisdiction, both as to law and fact, with such exceptions, and under such regulations as the Congress shall make.

The trial of all crimes, except in cases of impeachment, shall be by jury; and such trial shall be held in the state where the said crimes shall have been committed; but when not committed within any state, the trial shall be at such place or places as the Congress may by law have directed.

Sect. 3. Treason against the United States, shall consist only in levying war against them, or in adhering to their enemies, giving them aid and comfort. No person shall be convicted of treason unless on the testimony of two witnesses to the same overt act, or on confession in open court.

The Congress shall have power to declare the punishment of treason, but no attainder of treason shall work corruption of blood, ~~nor~~ *or* forfeiture, except during the life of the person attainted.

IV.

Sect. 1. Full faith and credit shall be given in each state to the public acts, records, and judicial proceedings of every other state. And the Congress may by general laws prescribe the manner in which such acts, records and proceedings shall be proved, and the effect thereof.

Sect. 2. The citizens of each state shall be entitled to all privileges and immunities of citizens in the several states.

A person charged in any state with treason, felony, or other crime, who shall flee from justice, and be found in another state, shall on demand of the executive authority of the state from which he fled be delivered up, ~~and~~ *to be* removed to the state having jurisdiction of the crime.

No person ~~legally~~ held to service or labour in one state, *under the Laws thereof,* escaping into another, shall in consequence of ~~regulations subsisting~~ *any Law or Regulation* therein be discharged from such service or labor, but shall be delivered up on claim of the party to whom such service or labour may be due.

Sect. 3. New states may be admitted by the Congress into this union; but no new state shall be formed or erected within the jurisdiction of any other state; nor any state be formed by the junction of two or more states, or parts of states, without the consent of the legislatures of the states concerned as well as of the Congress.

The Congress shall have power to dispose of and make all needful rules and regulations respecting the territory or other property belonging to the United States: and nothing in this Constitution shall be so construed as to prejudice any claims of the United States, or of any particular state.

Sect. 4. The United States shall guarantee to every state in this union a Republican form of government, and shall protect each of them against invasion; and on application of the legislature or *of the* executive *(when the Legislature cannot be convened)* against domestic violence.

V.

The Congress, whenever two-thirds of both houses shall deem *it* necessary, *shall propose Amendments to this Constitution,* or on the application ~~of two-thirds~~ of the legislatures *of two thirds* of the several states, shall ~~propose amendments to this constitution,~~ *call a Convention for proposing Amendments,* which *in either case,* shall be valid to all intents and purposes, as part ~~thereof,~~ *of this Constitution,* when ~~the same shall have been~~ ratified by ~~three-fourths at least of~~ the legislatures *of three fourths* of the several states, or by conventions in three-fourths thereof, as the one or the other mode of ratification may be proposed by the Congress: Provided, that no amendment which may be made prior to the year 1808 shall in any manner affect the *first* and *fourth* ~~sections~~ *Clauses* ~~of~~ *in the Ninth Section of the first* article; *and that no State, without its Consent, shall be deprived of it's equal Suffrage in the Senate.*

VI.

All debts contracted and engagements entered into before the adoption of this Constitution shall be as valid against the United States under this Constitution as under the confederation.

This constitution, and the laws of the United States which shall be made in pursuance thereof; and all treaties made, or which shall be made, under the authority of the United States, shall be the supreme law of the land; and the judges in every state shall be bound thereby, any thing in the constitution or laws of any state to the contrary notwithstanding.

The senators and representatives beforementioned, and the members of the several state legislatures, and all executive and judicial officers, both of the United States and of the several States, shall be bound by oath or affirmation, to support this constitution; but no religious test shall ever be required as a qualification to any office or public trust under the United States.

VII.

The ratification of the conventions of nine States, shall be sufficient for the establishment of this constitution between the States so ratifying the same.

Population and Constitution-Making, 1774–1792

Estimates of population were an issue in politics and constitution-making throughout the Revolutionary Era. In the First Continental Congress in 1774, the Virginia delegates, whose colony contained about twenty percent of the population of the thirteen colonies, demanded more votes than such small colonies as Rhode Island. They were outvoted by the delegates who insisted that they represented colonies, not numbers. The three largest states, Virginia, Pennsylvania, and Massachusetts, demanded voting according to population during the writing of the Articles of Confederation, but again they were defeated by men who insisted upon the independence and the equality of the states.

The writing of the Articles also involved a conflict between the Northern and the Southern states, for Northerners insisted that common expenses be shared according to total population, while Southerners insisted that slaves were property and should not be counted. The issue was evaded by an agreement to share expenses according to the value of land. The dispute was revived in 1783 when Congress proposed that the Articles be amended to share expenses according to population. Eventually, Southern delegates agreed that three-fifths of the slaves should be counted in sharing common expenses.

Such issues, in one form or another, came to a head in the Constitutional Convention in 1787. Once more the large and small states fought over whether voting in Congress should be by states or by population. The Northern and the Southern states battled over the issue of whether or not slaves should be counted in apportioning Representatives in the House of Representatives. Northern and Southern delegates also disagreed over whether prospective new western states should be represented according to population or should be prevented from ever having enough Representatives to outvote the original thirteen states. The question of population was also involved in the debates over the number of states to be required to ratify the Constitution before it could go into effect. Some argued that seven states were enough, while others insisted that such a requirement might make it possible for less than a majority of voters in the United States to ratify the Constitution.

The Constitution included several compromises involving population. Each state was given two votes in the Senate. The compromise over representation in the House of Representatives was embodied in Article I, section 2 of the Constitution. It provided that Representatives should be apportioned "by adding to the whole Number of free Persons, including those bound to Service for a Term of Years, and excluding Indians not taxed, three fifths of all other Persons." The "other Persons" were the slaves. Sixty-five members of the first House of Representatives were apportioned among the states by the Constitution. However, the Constitution provided for regular reapportionment. Southerners were convinced that the South and the Southwest would grow faster than the North; and, despite the objections of most Northern delegates, the Southerners secured the insertion in the Constitution of the requirement for a national census every ten years and the reapportionment of the House of Representatives after each census.

Americans had no more exact information about the population of the United States in 1787 than they had in 1774 when John Adams at the First Continental Congress noted in his diary that "it will not do in such a case, to take each other's word. It ought to be ascertained by authentic evidence, from records." No such records were available in 1787. The records of the Constitutional Convention contain a few scattered and partial estimates of population but no account of the actual numbers used by the Convention to apportion representation in the first House of Representatives.

A question concerning the basis of apportionment was raised in the South Carolina House of Representatives in January 1788. On 17 January Charles Cotesworth Pinckney gave the figures which he said the Convention had used. His speech was published in the Charleston *City Gazette* on 24 January. On 5 February the New York *Daily Advertiser,* without referring to the source, published the estimates with the statement that "the numbers in the different states, according to the most accurate accounts which could be obtained by the late Federal Convention were as follow." By May 1788 Pinckney's estimates had been published in at least twenty-eight newspapers from Maine to Georgia. Since there is no evidence that anyone contradicted the figures given by Pinckney, it seems likely that they were the estimates used by the Convention.

The first census act became law on 1 March 1790, and the census was completed by February 1792. In the meantime, North Carolina ceded the Southwest Territory (Tennessee) to the United States in 1790; in February 1791 Congress admitted Vermont to statehood as of 4 March 1791 and Kentucky to statehood as of 1 June 1792. Congress assigned the two new states two Representatives each, pending the completion of the census.

The first reapportionment act became law on 14 April 1792. It provided that after 3 March 1793 the House of Representatives would consist of one member for every 33,000 persons in each state "computed according to the rule prescribed by the Constitution. . . ."

The following table consists of five columns. Column I contains the estimates of population which, according to Charles Cotesworth Pinckney, were used by the Constitutional Convention in assigning Representatives to the states. Column II gives the number of Representatives apportioned by the Constitution of 1787. Column III is derived from the Census of 1790. Column III-A gives "the whole Number of free Persons, including those bound to Service for a Term of Years, and excluding Indians not taxed. . ." (The Constitution, Article I, section 2). Column III-B gives the total slave population. Column IV was obtained by adding to the nonslave population given in Column III-A, "three fifths of all other Persons" (The Constitution, Article I, section 2), that is, the slave population in Column III-B. Column V contains the number of Representatives assigned each state by the Reapportionment Act of 1792.

APPORTIONMENT OF HOUSE OF REPRESENTATIVES
1787, 1792

States and Territories	I Population Estimate Used by Convention	II Apportionment in Constitution	III Census of 1790 A Non-slave Population	III Census of 1790 B Slave Population	IV Population Basis for Reapportionment	V Apportionment by Act of 1792
NEW HAMPSHIRE	102,000	3	141,727	158	141,822	4
MASSACHUSETTS	360,000	8	475,327	0	475,327	14
RHODE ISLAND	58,000	1	67,877	948	68,446	2
CONNECTICUT	202,000	5	235,182	2,764	236,840	7
NEW YORK	238,000	6	318,796	21,324	331,590	10
NEW JERSEY	138,000	4	172,716	11,423	179,570	5
PENNSYLVANIA	360,000	8	430,636	3,737	432,878	13
DELAWARE	37,000	1	50,209	8,887	55,541	1
MARYLAND	218,000 (including 3/5ths of 80,000 Negroes)	6	216,692	103,036	278,514	8
VIRGINIA	420,000 (including 3/5ths of 280,000 Negroes)	10	454,983	292,627	630,559	19
NORTH CAROLINA	200,000 (including 3/5ths of 60,000 Negroes)	5	293,179	100,572	353,522	10
SOUTH CAROLINA	150,000 (including 3/5ths of 80,000 Negroes)	5	141,979	107,094	206,235	6
GEORGIA	90,000 (including 3/5ths of 20,000 Negroes)	3	53,284	29,264	70,842	2
Totals	2,573,000	65	3,052,587	681,834	3,461,686	101

States and Territories	I Population Estimate Used by Convention	II Apportionment in Constitution	III Census of 1790		IV Population Basis for Reapportionment	V Apportionment by Act of 1792
			A Non-slave Population	B Slave Population		
KENTUCKY			61,247	12,430	68,705	2
VERMONT			85,539	no data	85,539	2
NORTHWEST TERRITORY			no data	no data	no data	0
SOUTHWEST TERRITORY			32,274	3,417	34,324	0
Totals			179,060	15,847	188,568	4

VIII

The Report of the Constitutional Convention

17 September 1787

Introduction

The Convention completed its revision of the Report of the Committee of Style on Saturday afternoon, 15 September, and at six o'clock James Madison moved that the Constitution be adopted. The Convention agreed and ordered that the Constitution be engrossed and that 500 copies be printed.

The Constitution was engrossed by Jacob Shallus, assistant clerk of the Pennsylvania Assembly. The engrossed Constitution was read to the Convention on Monday morning, 17 September. James Wilson then read a speech written by Benjamin Franklin; and, still speaking for Franklin, he moved that the Constitution be signed "and offered the following as a convenient form viz. 'Done in Convention, by the unanimous consent of *the States* present the 17th. of Sepr. &c—In Witness whereof we have hereunto subscribed our names.'" Gouverneur Morris had suggested this form to Franklin to gain the support of the dissenting members and, failing that, to give the action the appearance of unanimity.

Before voting on the motion, the Convention changed the ratio of Representatives from one for each forty thousand to one for each thirty thousand according to the method prescribed in the Constitution, a change supported by George Washington in his only recorded speech in the Convention. The Convention then adopted Franklin's motion and resolved that the President of the Convention "retain the Journal and other papers [of the Convention], subject to the order of Congress, if ever formed under the Constitution."

Thirty-eight of the forty-one delegates still in attendance on the afternoon of 17 September, led by the President of the Convention, signed the Constitution. George Read signed for the absent John Dickinson, bringing the number of signers to thirty-nine. Edmund Randolph, George Mason, and Elbridge Gerry, who had given their reasons two days earlier, refused to sign. The Convention then adjourned *sine die* at four in the afternoon.

It is unclear when Shallus engrossed the form of signing and the last-minute changes described in the statement of errata placed to the left of the form of signing. The names of the states, listed next to the names of the signers, are in the handwriting of Alexander

Hamilton. Secretary William Jackson's attestation of the Constitution appears below the statement of errata.

On the evening of 17 September William Jackson delivered the Convention Journal and papers to George Washington. The following morning Jackson left by stage for New York City to deliver the engrossed Constitution and accompanying documents to the Confederation Congress.

A. THE PRESIDENT OF THE CONVENTION TO THE PRESIDENT OF CONGRESS, 17 September[1]

In Convention, September 17, 1787.

SIR, WE have now the honor to submit to the consideration of the United States in Congress assembled, that Constitution which has appeared to us the most adviseable.

The friends of our country have long seen and desired, that the power of making war, peace and treaties, that of levying money and regulating commerce, and the correspondent executive and judicial authorities should be fully and effectually vested in the general government of the Union: but the impropriety of delegating such extensive trust to one body of men is evident—Hence results the necessity of a different organization.

It is obviously impracticable in the foederal government of these States; to secure all rights of independent sovereignty to each, and yet provide for the interest and safety of all—Individuals entering into society, must give up a share of liberty to preserve the rest. The magnitude of the sacrifice must depend as well on situation and circumstance, as on the object to be obtained. It is at all times difficult to draw with precision the line between those rights which must be surrendered, and those which may be reserved; and on the present occasion this difficulty was encreased by a difference among the several States as to their situation, extent, habits, and particular interests.

In all our deliberations on this subject we kept steadily in our view, that which appears to us the greatest interest of every true American, the consolidation of our Union, in which is involved our prosperity, felicity, safety, perhaps our national existence, This important consideration, seriously and deeply impressed on our minds, led each State in the Convention to be less rigid on points of inferior magnitude, than might have been otherwise expected; and thus the Constitution, which we now present, is the result of a spirit of amity, and of that mutual deference and concession which the peculiarity of our political situation rendered indispensible.

That it will meet the full and entire approbation of every State is not perhaps to be expected; but each will doubtless consider, that had her interests been alone consulted, the consequences might have been particularly disagreeable or injurious to others; that it is liable to as few exceptions as could reasonably have been expected, we hope and believe; that it may promote the lasting welfare of that country so dear to us all, and secure her freedom and happiness, is our most ardent wish.

With great respect, WE have the honor to be SIR, Your Excellency's most Obedient and humble servants.

> George Washington, President.
> By unanimous Order of the
> Convention

1. Broadside (LT), PCC, Item 122, Resolve Book of the Office of Foreign Affairs, 1785–89, tipped in between pages 98–99, DNA. The original letter has been lost. The above is transcribed from the official copy of the Convention Report, printed by John McLean and attested by Charles Thomson. The letter was addressed to "HIS EXCELLENCY The President of Congress."

B. THE CONSTITUTION, 17 September[1]

We the People of the United States, in Order to form a more perfect Union, establish Justice, insure domestic Tranquility, provide for the common defence, promote the general Welfare, and secure the Blessings of Liberty to ourselves and our Posterity, do ordain and establish this Constitution for the United States of America.

Article. I.

Section. 1. All legislative Powers herein granted shall be vested in a Congress of the United States, which shall consist of a Senate and House of Representatives.

Section. 2. The House of Representatives shall be composed of Members chosen every second Year by the People of the several States, and the Electors in each State shall have the Qualifications requisite for Electors of the most numerous Branch of the State Legislature.

No Person shall be a Representative who shall not have attained to the Age of twenty five Years, and been seven Years a Citizen of the United States, and who shall not, when elected, be an Inhabitant of that State in which he shall be chosen.

Representatives and direct Taxes shall be apportioned among the several States which may be included within this Union, according to their respective Numbers, which shall be determined by adding to the whole Number of free Persons, including those bound to Service for a Term of Years, and excluding Indians not taxed, three fifths of all other Persons. The actual Enumeration shall be made within three Years after the first Meeting of the Congress of the United States, and within every subsequent Term of ten Years, in such Manner as they shall by Law direct. The Number of Representatives shall not exceed one for every thirty Thousand, but each State shall have at Least one Representative; and until such enumeration shall be made, the State of New Hampshire shall be entitled to chuse three, Massachusetts eight, Rhode-Island and Providence Plantations one, Connecticut five, New-York six, New Jersey four, Pennsylvania eight, Delaware one, Maryland six, Virginia ten, North Carolina five, South Carolina five, and Georgia three.

When vacancies happen in the Representation from any State, the Executive Authority thereof shall issue Writs of Election to fill such Vacancies.

The House of Representatives shall chuse their Speaker and other Officers; and shall have the sole Power of Impeachment.

Section. 3. The Senate of the United States shall be composed of two Senators from each State, chosen by the Legislature thereof, for six Years; and each Senator shall have one Vote.

Immediately after they shall be assembled in Consequence of the first Election, they shall be divided as equally as may be into three Classes. The Seats of the Senators of the first Class shall be vacated at the Expiration of the second Year, of the second Class at the Expiration of the fourth Year, and of the third Class at the Expiration of the sixth Year, so that one third may be chosen every second Year; and if Vacancies happen by Resignation, or otherwise, during the Recess of the Legislature of any State, the Executive thereof may make temporary Appointments until the next Meeting of the Legislature, which shall then fill such Vacancies.

No Person shall be a Senator who shall not have attained to the Age of thirty Years, and been nine Years a Citizen of the United States, and who shall not, when elected, be an Inhabitant of that State for which he shall be chosen.

The Vice President of the United States shall be President of the Senate, but shall have no Vote, unless they be equally divided.

The Senate shall chuse their other Officers, and also a President pro tempore, in the Absence of the Vice President, or when he shall exercise the Office of President of the United States.

The Senate shall have the sole Power to try all Impeachments.

When sitting for that Purpose, they shall be on Oath or Affirmation. When the President of the United States is tried, the Chief Justice shall preside: And no Person shall be convicted without the Concurrence of two thirds of the Members present.

Judgment in Cases of Impeachment shall not extend further than to removal from Office, and disqualification to hold and enjoy any Office of honor, Trust or Profit under the United States: but the Party convicted shall nevertheless be liable and subject to Indictment, Trial, Judgment and Punishment, according to Law.

Section. 4. The Times, Places and Manner of holding Elections for Senators and Representatives, shall be prescribed in each State by the Legislature thereof; but the Congress may at any time by Law make or alter such Regulations, except as to the Places of chusing Senators.

The Congress shall assemble at least once in every Year, and such Meeting shall be on the first Monday in December, unless they shall by Law appoint a different Day.

Section. 5. Each House shall be the Judge of the Elections, Returns and Qualifications of its own Members, and a Majority of each shall constitute a Quorum to do Business; but a smaller Number may adjourn from day to day, and may be authorized to compel the Attendance of absent Members, in such Manner, and under such Penalties as each House may provide.

Each House may determine the Rules of its Proceedings, punish its members for disorderly Behaviour, and, with the Concurrence of two thirds, expel a Member.

Each House shall keep a Journal of its Proceedings, and from time to time publish the same, excepting such Parts as may in their Judgment require Secrecy; and the Yeas and Nays of the Members of either House on any question shall, at the Desire of one fifth of those Present, be entered on the Journal.

Neither House, during the Session of Congress, shall, without the Consent of the other, adjourn for more than three days, nor to any other Place than that in which the two Houses shall be sitting.

Section. 6. The Senators and Representatives shall receive a Compensation for their Services, to be ascertained by Law, and paid out of the Treasury of the United States. They shall in all Cases, except Treason, Felony and Breach of the Peace, be privileged from Arrest during their Attendance at the Session of their respective Houses, and in going to and returning from the same; and for any Speech or Debate in either House, they shall not be questioned in any other Place.

No Senator or Representative shall, during the Time for which he was elected, be appointed to any civil Office under the Authority of the United States which shall have been created, or the Emoluments whereof shall have been encreased during such time; and no Person holding any Office under the United States, shall be a Member of either House during his Continuance in Office.

Section. 7. All Bills for raising Revenue shall originate in the House of Representatives; but the Senate may propose or concur with Amendments as on other Bills.

Every Bill which shall have passed the House of Representatives and the Senate shall, before it become a Law, be presented to the President of the United States; If he approve he shall sign it, but if not he shall return it, with his Objections to that House in which it shall have originated, who shall enter the Objections at large on their Journal, and proceed to reconsider it. If after such Reconsideration two thirds of that House shall agree to pass the Bill, it shall be sent, together with the Objections, to the other House, by which it shall likewise be reconsidered, and if approved by two thirds of that House, it shall become a Law. But in all such Cases the Votes of both Houses shall be determined by yeas and Nays, and the Names of the Persons voting for and against the Bill shall be entered on the Journal of each House respectively. If any Bill shall not be returned by the President within ten Days (Sundays excepted) after it shall have been presented to him, the Same shall be a Law, in like Manner as if he had signed it, unless the Congress by their Adjournment prevent its Return, in which Case it shall not be a Law.

Every Order, Resolution, or Vote to which the Concurrence of the Senate and House of Representatives may be necessary (except on a question of Adjournment) shall be presented to the President of the United States; and before the Same shall take Effect, shall be approved by him, or being disapproved by him, shall be repassed by two thirds of the Senate and House of Representatives, according to the Rules and Limitations prescribed in the Case of a Bill.

Section. 8. The Congress shall have Power To lay and collect Taxes, Duties, Imposts and Excises, to pay the Debts and provide for the common Defence and general Welfare of the United States; but all Duties, Imposts and Excises shall be uniform throughout the United States;

To borrow Money on the credit of the United States;

To regulate Commerce with foreign Nations, and among the several States, and with the Indian Tribes;

To establish an uniform Rule of Naturalization, and uniform Laws on the subject of Bankruptcies throughout the United States;

To coin Money, regulate the Value thereof, and of foreign Coin, and fix the Standard of Weights and Measures;

To provide for the Punishment of counterfeiting the Securities and current Coin of the United States;

To establish Post Offices and post Roads;

To promote the Progress of Science and useful Arts, by securing for limited Times to Authors and Inventors the exclusive Right to their respective Writings and Discoveries;

To constitute Tribunals inferior to the supreme Court;

To define and punish Piracies and Felonies committed on the high Seas, and Offences against the Law of Nations;

To declare War, grant Letters of Marque and Reprisal, and make Rules concerning Captures on Land and Water;

To raise and support Armies, but no Appropriation of Money to that Use shall be for a longer Term than two Years;

To provide and maintain a Navy;

To make Rules for the Government and Regulation of the land and naval Forces;

To provide for calling forth the Militia to execute the Laws of the Union, suppress Insurrections and repel Invasions;

To provide for organizing, arming, and disciplining, the Militia, and for governing such Part of them as may be employed in the Service of the United States, reserving to the States respectively, the Appointment of the Officers, and the Authority of training the Militia according to the discipline prescribed by Congress;

To exercise exclusive Legislation in all Cases whatsoever, over such District (not exceeding ten Miles square) as may, by Cession of particular States, and the Acceptance of Congress, become the Seat of the Government of the United States, and to exercise like Authority over all Places purchased by the Consent of the Legislature of the State in which the same shall be, for the Erection of Forts, Magazines, Arsenals, dock-Yards, and other needful Buildings;—And

To make all Laws which shall be necessary and proper for carrying into Execution the foregoing Powers, and all other Powers vested by this Constitution in the Government of the United States, or in any Department or Officer thereof.

Section. 9. The Migration or Importation of such Persons as any of the States now existing shall think proper to admit, shall not be prohibited by the Congress prior to the Year one thousand eight hundred and eight, but a Tax or duty may be imposed on such Importation, not exceeding ten dollars for each Person.

The Privilege of the Writ of Habeas Corpus shall not be suspended, unless when in Cases of Rebellion or Invasion the public Safety may require it.

No Bill of Attainder or ex post facto Law shall be passed.

No Capitation, or other direct, Tax shall be laid, unless in Proportion to the Census or Enumeration herein before directed to be taken.

No Tax or Duty shall be laid on Articles exported from any State.

No Preference shall be given by any Regulation of Commerce or Revenue to the Ports of one State over those of another: nor shall Vessels bound to, or from, one State, be obliged to enter, clear, or pay Duties in another.

No Money shall be drawn from the Treasury, but in Consequence of Appropriations made by Law; and a regular Statement and Account of the Receipts and Expenditures of all public Money shall be published from time to time.

No Title of Nobility shall be granted by the United States: And no Person holding any Office of Profit or Trust under them, shall, without the Consent of the Congress, accept of any present, Emolument, Office, or Title, of any kind whatever, from any King, Prince, or foreign State.

Section. 10. No State shall enter into any Treaty, Alliance, or Confederation; grant Letters of Marque and Reprisal; coin Money; emit Bills of Credit; make any Thing but gold and silver Coin a Tender in Payment of Debts; pass any Bill of Attainder, ex post facto Law, or Law impairing the Obligation of Contracts, or grant any Title of Nobility.

No State shall, without the Consent of the Congress, lay any Imposts or Duties on Imports or Exports, except what may be absolutely necessary for executing it's inspection Laws: and the net Produce of all Duties and Imposts, laid by any State on Imports or Exports, shall be for the Use of the Treasury of the United States; and all such Laws shall be subject to the Revision and Controul of the Congress.

No State shall, without the Consent of Congress, lay any Duty of Tonnage, keep Troops, or Ships of War in time of Peace, enter into any Agreement or Compact with another State, or with a foreign Power, or engage in War, unless actually invaded, or in such imminent Danger as will not admit of delay.

Article. II.

Section. 1. The executive Power shall be vested in a President of the United States of America. He shall hold his Office during the

Term of four Years, and, together with the Vice President, chosen for the same Term, be elected, as follows

Each State shall appoint, in such Manner as the Legislature thereof may direct, a Number of Electors, equal to the whole Number of Senators and Representatives to which the State may be entitled in the Congress: but no Senator or Representative, or Person holding an Office of Trust or Profit under the United States, shall be appointed an Elector.

The Electors' shall meet in their respective States and vote by Ballot for two Persons, of whom one at least shall not be an Inhabitant of the same State with themselves. And they shall make a List of all the Persons voted for, and of the Number of Votes for each; which List they shall sign and certify, and transmit sealed to the Seat of the Government of the United States, directed to the President of the Senate. The President of the Senate shall, in the Presence of the Senate and House of Representatives, open all the Certificates, and the Votes shall then be counted. The Person having the greatest Number of Votes shall be the President, if such Number be a Majority of the whole Number of Electors appointed; and if there be more than one who have such Majority, and have an equal Number of Votes, then the House of Representatives shall immediately chuse by Ballot one of them for President; and if no Person have a Majority, then from the five highest on the List the said House shall in like Manner chuse the President. But in chusing the President, the Votes shall be taken by States, the Representation from each State having one Vote; A quorum for this Purpose shall consist of a Member or Members from two thirds of the States, and a Majority of all the States shall be necessary to a Choice. In every Case, after the Choice of the President, the Person having the greatest Number of Votes of the Electors shall be the Vice President. But if there should remain two or more who have equal Votes, the Senate shall chuse from them by Ballot the Vice President.

The Congress may determine the Time of chusing the Electors, and the Day on which they shall give their Votes; which Day shall be the same throughout the United States.

No Persons except a natural born Citizen, or a Citizen of the United States, at the time of the Adoption of this Constitution, shall be eligible to the Office of President; neither shall any Person be eligible to that Office who shall not have attained to the Age of thirty five Years, and been fourteen Years a Resident within the United States.

In Case of the Removal of the President from Office, or of his Death, Resignation, or Inability to discharge the Powers and Duties of the said Office, the Same shall devolve on the Vice President, and the Congress may by Law provide for the Case of Removal, Death, Resignation or Inability, both of the President and Vice President, declaring what Officer shall then act as President, and such Officer shall act accordingly, until the Disability be removed, or a President shall be elected.

The President shall, at stated Times, receive for his Services, a Compensation, which shall neither be encreased nor diminished during the Period for which he shall have been elected, and he shall not receive within that Period any other Emolument from the United States, or any of them.

Before he enter on the Execution of his Office, he shall take the following Oath or Affirmation:—"I do solemnly swear (or affirm) that I will faithfully execute the Office of President of the United States, and will to the best of my Ability, preserve, protect and defend the Constitution of the United States."

Section. 2. The President shall be Commander in Chief of the Army and Navy of the United States, and of the Militia of the several States, when called into the actual Service of the United States; he may require the Opinion, in writing, of the principal Officer in each of the executive Departments, upon any Subject relating to the Duties of their respective Offices, and he shall have Power to grant Reprieves and Pardons for Offences against the United States, except in Cases of Impeachment.

He shall have Power, by and with the Advice and Consent of the Senate, to make Treaties, provided two thirds of the Senators present concur; and he shall nominate, and by and with the Advice and Consent of the Senate, shall appoint Ambassadors, other public Ministers and Consuls, Judges of the supreme Court, and all other Officers of the United States, whose Appointments are not herein otherwise provided for, and which shall be established by Law: but the Congress may by Law vest the Appointment of such inferior Officers, as they think proper, in the President alone, in the Courts of Law, or in the Heads of Departments.

The President shall have Power to fill up all Vacancies that may happen during the Recess of the Senate, by granting Commissions which shall expire at the End of their next Session.

Section. 3. He shall from time to time give to the Congress Information of the State of the Union, and recommend to their Consideration such Measures as he shall judge necessary and expedient; he may, on extraordinary Occasions, convene both Houses, or either of them, and in Case of Disagreement between them, with Respect to the Time of Adjournment, he may adjourn them to such Time as he shall think proper; he shall receive Ambassadors and other public Ministers; he shall take Care that the Laws be faithfully executed, and shall Commission all the Officers of the United States.

Section. 4. The President, Vice President and all civil Officers of the United States, shall be removed from Office on Impeachment for, and Conviction of Treason, Bribery, or other high Crimes and Misdemeanors.

Article III.

Section. 1. The judicial Power of the United States, shall be vested in one supreme Court, and in such inferior Courts as the Congress may from time to time ordain and establish. The Judges, both of the supreme and inferior Courts, shall hold their Offices during good Behaviour, and shall, at stated Times, receive for their Services, a Compensation, which shall not be diminished during their Continuance in Office.

Section. 2. The judicial Power shall extend to all Cases, in Law and Equity, arising under this Constitution, the Laws of the United States, and Treaties made, or which shall be made, under their Authority;—to all Cases affecting Ambassadors, other public Ministers and Consuls;—to all Cases of admiralty and maritime Jurisdiction;—to Controversies to which the United States shall be a Party;—to Controversies between two or more States;—between a State and Citizens of another State;—between Citizens of different States,—between Citizens of the same State claiming Lands under Grants of different States, and between a State, or the Citizens thereof, and foreign States, Citizens or Subjects.

In all Cases affecting Ambassadors, other public Ministers and Consuls, and those in which a State shall be Party, the supreme Court shall have original Jurisdiction. In all the other Cases before mentioned, the supreme Court shall have appellate Jurisdiction, both as to Law and Fact, with such Exceptions, and under such Regulations as the Congress shall make.

The Trial of all Crimes, except in Cases of Impeachment, shall be by Jury; and such Trial shall be held in the State where the said Crimes shall have been committed; but when not committed within any State, the Trial shall be at such Place or Places as the Congress may by Law have directed.

Section. 3. Treason against the United States, shall consist only in levying War against them, or in adhering to their Enemies, giving them Aid and Comfort. No Person shall be convicted of Treason unless on the Testimony of two Witnesses to the same overt Act, or on Confession in open Court.

The Congress shall have Power to declare the Punishment of Treason, but no Attainder of Treason shall work Corruption of Blood, or Forfeiture except during the Life of the Person attainted.

Article. IV.

Section. 1. Full Faith and Credit shall be given in each State to the public Acts, Records, and judicial Proceedings of every other State. And the Congress may by general Laws prescribe the Manner in which such Acts, Records and Proceedings shall be proved, and the Effect thereof.

Section. 2. The Citizens of each State shall be entitled to all privileges and Immunities of Citizens in the several States.

A Person charged in any State with Treason, Felony, or other Crime, who shall flee from Justice, and be found in another State, shall on Demand of the executive Authority of the State from which he fled, be delivered up, to be removed to the State having Jurisdiction of the Crime.

No Person held to Service or Labour in one State, under the Laws thereof, escaping into another, shall, in Consequence of any Law or Regulation therein, be discharged from such Service or Labour, but shall be delivered up on Claim of the Party to whom such Service or Labour may be due.

Section. 3. New States may be admitted by the Congress into this Union; but no new State shall be formed or erected within the Jurisdiction of any other State; nor any State be formed by the Junction of two or more States, or Parts of States, without the Consent of the Legislatures of the States concerned as well as of the Congress.

The Congress shall have Power to dispose of and make all needful Rules and Regulations respecting the Territory or other Property belonging to the United States; and nothing in this Constitution shall be so construed as to Prejudice any Claims of the United States, or of any particular State.

Section. 4. The United States shall guarantee to every State in this Union a Republican Form of Government, and shall protect each of them against Invasion; and on Application of the Legislature, or of the Executive (when the Legislature cannot be convened) against domestic Violence.

Article. V.

The Congress, whenever two thirds of both Houses shall deem it necessary, shall propose Amendments to this Constitution, or, on the Application of the Legislatures of two thirds of the several States, shall call a Convention for proposing Amendments, which, in either Case, shall be valid to all Intents and Purposes, as Part of this Constitution, when ratified by the Legislatures of three fourths of the several States, or by Conventions in three fourths thereof, as the one or the other Mode of Ratification may be proposed by the Congress; Provided that no Amendment which may be made prior to the Year One thousand eight hundred and eight shall in any Manner affect the first and fourth Clauses in the Ninth Section of the first Article; and that no State, without its Consent, shall be deprived of it's equal Suffrage in the Senate.

Article. VI.

All Debts contracted and Engagements entered into, before the Adoption of this Constitution, shall be as valid against the United States under this Constitution, as under the Confederation.

This Constitution, and the Laws of the United States which shall be made in Pursuance thereof; and all Treaties made, or which shall be made, under the Authority of the United States, shall be the supreme Law of the Land; and the Judges in every State shall be bound thereby, any Thing in the Constitution or Laws of any State to the Contrary notwithstanding.

The Senators and Representatives before mentioned, and the Members of the several State Legislatures, and all executive and judicial Officers; both of the United States and of the several States, shall be bound by Oath or Affirmation, to support this Constitution; but no religious Test shall ever be required as a Qualification to any Office or public Trust under the United States.

Article. VII.

The Ratification of the Conventions of nine States, shall be sufficient for the Establishment of this Constitution between the States so ratifying the Same.

The Word, "the," being interlined between the seventh and eighth Lines of the first Page, The Word "Thirty" being partly written on an Erazure in the fifteenth Line of the first Page, done in Convention by the Unanimous Consent of the States present the Seventeenth Day of September in the Year of our Lord one thousand seven hun-

The Words "is tried" being interlined between the thirty second and thirty third Lines of the first Page and the Word "the" being interlined between the forty third and forty fourth Lines of the second Page.

dred and Eighty seven and of the Independance of the United States of America the Twelfth In Witness whereof We have hereunto subscribed our Names,

Attest William Jackson Secretary

Go: Washington—Presidt.
and deputy from Virginia

Delaware
- Geo: Read
- Gunning Bedford junr
- John Dickinson
- Richard Bassett
- Jaco: Broom

Maryland
- James McHenry
- Dan of St Thos. Jenifer
- Danl Carroll

Virginia
- John Blair—
- James Madison Jr.

North Carolina
- Wm. Blount
- Richd. Dobbs Spaight.
- Hu Williamson

South Carolina
- J. Rutledge
- Charles Cotesworth Pinckney
- Charles Pinckney
- Pierce Butler

Georgia
- William Few
- Abr Baldwin

New Hampshire
- John Langdon
- Nicholas Gilman

Massachusetts
- Nathaniel Gorham
- Rufus King

Connecticut
- Wm: Saml. Johnson
- Roger Sherman

New York. . . Alexander Hamilton

New Jersey
- Wil: Livingston
- David Brearley
- Wm. Paterson.
- Jona: Dayton

Pensylvania
- B Franklin
- Thomas Mifflin
- Robt Morris
- Geo. Clymer
- Thos. FitzSimons
- Jared Ingersoll
- James Wilson
- Gouv. Morris

1. Engrossed MS (LT), RG 11, DNA.

C. RESOLUTIONS OF THE CONVENTION RECOMMENDING THE PROCEDURES FOR RATIFICATION AND FOR THE ESTABLISHMENT OF GOVERNMENT UNDER THE CONSTITUTION BY THE CONFEDERATION CONGRESS, 17 September[1]

In Convention Monday September 17th. 1787.

Present The States of New Hampshire, Massachusetts, Connecticut, Mr. Hamilton from New York, New Jersey, Pennsylvania, Delaware, Maryland, Virginia, North Carolina, South Carolina and Georgia.

RESOLVED, That the preceeding Constitution be laid before the United States in Congress assembled, and that it is the Opinion of this Convention, that it should afterwards be submitted to a Convention of Delegates, chosen in each State by the People thereof, under the Recommendation of its Legislature, for their Assent and Ratification; and that each Convention assenting to, and ratifying the Same, should give Notice thereof to the United States in Congress assembled.

Resolved, That it is the Opinion of this Convention, that as soon as the Conventions of nine States shall have ratified this Constitution, the United States in Congress assembled should fix a Day on which Electors should be appointed by the States which shall have ratified the same, and a Day on which the Electors should assemble to vote for the President, and the Time and Place for commencing Proceedings under this Constitution. That after such Publication the Electors should be appointed, and the Senators and Representatives elected: That the Electors should meet on the Day fixed for the Election of the President, and should transmit their Votes certified, signed, sealed and directed, as the Constitution requires, to the Secretary of the United States in Congress assembled, that the Senators and Representatives should convene at the Time and Place assigned; that the Senators should appoint a President of the Senate, for the sole Purpose of receiving, opening and counting the Votes for President; and, that after he shall be chosen, the Congress, together with the President, should, without Delay, proceed to execute this Constitution.

By the Unanimous Order of the Convention

W. Jackson Secretary.   Go: Washington Presidt.

1. Engrossed MS (LT), RG 11, DNA.

D. TRANSMITTAL OF THE CONSTITUTION FROM THE CONVENTION IN PHILADELPHIA TO THE CONFEDERATION CONGRESS IN NEW YORK, 17–20 September

William Jackson to George Washington, Monday Evening, 17 September (excerpt)[1]

Major Jackson presents his most respectful compliments to General Washington. . . .

Major Jackson, after burning all the loose scraps of paper which belong to the Convention, will this evening wait upon the General with the Journals and other papers which their vote directs to be delivered to His Excellency.[2]

George Washington Diary, Monday, 17 September (excerpt)[3]

The business being thus closed, the members adjourned to the City Tavern, dined together and took a cordial leave of each other. After which I returned to my lodgings, did some business with, and received the papers from the Secretary of the Convention, and retired to meditate on the momentous work which had been executed, after not less than five, for a large part of the time six, and sometimes 7 hours sitting every day ([except] Sundays and the ten days' adjournment to give a committee opportunity and time to arrange the business) for more than four months.

Noah Webster Diary, Philadelphia, Tuesday, 18 September[4]

General Washington leaves town. Dr. Franklin presents the Speaker of the House of Assembly in Pennsylvania with the federal system which is read. Bells ring. All America waits anxiously for the plan of government.

Philadelphia Pennsylvania Packet, 18 September

We have the heartfelt pleasure to inform our fellow citizens that the Federal Convention adjourned yesterday, having completed the object of their deliberations. And we hear that Major W[illiam] Jackson, the Secretary of that honorable body, leaves this city for New York this morning in order to lay the great result of their proceedings before the United States in Congress.

William Samuel Johnson Diary, 18, 19 September (excerpts)[5]

18th. Set out at 10 o'clock in the stage, Governor [William] Livingston, [William] Few, [Abraham] Baldwin, [William] Jackson, etc. in company came to [New] Brunswick. Cold.

. . . .

19th. Violent storm. Set out in it at 6 and arrived in New York at [2?].

New York Daily Advertiser, 20 September

We are informed, from good authority, that the FEDERAL CON-

VENTION completed their business on Monday last; and that their proceedings will be immediately laid before Congress. We purpose to give the whole of their proceedings in tomorrow's paper.

1. RC, Washington Papers, DLC.
2. For the disposal of the Convention Journals and papers, see Farrand, II, 641, 648.
3. MS, Washington Papers, DLC. The parentheses have been inserted by the editors. Washington rewrote the above entry from his rough diary which reads: "Met in Convention and signed the proceedings—all except Governor Randolph, Colonel Mason and Mr. Gerry. Dine all together at the City Tavern and returned to my lodgings."
4. MS, Webster Diary, NN.
5. MS, Johnson Papers, CtHi.

IX

The Confederation Congress
and the Constitution

20–28 September 1787

Introduction

The Constitution was read to Congress on Thursday, 20 September, and the following Wednesday, 26 September, was assigned for its consideration. Between the 20th and the 26th, Congress considered such matters as Indian relations, finance, the Western Territory, foreign affairs, and private petitions. On 24 September, the Rhode Island General Assembly's explanation of its refusal to send delegates to the Convention at Philadelphia was read to Congress (VI:M above).

Under the Articles of Confederation, each state could send from two to seven delegates to Congress, and a majority of each delegation was necessary for the state's vote to be counted. An evenly split delegation went on the rolls as "divided." If only a single member from a state was present, the vote was not counted. Therefore, on 13 August, prior to the end of the Convention, the President of Congress, Arthur St. Clair, had urged the states to be fully represented (LMCC, VIII, 638). As a result, every state except Rhode Island and Maryland had at least two members present by 26 September.

Of the thirty-three members of Congress who attended between 20 and 28 September, ten had attended the Constitutional Convention. William Pierce of Georgia left the Convention on 1 July and returned to Congress. Nathaniel Gorham, Rufus King, William Samuel Johnson, and William Few had returned by 20 September; while Nicholas Gilman, John Langdon, James Madison, William Blount, and Pierce Butler had returned before the 26th. All of these delegates, except Pierce, had signed the Constitution on 17 September. Two other members of Congress, Richard Henry Lee and Abraham Clark, had been elected to the Convention but refused to attend.

Other Convention delegates who were not members of Congress were also in New York. Among them were Gouverneur Morris, Charles Cotesworth Pinckney, John Rutledge, Elbridge Gerry, and possibly Alexander Hamilton, Charles Pinckney, and Abraham Baldwin.

The proceedings of Congress from 20 to 28 September are reconstructed from several sources: the rough manuscript Journals, motions made and papers read in Congress, Melancton Smith's notes of debates, letters written by members of Congress, and letters written by non-members.

The printed *Journals of Congress,* which Secretary Charles Thomson sent to the state executives on 28 November, provide almost no information about the proceedings of Congress on the Constitution. The entry for the 20th does not mention that the Constitution was read that day. The only entry for the 26th, when the debate on the Constitution began, concerns payment for Nathaniel Twining, who carried mails by stagecoach, and includes a roll-call vote on that issue. The entry for the 27th states: "Congress assembled. Present as before." The printed *Journals* for the 28th contain the text of the Constitution, the documents sent with it from the Convention, and the resolution of Congress submitting the Constitution to the states.

Thus, so far as the public was informed by official sources, Congress merely received and transmitted the Constitution on 28 September. The New York newspapers, which usually printed rather full accounts of the proceedings of Congress, virtually ignored the events of 26–28 September. They printed only Congress' resolution of 28 September transmitting the Constitution to the states. They gave no hint that debates took place; nor, for the most part, did other newspapers throughout the United States. The first widely circulated public reference to the fact that a debate had occurred appeared in Samuel Bryan's "Centinel" II in the Philadelphia *Freeman's Journal* on 24 October (CC:190). Bryan evidently had received the information from a member of Congress. Only one other isolated newspaper account in the Boston *American Herald,* 19 November, disclosed the controversy that had occurred in Congress. Consequently, the general public did not become aware of the extent of the controversy until the publication of Richard Henry Lee's proposed amendments and his letter of 16 October to Governor Edmund Randolph in the Petersburg *Virginia Gazette* on 6 December (CC:325).

With the exception of the entry for 27 September, the rough manuscript Journals reveal no more than the printed *Journals.* The Journals for the 27th contain motions for the transmittal of the Constitution to the states made by Richard Henry Lee, Abraham Clark, and Edward Carrington, and a roll-call vote. However, they do not contain Richard Henry Lee's motion offering amendments to the Constitution. Abraham Clark stated that Lee's motion for amendments "will do injury by coming on the Journal"; therefore at the end of the day, evidently on orders from Congress, lines were drawn through the manuscript Journals, thus removing the motion from the official record.

Melancton Smith's notes of the debates are the most complete record of discussion and action in Congress. In recording the arguments of his fellow delegates, Smith placed all motions in the proper order, although he did not summarize all of them. Smith's notes are undated, but comparison with the rough manuscript Journals of 27 September indicates that they cover the events of that day. Nathan Dane's motion, to which Smith refers at the beginning of his notes, was evidently presented on the 26th, because the Journals for the 27th begin with Richard Henry Lee's substitute motion.

In editing Melancton Smith's notes of debates, punctuation has been added and abbreviations have been spelled out. Brackets with question marks are used to indicate uncertain readings of abbreviations, and words have been added in brackets to provide clarity.

Melancton Smith's manuscript notes are a unique source without which it would be impossible to present the version of events in Congress printed below. They were secured by the New York State Library in 1959 and were published by Julius Goebel, Jr., as "Melancthon Smith's Minutes of Debates on the New Constitution," *Columbia Law Review*, LXIV (January 1964), 26–43. On the whole, the version of Smith's notes printed below and that printed by Goebel are similar, although some of Smith's abbreviations are interpreted differently.

Members of Congress in Attendance, 20–28 September[1]

CONNECTICUT
Joseph Platt Cooke
William Samuel Johnson

DELAWARE
Dyre Kearney
Nathaniel Mitchell

GEORGIA
William Few
William Pierce

MARYLAND
David Ross

MASSACHUSETTS
Nathan Dane
Nathaniel Gorham
Rufus King

NEW HAMPSHIRE
Nicholas Gilman
John Langdon

NEW JERSEY
Lambert Cadwalader
Abraham Clark
James Schureman

NEW YORK
Melancton Smith
John Haring
Abraham Yates

NORTH CAROLINA
John Baptiste Ashe
William Blount
Robert Burton

PENNSYLVANIA
John Armstrong, Jr.
William Bingham
William Irvine
Arthur St. Clair

RHODE ISLAND
Unrepresented

SOUTH CAROLINA	VIRGINIA
Pierce Butler	Edward Carrington
Daniel Huger	William Grayson
John Kean	Henry Lee
	Richard Henry Lee
	James Madison

1. The names of members of Congress who were members of the Constitutional Convention have been set in italic type.

A. PROCEEDINGS OF CONGRESS ON THE CONSTITUTION, 20–28 September

Journals of Congress, Thursday, 20 September[1]

Congress assembled. Present: Massachusetts, Connecticut, New York, New Jersey, Pennsylvania, Delaware, Virginia, North Carolina, and Georgia and from Maryland Mr. [David] Ross and from South Carolina Mr. [Daniel] Huger.

Despatch Book, 20 September[2]

Received	Dates	From whom	Subjects, etc., etc.
1787 September 20	September 17	Convention of the states	with new frame of government

William Bingham to Thomas FitzSimons, New York, 21 September[3]

You expressed a desire of knowing what reception the conventional government would meet with in Congress, and whether there was a prospect of its passing thro the necessary formalities in Congress, previous to the adjournment of our legislature.

It was yesterday received and read in Congress, and Wednesday next fixed as the day for its consideration. If I had been present, I should certainly have opposed its postponement to so distant a day. As from inquiry I find that every state on the floor of Congress is disposed to adopt it, I will endeavor to bring on the question immediately. I shall urge as an argument the favorable disposition of our Assembly, which is now in session. I will inform you of the results as soon as possible.

Roger Alden Memorandum, New York, 21 September[4]

The budget was opened yesterday and the important secret is now exposed to public view, and I hope it will be approved by every individual. I find it meets with the approbation of many of those gentlemen of whose opinion and for whose judgment I have the highest respect, but where we may expect opposition is easy to be conjectured. I can readily make three classes: great men of our own who will lose their consequence, little great men, conscious of their own talents who know they have not abilities to become really great men, and all those who are really enemies to the happiness of the country or have exposed themselves by their crimes, idleness and wickedness to the just laws of society.

Edward Carrington to James Madison, New York, 23 September[5]

The gentlemen who have arrived from the Convention inform us that you are on the way to join us.[6] Lest, however, you may, under a supposition that the state of the delegation is such as to admit of your absence, indulge yourself in leisurely movements, after the fatiguing time you have had, I take this precaution to apprise you that the same schism which unfortunately happened in our state in Philadelphia threatens us here also. One of our colleagues Mr. R[ichard] H[enry] Lee is forming propositions for essential alterations in the Constitution, which will, in effect, be to oppose it. Another, Mr. [William] Grayson, dislikes it and is, at best, for giving it only a silent passage to the states. Mr. H[enry] Lee joins me in opinion that it ought to be warmly recommended to insure its adoption. A lukewarmness in Congress will be made a ground of opposition by the unfriendly in the states. Those who have hitherto wished to bring the conduct of Congress into contempt, will in this case be ready to declare it truly respectable.

Next Wednesday [26 September] is fixed for taking under consideration this business, and I ardently wish you could be with us.

The New York faction is rather active in spreading the seeds of opposition. This, however, has been expected, and will not make an impression so injurious as the same circumstance would in some other states. Colonel [Alexander] Hamilton has boldly taken his ground in the public papers and, having truth and propriety on his side, it is to be hoped he will stem the torrent of folly and iniquity.[7]

I do not implicitly accede, in sentiment, to every article of the scheme

proposed by the Convention, but I see not how my utmost wishes
are to be gratified until I can withdraw from society. So long as I
find it necessary to combine my strength and interests with others,
I must be satisfied to make some sacrifices to the general accomoda-
tion.

Journals of Congress, Monday, 24 September

Congress assembled. Present as before [i.e., Massachusetts, Connecticut, New York, New Jersey, Pennsylvania, Delaware, Virginia, North
Carolina, South Carolina, and Georgia, and from Maryland David
Ross].
[The Rhode Island General Assembly's explanation of its refusal
to send delegates to the Convention was read to Congress (VI:M
above).]

Journals of Congress, Wednesday, 26 September

Congress assembled. Present as before [i.e., New Hampshire, Massachusetts, Connecticut, New York, New Jersey, Pennsylvania, Delaware, Virginia, North Carolina, South Carolina, and Georgia, and
from Maryland David Ross].

Melancton Smith's Notes, 26 September[8]

On the Constitution reported by the Convention. The motion of
Nathan Dane for sending forward the Constitution with an opinion,
received.

Nathan Dane's Motion, 26 September[9]

Whereas Congress Sensible that there were defects in the present
Confederation; and that several of the States were desirous that a
Convention of Delegates should be formed to consider the same, and
to propose necessary alterations in the federal Constitution; in February last resolved that it was expedient that a Convention of the
States should be held for the Sole and express purpose of revising
the articles of Confederation and reporting to Congress and the several legislatures such alterations and provisions therein, as Should
when agreed to in Congress, and be confirmed by the States, render the
federal Constitution adequate to the exigencies of Government, and
the preservation of the union—[10]

And whereas it appears by Credentials laid before Congress, that twelve States appointed Delegates who assembled in Convention accordingly, and who did on the 17th. instant, by the unanimous consent of the States then present in convention agree upon, and afterwards lay before Congress, a Constitution for the United States, to be submitted to a convention of Delegates, chosen in each State by the people thereof, under the recommendation of its legislature, for their assent and ratification which constitution appears to be intended as an entire system in itself, and not as any part of, or alteration in the Articles of Confederation;—to alterations in which articles, the deliberations and powers of Congress are, in this Case, constitutionally confined—and whereas Congress cannot with propriety proceed to examine and alter the said Constitution proposed, unless it be with a view so essentially to change the principles and forms of it, as to make it an additional part in the said Confederation and the members of Congress not feeling themselves authorised by the forms of Government under which they are assembled, to express an opinion respecting a system of Government no way connected with those forms; but conceiving that the respect they owe their constituents and the importance of the subject require, that the report of the Convention should, with all convenient dispatch, be transmitted to the Several States to be laid before the respective legislatures ther[eof,] therefore

Resolved that there be transmitted to the Supreme executive of each State a copy of the report of the Convention of the States lately Assembled in the City of Philadelphia signed by their deputies the seventeenth instant including their resolutions and their letter directed to the president of Congress—

Melancton Smith's Notes, 26 September[11]

Pierce Butler: Wishes to know the motives that produced the motion. He thinks it is calculated to disapprove [the Constitution].

Nathan Dane: Asks to know what words are objectionable.

1. The consolidation [is] imperfect and will not work.

2. If it does, it will not work on free principles. It must be supported by a standing army. It will oppress the honest and industrious, [and] it will advantage a few. Is not averse to examination, is open to conviction, and, if convinced, will support it. Is willing the present motion should be amended so as to be neutral. If it [the Constitution] is to be approved, it will be moved to take it up by paragraphs, objections stated, [and] amendments moved. Congress [has] no constitutional right to consider [the Constitution].

Journals of Congress, Thursday, 27 September

Congress assembled. Present as before.

According to order Congress resumed the consideration of the form of a Constitution for the United States of America and transmitted to Congress by the Convention of the states held at Philadelphia pursuant to the resolve of the twenty-first day of February last.

Melancton Smith's Notes, 27 September

Richard Henry Lee: Every man to see with his own eyes; to judge for themselves. Congress, acting under the present Constitution definitely limiting their powers, have no right to recommend a plan subverting the government. This remark felt, as a gentleman yesterday justify, by the necessity of the case. This [is] dangerous because this principle has been abused to bad 100 times [to one] where it is used for good. The Impost [of 1781][12] referred [to] as an instance to justify; that [was] within the powers [of Congress; it was] sent to [receive?] the approval of 13 states; and within this line this [Constitution] by [the approval of] nine [states]. This plan proposes [to] destroy the Confederation of 13 and [to] establish a new one of 9. Yet it would be indecent not to send it to the states for 12 states sent delegates [to the Federal Convention], as he understands, to amend the present government. Men of respected characters have agreed upon this. It [the Constitution] should be forwarded. A gentleman yesterday said the Confederation says nothing of [a] convention. It is true it does not point [to] a convention, but it does not forbid [this?] to be proposed by one, or any other way. Congress is only to agree. If this was not destructive, but an amendment, Congress might consider [the Constitution]. Proposes a resolution, stating that as Congress have no right under the Confederation to recommend alterations of the Confederation unless agreed to by 13 states, and this [Constitution] proposes an amendment by 9.

Richard Henry Lee's Motion, Journals of Congress, 27 September[13]

And a motion being made by Richard Henry Lee, seconded by Melancton Smith in the words following: "Resolved, That Congress after due attention to the Constitution under which this body exists and acts find that the said Constitution in the thirteenth article thereof limits the power of Congress to the amendment of the present Confederacy of thirteen states, but does not extend it to the creation of a new confederacy of nine states; and the late Convention having been constituted under the authority of twelve states in this Union it is deemed respectful to transmit, and it is accordingly ordered, that the plan of a new Federal Constitution laid before Congress by the said Convention be sent to the executive of every state in this Union to be laid before their respective legislatures."

Melancton Smith's Notes, 27 September

Rufus King: Recommends moderation and is sorry Mr. Dane is intemperate.

Henry Lee: Approves the motion of Richard Henry Lee as bringing the point to view: whether it shall be passed with investiture or without. Thinks Mr. Dane has not appeared intemperate.

Richard Henry Lee: At a loss to understand Mr. King. Feel his pulse and he will find no inte[mperance?]. Congress must do something. Some think it [the Constitution] must be approved. Some think we have no right to determine. He [thought?] his motion neutral. If he is called to approve, his conscience will oblige him to declare his sentiments. He is candid, not sinister.

Abraham Clark: Don't like any proposal yet made. He can't approve it [the Constitution], but thinks it will answer no purpose to alter it. Will not oppose it in any place. Prefers a resolution to postpone [Lee's motion] to take up one, barely to forward a copy to the states, to be laid before the legislatures to be referred to conventions.

Abraham Clark's Motion, Journals of Congress, 27 September

A motion was made by Abraham Clarke seconded by Nathaniel Mitchel to postpone the consideration of that motion [Lee's] in order to take up the following: "That a copy of the Constitution agreed to and laid before Congress by the late Convention of the several states with their resolutions and the letter accompanying the same be transmitted to the executives of each state to be laid before their respective legislatures in order to be by them submitted to conventions of delegates to be chosen agreeably to the said resolutions of the Convention."[14]

Melancton Smith's Notes, 27 September

Richard Henry Lee: The resolution moved is an approval.

Abraham Clark: Does not mean to approve the plan, but [only] the resolution of [the Federal] Convention [which stated that the

Constitution was] to be laid before the conventions of the states. By that we only approve that it [the Constitution] be laid before the states, but does not recommend that [it] be ratified. We may take it up and alter it.

Nathaniel Gorham: Hopes it [Lee's motion] will be postponed as it is plainer. The resolution of Mr. Lee states [that] we cannot take it [the Constitution] up and will prevent Congress from setting the government to work if 9 or 10 states agree to it. Therefore there must be war. The new government must raise troops to overset Congress.

William Grayson: The motion from Virginia [is] better than [that from New] Jersey. The one from Jersey just forwards the proposal by a bare implicit approbation; the one [from] Virginia gives a reason why it don't approve and leaves the adv[ocates?] to say Congress would have approved, if they could. In favor of the motion from Virginia. Is in favor of the new Constitution. This [Confederation] proposes a mode of altering. If we depart from the mode in this case, it will form a precedent from doing it in the old one—[in] the [way the] 13th Article [found?]. 9 states may agree to the new [Constitution]; the other 4 ought to be left in possession of this [Confederation] if they choose and not [be] forced to come in. Does not think there has yet been any departure from the Confederation. Congress had a right to refer to any body to report. Keep the present [Confederation] until you get a better.

Against the Constitution. It affects his state. Personal right[s] not in the danger some fear. Bills of rights essential in monarchies. The government is democratic all [over?]. Liberty as safe as in the hands of Rhode Island if gentlemen embarrassed respecting personal liberty. But can't say so as to property, an idea taken up, [but] never admitted in [the] Confederation. Majority never governs—the Netherlands instanced. Nine states should have been required [to alter the Confederation?]. The representation in the Senate inequal.

Richard Henry Lee: It is objected that if this Congress cannot decide now, a new, a future one cannot. [This argument] has not force, for this is a first principle that the majority of the people have a right to make a new one. If 9 states agree, the majority of the people [agree].

Henry Lee: Will vote for the postponement [of Lee's motion] because he supposes we have a right to decide from the great principle of necessity or the salus populi. This necessity justifies the measure. Congress and all the states have decided it. Are the laws of Congress paramount to the constitutions of the different states?

Nathan Dane: Wishes to steer in the channel of neutrality, yet suggest whether a motion which brings into view so materially the question of 9 states [should be adopted]. Prefers the Jersey [motion].

Understands the clause which makes the clause declaring the Constitution [the] supreme law, [is] different from the Convention [draft].[15]

Richard Henry Lee: We live in an enlightened age. People will understand us. To accommodate, has left out the words 9 and 13. Will consent they may be put out. The doctrine of salus populi [is] dangerous. [It] has been in the [mouths] of all tyrants. If men may do as they please, from this argument all constitutions [are] useless. All tyrants have used it.

James Madison: Can't accede to it [Lee's motion]. [It] is not respectful to the Convention. After what has been done, if Congress does not agree, [it] implies a disagreement. Congress from former acts do not object to a national government. If either [Lee's or Clark's] motion is adopted it implies disap[probation]. The question is, whether on the whole it is best to adopt it, and [we] ought to say so. The powers of [the] Convention [are] the same as of Congress. The reason of Convention [was] that they might not be interrupted; and that persons might be admitted [to the Convention] whether or not [they] be in Congress, and to prevent jealousies. If this House can't approve [the Constitution], it says the crisis is not yet arrived and implies a disapp[robation]. [In] a great many instances, Congress have recommended what they have no right [to recommend]

Richard Henry Lee: The Convention have not proceeded as this House were bound [by the Articles of Confederation]. It is to be agreed to by the states and means the 13 [states]. But this [Constitution] recommends a new confederacy of 9 [states]. The Convention [had] no more powers than Congress, yet if 9 states agree [the Constitution] becomes supreme law. Knows no instance on the Journals, as he remembers, opposing the Confederacy. The Impost [of 1781] was to be adopted by 13 [states]. The resolution from [New] Jersey approves [the Constitution] for Congress don't send out anything but such as they approve.

Abraham Clark: Unhappy to differ from [Richard Henry] Lee. He reveres his judgment. If his objection [is] good, his own proposal [is] liable to the like objection.

William Samuel Johnson: Hardly possible to send it out without approving or disapproving. For this reason, Mr. Lee's motion [ought to be postponed]. Congress ought to approve or disapprove. They may do it. It is their duty to do it. The people will see [that] we, that Congress, act without power in the case of 9 or 13 [states]. They will see, that the act of [21] February [calling the Convention] was departing from the Constitution. [The] Confederation says Congress was to make alterations.[16] Congress appoint a Convention to do it. He saw it so at the time and opposed it.[17] The argument then was salus populi. Nothing from Congress would do. The proposal from [the] Convention [is] not a proposal to 9 [states] but to all. It is hoped all will [agree]. Mr. Lee says, if 9 agree to alter by the people; this says, if 9 do in this case, we will set it going on the principle of majority. On the principle of Congress referring to the Convention, they are a committee and have made report. Congress then must approve or disapprove. It don't imply an approbation of all its parts, but the best upon the whole, a matter of accommodation. We say it is better than the present [constitution], better than running the risk of another.

James Madison: Did not say the Convention moved exactly in the line of their appointment. Congress did depart from the idea of [a] federal and recommend a national government in February 1781.[18] Congress did [so] from the principle [of] salus populi. The western country, its sale and government, [is] an instance of exceeding powers, as Congress have in many instances exceeded their power. If it does not in this instance approve, it will imply disapproval.

Richard Henry Lee: The western country was once Virginia's. She gave it to Congress. Congress sells it as she had a right. The government [is] temporary and not inconsistent.[19]

If I understand, gentlemen, this [Constitution] is to be adopted and no other, with[out] alterations. Why so? [There are] good things in it, but many bad. So much so that, he says here as he will say everywhere, that if adopted, civil liberty will be in eminent danger. The greatest parts of difficulty arises from debt. If that was removed, and [the government] could make treaties without the limitations, and to regulate the trade with reasonable limits—but at all events, he sees not the necessity of pressing this [Constitution] without any amendments. Thinks the [state] conventions had best have had the liberty to alter [the Constitution].

Pierce Butler: The question ought to be on the whole—no amendments. The objections [are] not pointed [out]. Dane has leading objections but declines naming them. Lee [says the Constitution is] dangerous to civil liberty. The Convention could have made a better—but that this [is] best on the whole. [Congress] have no power and it will answer no purpose to alter. The state of the country [is] contemptible abroad and on the eve of anarchy at home. Anarchy will follow if it [the Constitution] is not adopted.

Vote to Postpone Richard Henry Lee's Motion, Journals of Congress, 27 September

On the question to postpone [Lee's motion] for the purpose above mentioned [for considering Abraham Clark's motion] the yeas and nays being required by Richard Henry Lee:

NEW HAMPSHIRE			DELAWARE		
Langdon	ay	ay	Kearny	ay	ay
Gilman	ay		Mitchell	ay	
MASSACHUSETTS			**MARYLAND**		
Gorham	ay		Ross	ay	
King	ay	ay			
Dane	ay		**VIRGINIA**		
			Grayson	no	
CONNECTICUT			Madison	ay	
Johnson	ay	ay	R H Lee	no	ay
Cook	ay		Carrington	ay	
			H Lee	ay	
NEW YORK					
Smith	no		**NORTH CAROLINA**		
Haring	no	no	Blount	ay	
Yates	no		Ashe	ay	ay
			Burton	ay	
NEW JERSEY					
Cadwallader	ay		**SOUTH CAROLINA**		
Clarke	ay	ay	Kean	ay	
Schurman	ay		Huger	ay	ay
			Butler	ay	
PENNSYLVANIA					
St. Clair	ay		**GEORGIA**		
Irvine	ay		Few	ay	ay
Bingham	ay	ay	Pierce	ay	
Armstrong	ay				

So it was resolved in the affirmative.

Edward Carrington's Motion, Journals of Congress, 27 September

On motion of Edward Carrington seconded by William Bingham, the motion of Abraham Clarke was postponed to take into consideration the following motion, viz.: "Congress proceeded to the consideration of the Constitution for the United States by the late Convention held in the city of Philadelphia and thereupon resolved that Congress do agree thereto and that it be recommended to the legislatures of the several states to cause conventions to be held as speedily as may be to the end that the same may be adopted, ratified and confirmed."

Melancton Smith's Notes, 27 September

The motion from Richard Henry Lee was postponed, and then a motion was made by Edward Carrington.

Henry Lee: Thinks the matter [the Constitution] was to be taken up [by Congress] in its parts, but cannot agree to it in all its parts, without [an] examination by paragraphs and propose [such?] amendments [as] are necessary. Congress will subject themselves to disgrace by voting on a matter which they have not examined. Moves to postpone [Carrington's motion] and [have the Constitution] taken up by paragraphs.

Nathaniel Gorham: Thinks not necessary to take up [the Constitution] by paragraphs. Every gentleman may propose amendments. No necessity of a bill of rights, because a bill of rights in state governments was intended to retain certain powers [in the people] as the legislatures had unlimited powers.

James Madison: The business is open to consideration. Should feel delicacy if he had not assented in Convention though he did not approve it.[20] Gentlemen have said this is in the situation of a bill agreed to by one house. This principle will oppose amendments because the act if altered will not be the act of both. It must be altered in all stages. It may be, but it cannot succeed, nor any other alteration if all are to agree in this manner. [The] Confederation was proposed without alteration. No probability of Congress agreeing in alterations. Those who disagree, differ in their opinions. A bill of rights [is] unnecessary because the powers are enumerated and only extend to certain cases, and the people who are to agree to it are to establish this.[21]

Richard Henry Lee: It is admitted and [a] fact that this [Constitution] was to be sent to Congress, but surely it was to be considered and altered, and not to be sent forward without. The bill of rights will be brought forward. [A bill of rights] not necessary in [the] Confederation because it is expressly declared [that] no power should be exercised, but such as is expressly given, and therefore no constructive power can be exercised. To prevent this [is] the great use of a bill of rights.

Rufus King: The House cannot constitutionally make alterations.

The idea of [the] Convention originated in the states, and this led the House to agree. They proposed the Convention should propose alterations, which when agreed to here and confirmed by the states [should be adopted], and therefore [Congress] are to agree or disagree to the alterations and cannot alter [the Constitution] consistently with their own act. Congress have taken their line, but in consequence of that [decision they are put?]. The majority of the people, it is said [by Richard Henry Lee], may alter, and if they have manifested a desire to change, this House may advise it, as it is not obligatory. We may advise as any other body of men. To satisfy forms it was ordered to pass this House. They may agree or disagree. If they do disagree it will not prevent them [the states] to accept. If they [Congress] agree it will give weight.

Richard Henry Lee: Strangest doctrine he ever heard, that [in] referring a matter of report, that no alterations should be made. The idea the common sense of man. The states and Congress, he thinks, had the idea that Congress was to amend if they thought proper. He wishes to give it a candid inquiry, and proposes such alterations as are necessary. If the gentleman [King] wishes it should go forth without amendments, let it go with all its imperfections on its head, and the amendments by themselves. To insist that it should go as it is without amendments is like presenting a hungry man 50 dishes and insisting he should eat all or none.

James Madison: A circumstance distinguishes this report from others. The Convention was not appointed by Congress, but by the people from whom Congress derive their power. Congress only to concur. Admits Congress may alter, but if they do alter, it is not the act of Convention but of Congress; and excludes [the] Convention entirely and confines the House in the trammels of the Confederation. Not unusual to propose things in the lump. So the Confederation was presented.

Richard Henry Lee: A report implies a right to consider on the whole or part. The Confederation went in such way as to admit of objections, and most states proposed them.[22] If it is amended, he thinks it will be more likely to succeed, as capital objections will probably be removed. The idea seems to be, this must be agreed to or nothing else. Why this idea? This supposes all wisdom centers in the Convention.

Nathaniel Gorham: Why does not the gentleman propose his amendments? Then the question of the expediency of the amendments will be considered.

William Samuel Johnson: The term of report: a general expression, not meant as in cases where [a] report is made to Congress.

The people and Congress agree the alterations shall be made by Convention, and the nature of things forbids any alteration as it will make it no act of Convention. Congress are not to judge in the last resort, but the people; and therefore it must be approved or disapproved in the whole.

Richard Henry Lee: Is it the idea of Convention that not only Congress but the states must agree in the whole, or else to reject it? And it seems all idea of amendments are precluded.

James Madison: The proper question is whether any amendments shall be made, and that the House should decide. Suppose alterations sent to the states. The Arts. [Articles of Confederation][23] requires the delegates [in Congress] to report [alterations] to them [i.e., the state legislatures]. There will be two plans. Some will accept one and some another. That will create confusion and proves it was not the intent of the state.

Richard Henry Lee: Some admit the right but doubt the expediency and proposes amendments.

Richard Henry Lee's Proposed Amendments, 27 September[24]

It having been found from Universal experience that the most express declarations and reservations are necessary to protect the just rights and liberty of Mankind from the Silent, powerful, and ever active conspiracy of those who govern—And it appearing to be the sense of the good people of America by the various Bills or Declarations of rights whereon the governments of the greater number of the States are founded, that such precautions are proper to restrain and regulate the exercise of the great powers necessarily given to Rulers—In conformity with these principles, and from respect for the public sentiment on this subject it is submitted

That the new Constitution proposed for the Government of the U. States be bottomed upon a declaration, or Bill of Rights, clearly and precisely stating the principles upon which this Social Compact is founded, to wit;

That the rights of Conscience in matters of Religion shall not be violated—

That the freedom of the Press shall be secured—

That the trial by Jury in Criminal and Civil cases, and the modes prescribed by the Common Law for safety of Life in Criminal prosecutions shall be held sacred—

That standing Armies in times of peace are dangerous to liberty, and ought not to be permitted unless assented to by two thirds of the Members composing each House of the legislature under the new constitution—

That Elections of the Members of the Legislature should be free and frequent—

That the right administration of justice should be secured by the freedom and independency of the Judges—

That excessive Bail, excessive Fines, or cruel and unusual punishments should not be demanded or inflicted—

That the right of the people to assemble peaceably for the purpose of petitioning the Legislature shall not be prevented—

That the Citizens shall not be exposed to unreasonable searches, seizures of their papers, houses, persons, or property.

And whereas it is necessary for the good of Society that the administration of government be conducted with all possible maturity of judgement; for which reason it hath been the practise of civilized nations, and so determined by every State in this Union, that a Council of State or Privy Council should be appointed to advise and assist in the arduous business assigned to the Executive power—therefore, that the New Constitution be so amended as to admit the appointment of a Privy Council, to consist of Eleven Members chosen by the President, but responsible for the advise [sic] they may give—for which purpose the Advice given shall be entered in a Council Book and signed by the Giver in all affairs of great concern. and that the Counsellors act under an Oath of Office—

In order to prevent the dangerous blending of the Legislative and Executive powers, and to secure responsibility—The Privy Council and not the Senate shall be joined with the President in the appointment of all Officers Civil and Military under the new Constitution—

That it be further amended so as to omit the Creation of a Vice President, whose duties, as assigned by the Constitution, may be discharged by the Privy Council (except in the instance of presiding in the Senate, which may be supplied by a Speaker chosen from the body of Senators by themselves as usual) and thus render unnecessary the establishment of a Great Officer of State who is sometimes to be joined with the Legislature and sometimes to administer the Executive power, rendering responsibility difficult, and adding unnecessarily to the Aristocratic influence; besides giving unjust and needless preeminence to that state from whence this Officer may come.

That such parts of the new Constitution be amended as provide imperfectly for the trial of Criminals by a Jury of the Vicinage, and to supply the omission of a Jury trial in Civil causes or disputes about property between Individuals where by the Common law it is directed, and as generally it is secured by the several State Constitutions.

That such other parts be amended as permit the vexatious and oppressive calling of Citizens from their own Country in all cases of controversy concerning property between Citizens of different States, and between Citizens and foreigners, to be tried in far distant Courts, and as it may be, without a Jury. Whereby in a multitude of Cases, the circumstances of distance and expence may compel men to submit to the most unjust and ill founded demands.

That in order to secure the rights of the people more effectually from oppression, the power and respectability of the House of Representatives be increased, by increasing the number of Delegates to that House where the democratic interest will chiefly reside.

That the New Constitution be so altered as to increase the number of Votes necessary to determine questions relative to the creation of new or the amendment of old Laws, as it is directed in the choice of a President where the Votes are equal from the States; it being certainly as necessary to secure the Community from oppressive Laws as it is to guard against the choice of an improper President. The plan now admitting of a bare majority to make Laws, by which it may happen that 5 States may Legislate for 13 States tho 8 of the 13 are absent—

That the new Constitution be so amended as to place the right of representation in the Senate on the same ground that it is placed in the House of Delegates thereby securing equality of representation in the Legislature so essentially necessary for good government.

Melancton Smith's Notes, 27 September

Nathan Dane: The gentlemen from the Convention are pushing the business by refinements. [Is] that the common sense of the country? If the House mean to preclude amendments, the gentleman [i.e., Dane] will stand excused to vote in the negative.

Edward Carrington: When he made the motion, supposed every man had a right to examine [the Constitution]. He had considered and made up his mind. If any gentleman has not made up his mind, he ought to have a liberty of amending. For though he thinks it inexpedient to amend, as he fears it would defeat the whole. Important amendments are offered by a member. He ought to have a right to support them.

Abraham Clark: The motion by Mr. Lee for amendments will do injury by coming on the Journal, and therefore the House, upon cool reflection, will think it best to agree to send it [the Constitution] out without agreeing.

William Grayson: It is a curious situation. It is urged all alterations are precluded. Has not made up his mind, and thinks it precipitant to urge a decision in two days on a subject [which] took 4 months. If we have no right to amend, then we ought to give a silent passage, for if we cannot alter, why should we deliberate. His opinion [is that] they should stand solely upon the opinion of [the] Convention. The salus populi much talked of. This Constitution will not remove our difficulties—the great defects a disinclination to pay money. That removed, our great difficulty would be over. No necessity to urge a hasty decision. In 2 or 3 years we should get a good government.

Journals of Congress, Friday, 28 September

Congress assembled. Present: New Hampshire, Massachusetts, Connecticut, New York, New Jersey, Pennsylvania, Delaware, Virginia, North Carolina, South Carolina, and Georgia and from Maryland Mr. [David] Ross.

Congress having received the report of the Convention lately assembled in Philadelphia.

"Resolved unanimously, That the said report with the resolutions and letter accompanying the same be transmitted to the several legislatures in order to be submitted to a convention of delegates chosen in each state by the people thereof in conformity to the resolves of the Convention made and provided in that case."

Charles Thomson, Circular Letter to the Executives of the States, New York, 28 September[25]

In obedience to an unanimous resolution of the United States in Congress assembled, a copy of which is annexed, I have the honor to transmit to Your Excellency, the report of the Convention lately assembled in Philadelphia, together with the resolutions and letter accompanying the same; and have to request that Your Excellency will be pleased to lay the same before the legislature, in order that it may be submitted to a convention of delegates chosen in your state by the people of the state in conformity to the resolves of the Convention, made and provided in that case.

1. Congress had not met since Friday, 14 September, and the rough Journals for the 20th contain only this entry. On the 20th, in addition to receiving the Constitution and assigning Wednesday, 26 September for its consideration, Congress agreed to pay certain expenses of the Convention as requested by the Convention on 5 September (JCC, XXXIII, 487–88). Lastly, Congress received and read replies from state executives to the letter from the President of Congress of 13 August requesting the states to send delegates to Congress.

2. PCC, Item 185, Despatch Books, IV, 17, DNA.

3. RC, Gratz Collection, PHi. FitzSimons, a member of the Pennsylvania Assembly, endorsed the letter as received on 24 September.

4. PCC, Item 55, Records of the Office of Congress, 1781–89, f. 207, DNA. Alden, Deputy Secretary of Congress, addressed the document to "Dear Sir," but he possibly intended it as a memorandum since it remains in the papers of Congress.

5. RC, Madison Papers, DLC.

6. Madison was on the way to New York, where he arrived on 24 September (Madison to James Madison, Sr., 30 September, IX:B below).

7. Hamilton published an anonymous attack on Governor George Clinton in the New York *Daily Advertiser* on 21 July. He followed this with another anonymous article on 15 September, answering a writer who had defended Clinton (Syrett, IV, 229–32, 248–53; see also CC:52).

8. MS, Melancton Smith Papers, N. See note 11 below.

9. MS (LT), PCC, Item 36, Motions Made in Congress, 1777–88, DNA. This document is endorsed "Mr. Dane's Motion respect[in]g New Constitution Oct. 1787." The endorsement may mean that Dane delivered his motion to Secretary Thomson in October.

10. For Congress' resolution of 21 February, see V:C above.

11. Smith's notes are placed on 26 September because the Journals for the 27th indicate that the first speaker was Richard Henry Lee. Thus the Butler and Dane speeches appear to have been given on the 26th.

12. For the Impost, see IV:A above.

13. Lee's draft motion is in PCC, Item 36, Motions Made in Congress, 1777–88, DNA. With minor variations in punctuation and capitalization, Lee's draft and the version in the Journals are almost identical. In his draft Lee crossed out the word "system" and inserted "Confederacy of Nine States."

14. Ten months later, on 23 July 1788, Clark explained in a letter to Thomas Sinnickson of Salem, N. J., that "I never liked the system in all its parts. I considered it from the first, more a consolidated government than a federal, a government too expensive and unnecessarily oppressive in its operation; creating a judiciary undefined and unbounded. With all these imperfections about it, I nevertheless wished it to go to the states from Congress just as it did, without any censure or commendation, hoping that in case of a general adoption, the wisdom of the states would soon amend it in the exceptionable parts" (LMCC, VIII, 764–65).

15. Dane probably referred to the report of the Committee of Detail, 6 August (for the evolution of the "supreme law" clause see VII:D, F, G, H, I above).

16. See the Articles of Confederation, Article XIII (II:B above).

17. See James Madison, Notes of Debates in Congress, 21 February 1787 (V:D above).

18. See Amendment to Give Congress Coercive Power over the States and Their Citizens, 16 March 1781 (IV:B above).

19. Madison and Lee are referring to the ordinances for the Western Territory of 1784, 1785, and 1787 (IV:F, I, K above).

20. We have not been able to determine the Convention action referred to by Madison.

21. For similar arguments, see William Pierce to St. George Tucker, 28 September (CC:106); and James Wilson's speech of 6 October (RCS:Pa., also in CC:134).

22. See III above.

23. The abbreviation is unclear in the manuscript. It can also be read as "Acts," in which case the sentence would read: "The [states'] acts requires the delegates [to the Convention] to report to them [i.e., the state legislatures]."

24. RC (LT). Enclosed in Richard Henry Lee to Elbridge Gerry, 29 September

1787, Signers of the Constitution, Americana Room, DNDAR. The document is transcribed literally, except that each amendment is placed in a paragraph. Lee also sent copies of his amendments in letters to George Mason, 1 October; William Shippen, Jr., 2 October; and Samuel Adams, 27 October (letters printed IX:B below). For the printing and distribution of the amendments, see CC:325.

    25. FC, PCC, Item 18, Letter Books of the Secretary of Congress, Letter Book B, 129, DNA. Roger Alden, Deputy Secretary, endorsed the letter, "transmitting the Report of the Convention." Enclosed with this letter was a handwritten copy of the first three paragraphs in the rough manuscript Journals for 28 September and the four-page official broadside, attested by Thomson. The broadside, printed by John McLean of the New York *Independent Journal*, included the Constitution, the resolutions and letter of the Convention, and the three paragraphs from the rough Journals of Congress. The proceedings of Congress were reprinted over three dozen times from Vermont to Georgia before the end of October.

B. COMMENTARIES BY MEMBERS OF CONGRESS ON THE PROCEEDINGS OF CONGRESS ON 26–28 September

Richard Henry Lee to Elbridge Gerry, New York, 29 September[1]

According to your request I now enclose you the amendments that I proposed to the new Constitution.[2] I incline to think that unless some such alterations and provisions as those are interposed for the security of those essential rights of mankind without which liberty cannot exist, we shall soon find that the new plan of government will be far more inconvenient than anything sustained under the present government. And that to avoid Scylla we shall have fallen upon Charybdis.

James Madison to James Madison, Sr., New York, 30 September (excerpt)[3]

By Mr. [John] Blair who left Philadelphia immediately after the rising of the Convention, I sent to the care of Mr. F[ontaine] Maury a copy of the new Constitution proposed for the United States.[4] Mr. Blair set out in such haste that I had no time to write by him, and I thought the omission of the less consequence as your last letter led me to suppose that you must about that time be absent on your trip to Frederick. . . . I arrived here on Monday last [24 September]. The act of the Convention was then before Congress. It has been since taken up and, by a unanimous vote, forwarded to the states to be proceeded on as recommended by the Convention. What reception this new system will generally meet with cannot yet be pronounced.

James Madison to George Washington, New York, 30 September[5]

I found on my arrival here that certain ideas unfavorable to the act of the Convention, which had created difficulties in that body, had made their way into Congress. They were patronized chiefly by Mr. R[ichard] H[enry] L[ee] and Mr. [Nathan] Dane of Massachusetts. It was first urged that as the new Constitution was more than an alteration of the Articles of Confederation under which Congress acted, and even subverted these Articles altogether, there was a constitutional impropriety in their taking any positive agency in the work. The answer given was that the resolution of Congress in February had recommended the Convention as the best mean of obtaining a firm *national government*; that as the powers of the Convention were defined by their commissions in nearly the same terms with the powers of Congress given by the Confederation on the subject of alterations, Congress were not more restrained from acceding to the new plan, than the Convention were from proposing it. If the plan was within the powers of the Convention it was within those of Congress; if beyond those powers, the same necessity which justified the Convention would justify Congress; and a failure of Congress to concur in what was done would imply either that the Convention had done wrong in exceeding their powers, or that the government proposed was in itself liable to insuperable objections; that such an inference would be the more natural, as Congress had never scrupled to recommend measures foreign to their constitutional functions, whenever the public good seemed to require it; and had in several instances, particularly in the establishment of the new western governments, exercised assumed powers of a very high and delicate nature, under motives infinitely less urgent than the present state of our affairs, if any faith were due to the representations made by Congress themselves, echoed by 12 states in the Union, and confirmed by the general voice of the people. An attempt was made in the next place by R.H. L[ee] to amend the act of the Convention before it should go forth from Congress. He proposed a bill of rights, provision for juries in civil cases and several other things corresponding with the ideas of Colonel [George] Mason. He was supported by Mr. Me[lancton] Smith of this state. It was contended that Congress had an undoubted right to insert amendments, and that it was their duty to make use of it in a case where the essential guards of liberty had been omitted. On the other side the right of Congress was not denied, but the inexpediency of exerting it was urged on the following grounds: 1. That every circumstance indicated that the introduction of Congress as a party to the reform was intended by the states merely as a matter of form and respect. 2. That it was evident from the contradictory objections which had been expressed by the different members who had animadverted on the plan, that a discussion of its merits would consume much time, without producing agreement even among its adversaries. 3. That it was clearly the intention of the states that the plan to be proposed should be the act of the Convention with the assent of Congress, which could not be the case, if alterations were made, the Convention being no longer in existence to adopt them. 4. That as the act of the Convention, when altered would instantly become the mere act of Congress, and must be proposed by them as such, and of course be addressed to the legislatures, not conventions of the states, and require the ratification of thirteen instead of nine states, and as the unaltered act would go forth to the states directly from the Convention under the auspices of that body—some states might ratify one and some the other of the plans, and confusion and disappointment be the least evils that could ensue. These difficulties which at one time threatened a serious division in Congress and popular alterations with the yeas and nays in the Journals, were at length fortunately terminated by the following resolution: "Congress having received the report of the Convention lately assembled in Philadelphia, resolved *unanimously* that the said report, with the resolutions and letter accompanying the same, be transmitted to the several legislatures, in order to be submitted to a convention of delegates chosen in each state by the people thereof, in conformity to the resolves of the Convention made and provided in that case." Eleven states were present, the absent ones Rhode Island and Maryland.[6] A more direct approbation would have been of advantage in this and some other states, where stress will be laid on the agency of Congress in the matter, and a handle taken by adversaries of any ambiguity on the subject. With regard to Virginia and some other states, reserve on the part of Congress will do no injury. The circumstance of unanimity must be favorable everywhere.

The general voice of this city seems to espouse the new Constitution. It is supposed, nevertheless, that the party in power is strongly opposed to it. That [the] country must finally decide, the sense of which is as yet wholly unknown. As far as Boston and Connecticut has been heard from, the first impression seems to be auspicious. I am waiting with anxiety for the echo from Virginia but with very faint hopes of its corresponding with my wishes.[7]

.   .   .   .

P.S. A small packet of the size of 2 vol. 8.° addressed to you lately came to my hands with books of my own from France. General [Charles Cotesworth] Pinkney has been so good as to take charge of them. He set out yesterday for South Carolina and means to call at Mount Vernon.[8]

Richard Henry Lee to George Mason, New York, 1 October (excerpt)[9]

I have waited until now to answer your favor of September 18th[10] from Philadelphia, that I might inform you how the Convention plan of government was entertained by Congress. Your prediction of what would happen in Congress was exactly verified. It was with us, as with you, this or nothing; and this urged with a most extreme intemperance. The greatness of the powers given and the multitude of places to be created produces a coalition of monarchy men, military men, aristocrats, and drones whose noise, impudence and zeal exceeds all belief—whilst the commercial plunder of the South stimulates the rapacious trader. In this state of things, the patriot voice is raised in vain for such changes and securities as reason and experience prove to be necessary against the encroachments of power upon the indispensable rights of human nature. Upon due consideration of the Constitution under which we now act, some of us were clearly of opinion that the 13th Article of the Confederation precluded us from giving an opinion concerning a plan subversive of the present system and eventually forming a new confederacy of nine instead of 13 states. The contrary doctrine was asserted with great violence in expectation of the strong majority with which they might send it forward under terms of much approbation. Having procured an opinion that Congress was qualified to consider, to amend, to approve or disapprove, the next game was to determine that tho a right to amend existed, it would be highly inexpedient to exercise that right; but merely to transmit it with respectful marks of approbation. In this state of things I availed myself of the right to amend and moved the amendments, a copy of which I send herewith, and called the ayes and nays to fix them on the Journal. This greatly alarmed the majority and vexed them èxtremely, for the plan is to push the business on with great dispatch and with as little opposition as possible; that it may be adopted before it has stood the test of reflection and due examination. They found it most eligible at last to transmit it merely, without approving or disapproving; provided nothing but the transmission should appear on the Journal. This compromise was settled and they took the opportunity of inserting the word "*unanimously*," which applied only to simple transmission, hoping to have it mistaken for an unanimous approbation of the thing.

It states that Congress having received the Constitution unanimously transmit it, etc. It is certain that no approbation was given.

Richard Henry Lee to William Shippen, Jr., New York, 2 October (excerpt)[11]

I have considered the new Constitution with all the attention and candor that the thing and the times render necessary, and I find it impossible for me to doubt, that in its present state, unamended, the adoption of it will put civil liberty and the happiness of the people at the mercy of rulers who may possess the great unguarded powers given. And I assure you that confidence in the moderation or benignity of power is not a plant of quick growth in a reflecting bosom. The necessary alterations will by no means interfere with the general nature of the plan, or limit the power of doing good; but they will restrain from oppression the wicked and tyrannic. If all men were wise and good there would be no necessity for government or law. But the folly and the vice of human nature renders government and laws necessary for the many, and restraints indispensable to prevent oppression from those who are entrusted with the administration of one and the dispensation of the other. You will see herewith the amendments that appeared to me necessary.[12] They are submitted to you and my excellent old friend at Germantown. Perhaps they may be submitted to the world at large. My good old friend has made himself better acquainted with Hippocrates than with Plato, and re-lying upon the goodness of his own heart, without reflecting upon the corrupting and encroaching nature of power, he is willing to trust to its fangs more than experience justifies. The malady of human nature in these states now seems to be as it was in the years of 1778 and 1779 with respect to the effect produced by a certain combination. The malady that I mean is a temporary insanity. I wish that the present may subside with as little public injury as it formerly did, altho that was not small in all its branches.

Nathan Dane to Caleb Strong, New York, 10 October (excerpt)[13]

You have seen, I suppose, the resolution of Congress relative to the new Constitution. It was considered as an entire new system, on its passage from the Convention to the people, and altogether extraneous to the powers of Congress. The warmest friends of it appeared to be extremely impatient to get it thro Congress, even the first day that it was taken up. They wanted Congress to approve of it, but objected to any examination of it by paragraphs in the usual mode of doing business. Very few members wanted any alterations and after two days' debates Congress unanimously agreed the proper measure was to transmit it to the states to be laid before conventions of the people. Had Congress been of opinion that it was a subject within their cognizance, and taken time to examine it as so respectable a body ought always to do [in] such important cases, I think it is highly probable that Congress would have very fully approved of the plan proposed, and on the principles which actuated the Convention.

Edward Carrington to Thomas Jefferson, New York, 23 October (excerpt)[14]

When the report was before Congress, it was not without its direct opponents, but a great majority were for giving it a warm approbation. It was thought best, however, by its friends, barely to recommend to the several legislatures, the holding of conventions for its consideration, rather than send it forth with even a single negative to an approbatory act. The people do not scrutinize terms. The unanimity of Congress in recommending a measure to their consideration, naturally implies approbation; but any negative to a direct approbation would have discovered a dissension, which would have been used to favor divisions in the states. It certainly behooved Congress to give a measure of such importance and respectable birth, a fair chance in the deliberations of the people, and I think the step taken in that body well adapted to this idea.

James Madison to Thomas Jefferson, New York, 24 October (excerpt)[15]

When the plan came before Congress for their sanction, a very serious effort was made by R[ichard] H[enry] Lee and Mr. [Nathan] Dane from Massachusetts to embarrass it. It was first contended that Congress could not properly give any positive countenance to a measure which had for its object the subversion of the Constitution under which they acted. This ground of attack failing, the former gentleman urged the expediency of sending out the plan with amendments, and proposed a number of them corresponding with the objections of Colonel [George] Mason. This experiment had still less effect. In order however to obtain unanimity, it was necessary to couch the resolution in very moderate terms.

Richard Henry Lee to Samuel Adams, New York, 27 October (excerpt)[16]

Major [Winthrop] Sergeant delivered me the letter that you were pleased to write me on the 8th instant, by which I see that you supposed me to have been a member of the late Convention.[17] I did early decline being a member of that body, because I was a member of Congress, and the proposed plan stated, that Congress should review, and if they approved, transmit the proposed *amendments to the Confederation,* (for that was the idea, and indeed the only idea that the present federal plan admits of, or that the powers delegated to the Convention countenanced) to the 13 states for approbation and ratification. In this view of the business, it appeared to me an inconsistency that the same men should in New York review their own doings at Philadelphia. And this opinion was fully verified when the members of Convention came to Congress in such numbers with their own plan, that the votes of 3 states were Convention votes, 2 others divided by conventioneers, and conventioneers mingled with many other states. It is sir most obvious, that the Constitution proposed by the Convention could not have a dispassionate and impartial consideration in Congress. And indeed it had not. In my letter to you of the 5th instant, I sent you the amendments that I proposed in Congress; if they, with my letter should have miscarried, our friend Mr. [Elbridge] Gerry can furnish you with them.[18]

1. RC, Signers of the Constitution, Americana Room, DNDAR. Endorsed: "Colo R H Lees propositions to amend ye Constitution Sepr 1787." Gerry had been in New York City since 20 September.
2. The amendments are printed in the Proceedings of Congress, 27 September, IX:A above.
3. RC, Madison Papers, DLC.
4. Blair, a Virginia delegate to the Convention, had left Philadelphia with George Washington on 18 September (MS, Washington Diary, Washington Papers, DLC).
5. RC, Washington Papers, DLC.
6. Maryland was not represented. David Ross was the only Maryland delegate present.
7. For Washington's reply of 10 October, see RCS:Va.
8. General Pinckney arrived at Mount Vernon on 11 October (MS, Washington Diary, Washington Papers, DLC).
9. RC, Mason Papers, Rare Book Room, DLC (printed CC:117). The last page is endorsed "Richd H Lee 1787" and addressed to "George Mason esquire of Gunston Hall in Fairfax County." A postmark, "ALEX, NOV 2," also appears.
10. This letter has not been located. In it Mason probably outlined his objections to the Constitution (Rutland, III, 999n).
11. RC, Autograph Collection, PHi (printed CC:122).
12. See note 2 above.

13. RC, Strong Manuscripts, MNF (printed CC:144).
14. RC, Jefferson Papers, DLC (printed CC:185).
15. RC, Jefferson Papers, DLC (printed CC:187).
16. RC, Samuel Adams Papers, NN (printed CC:199). On 3 December 1787 (CC:315) Adams replied to this and an earlier letter of 5 October (CC:132).
17. Sargent of Massachusetts, who delivered Adams's letter of 8 October (not located), had been appointed Secretary of the Western Territory by Congress on 5 October (JCC, XXXIII, 610).
18. See note 2 above.

C. PUBLIC AND PRIVATE COMMENTARIES ON THE PROCEEDINGS OF CONGRESS ON 26–28 September

Antoine de la Forest to Comte de Montmorin, New York, 28 September (excerpt)[1]

This work, sir, has been considered by Congress for eight days and has been debated at length. Many people think that there is absolutely no need of a strong government in the United States for the welfare of the people and objections are being made to the proposed one. It has just been agreed by Congress today that this body has recommended to all the legislatures to submit the Constitution to the people in each state.

It was foreseen in the Convention at Philadelphia that if the new government was referred to the legislatures for their adoption, the latter would be astonished by the curtailments made in their powers and would reluctantly consent to allow themselves to be stripped of their powers for the common good. It was consequently preferred to ask for a special assembly of the people in each state. These assemblies, convened for the moment, exercising no powers, will not contain the legislatures' jealousy. It is known that the people are fairly generally disaffected with the shadow of government which now exists and are everywhere disposed to adopt a more effective one; the patriotism of the principal officers of some states is counted on much less. Moreover, it was to be expected that a general constitution which is to subordinate all the clauses contained in the individual state constitutions was agreed to by those to whom [———] is concerned to affect the latter.

Article 7 of the proposed Constitution states that the ratification of 9 states will be sufficient to establish it among the states that have ratified. It is thought that those which refused to ratify it after the accession of 9 others will consequently be excluded from laws and treaties of the Union.

Erkuries Beatty Diary, Philadelphia, Saturday, 29 September (excerpt)[2]

General [William] Irvine arrived this evening from New York. Says there is a majority in Congress that wishes the new Confederation to be adopted as it is, but every member from New York is against it as it stands, altho they have recommended calling a convention of the different states.

Phineas Bond to the Marquis of Carmarthen, Philadelphia, 29 September (excerpt)[3]

My last letter to Your Lordship enclosed the Constitution of government recommended to the consideration of Congress by the Convention of the states, which terminated on the 17th inst. Yesterday, my lord, the Congress in which there was a full representation from 11 states (1 member from Maryland—Rhode Island unrepresented) the report of the Convention and their letter and resolutions were by an unanimous resolve ordered to be transmitted to the several states for the purpose of being submitted to a convention of each, conformable to the recommendation of the Convention: so that, as far as the power of Congress goes, this amounts to a complete adoption of the Constitution on their part.

Extract of a Letter from a Member of the Constitutional Convention, New York, 29 September[4]

Yesterday Congress passed the Constitution agreed on by the Federal Convention, and resolved to transmit it to the several states for the assent and ratification of state conventions to be chosen in each state. I have no doubt but that it will be very soon adopted by a large majority of the states, and I shall set out for South Carolina tomorrow, that I may be present when it is considered by our state. I think it a good Constitution; I am sure every person must think it an *honest* one, and all men of integrity must approve of those articles which declare, that "all treaties made, or which shall be made by the authority of the United States shall be the supreme law of the land" and "that no State shall emit bills of credit, make any thing but gold or silver coin a tender in payment of debts; pass any bill of attainder, ex post facto law, or law impairing the obligation of contract." So that in future we shall be free from the apprehensions of paper money, pine barren acts, and installment laws.

New York Daily Advertiser, 29 September[5]

Yesterday Congress resolved unanimously, eleven states being present, that the new Constitution is to be transmitted to the legislatures of the several states, in order to be submitted to a convention of delegates to be chosen by the people, agreeably to the mode prescribed by the Convention.

Don Diego de Gardoqui to Conde de Floridablanca, New York, 30 September (excerpt)[6]

The results of the Convention in Philadelphia have been seen and examined by Congress, and after some debate during the three days which its meeting has lasted, Congress simply determined that it (the results of the Convention) be sent to the respective states.

They generally flatter themselves, that the new system of government will be adopted, in spite of the fact that they believe that it will have some opposition.

No one doubts that General Washington will be the first President and that perhaps they will reelect him successively.

Arthur Lee to John Adams, New York, 3 October (excerpt)[7]

Congress, having three states represented by those who were members of Convention and three of the most influential each in three other states, resolved to send it on without any recommendation, because its opponents insisted upon having their reasons on the Journals if they offered to recommend it. The states present were New Hampshire (2 Convention men), Massachusetts (2 Convention, one not), Connecticut (one Convention, one not), New York, New Jersey, Pennsylvania, Delaware, Virginia (1 Convention, 3 not), North Carolina (one Convention, one not), South Carolina (one Convention, 2 not), Georgia (2 Convention).

Pennsylvania Herald, 6 October (excerpt)[8]

It is said, that the resolution of Congress, after much altercation, was produced as a compromise between those who were for adopting and those who were for rejecting it. The cool and formal language of the resolution seems indeed to corroborate that assertion.

Louis Guillaume Otto to Comte de Montmorin, New York, 23 October (excerpt)[9]

The dissolution of the General Convention having caused a great number of members of Congress to return to New York, this assembly has resumed its sessions. It has begun by debating the plan of the new government, but discovering that the opposition was very strong, they limited themselves to referring this plan to the different states without either approving or disapproving it. It is surprising to see that Congress itself is not in agreement over the great powers which the new Constitution allots it. Mr. Richard Henry Lee, former President, is at the head of the opposition. Although elected a member of the Philadelphia Convention, he continually refused to attend it. He does not find the situation of the United States so hopeless, that one might have need of recourse to violent remedies. He disapproves especially that the government might have been accorded immense powers without preceding the Constitution with a *bill of rights*, which has always been regarded as the palladium of a free people. "If," he said, "in place of a virtuous and patriotic President we are given a William the Conqueror, what will become of liberty? How to prevent usurpation? Where is the contract between the nation and the government? The Constitution makes mention only of those who govern, never of the rights of the governed." This new Gracchus, sir, has all the necessary talents for making an impression. He has against him men equally distinguished by their merit, their learning, their services; but he pleads the cause of the people.

Whatever may be, sir, the determination of the states, the present Congress continues its ordinary pursuits. It just addressed new requisitions to the states for the sum of three million piastres, it made particular mention of the interest due Holland and it upheld that the funds destined for her be used in a completely different way. The continental treasury is likewise drained so that the commissioners don't know how to satisfy the most pressing needs. The moment of effectively making good the debts to His Majesty has not yet come. On this point of view the proposed government would certainly be more favorable towards us.

General Sinclair [Arthur St. Clair], present President of Congress, was just named governor of the Western Lands. The other civil officers are also elected and on the point of departing for their destination. Many officers of the army and a great number of adventurers are flocking to set up businesses there. The abundant population of the Northern States and all the malcontents are moving there in large numbers, and the banks of the Ohio will soon be covered with planta-tions. The authority of Congress will be upheld there by a corps of troops, which the proximity and the plunderings of the savages render indispensable, and this assembly will surely be more respected there than in its own lobbies.

1. RC (Tr), Correspondance Consulaires, New York, BI 909, ff. 284–85, Archives Nationales, Paris, France. Antoine René Charles Mathurin de la Forest was French Consul for New York, New Jersey, and Connecticut. The Comte de Montmorin was France's Minister of Foreign Affairs.

2. Misc. MSS Boxes, Box of Beatty Diaries, Diary of 3 July–25 October, NHi. For a longer excerpt from this diary see Mfm:Pa. 82. Lieutenant Beatty was pay-master for the 1st United States Infantry in the Western Territory. He was in Philadelphia on army business.

3. RC, Foreign Office, Class 4, America, Volume 5, ff. 286–87, Public Record Office, London, England. Printed: J. Franklin Jameson, ed., "Letters of Phineas Bond, British Consul At Philadelphia, To The Foreign Office of Great Britain, 1787, 1788, 1789," American Historical Association Annual Report . . . 1896 (2 vols., Washington, D.C., 1897), I, 546–49. Another section of this letter is printed in Mfm:Pa. 83. Bond was Great Britain's Consul for New York, New Jersey, Pennsylvania, Delaware, and Maryland. He was a native Pennsylvanian who was attainted for treason in 1778. He left for England that year and returned to Penn-sylvania in 1786 after being appointed Consul. The Marquis of Carmarthen (the Duke of Leeds after 23 March 1789) was Foreign Secretary in the cabinet of William Pitt the Younger.

4. This item, printed in the Charleston Columbian Herald, 14 February 1788 under the dateline "LONDON, December 6," was entitled "Extract of a letter from an eminent Member of the late Convention at Philadelphia, dated New-York, Sept. 29, 1787." The letter could have been written by any of South Carolina's four delegates to the Constitutional Convention (Charles Cotesworth Pinckney, John Rutledge, Pierce Butler, and Charles Pinckney), all of whom were in New York on 29 September. The letter was probably written by Rutledge to his son John Rut-ledge, Jr., who was in London.

5. By 22 October this account was reprinted sixteen times in New England, twice in New York, and once in South Carolina.

6. RC (Tr), Dispatch No. 213, Estado, Legajo 3893 bis, Apartado No. 6, Archivo Histórico Nacional, Madrid, Spain. Gardoqui, Spanish minister to the United States, arrived in America in 1785 to negotiate a treaty with Congress. Floridablanca was Spain's Secretary of State.

7. RC, Adams Family Papers, MHi (printed CC:127).

8. For the entire article see Mfm:Pa. 109. The writer of this item possibly ob-tained this information from William Irvine, one of Pennsylvania's delegates to Congress. Irvine had arrived in Philadelphia on 29 September and remained there for a few days in order to obtain payment for his congressional services.

9. RC (Tr), Correspondance Politique, États-Unis, Volume 32, ff. 381–82, Archives du Ministère des Affaires Étrangères, Paris, France. Otto had been France's chargé d'affaires since 1785 and its principal diplomatic representative in America until the arrival of the Comte de Moustier early in 1788.

Index

NOTE: The sub-entries "Convention proposals" and "Convention proposals rejected" in this index refer only to the proposals in the Constitutional Convention embodied in the formal resolutions and drafts printed in this volume, not to the many proposals recorded in the notes of the debates in the Convention.

ADAMS, ANDREW (Conn.)
signer, Articles of Confederation, 94
ADAMS, JOHN (Mass.)
favors strong central government, 55; on committee to draft Declaration of Independence, 72; signer, Declaration of Independence, 76; advocates census, 298
—letter to, 351
ADAMS, SAMUEL (Mass.)
53, 55; on sovereignty of colonial legislatures, 52; opposes Galloway Plan, 52; signer, Declaration of Independence, 76; on committee to draft confederation, 78; signer, Articles of Confederation, 94; and R.H. Lee's amendments (1787), 342n
—letter from, 349n
—letter to, 348
ADAMS, THOMAS (Va.)
signer, Articles of Confederation, 94
ADDRESS TO THE PEOPLE
Convention instructs Committee of Style to draft, 270, 284; draft rejected, 285
ADMIRALTY COURTS
Declaration of Independence denounces lack of jury trial in, 74; Draft Articles give Congress power to create, 82; Pinckney Plan recommends establishment of in each state, 247
AGRARIAN DISCONTENT
and calling of Constitutional Convention, 178–79
AGREEMENTS, INTERSTATE
See Interstate relations
ALDEN, ROGER (Conn.)
id., 341n; on Constitution, 326
ALLIANCES, FOREIGN
See Treaties
AMBASSADORS
Draft Articles, 79, 82; Articles prohibit states from appointing or receiving, 88; Articles give Congress power to appoint and receive, 89; Convention proposals concerning, 252, 254, 265, 266, 267, 277, 279, 280,

281, 293, 294; Constitution gives President power to appoint, with approval of Senate, and power to receive, 313, 314; Constitution gives Supreme Court original jurisdiction over cases involving, 314
AMENDMENTS TO ARTICLES OF CONFEDERATION
Procedures for, 177–78, 192, 193; Draft Articles, 85–86; Articles, 93; South Carolina amendments to Articles, 123; Rhode Island refusal to appoint delegates to Convention, 226, 227–28; debates in Congress, 327–28, 329–30, 331–33, 344, 345, 348
Proposed by states (1778–79), 55–56, 96; Maryland, 97–100; Massachusetts, 103–5; Rhode Island, 105–9; Connecticut, 109–11; New Jersey, 113–18; Pennsylvania, 119; South Carolina, 121–23; Georgia, 126–28; Delaware, 130–31
Proposed or considered by Congress (1781–86), 63–67, 176–79, 192–94; Impost of 1781, 140–41; amendment giving Congress coercive power (1781), 141–43, 333, 341n; amendment to share expenses according to population, 148–50, 240, 258; amendment giving Congress power to regulate commerce (1785), 154–56; seven amendments of grand committee of Congress (1786), 163–68; call for a convention to revise and amend Articles (1786–87), 178–79, 185–90, 192
Proposed in Constitutional Convention: New Jersey Amendments, 234–35, 250–53
Public and private debate on need for, 176–79, 192–94
AMENDMENTS TO CONSTITUTION
Procedures for, 270; Virginia Resolutions, 245; Pinckney Plan, 247; Amended Virginia Resolutions, 250; Resolutions of 24 July, 259–60; Committee of Detail, 269; Amend-

ed Committee of Detail, 283; Amended Committee of Style, 295; Constitution, 316 Proposed and debated in Congress, 323, 326, 328, 333, 335–40, 342, 343–44, 345, 346, 347, 348, 352; R. H. Lee amendments (1787), 323, 326, 337–40, 343, 345, 346, 347; distribution of Lee amendments, 342, 342n, 345, 346, 348

ANNAPOLIS CONVENTION
67, 177; called by Virginia, 177, 180–81; Northern distrust of, 177; delegates to, 177, 181–82, 185; members of in Constitutional Convention, 177; proceedings and report of, 177, 181–85; proposes convention to revise Articles of Confederation, 177, 183–85, 192; legality of its call for a convention, 177–78, 192–93; Congress and report of, 178–79, 185–90, 192; report of and appointment of delegates to Constitutional Convention, 193–94, 196–97, 208n

APPELLATE JURISDICTION
See Captures on land and sea; Judiciary, 1776–1787; Judiciary under Constitution

APPROPRIATIONS
rules in Articles governing Congress, 91, 92; Convention proposals concerning, 258, 262, 274, 275, 289, 290; rules in Constitution governing Congress, 310, 311

ARMSTRONG, JOHN, JR. (Pa.)
member of Congress (1787), 324

ARMY
Draft Articles, 80, 82, 83, 84; Articles give Congress power over and limit power, 89, 91–92, 92; Articles give states power over and limit power, 88, 89, 91, 91–92; proposed changes in Congress' power over, 103–4, 104, 116, 117, 119, 122, 145, 164–65; proposed changes in states' power over, 122; Convention proposals concerning, 238, 247, 252, 254, 255, 264, 267, 268, 275, 280, 282, 289, 291, 292; Constitution gives Congress power to raise and support with a two-year limitation on appropriations, 310; Constitution prohibits states from keeping without consent of Congress, 311; Constitution makes President commander in chief, 313

ARMY, STANDING
fear of, 56, 74, 110, 110–11, 114, 117, 328, 337–38

ARTICLES OF CONFEDERATION (DRAFT)
nature of debates over, in Congress (1776–77), 53–55; members of committee that drafted, 53, 78; presented to Congress, 78; text of, 79–86. See also Congress, Second Continental

ARTICLES OF CONFEDERATION
evolution of, 53–55, 72, 78, 297; members of Congress who played key roles in writing of, 53; submission of to states, 55, 78; publication of, 78, 96, 101, 125; draft of, 79–86; text of, 86–93; signers of, 94
Ratification, provisions for: Draft Articles, 85–86; Articles, 93
Ratification of by states (1778–81), 56–57, 96–97, 124; New Hampshire, 101–2; Massachusetts, 102–5; Rhode Island, 105–9; Connecticut, 109–11; New York, 111–13; Pennsylvania, 118–20; Virginia, 120; South Carolina, 121–23; North Carolina, 124–26; Georgia, 126–28; New Jersey, 128–30; Delaware, 130–35; Maryland, 135–37
Amendments, procedures for, 85–86, 93, 123, 177–78, 192, 193, 226, 227–28, 327–28, 329–30, 331–33, 344, 345, 348. See also Amendments to Articles of Confederation
Amendments proposed by states (1778–79), 55–56, 96, 97–100, 103–5, 105–9, 109–11, 113–18, 119, 121–23, 126–28, 130–35. See also Amendments to Articles of Confederation
Amendments proposed or considered by Congress (1781–86), 63–67, 140–41, 141–43, 148–50, 154–56, 163–68. See also Amendments to Articles of Confederation
Constitutional Convention and, 260; state acts appointing delegates to, 193–94; Rhode Island refusal to appoint delegates, 226, 227–28; abandoned by, 233–35; Virginia Resolutions, 243; New Jersey Amendments, 250–53
Congress (1787) and, 322, 329–30, 335, 343, 348

ASHE, JOHN BAPTISTE (N.C.)
member of Congress (1787), 324

ATTAINDER, BILL OF
Convention proposals concerning, 237, 276, 281, 290, 291; Constitution prohibits Congress and states from passing, 311

BAIL, RIGHT OF
Northwest Ordinance protects against excessive bail being demanded, 62, 172; R. H. Lee amendments (1787) propose protection from excessive bail, 338

BALDWIN, ABRAHAM (Ga.)
269n; delegate, Constitutional Convention, 204, 230; signer, Constitution, 317

BANISTER, JOHN (Va.)
signer, Articles of Confederation, 94

BANKRUPTCIES
Convention proposals concerning, 275, 289; Constitution gives Congress power to make uniform laws governing, 309

BARTLETT, JOSIAH (N.H.)
signer, Declaration of Independence, 76; on committee to draft confederation, 78; signer, Articles of Confederation, 94

BASSETT, RICHARD (Del.)
delegate, Annapolis Convention, 177, 182, 185; delegate, Constitutional Convention, 203, 230; signer, Constitution, 317

BEATTY, ERKURIES (Pa.)
id., 353n
—diary of, 350

BEDFORD, GUNNING, JR. (Del.)
64, 65; delegate, Constitutional Convention, 203; signer, Constitution, 317

BENSON, EGBERT (N.Y.)
187n; delegate, Annapolis Convention, 177, 181, 185

BICAMERALISM
See Congress under Constitution: organization

BILL OF RIGHTS
in Northwest Ordinance, 62, 172–73; Constitutional Convention rejects, 285; debates in Congress on, 331, 335–37, 339; R. H. Lee proposes in Congress (1787), 337–38, 343, 352. See also Amendments to Constitution

BILLS OF CREDIT
See Money

BINGHAM, WILLIAM (Pa.)
324; favors sub-confederacies, 189; on reception of Constitution by Congress, 325
—letter from, 325

BLAIR, JOHN (Va.)
id., 348n; delegate, Constitutional Convention, 198, 230; signer, Constitution, 317; carries Constitution to Virginia, 342

BLAND, THEODORICK (Va.)
opposes counting three-fifths of slaves in apportioning expenses (1783), 149

BLOODWORTH, TIMOTHY (N.C.)
67; on committee to prepare amendments to Articles of Confederation (1786), 163–64

BLOUNT, WILLIAM (N.C.)
67, 322, 324; on committee to consider Annapolis Convention report, 185; delegate, Constitutional Convention, 202n, 230; signer, Constitution, 317

BOND, PHINEAS (Great Britain)
id., 353n
—letter from, 350

BOUDINOT, ELIAS (N.J.)
authorized to ratify Articles of Confederation, 129

BOUNTIES, MILITARY
Land Ordinance (1785), 159, 161–62

BOWDOIN, JAMES (Mass.)
208n, 209n

BRAXTON, CARTER (Va.)
signer, Declaration of Independence, 76

BREARLEY, DAVID (N.J.)
delegate, Constitutional Convention, 195, 196, 230; chairman, Committee on Postponed Parts, 270; signer, Constitution, 317

BROOM, JACOB (Del.)
delegate, Constitutional Convention, 203, 230; signer, Constitution, 317

BRYAN, SAMUEL (Pa.)
as "Centinel," comments on debates in Congress, 323

BURKE, THOMAS (N.C.)
opposes establishment of precedents for exercise of congressional power, 55; proposes Article II of Articles of Confederation, 55

BURTON, ROBERT (N.C.)
member of Congress (1787), 324

BUTLER, PIERCE (S.C.)
322, 325, 353n; delegate, Constitutional Convention, 215, 230; signer, Constitution, 317; in debates in Congress on Constitution, 328, 333, 341n

CABINET
See Departments, executive

CADWALADER, LAMBERT (N.J.)
324; on committee to consider Annapolis Convention report (1787), 185

CANADA
Declaration of Independence denounces arbitrary government in, 74; Draft Articles, 85; Articles provide for admission of into Union, 93; territorial lands of U.S. reserved for refugees from, 162

CANALS
Convention rejects power of Congress to issue charters of incorporation for, 285

CAPITAL, FEDERAL
Convention proposals concerning, 275, 289–90; Constitution gives Congress exclusive control over a ten-mile square area for, 310. *See also* Federal sites

CAPTURES ON LAND AND SEA
Draft Articles, 82; Articles grant Congress power to establish rules concerning and to create courts of appeal in cases involving, 89; proposed change in Articles, 145; Convention proposals concerning, 244–45, 247, 252, 254, 264, 267, 275, 281, 289, 294; Constitution gives Congress power to make rules concerning, 310; Constitution gives U.S. judiciary jurisdiction in admiralty and maritime cases, 314

CARMARTHEN, MARQUIS OF (Great Britain)
id., 353n
—letter to, 350

CARRINGTON, EDWARD (Va.)
323, 325; in debates in Congress on Constitution, 334–35, 339, 347
—letters from, 326–27, 347

CARROLL, CHARLES, OF CARROLLTON (Md.)
58, 217, 222n; signer, Declaration of Independence, 76; resigns as delegate to Constitutional Convention, 195, 223n

CARROLL, DANIEL (Md.)
64; signer, Articles of Confederation, 94, 136; delegate, Constitutional Convention, 222, 223n, 230; signer, Constitution, 317

CASWELL, RICHARD (N.C.)
125–26, 126n, 130; resigns as delegate to Constitutional Convention, 52, 195, 202, 202n
—letter from, 126
—letter to, 125

CENSUS (LAND)
56; Rhode Island and New Jersey amendments to Articles recommend

census at least every five years to determine each state's share of expenses, 105–6, 108, 114–15, 117; South Carolina amendment to Articles recommends census at least every ten years to determine each state's share of expenses, 122

CENSUS (POPULATION)
56, 297–301; Draft Articles provide for triennial census of white inhabitants for purpose of apportioning common expenses, 80; New Jersey amendment to Articles recommends census at least every five years to determine quota of troops supplied by each state, 116, 117; committee of Congress (1781) recommends census of white inhabitants, 144; amendment to Articles to share expenses according to population provides for triennial census, 150; Convention proposals concerning, 241, 258, 264–65, 265, 271–72, 276, 286, 290; Constitution requires census within three years after first meeting of Congress and every ten years thereafter as basis for apportionment of Representatives and direct taxes, 306–7; Constitution requires capitation and other direct taxes be laid in proportion to census, 311

CHASE, JEREMIAH TOWNLEY (Md.)
on committee to draft Ordinance of 1784, 150

CHASE, SAMUEL (Md.)
53, 58, 223n; signer, Declaration of Independence, 76

CHIEF JUSTICE OF THE UNITED STATES
See Judiciary under Constitution

CITIZENSHIP
55; Convention proposals concerning, 260, 261, 262, 271, 272, 279, 286, 287, 292; Constitution requires as qualification for Representative, Senator, and President, 306, 307, 312. *See also* Naturalization

CLARK, ABRAHAM (N.J.)
53, 323, 324; signer, Declaration of Independence, 76; delegate, Annapolis Convention, 177, 181, 185; refuses appointment as delegate to Constitutional Convention, 177, 195, 196n, 322; in debates in Congress on Constitution, 330, 332, 334, 339, 341n; supports amendments to Constitution, 341n
—letter from, 341n

CLINGAN, WILLIAM (Pa.)
signer, Articles of Confederation, 94, 118

CLINTON, GEORGE (N.Y.)
113n, 213n, 341n

CLYMER, GEORGE (Pa.)
53; signer, Declaration of Independence, 76; delegate, Constitutional Convention, 199–200, 230; signer, Constitution, 317

COLLINS, JOHN (R.I.)
227, 229n; signer, Articles of Confederation, 94

COMITY, INTERSTATE
See Interstate relations

COMMANDER IN CHIEF
Articles give Congress power to appoint with assent of nine states, 92; territorial governor to be commander in chief of militia, 170; Convention proposals concerning, 238, 252, 254, 267, 280, 292; Constitution makes President commander in chief of army and navy of U.S. and of militia when in service of U.S., 313

COMMERCE
52, 54, 56, 60–61, 64–67, 74, 75, 177, 180–81, 182–85, 192, 196, 205, 226, 227, 305, 333, 345

Draft Articles: Congress may not levy import and export duties, 83

Articles: guarantee citizens of each state equal commercial privileges in all other states, 87; states may not levy duties or restrictions on property of U.S. or any other state, 87; states may not levy import and export duties interfering with stipulations in U.S. treaties, 88; U.S. commercial treaties may not restrict right of states to impose same duties on foreigners their citizens are subject to, and to export and import any goods or commodities whatever, 89; Congress may regulate trade with Indians not members of any state, provided legislative rights of states within their limits are not infringed or violated, 91

Proposed changes in Articles: Congress to have exclusive power to regulate foreign trade with revenue used to build navy and fortify seacoasts, 114, 117; Congress to levy import duties to pay public debt, 140–41; Congress to levy

embargoes in wartime, 141, 142–43, 145; Congress to levy import duties for twenty-five years, 146–48; Congress to prohibit importation of goods in vessels of nations not having commercial treaties with U.S. and to prohibit foreigners from importing goods not produced in their own nations, 153–54; Congress to regulate trade with foreign nations and among states and levy import and export duties, provided that duties are not discriminatory, 154–56, 164; duties collected by Congress to be consistent with state constitutions and given to states in which paid, 164; right of states to levy embargoes in times of scarcity may not be restrained, 164; Congress to establish federal judicial court to have appellate jurisdiction in cases involving regulation of commerce and collection of revenue from such regulation, 167

Northwest Ordinance: navigable waters leading to Mississippi and St. Lawrence rivers to remain free, 173

Convention proposals concerning, 241–42, 246, 247, 251, 252, 264, 265, 268, 274, 276, 282, 285, 289, 290, 291

Convention proposals rejected: two-thirds vote to pass navigation acts, 242, 265, 276, 285; states to levy embargoes in times of scarcity, 246; state courts to have original jurisdiction in cases involving regulation of commerce, 247, 251; states to levy import and export duties with consent of Congress, 268, 282; Congress to grant charters of incorporation to build canals, 285

Constitution: Congress to lay and collect duties and imposts uniformly throughout U.S., 309; Congress to regulate commerce with foreign nations, among the states, and with Indian tribes, 309; Congress may not prohibit before 1808 the migration or importation of "such Persons" as states may think fit to admit, but may impose a duty on "each Person" imported, 310; Congress may not levy export duties, 311; Congress may not give preference to ports of one state over another, 311; Congress may not require vessels bound to or from any state to enter, clear, or pay duties in another, 311; with consent of Congress states may levy import and export duties to execute inspection laws, 311; states may not levy tonnage duties without consent of Congress, 311

COMMITTEE OF DETAIL
64, 232, 236, 242, 332, 341n; background and membership of, 255, 260; resolutions submitted to, 255–60; report of, 260–69; report of, amended, 270–84

COMMITTEE OF STYLE
236; background and membership of, 270; amended report of Committee of Detail submitted to, 270–84; to draft address to people, 270, 284, 284n; work of described, 284–85; amended report of, 284–96; changes adopted in report of, 285, 304; changes rejected in report of, 285

CONFEDERACIES
desire for sub-confederacies, 189, 190n

CONGRESS, FIRST CONTINENTAL
Galloway Plan in, 52; debate in on sovereignty, 52; membership of, 52–53; members of in Constitutional Convention, 52–53; debate in on regulation of commerce, 65; debate in on population and representation, 297

CONGRESS, SECOND CONTINENTAL
debates on independence and adoption of Declaration of Independence, 53, 72; members of who wrote Articles and sat in Constitutional Convention, 53; debates on Articles of Confederation (1776–77), 53–55; attempts to increase powers of (1777), 55; adopts and transmits Articles to states, 55, 78, 96; rejects state amendments to Articles (1778–79), 55–56, 96, 97–100, 102–5, 105–9, 109–11, 113–18, 119, 121–23, 126–28, 130–31, 133–34; accepts state ratifications of Articles (1778–81), 56, 57, 96–97, 101–2, 102–5, 105–9, 109–11, 111–13, 118–20, 120, 121–23, 124, 124–26, 126–28, 128–30, 130–35, 135–37; requests state land cessions and outlines provisions for new states (1780), 58; adopts Impost of 1781, 63, 140–41, 329; roll calls on Maryland and Delaware amendments to Articles, 100, 133–34

CONGRESS UNDER ARTICLES OF CONFEDERATION
Organization
—Articles of Confederation: adjournment of, 92; Committee of the States, 91, 92; compensation of members, 87; dual officeholding prohibited, 87, 89; election of members, 87; journal of, 92; meeting of, 87, 92; members not to receive presents, etc. from foreign nations, 88; number of states required to decide questions, 92, 93; President of, 91; privileges of members, 87–88; recall of members, 87; representation in, 87; Secretary of, 90; each state has one vote, 87; term of members, 87
—Proposed changes in Articles: to fix date for election of members, 121, 167; date of meeting, 121; discipline for non-attendance of members, 167–68; number of delegates, 105, 121; number of votes required to decide questions, 103, 104, 116–17, 123, 145, 152, 156, 164, 251; to require oaths to support Confederation, 113–14; to require oaths not to receive presents, etc. from foreign nations, 144; to require roll-call votes on every question, 123; term of delegates, 121; term of President, 123

Powers
Ambassadors, to appoint and receive, 89
Amendments to Articles, to propose, 93
Appropriations, to pass acts concerning, 91, 92
Army, to raise, regulate, and support, 89, 91, 91–92, 92
Bills of credit, to emit, 91, 92
Canada and other English colonies, provision to admit into Union, 93
Civil officers, to appoint, 91
Commander in chief, to appoint, 92
Commerce, to regulate with Indian tribes, 91
Courts, to create to try cases of piracy and felony on high seas, 89; to settle appeals in cases of captures, 89; to settle disputes among states over lands and boundaries and controversies

concerning private rights of soil, 89–90, 90–91
Debt, to pay, 93
Expenses of U.S., to requisition states for money to meet, 89, 91, 92
Marque and reprisal, to grant letters of, 89, 92
Military and naval officers, to appoint, 91, 92
Money, to borrow, 91, 92
Money, to regulate value of coin struck by U.S. and by states, 91, 92
Navy, to raise and equip, 91, 92
Peace, to make, 89
Post office, to establish and regulate, 91
Taxes, to levy for post office, 91
Treaties, confederations, and alliances, to enter into, 88, 89, 92
War, to declare, 88, 89, 92
Weights and measures, to fix standard of, 91
Proposed additional powers (1778–87):
52, 55–56, 56, 60–61, 63–64, 64–67, 333, 341n; to fix western limits of states, 97–98, 99, 130, 133–34; to control ungranted western lands for benefit of states, 87, 99–100, 106, 108–9, 115–16, 117, 130, 133–34; to regulate commerce with foreign nations and among states, 114, 117, 153–54, 154–56, 164, 167, 177, 180–81, 182–85, 192, 196, 205, 226, 227; to use money from regulation of commerce to build navy and fortify seacoasts, 114, 117; to define piracies and felonies on high seas, 122–23; to decide disputes between two or more states over boundaries, jurisdiction, or any other cause, 123; to levy import duties, 140–41, 146–48, 155, 164, 251; to levy embargoes in wartime, 141, 142–43, 145; to use force to compel states to fulfill federal obligations, 141–43; to establish plan for equipping and governing militia, 144; to establish a mint, 144; to appoint a committee for Indian affairs, 144; to take a census of white inhabitants, 144; to impress property for service of U.S. during "present War," 145; to appoint tax collectors and assessors and direct accounting of state taxes to meet congressional requisitions, 145, 164–65, 165–66, 251; to admit new states, 145, 253; to stipulate in treaties for the establishment of consular power without reference to individual states, 145; to seize property of states delinquent in raising of men and money, 145; to abolish restrictions on power to make commercial treaties, 155; to levy export duties, 155, 164; to increase number of troops of states failing to meet quotas in time, 164–65; to define and punish treason, 166–67; to appoint judges of federal judicial court, 167; to appoint and remove federal executive, 252; to establish a uniform rule of naturalization, 253
Restraints
54, 54–55; may exercise only expressly delegated powers, 86; may not grant titles of nobility, 88; may not appoint officers of or under rank of colonel of troops raised for common defense, 89; commercial treaties shall not restrain states from levying same duties on foreigners as their citizens are subject to, and shall not prohibit exportation and importation of any goods or commodities, 89; may not deprive any state of territory for benefit of United States, 90
Proposed additional restraints (1778–79)
56; to forbid standing army in peacetime, 110, 110–11, 114, 117; to report post office accounts to state legislatures annually, 119; to give states greater control over troops raised for common defense, 122; deletion of power to create courts to try piracies, 122–23; to have state courts rather than Congress-appointed court determine controversies over private right of soil, 130–31, 133–34
CONGRESS UNDER ARTICLES: AND THE CONSTITUTIONAL CONVENTION
calls Convention to revise and amend Articles, 67, 179, 185–90, 194, 207, 208n, 209, 209n, 210–11, 213, 214, 215–16, 217, 222, 232, 233, 234; Congress required to approve work of

Convention, 193–94, 197, 199–200, 203, 204, 205, 207, 209, 211, 213, 214, 216, 217, 222, 223, 245, 250, 259–60, 269; requirement rejected by Convention, 270, 283; and Rhode Island refusal to send delegates to Convention, 194, 225–29, 322, 327

CONGRESS UNDER ARTICLES: AND THE CONSTITUTION
Constitution received from Constitutional Convention, 305, 319, 319–20, 322, 323, 325, 326; debate on amendments to Constitution, 323, 326, 328, 333, 335–40, 342, 343–44, 345, 346, 347, 348, 352; debate on procedure for ratifying Constitution, 323, 327–28, 329, 329–30, 330, 330–33, 334, 334–35, 340, 342, 344, 345, 347, 348, 349, 350, 351, 352; debate on right of Congress to consider Constitution, 327–28, 328, 329, 329–30, 330–33, 334, 343-44, 345, 346–47, 347; debate on transmitting Constitution to states for approval, 323, 327–28, 328, 329, 329–30, 330, 330–33, 334, 334–35, 335–37, 337–39, 339–40, 340, 342, 343–44, 345–46, 346–47, 347, 348, 349, 350, 351, 352; delegates to, present during debate, 322, 323–24, 324–25, 340n, 344, 350; and establishment of new government, 245, 250, 259, 269, 283–84, 318; and first federal elections, 269, 283–84, 318

CONGRESS UNDER ARTICLES: EXTRA-CONSTITUTIONAL ACTS
calls Constitutional Convention, 67, 177–78, 179, 185–90, 192–93, 194, 232, 233, 234, 327–28, 329, 329–30, 330–33, 334, 343–44, 345, 346–47, 347; creates national domain, 57–63, 150–53, 156–63, 168–74, 333, 341n, 343; transmits Constitution to states for approval, 323, 327–28, 328, 329, 329–30, 330, 330–33, 334, 334–35, 335–37, 337–39, 339–40, 340, 342, 343–44, 345–46, 346–47, 347, 348, 349, 350, 351, 352

CONGRESS UNDER CONSTITUTION: ORGANIZATION
Convention proposals, 232, 242, 243, 244, 246, 247, 248, 249, 251, 253, 256, 259, 261, 263, 264, 265, 266, 268, 271, 274, 275, 276, 278, 279, 282, 283, 285, 288, 288–89, 289, 293, 295
Convention proposals rejected: two-thirds vote required to pass navigation acts, 242, 265, 276, 285;

majority vote to override presidential veto, 244; to elect President by joint ballot, 246, 266, 278; to require more than a majority vote on important questions, 247, 251; to elect Treasurer by joint ballot, 264, 275, 285, 289; to require two-thirds vote of members present to admit new states, 268, 282; to require three-fourths vote to override presidential veto, 274, 285, 288–89
Constitution: bicameralism of, 306; two-thirds vote required to override presidential veto, 309; yeas and nays to be recorded when overriding presidential veto, 309; to receive State of the Union message, 313; two-thirds vote required to recommend amendments, 316
See also House of Representatives under Constitution: organization; Senate under Constitution: organization

CONGRESS UNDER CONSTITUTION: OBLIGATIONS
Convention proposals, 237, 241, 245, 250, 258, 259, 264–65, 265, 269, 271–72, 276, 283, 286, 290, 295
Constitution: to reapportion House of Representatives after each decennial census, 306–7; to apportion direct taxes among states according to population, 306–7; to take census three years after first meeting of Congress and every ten years thereafter, 306–7; to guarantee each state a republican form of government, 315; to protect states against insurrections and invasions, 315; at request of two-thirds of state legislatures, to call a constitutional convention to propose amendments to Constitution, 316; to pay public debt, 316

CONGRESS UNDER CONSTITUTION: POWERS
Convention proposals, 236–37, 237–38, 241, 243, 244, 245, 246, 246–47, 247, 248–49, 249, 250, 251, 252, 253, 254, 255, 257, 258, 259, 261, 262, 263–64, 264, 266, 267–68, 268, 268–69, 269, 270, 271, 272, 274, 274–76, 276, 278, 279, 280, 281, 282, 283, 284, 285, 287, 288, 289–90, 290, 291, 292, 293, 294, 295, 298
Convention proposals rejected: to veto state laws, 236, 244, 246, 249, 257; to elect President, 237–38, 244,

246, 249, 252, 258, 266, 269, 278, 284; to requisition states to raise money for expenses of United States, 243, 247, 251; to appoint judges, 244, 247; to be last resort on appeals in disputes between two or more states, 246–47; to create executive departments, 247; to create admiralty courts, 247; to remove President, 252; to appoint Treasurer, 264, 275, 285, 289; to emit bills of credit, 264, 275; to establish jurisdiction of inferior courts, 267–68, 281; to grant charters of incorporation to build canals, 285; to establish nonsectarian national university, 285

Constitution

Amendments, to propose to Constitution, 316

Appropriation bills, to pass, 310, 311

Army, to raise, regulate, and support, 310

Bankruptcies, to make uniform laws governing, 309

Capital, federal, exclusive control over, 310

Captures on land and sea, to make rules concerning, 310

Civil officers, to appoint, 313

Coin, foreign, to regulate value of, 310

Commerce, to regulate with foreign nations, among states, and with Indians, 309

Copyrights and patents, to provide for, 310

Counterfeiting, to provide for punishment of, 310

Debt, public, to obtain revenue for payment of, 309

Elections, federal, to make or alter regulations concerning times, places, and manner of, 308

Excises, to lay and collect, 309

Federal sites, to exercise exclusive control over arsenals, dockyards, forts, magazines, etc., 310

Full faith and credit, to pass general laws prescribing manner in which each state gives full faith and credit to laws, etc. of every other state, 315

Import duties, to lay and collect, 309, 310

Inferior courts, to create, 310, 314

Insurrections, to provide for calling forth militia to suppress, 310

Invasions, to provide for callng forth militia to repel, 310

Law of nations, to define and punish offenses against, 310

Laws of the United States, to provide for calling forth militia to execute, 310

Marque and reprisal, to grant letters of, 310

Militia, to provide for calling forth, organizing, arming, and disciplining, 310

Money bills, to pass, 309

Money, to borrow, 309

Money, to coin and regulate value of, 310

Naturalization, to establish uniform rule for, 309

Navy, to raise, regulate, and support, 310

Necessary and proper clause: to pass laws necessary and proper to execute powers of, 310

Piracies, to define and punish, 310

Post offices and post roads, to establish, 310

President, to provide for succession of, 313

Reapportionment, of House of Representatives after decennial census, 306–7

State laws, to approve certain enumerated ones, 311

States, to provide for admission of, 315

Supreme Court, to regulate appellate jurisdiction of, 314

Taxes, to lay and collect, 309

Territories, to dispose of and make rules and regulations concerning, 315

Treason, to declare punishment of, 315

Trial by jury, to name places to hold for crimes not committed in any state, 314

Veto, presidential, to override by by two-thirds vote, 309

War, to declare, 310

Weights and measures, to fix standard of, 310

See also House of Representatives under Constitution: powers; Senate under Constitution: powers

CONGRESS UNDER CONSTITUTION: RE-
STRAINTS
Convention proposals, 237, 238, 242,
244, 249, 254, 258, 259, 262, 263–64,
264, 265, 266, 267, 269, 274, 275,
276, 279–80, 280, 281, 282, 283, 285,
287, 288–89, 289, 290, 291, 292, 293,
294, 295, 296
Constitution
Appropriations bills required to
withdraw money from Treasury,
311
Army appropriations limited to
two years, 310
Bills of attainder forbidden, 311
Capitation and other direct taxes
to be laid in proportion to census, 311
Commerce, may not discriminate
among states and vessels in regulation of, 311
Export duties prohibited on articles exported from states, 311
Ex post facto laws forbidden, 311
Habeas corpus, writ of not to be
suspended except in cases of
invasion and rebellion, 310–11
Judges' compensation may not be
diminished while in office, 314
Laws of may be vetoed by President, 309
President's compensation may not
be increased or diminished while
in office, 313
Religious tests may not be required for any office or public
trust under United States, 316
Senators' places of election may
not be altered, 308
Sessions of may be convened by
President, and adjourned by him
when two houses disagree on
date, 313–14
Slaves, importation of may not be
forbidden before 1808, 310
States: no new states shall be
formed within jurisdiction of
other states without consent
of state legislatures, 315; no new
states shall be formed by junction of two or more states, or
parts of states, without consent
of state legislatures, 315; no state
shall be deprived of equal suffrage in Senate without its consent, 316
Titles of nobility forbidden, 311
Treason: defined by Constitution,

314–15; requirement for conviction of, 315; punishment of shall
not work corruption of blood
or forfeiture during life of attainted person, 315
See also Senate under Constitution:
restraints
CONNECTICUT
147, 248, 251; proposes amendments
to Articles, 56, 109–11; ratifies Articles, 109–11, 124; opposes Constitutional Convention, 179, 189; opposes
stronger central government, 190;
appoints delegates to Convention,
194, 215–16; and compromise on
trade regulation and slave trade, 242;
allotted five Representatives by Constitution, 257, 261, 271, 286, 300, 307;
allotted seven Representatives after
Census of 1790, 300; delegates in
Congress (1787), 324; supports Constitution, 344
CONSTITUTION, EVOLUTION AND ESTAB-
LISHMENT OF
Resolutions and proposals: Virginia
Resolutions, 232, 233–35, 236–37,
243–45; Pinckney Plan, 245–47, 255;
Amended Virginia Resolutions,
234, 235, 236, 247–50, 255, 256;
New Jersey Amendments, 234–35,
248, 250–53, 255; Hamilton Plan,
253–55; Resolutions of 24 July,
255–60
Drafts of: Committee of Detail, 236,
242, 260–69; Amended Committee
of Detail, 270–84; Amended Committee of Style, 284–96, 304
Adoption of by Constitutional Convention, 304–5
Text of, 306–17; errata in, 316–17;
attestation clause, 316–17; signers,
non-signers of, 304, 317, 320n
Letter and resolutions accompanying
transmittal to Congress, 284–85,
305–6, 317–18
Transmittal of to Congress, 305, 318–
20
Publication of, 320, 342n
Congress and: received and read,
322, 325; actions upon, 322–42;
sent to states, 340, 342, 342n, 344,
345–46, 347, 350, 351; commentaries
on actions by members of, 342–49;
commentaries on actions by non-
members of, 349–53. See also Congress under Articles: and the Constitution
Opposition to, 326, 343, 344, 347, 350,
351, 352

Support for, 325, 326, 344, 345, 346–47, 348, 349, 350, 351

Ratification of, provisions for, 233, 235, 245, 250, 259–60, 269, 270, 283, 296, 316, 317–18, 323, 327–28, 329, 329–30, 330, 330–33, 334, 334–35, 340, 342, 344, 345, 347, 348, 349, 350, 351, 352

New federal government, procedures for establishment of, 245, 250, 259, 269, 283–84, 318

Oaths required by Constitution (President and federal officeholders), 238–39, 245, 250, 259, 267, 269, 280, 283, 292, 296, 313, 316

CONSTITUTIONAL CONVENTION

Proposals for (1781–87), 66, 67, 163, 176–77, 192–93, 232; by Annapolis Convention, 177–78, 181–85, 192

Opposition to (1781–87), 177, 178, 179, 188–90, 192

Legality of questioned, 177–78, 188–90, 192–93; debated in Congress, 327–28, 328, 329, 329–30, 330–33, 334, 343–44, 345, 346–47, 347

Impact of agrarian discontent on calling of (1786–87), 178–79

Congress calls (1787), 67, 179, 185–90, 194, 232, 233, 234

Election of delegates to, 178, 179, 193–94; New Jersey, 195–96; Virginia, 196–98; Pennsylvania, 199–200; North Carolina, 200–2; Delaware, 203–4; Georgia, 204; Massachusetts, 205–9; New York, 209–13; South Carolina, 213–15; Connecticut, 215–16; Maryland, 216–23; New Hampshire, 223–25; Rhode Island refuses to elect, 225–29, 322, 327

Elections to, refused, 195, 196n, 198n, 202n, 215n, 216n, 223n, 348, 352

Delegates as members of: First Continental Congress, 52–53; Second Continental Congress, 53; Confederation Congress (1781–86), 64, 65, 67, 260; Annapolis Convention, 177; Confederation Congress (September 1787), 322, 324–25, 326, 348, 351, 352

Restrictions upon: resolution of Congress of 21 February 1787, 179, 187, 194, 233, 234, 235; state acts appointing delegates to Convention, 193–94, 197, 199–200, 203, 204, 205, 207, 208n, 209, 209n, 210–11, 213, 214, 215–16, 217, 222, 223–24, 225

Meeting, officers, and rules of, 232–33

Attendance in, 195, 230, 232

Issues in: abandonment of Articles of Confederation, 233, 233–34; ratification of Constitution by state conventions, 233, 235; rejection of congressional approval of Constitution, 233, 235, 270; state versus national sovereignty, 233–35, 236–37, 238, 239; balance of power among branches, 236, 237–39; congressional veto of state laws, 236; use of armed force against states, 236–37; republican government guaranteed to states, 237; economic restraints upon states, 237; supremacy of Constitution, 237; powers of Congress, 237–38, 285; Presidency, 237–39, 270, 285; large versus small states over representation in House, 239, 240–41, 241–42, 285, 297–98; large versus small states over representation in Senate, 239–40, 240, 242, 297; North versus South over slavery and representation, 240–41; North versus South over congressional regulation of commerce, 241, 242, 285; North versus South over census, 241; North versus South over slave trade, 241–42; North versus South over levying of export duties, 242, 285; address to the people, 270, 284–85; transmittal of Constitution to states, 284–85; treasurer, 285; taxation, 285; bill of rights, 285; liberty of the press, 285; charters of incorporation for canals, 285; national university, 285

Resolutions and proposals in: Virginia Resolutions, 232, 233–35, 236–37, 243–45; Pinckney Plan, 245–47, 255; Amended Virginia Resolutions, 234, 235, 236, 247–50, 255, 256; New Jersey Amendments, 234–35, 248, 250–53, 255; Hamilton Plan, 253–55; Resolutions of 24 July, 255–60

Drafts of Constitution: Committee of Detail, 236, 242, 260–69; Amended Committee of Detail, 270–84; Amended Committee of Style, 284–96, 304

Adopts Constitution, 304–5

Text of Constitution, 306–17

Letter and resolutions transmitting Constitution to Congress, 284–85, 305–6, 317–18, 318–20, 330

Journals and papers, disposition of, 305, 318–19

Adjourns, 319–20
Expenses of, 340n
CONSTITUTIONAL CONVENTIONS
350; Convention proposals concerning, 269, 283, 295; Constitution provides that Congress shall call convention to propose amendments on request from two-thirds of state legislatures, 316
CONSTITUTIONS, COLONIAL
Declaration of Independence denounces British violation of colonial charters, 74
CONSULS
See Ambassadors
CONTRACTS
obligation of: 350; Northwest Ordinance prohibits territories from impairing, 62, 172–73; Convention proposals concerning, 237, 291; Constitution prohibits states from passing laws impairing, 311
CONVENTIONS, STATE
350; Convention proposals concerning, 233, 235, 245, 250, 259–60, 269, 283, 295, 296; Constitution requires legislatures or conventions of three-fourths of the states to ratify amendments to Constitution, 316; Constitution provides that ratification by nine state conventions is sufficient to establish the Constitution among the ratifying states, 316; Convention Resolution of 17 September recommends that Constitution be laid before Congress and submitted to state conventions, 317–18; in debates in Congress on Constitution, 323, 327–28, 329–30, 330, 330–33, 334, 334–35, 340, 344, 345, 347, 348, 349, 351, 352. See also Amendments to Constitution; Constitution, evolution and establishment of
COOKE, JOSEPH PLATT (Conn.)
member of Congress (1787), 324
COPYRIGHTS
Convention proposals concerning, 275, 289; Constitution gives Congress power to provide for, 310
CORPORATIONS
Convention rejects power of Congress to charter, 285
COUNCIL OF REVISION
Convention proposal for rejected, 237, 244, 246
COUNTERFEITING
See Money
COXE, TENCH (Pa.)
delegate, Annapolis Convention, 177, 181, 185

CREDITORS, PUBLIC
157; support strong central government, 176

DANA, FRANCIS (Mass.)
96; signer, Articles of Confederation, 94; delegate, Constitutional Convention, but does not attend, 195, 206, 207
DANE, NATHAN (Mass.)
67, 178, 188n, 324; as principal draftsman of Northwest Ordinance (1787), 61; on committee to prepare amendments to Articles of Confederation (1786), 163–64, 168n; on committee to consider Annapolis Convention report, 185; opposition to call for a convention by Confederation Congress, 189, 208n; in debates in Congress on Constitution, 327–28, 330, 331–32, 333, 341n, 343, 346–47; supports amendments to Constitution, 339
—letter from, 346–47
DAVIE, WILLIAM R. (N.C.)
delegate, Constitutional Convention, 202, 230
DAYTON, JONATHAN (N.J.)
delegate, Constitutional Convention, 196n, 230; signer, Constitution, 317
DEBT, PUBLIC
59, 63, 157, 333, 352; Draft Articles, 81; Articles require Congress to pay, 93; proposed methods of payment, 115–16, 117, 141, 144, 146–47; obligation of territories to pay share of, 152, 173; Convention proposals concerning, 269, 274, 282, 289, 295; Constitution provides for payment of, 309; Constitution requires payment of debt contracted under the Confederation, 316
DECLARATION OF INDEPENDENCE
background of, 53, 72; members of committee that drafted, 72; text of, 73–75; signers of, 76; and New Jersey amendments to Articles (1778), 114, 116
DELAWARE
124, 147, 248, 251; supports congressional power to fix western boundaries of states, 54; proposes amendments to Articles, 55–56, 130–31; ratifies Articles, 96, 130–35; appoints delegates to Annapolis Convention, 177, 183; appoints delegates to Constitutional Convention, 193, 203–4; requires Congress to approve work of Convention, 193, 203; requires Convention to retain equality of

states provided for in Articles, 203; and compromise on trade regulation and slave trade, 242; allotted one Representative by Constitution, 257, 261, 271, 286, 300, 307; allotted one Representative after Census of 1790, 300; delegates in Congress (1787), 324

DEPARTMENTS, EXECUTIVE
Convention proposals concerning, 246, 247, 254, 280, 292–93; Constitution allows President to require written opinions from, 313. *See also* Navy; President under Constitution: powers; State, department of; Treasury under Constitution; War, department of

DICKINSON, JOHN (Del., Pa.)
52, 53; writes draft of Articles of Confederation, 53, 78, 86n; signer, Articles of Confederation, 94, 132; chairman, Annapolis Convention, 177, 182, 185, 185n, 186; delegate, Constitutional Convention, 203, 230; and drafting of New Jersey Amendments, 250; signer (by proxy), Constitution, 304, 317

DRAYTON, WILLIAM HENRY (S.C.)
signer, Articles of Confederation, 94; and amendments to Articles of Confederation, 123n

DUANE, JAMES (N.Y.)
52, 53, 211–12; supports Galloway Plan, 52; on committee to revise and arrange Articles of Confederation and prepare circular letter to states, 78; signer, Articles of Confederation, 94; on committee to increase powers of Congress (1781), 141; on committee to prepare government ordinance of 1784, 150

DUER, WILLIAM (N.Y.)
signer, Articles of Confederation, 94

DUVALL, GABRIEL (Md.)
resigns as delegate to Constitutional Convention, 195, 223n

ELECTIONS, FEDERAL
Convention proposals concerning, 238, 243, 246, 248, 253–54, 256, 261, 262, 272, 278–79, 287, 291–92; Constitution's provisions for, 308, 312; R. H. Lee amendments (1787) propose that congressional elections be free and frequent, 338

ELECTIONS, FIRST FEDERAL
Convention proposals concerning, 269, 283–84; Convention Resolution of 17 September, 318

ELECTORS, PRESIDENTIAL
Convention proposals concerning, 238, 278–79, 291–92; Constitution's provisions for, 312; Convention Resolution of 17 September, 318

ELLERY, WILLIAM (R.I.)
133; signer, Declaration of Independence, 76; signer, Articles of Confederation, 94, 105, 107

ELLSWORTH, OLIVER (Conn.)
64; on committee for carrying the Confederation into effect (1781), 143, 260; delegate, Constitutional Convention, 216, 230; moves in Convention for equal representation of states in Senate, 239; and drafting of New Jersey Amendments, 250; on Committee of Detail, 255, 260

EMBARGOES
proposed changes in states' power under Articles to lay, 121, 164; proposed changes giving Congress power to lay and limits on power, 141, 142–43, 145; convention proposal concerning, 246

ENUMERATED POWERS OF CONGRESS
Convention proposals, 264, 274–76, 289–90; Constitution's listing of, 309–10

EXPENSES, U.S.
54, 56, 64, 66, 217, 240, 297; Draft Articles give Congress power to apportion among states according to population, 80, 81, 83, 84; Articles give Congress power to apportion among states according to land values, 89, 91, 92; proposed changes in Articles concerning, 97, 99, 103, 104, 105–6, 108, 109–10, 110, 114–15, 117, 122, 144, 145, 148–50, 165–66, 167; territories to pay a portion of, 152, 173; Convention proposals concerning, 243, 244–45, 247, 251, 252

EXPORT DUTIES
Draft Articles, 80, 83; Articles limit states' power to levy, 87, 88; proposed grants of congressional power to levy, 155, 164; Convention proposals concerning, 242, 246, 265, 282, 285, 290, 291; Constitution prohibits Congress from levying, 311; Constitution prohibits states from levying except for executing inspection laws, 311. *See also* Taxation

EX POST FACTO LAWS
Convention proposals concerning, 237, 276, 281, 290, 291, 350; Constitution prohibits Congress and states from passing, 311

EXTRADITION
See Interstate relations

FEDERAL CAPITAL
See Capital, federal

FEDERAL SITES
Convention proposals concerning, 275, 289–90; Constitution gives Congress sole control over arsenals, dockyards, forts, magazines, etc., 310

FEDERAL–STATE RELATIONS
See States under Articles of Confederation; States under Constitution

FEW, WILLIAM (Ga.)
67, 322, 324; on committee to consider Annapolis Convention report, 185; delegate, Constitutional Convention, 204, 230; signer, Constitution, 317

FITZSIMONS, THOMAS (Pa.)
id., 341; mentioned, 64; on committee on Impost of 1783, 146; delegate, Constitutional Convention, 199–200, 230; signer, Constitution, 317
—letter to, 325

FLORIDABLANCA, CONDE DE (Spain)
id., 353n
—letter to, 351

FLORIDA, EAST AND WEST
Georgia calls for admission into Union, 127, 128

FLOYD, WILLIAM (N.Y.)
signer, Declaration of Independence, 76

FOREST, ANTOINE DE LA (France)
id., 353n
—letter from, 349

FORREST, URIAH (Md.)
on committee to consider Annapolis Convention report, 185

FRANKLIN, BENJAMIN (Pa.)
53, 118, 319; on committee to draft Declaration of Independence, 72; signer, Declaration of Independence, 76; in Europe, 120n; delegate, Constitutional Convention, 200n, 230; supports need for congressional approbation of Constitution, 270; speech in Convention on form of signing Constitution, 304; signer, Constitution, 317

FULL FAITH AND CREDIT
Articles require each state to give full faith and credit to the acts, records, and judicial proceedings of every other state, 87; proposed change in Articles, 144; Convention proposals concerning, 246, 268, 282, 294; Constitution requires each state to give full faith and credit to the acts, records, and judicial proceedings of every other state, 315

GALLOWAY, JOSEPH (Pa.)
delegate, First Continental Congress, 52; plan of union, supported and opposed, 52

GARDOQUI, DON DIEGO DE (Spain)
id., 353n; treaty negotiations with John Jay, 60, 65, 67, 164, 241
—letter from, 351

GENERAL WELFARE CLAUSE
Convention proposals, 274, 289; Constitution, 309

GEORGIA
124, 147, 248, 251; proposes amendments to Articles, 56, 126–27; ratifies Articles, 96, 126–28; appoints delegates to Constitutional Convention 193, 204; requires Congress to approve work of Convention, 193, 204; and compromise on trade regulation and slave trade, 242; allotted three Representatives by Constitution, 257, 261, 271, 286, 300, 307; allotted two Representatives after Census of 1790, 300; delegates in Congress (1787), 324

GERRY, ELBRIDGE (Mass.)
53, 65, 66, 322; signer, Declaration of Independence, 76; signer, Articles of Confederation, 94; on committee to prepare grant of temporary power to Congress to regulate commerce (1784), 153; on committee to prepare amendment to grant Congress power to regulate commerce (1785), 155; on committee to draft Land Ordinance (1785), 156; delegate, Constitutional Convention, 206, 207, 230; refuses to sign Constitution, 234, 270, 304, 320n; and R. H. Lee amendments (1787), 341–42n, 342, 348, 348n
—letter to, 342

GILMAN, NICHOLAS (N.H.)
322, 324; delegate, Constitutional Convention, 224, 225n, 230; signer, Constitution, 317

GORHAM, NATHANIEL (Mass.)
64, 67, 242, 324; chairman, committee to prepare Impost of 1783, 146; delegate, Constitutional Convention, 206, 207, 230; on Committee of Detail, 255; signer, Constitution, 317; in debates in Congress on Constitution, 322, 331, 335, 336

GOVERNORS, STATE
Convention proposals concerning, 255, 262, 266–67, 272, 280, 286; Constitution gives governors power to fill Senate vacancies during recess of state legislatures, 307
GRAYSON, WILLIAM (Va.)
61, 67, 325; drafts Land Ordinance (1785) and credits passage to pressure from public creditors, 157; signs Northwest Ordinance as chairman of committee, 174; on committee to consider Annapolis Convention report, 185; in debates in Congress on Constitution, 326, 331, 339–40
GREAT BRITAIN
Declaration of Independence attacks policies of, 73–75; Order–in–Council (1783) of, 65, 153–54
GREENE, NATHANAEL (R.I.)
proposes convention to create central government (1780), 176
GWINNETT, BUTTON (Ga.)
signer, Declaration of Independence, 76; on committee to draft confederation, 78

HABEAS CORPUS, WRIT OF
proposed amendment of 1786 to guarantee privilege of, 167; Northwest Ordinance guarantees privilege of, 172; Convention proposals concerning, 281, 290; Constitution prohibits Congress from suspending except in cases of rebellion or invasion, 310–11
HALL, LYMAN (Ga.)
signer, Declaration of Independence, 76
HAMILTON, ALEXANDER (N.Y.)
64, 149, 304–5, 322; on committee on Impost of 1783, 146; proposes convention to create strong central government (1780), 176; delegate, Annapolis Convention, and drafts report, 177, 181, 185, 185n; writes New York instructions to delegates in Congress for calling a constitutional convention, 187n; delegate, Constitutional Convention, 211–13, 230, 232; plan of government, 253–55; on Committee of Style, 270; supports need for congressional approbation of Constitution, 270; signer, Constitution, 317; publishes attacks on Governor George Clinton, 326, 341n
HAMILTON PLAN
background of, 253; text of, 253–55

HANCOCK, JOHN (Mass.)
53; signer, Declaration of Independence, 76; signer, Articles of Confederation, 94
HANSON, JOHN (Md.)
signer, Articles of Confederation, 94, 136
HARING, JOHN (N.Y.)
67; member of Congress (1787), 324
HARNETT, CORNELIUS (N.C.)
signer, Articles of Confederation, 94
HARRISON, BENJAMIN (Va.)
signer, Declaration of Independence, 76
HART, JOHN (N.J.)
signer, Declaration of Independence, 76
HARVIE, JOHN (Va.)
signer, Articles of Confederation, 94
HENRY, JOHN (Md.)
223n; on committee to prepare amendments to Articles of Confederation (1786), 163–64
HENRY, PATRICK (Va.)
52; opposes Galloway Plan, 52; and call for Annapolis Convention, 181; refuses appointment as delegate to Constitutional Convention, 195, 198n —letter from, 181
HEWES, JOSEPH (N.C.)
signer, Declaration of Independence, 76; on committee to draft confederation, 78
HEYWARD, THOMAS, JR. (S.C.)
signer, Declaration of Independence, 76; signer, Articles of Confederation, 94
HIGGINSON, STEPHEN (Mass.)
id., 177; mentioned, 232; on Annapolis Convention, 177
HOLTEN, SAMUEL (Mass.)
opposes a national convention (1785), 66; signer, Articles of Confederation, 94
HOOPER, WILLIAM (N.C.)
signer, Declaration of Independence, 76
HOPKINS, STEPHEN (R.I.)
105; signer, Declaration of Independence, 76; on committee to draft confederation, 78
HOPKINSON, FRANCIS (N.J.)
signer, Declaration of Independence, 76; on committee to draft confederation, 78
HOSMER, TITUS (Conn.)
signer, Articles of Confederation, 94

HOUSE OF REPRESENTATIVES UNDER CONSTITUTION: ORGANIZATION
Convention proposals, 239, 240–41, 243, 246, 248, 249, 253, 255, 256, 257–58, 259, 260, 261, 261–62, 262, 263, 266, 269, 271, 271–72, 272, 273, 274, 278, 279, 279–80, 283, 285, 286, 287, 287–88, 288, 291, 292, 293, 296, 297–99, 300–1, 304
Convention proposals rejected: recall of members, 243; members to be ineligible for office under state or federal governments until one year after terms expire, 243, 248, 256; property qualifications for members, 255, 260, 262, 273; payment of members by states, 263, 273
Constitution: adjournment of, 308, 313–14; apportionment of among states in first Congress, 307; compensation of members, 308; contested elections, 308; discipline of members, 308; election to, 306, 308; electors of, qualifications for, 306; journal of, 308; meeting of, 308, 313–14; officers of, 307; privileges of members, 308; procedures of, 308; qualifications of members, 306, 308; quorum in, 308, 312; representation in and reapportionment of, 306–7; term of members, 306; vacancies in, 307
—restraints upon members: dual officeholding prohibited, 309; may not accept presents, etc. from foreign nations, 311; cannot serve as presidential Electors, 312; to take oath to support Constitution, 316
—voting in: two–thirds vote required to expel members, 308; yeas and nays to be recorded, 308, 309; majority of states required to elect President, 312
HOUSE OF REPRESENTATIVES UNDER CONSTITUTION: POWERS
Convention proposals, 243, 244, 246, 247, 248, 256, 258, 261–62, 262, 263, 267, 272, 274, 275, 278–79, 280, 286, 288, 291–92, 293
Convention proposals rejected: to elect Senators, 243, 246
Constitution: to have sole power of impeachment, 307; to initiate money bills, 309; to elect President if Electors fail to elect, 312
See also Congress under Constitution: powers

HOUSTON, WILLIAM C. (N.J.)
65; delegate, Annapolis Convention, 177, 181, 185; delegate, Constitutional Convention, 195, 196, 230
HOUSTOUN, WILLIAM (Ga.)
65, 67; on committee to grant commercial powers to Congress (1785), 155; on committee to prepare amendments to Articles of Confederation, 163–64; delegate, Constitutional Convention, 204, 230
HOWELL, DAVID (R.I.)
on committee to draft Ordinance of 1784, 150; on committee to draft Land Ordinance (1785), 156
HUGER, DANIEL (S.C.)
member of Congress (1787), 325
HUNTINGTON, SAMUEL (Conn.)
150; signer, Declaration of Independence, 76; signer, Articles of Confederation, 94
HUTSON, RICHARD (S.C.)
signer, Articles of Confederation, 94

IMMIGRATION
Convention proposals concerning, 265, 276, 290; Constitution forbids Congress to prohibit before 1808 the migration or importation of "such Persons" as states may think fit to admit, but may impose a duty on "each Person" imported, 310
IMPEACHMENT OF FEDERAL OFFICIALS
proposed amendment of 1786 to give Congress power to establish a court to try impeachments for misconduct, 167; Convention proposals concerning, 245, 247, 249–50, 252, 254–55, 259, 262, 267, 268, 272, 277, 280, 281, 286, 287, 293; Constitution gives House of Representatives sole power of, 307; Constitution gives Senate power to try cases of, 307–8; Constitution limits judgment in impeachment trials to removal from office and disqualification from holding a U.S. office, but those removed are liable to punishment according to law, 308; Constitution forbids President to pardon those impeached and removed from office, 313; Constitution provides that the President, Vice President, and civil officers may be impeached and removed from office upon conviction for treason, bribery, or other high crimes and misdemeanors, 314
IMPORT DUTIES
Draft Articles, 80, 83; Articles limit

states' power to levy, 87, 88; proposed grants of congressional power to levy, 140–41, 146–48, 155–56, 164; Convention proposals concerning, 246, 251, 264, 268, 274, 276, 282, 289, 290, 291; Constitution grants Congress power to levy, 309, 310; Constitution prohibits states from levying except for executing inspection laws, 311.
See also Taxation

IMPOST OF 1781
background of, 63, 140; failure of states to ratify, 63, 140, 146; text of, 140–41; in debates in Congress on Constitution (1787), 329, 332

IMPOST OF 1783
176; background of, 64, 146; status of in 1786, 66, 198n; text of, 146–48; New York refuses to ratify under conditions specified by Congress, 66, 189, 190n; Congress resubmits to nonassenting states, 198n; and Rhode Island refusal to appoint delegates to Convention, 226, 227

INCORPORATION, CHARTERS OF
Convention rejects power of Congress to grant, 285

INDENTURED SERVANTS
proposed changes under Articles, 148, 150; draft Ordinance of 1784 recommends prohibition of, 150; prohibited in territories, 174; runaways from other states to be returned, 174; Convention proposals concerning, 240, 249, 251, 257, 265, 276, 282, 286, 295; Constitution includes in formula for taxation and representation in House of Representatives, 307; Constitution provides for return of runaways, 315

INDIANS
Declaration of Independence denounces British incitement of, 75; Draft Articles exclude in apportioning expenses according to population, 80; Draft Articles prohibit further purchases of land from until boundaries of states are ascertained, 81; Draft Articles, 81, 82; Articles give Congress sole power to regulate commerce with and manage affairs with Indians not members of any state, provided that the legislative right of any state within its limits is not infringed or violated, 91; Articles allow states to engage in war with only in cases of imminent attack, 88;

proposed changes in Articles, 144, 148, 149, 150; lands of, 151, 156, 162, 170, 173; Convention proposals concerning, 240, 249, 251, 257, 265, 274, 276, 286, 289; Constitution excludes in formula for taxation and representation in House of Representatives, 307; Constitution gives Congress power to regulate trade with, 309.
See also Commerce; Territory of the United States

INFERIOR COURTS
See Judiciary under Constitution

INGERSOLL, JARED (Pa.)
delegate, Constitutional Convention, 199–200, 230; signer, Constitution, 317

INSPECTION LAWS
Convention proposal concerning, 285, 291; Constitution gives states power to levy export and import duties to execute inspection laws, but subject to revision by Congress, 311

INSURRECTIONS, DOMESTIC
Galloway Plan provides for suppression of, 52; Declaration of Independence denounces British for incitement of, 75; Convention proposals concerning, 237, 247, 259, 264, 269, 275, 283, 289, 295; Constitution empowers Congress to call militia to suppress, 310; Constitution guarantees states protection from, 315

INTERSTATE COMMERCE
See Commerce

INTERSTATE RELATIONS
Comity among states: Draft Articles, 80; Articles require, 87; proposed changes in Articles, 56, 97, 99, 121, 127, 128, 144; Convention proposals concerning, 246, 253, 268, 282, 294; Constitution requires, 315
Extradition of criminals: Articles provide for, 87; proposed change in Articles, 144; Convention proposals concerning, 268, 282, 294; Constitution provides for, 315
Fugitive slaves: in Northwest Ordinance, 174; Convention proposal concerning, 282, 295; Constitution provides for return of, 315
Full faith and credit: Articles require, 87; proposed change in Articles, 144; Convention proposals concerning, 246, 268, 282, 294; Constitution requires, 315
Landed vs. landless states: western lands, 54–55, 55–56, 56–57, 57–59

Large vs. small states: balance of power between, 53–54, 236; and nature of central government, 234; and representation in House of Representatives, 239, 297, 298; and suffrage in Senate, 239–40, 297

North vs. South: regulation of commerce, 54, 60, 65, 67, 154–55, 163–64, 177, 241–42, 345; apportionment of expenses among states, 54, 64; creation of new western states, 60–61, 156–57, 241–42; nature of central government, 189–90; balance of power between, 236; representation in Congress, 240–41, 241–42, 297–98

Treaties, confederations, and alliances among states: Draft Articles, 79; Articles prohibit without consent of Congress, 88; Convention proposals concerning, 268, 282, 291; Constitution prohibits, 311

INVASION, FOREIGN
Draft Articles, 81; Articles give states power to repel, 88; Convention proposals concerning, 237, 259, 264, 268, 269, 275, 282, 283, 289, 291, 295; Constitution gives Congress power to call militia to repel, 310; Constitution gives states power to repel, 311; Constitution guarantees states protection from, 315

IRVINE, WILLIAM (Pa.)
324, 353n; on committee to consider Annapolis Convention report, 185; on reaction to Constitution in Congress and in New York, 350

JACKSON, WILLIAM (Pa.)
as secretary, Constitutional Convention, 195, 232, 250n, 270, 305, 317, 318, 319
—letter from, 318

JAY–GARDOQUI TREATY NEGOTIATIONS
delays consideration of ordinance for Northwest Territory, 60; North-South dispute over, 65, 241; blocks consideration of amendments of 1786, 67, 163–64, 241

JAY, JOHN (N.Y.)
52, 232; supports Galloway Plan, 52; treaty negotiations with Spanish minister Gardoqui and consequences, 60, 65, 67, 163–64, 241; becomes Secretary for Foreign Affairs, 155; opposes Constitutional Convention unless called by Congress, 177–78, 192–93
—letter to, 132–33

JEFFERSON, THOMAS (Va.)
draft constitution of Virginia and western lands (1776), 57; chief architect of Ordinance of 1784, 59, 150; on committee to draft Declaration of Independence, 72; signer, Declaration of Independence, 76; on committee to grant Congress power to regulate commerce (1784), 153; drafts report for Land Ordinance (1785), 156
—letters to, 60, 347

JENIFER, DANIEL OF ST. THOMAS (Md.)
delegate, Constitutional Convention, 222, 223n, 230; signer, Constitution, 317

JOHNSON, THOMAS (Md.)
217, 222n, 223n; opposes terms of Virginia cession of Northwest Territory, 58

JOHNSON, WILLIAM SAMUEL (Conn.)
65, 67, 324; on committee to prepare amendment granting Congress commercial powers (1785), 155; on committee to prepare amendments to Articles of Confederation (1786), 163–64; opposes Congress calling Constitutional Convention, 179, 189; delegate, Constitutional Convention, 216, 216n, 230; chairman, Committee of Style, 270, 284; signer, Constitution, 317; in debates in Congress on Constitution, 322, 332–33
—diary of, 319

JONES, WALTER (Va.)
180, 181, 181n

JONES, WILLIE (N.C.)
refuses appointment as delegate to Constitutional Convention, 195, 202, 202n

JUDICIARY, 1776–1787
Declaration of Independence denounces British refusal to assent to laws for establishing judiciary powers, 74; Articles of Confederation give Congress power to establish courts to try cases of piracy, disputes among states over boundaries and lands, and private rights to soil, 89, 89–90, 90–91; proposed changes in Articles concerning piracy and land courts, 122–23, 123, 130–31, 133–34; proposed amendments to Articles for establishment of a federal judicial court to try and punish federal officers for misconduct, to hear cases on appeal from state courts involving treaties, law of nations, regulation of com-

merce, collection of federal revenues, and cases to which U.S. is a party, 166–67; Northwest Ordinance provides for establishment of court in Northwest Territory, 169–70; judges of Northwest Territory to take oath of fidelity and of office, 172

JUDICIARY UNDER CONSTITUTION
Convention proposals concerning, 237, 238, 244, 244–45, 247, 249, 249–50, 252, 254, 254–55, 255, 259, 260, 264, 265, 265–66, 266, 267, 267–68, 268, 275, 276, 277, 277–78, 278, 279, 280, 281, 287, 289, 290, 293, 293–94, 294

Convention proposals rejected: judges to serve with President on Council of Revision to veto laws of Congress, 237, 238, 244; judges to be appointed by Congress, 237, 244, 247; inferior courts to have original jurisdiction and Supreme Court only appellate jurisdiction, 244–45; jurisdiction in cases involving collection of national revenue, 244–45, 247, 249–50, 252, 254, 259; jurisdiction in cases involving impeachment of national officers, 244–45, 247, 249–50, 252, 254–55, 259, 267, 268, 280, 281; jurisdiction in cases involving peace and harmony of U.S., 244–45, 249–50, 259; jurisdiction in cases involving regulation of commerce, 247, 252; establishment of admiralty courts in each state, 247; judges to be appointed by Senate, 249, 259, 265–66, 266, 277–78, 278; judges prohibited from holding other offices or appointments during tenure, or an unspecified number of years thereafter, 252; property qualifications for judges, 255, 260; upon request of states, Senate to establish court to settle disputes among states over lands granted by different states, 265–66, 266, 277–78, 278; jurisdiction of inferior courts to be determined by Congress, 267–68, 281

Constitution
—Judicial power: to be vested in one supreme court and in such inferior courts as Congress shall ordain and establish, 310, 314
—Judges: Chief Justice to preside at impeachment trial of President, 308; may not accept presents, etc.

from foreign nations, 311; to be appointed by President and approved by Senate, 313; to hold office during good behavior, 314; to receive compensation which shall not be diminished while in office, 314
—Jurisdiction: judicial power shall extend to all cases in law and equity arising under the Constitution, laws, treaties of U.S., to all cases affecting ambassadors and other public ministers and consuls, to cases of admiralty and maritime jurisdiction, to controversies to which U.S. is a party, to controversies between two or more states, between a state and citizens of another state, between citizens of different states, between citizens of same state claiming lands under grant of different states, and between a state, or citizens thereof, and foreign states, citizens, or subjects, 314
—Supreme Court: shall have original jurisdiction in cases involving ambassadors, other public ministers and consuls, and those in which a state is a party, 314; shall have appellate jurisdiction as to law and fact in all other cases within the judicial power of the U.S., subject to such exceptions and regulations as Congress shall make, 314
—Treason: Constitution defines and specifies evidence required for conviction of, 314–15

JURY TRIAL
Declaration of Independence denounces British for depriving colonies of jury trial in many cases, 74; proposed amendment of 1786 guarantees that the trial of fact by jury trial shall be held sacred, 167; Northwest Ordinance guarantees, 172; Convention proposals concerning, 268, 281, 294; Constitution requires in all criminal cases other than impeachments, 314; R. H. Lee proposed amendments (1787) concerning, 337, 338–39, 343

KEAN, JOHN (S.C.)
member of Congress (1787), 325
KEARNEY, DYRE (Del.)
member of Congress (1787), 324

KENTUCKY
seeks statehood, 241; admitted as state, 298; allotted two Representatives upon admission into Union, 298, 301

KING, RUFUS (Mass.)
65, 67, 192, 208n, 243, 253, 324; opposes calling a continental convention (1785-87), 66, 178; on committee to prepare amendment to grant Congress commercial powers (1785), 155; on calling of Annapolis Convention (1786), 177; delegate, Constitutional Convention, 206, 207, 230; in debates in Convention, 239-40, 240-41; on Committee of Style, 270; signer, Constitution, 317; in debate in Congress on Constitution, 322, 330, 335-36

LANDED VS. LANDLESS STATES
See Interstate relations

LAND ORDINANCE OF 1785
61, 168; as an extra-constitutional act of Congress, 57, 62, 333, 341n, 343; background of, 59-60, 156-57; publication of, 151, 157; text of, 157-63. See also Northwest Ordinance (1787); Ordinance of 1784; Territory of the United States

LANGDON, JOHN (N.H.)
322, 324; delegate, Constitutional Convention, 224, 225n, 230; signer, Constitution, 317

LANGWORTHY, EDWARD (Ga.)
signer, Articles of Confederation, 94

LANSING, JOHN, JR. (N.Y.)
65, 253; delegate, Constitutional Convention, 211-13, 230, 232; denies right of Convention to create national government, 235; and drafting of New Jersey Amendments, 250

LARGE VS. SMALL STATES
See Interstate relations

LAURENS, HENRY (S.C.)
signer, Articles of Confederation, 94; as president of Congress signs pamphlet version of Articles sent to states, 96; refuses appointment as delegate to Constitutional Convention, 195, 215, 215n
—letter to, 126

LAW, RICHARD (Conn.)
on committee to revise draft Articles of Confederation (1777), 78

LAWS, COLONIAL
Declaration of Independence denounces restraints placed upon passage of, 73, 74

LAWS OF THE UNITED STATES
63-64, 236; Draft Articles, 83-84; Articles provide for enactment of, 92; proposed changes in Articles, 103, 104, 116-17, 117, 123, 141-43, 144-45, 145, 164-65, 165-66; Convention proposals concerning, 237, 238, 244, 246, 248, 249, 251, 252-53, 254, 255, 256, 257, 258, 259, 261-62, 263, 263-64, 265, 266, 267, 272, 273-74 275, 277, 279, 280, 281, 288, 288-89, 293, 296; Constitution provides for enactment of, 309, 310, 313; Constitution provides for enforcement of, 310, 314; Constitution gives U.S. courts jurisdiction over cases involving, 314; Constitution declares laws of U.S. to be supreme law of land, 316. See also Congress under Articles of Confederation; Congress under Constitution; Judiciary under Constitution; President under Constitution; Supremacy clause of Constitution

LEE, ARTHUR (Va.)
and three-fifths clause of amendment to apportion expenses (1783), 149; dropped from committee to give Congress power to regulate commerce (1784), 153
—letter from, 351

LEE, FRANCIS LIGHTFOOT (Va.)
signer, Declaration of Independence, 76; signer, Articles of Confederation, 94

LEE, HENRY (Va.)
325; on committee to prepare amendments to Articles of Confederation (1786), 163-64; in debates in Congress on Constitution, 326, 330, 331, 335

LEE, RICHARD HENRY (Va.)
52, 53, 61, 325; opposes Galloway Plan, 52; moves for independence and for a confederation, 53, 72, 78; and Articles of Confederation, 54, 55, 78, 96; on committee to draft Northwest Ordinance (1787), 61; signer, Declaration of Independence, 76; signer, Articles of Confederation, 94; signs Land Ordinance (1785) as President of Congress, 163; refuses appointment as delegate to Constitutional Convention, 195, 198n, 322, 352; in debates in Congress on Constitution, 323, 324, 326, 329-49, 352; transmittal of his amendments to Constitution, 341n, 342n, 342, 345, 346, 348, 348n
—letters from, 342, 345-46, 346, 348

LEGAL TENDER
Convention proposals concerning, 268, 281, 282, 290–91; Constitution prohibits states from making anything but gold and silver a tender in payment of debts, 311. *See also* Money

LEGISLATURES, COLONIAL
sovereignty of, 52; Declaration of Independence denounces restraints upon and dissolution of, 73–74

LEWIS, FRANCIS (N.Y.)
signer, Declaration of Independence, 76; signer, Articles of Confederation, 94

LIVERMORE, SAMUEL (N.H.)
on committee to prepare amendments to Articles of Confederation (1786), 163–64

LIVINGSTON, PHILIP (N.Y.)
signer, Declaration of Independence, 76

LIVINGSTON, ROBERT R. (N.Y.)
211–12; on committee to draft Declaration of Independence, 72; on committee to draft confederation, 78

LIVINGSTON, WILLIAM (N.J.)
52–53, 117n, 129n; delegate, Constitutional Convention, 196n, 230; signer, Constitution, 317

LONG, PIERSE (N.H.)
225n

LOVELL, JAMES (Mass.)
on committee to arrange Articles of Confederation and prepare circular letter to states, 78; signer, Articles of Confederation, 94

LYNCH, THOMAS, JR. (S.C.)
signer, Declaration of Independence, 76

McCLURG, JAMES (Va.)
delegate, Constitutional Convention, 198n, 230

McHENRY, JAMES (Md.)
65, 243; delegate, Constitutional Convention, 222, 223n, 230; signer, Constitution, 317

McKEAN, THOMAS (Del., Pa.)
signer, Declaration of Independence, 76; on committee to draft confederation, 78; signer, Articles of Confederation, 94, 132–33

MADISON, JAMES (Va.)
57, 63–64, 232, 322, 325; and Virginia cession of Northwest Territory, 59; on committee on coercive powers (1781), 141; on committee on Impost of 1783, 146; and counting three-fifths of slaves in apportioning expenses (1783), 149; delegate, Annapolis Convention, 177, 180–81, 182, 185; delegate, Constitutional Convention, 198, 230, 322; in debates in Convention, 236, 238, 239, 240, 304, 335, 341n; on representation of three-fifths of slaves (1787), 240; on Committee of Style, 270, 284; signer, Constitution, 317; in debates in Congress on Constitution, 332–33, 335, 336–37, 341n
—letters from, 342, 343–45, 347
—letters to, 155, 192, 326–27
—notes of debates in Congress, February 1787, 188–90
—notes of debates in Constitutional Convention, 243, 243–45, 251–53, 255, 270

MADISON, JAMES, SR. (Va.)
—letter to, 342

MANNING, JAMES (R.I.)
on committee to prepare amendments to Articles of Confederation (1786), 163–64

MARCHANT, HENRY (R.I.)
signer, Articles of Confederation, 94, 105, 107, 108

MARQUE AND REPRISAL, LETTERS OF
Draft Articles, 81, 82, 84; Articles prohibit states from granting except after declaration of war by Congress, 88; Articles give Congress power to grant with assent of nine states, 89, 92; proposed changes in Articles, 145, 156; Convention proposals concerning, 268, 275, 281, 289, 290; Constitution gives Congress power to grant, 310; Constitution prohibits states from granting, 311

MARTIN, ALEXANDER (N.C.)
delegate, Constitutional Convention, 202, 230

MARTIN, LUTHER (Md.)
delegate, Constitutional Convention, 222, 223n, 230; and drafting of New Jersey Amendments, 250

MARYLAND
147, 176, 248, 251, 322, 344, 350; supports congressional power to fix boundaries of states, 54; proposes amendments to Articles, 55, 96, 97–100; refuses to ratify Articles over issue of western lands, 56, 58, 124; ratifies Articles, 56–57, 97, 135–37; opposes terms of Virginia cession of "Old Northwest," 58–59; appoints delegates to Constitutional Convention, 194, 216–23; requires Congress

to approve work of Convention, 194, 217, 222; and compromise on trade regulation and slave trade, 242; allotted six Representatives by Constitution, 257, 261, 271, 286, 300, 307; allotted eight Representatives after Census of 1790, 300; delegates in Congress (1787), 324

MASON, GEORGE (Va.)
delegate, Annapolis Convention, 181; delegate, Constitutional Convention, 198, 230; in debates in Convention, 242; refuses to sign Constitution, 304, 320n; and R. H. Lee amendments (1787), 342n, 343, 347
—letter to, 345–46, 348n

MASSACHUSETTS
147, 239, 248, 251, 297; proposes amendments to Articles, 56, 103–4; legislature proposes a constitutional convention (1785), 66; ratifies Articles, 102–5, 124; delegates from do not attend Annapolis Convention, 177, 183; legislature and Annapolis Convention report, 208n; Shays's Rebellion in, 178–79; delegates in Congress oppose a constitutional convention (1786-87), 178, 189, 192; delegates in Congress move for a constitutional convention (1787), 179, 187, 188, 189, 190n; elects delegates to Constitutional Convention, 194, 205–9; places limitations on Convention, 194, 207; requires Congress to approve work of Convention, 205, 207; and compromise on trade regulation and slave trade, 242; allotted eight Representatives by Constitution, 257, 261, 271, 286, 300, 307; allotted fourteen Representatives after Census of 1790, 300; delegates in Congress (1787), 324

MATHEWS, JOHN (S.C.)
signer, Articles of Confederation, 94

MERCER, JOHN FRANCIS (Md.)
64; delegate, Constitutional Convention, 222, 223n, 230

MIDDLETON, ARTHUR (S.C.)
signer, Declaration of Independence, 76

MIFFLIN, THOMAS (Pa.)
53, 64; delegate, Constitutional Convention, 199–200, 230; signer, Constitution, 317

MILITIA
Draft Articles, 80; Articles require that states maintain, 88; proposed changes in Articles, 144; Northwest Ordinance makes territorial governor commander in chief of, 170; Convention proposals concerning, 237, 246, 247, 254, 255, 264, 267, 275, 280, 289, 292; Constitution gives Congress power to call forth, organize, arm, and discipline, 310; Constitution gives states power to appoint officers of and to provide training of, 310; Constitution makes President commander in chief of militia when in the service of the United States, 313

MINERALS
Congress' rights to in western lands, 160

MINT
proposal for establishment of, 144

MITCHELL, NATHANIEL (Del.)
324, 330; on committee to consider Annapolis Convention report (1787), 185

MITCHELL, STEPHEN MIX (Conn.)
67; opposes calling convention, 179, 189; on committee to consider Annapolis Convention report (1787), 185

MONEY
63; Draft Articles, 82, 83, 84; Articles give Congress power to emit bills of credit, 91, 92; Articles give Congress power to coin and to regulate alloy and value of, 91, 92; Articles give Congress power to borrow, 91, 92; Articles give Congress power to regulate alloy and value of states' coin, 91, 92; proposed changes in Articles, 144, 145; Convention proposals concerning, 237, 247, 258, 261–62, 264, 268, 272, 274, 275, 281, 282, 289, 290, 291; Convention rejects power of Congress to emit bills of credit, 275; Constitution gives Congress power to borrow, 309; Constitution gives Congress power to coin and regulate value of, and value of foreign coin, 310; Constitution gives Congress power to provide the punishment for counterfeiting, 310; Constitution prohibits states from coining or emitting bills of credit, 311; Constitution prohibits states from making anything but gold and silver a tender in payment of debts, 311

MONEY BILLS
Convention proposals concerning, 258, 261–62, 272, 274, 288; Constitution gives House of Representatives

sole power to originate revenue bills but allows Senate to amend, 309. *See also* House of Representatives under Constitution: powers; Senate under Constitution: restraints

MONROE, JAMES (Va.)
67; and sectionalism and the Northwest Territory, 60–61; on committee on commercial powers (1785), 155; opposes a continental convention (1786), 192
—letter from, 155

MONTMORIN, COMTE DE (France)
id., 353n
—letters to, 349, 352–53

MORRIS, GOUVERNEUR (N.Y., Pa.)
96; signer, Articles of Confederation, 94; delegate, Constitutional Convention, 199–200, 230, 322; in debates in Convention, 234, 238, 241, 242, 304; opposes requirement of congressional approval of Constitution, 235; on Committee of Style, 270, 284, 285; signer, Constitution, 317

MORRIS, LEWIS (N.Y.)
signer, Declaration of Independence, 76

MORRIS, ROBERT (Pa.)
53, 58; signer, Declaration of Independence, 76; signer, Articles of Confederation, 94, 118; delegate, Constitutional Convention, 199–200, 230; signer, Constitution, 317

MORTON, JOHN (Pa.)
signer, Declaration of Independence, 76

NATIONAL DOMAIN
See Territory of the United States

NATURALIZATION
Declaration of Independence denounces Britain for preventing naturalization of foreigners, 74; Convention proposals concerning, 253, 264, 275, 289; Constitution gives Congress power to establish uniform rules of, 309. *See also* Citizenship

NAVY
Draft Articles, 80, 81, 82, 83, 84; Articles prohibit states from maintaining in time of peace except for defense, 88; Articles give Congress power over, 91, 92; proposed changes in Articles, 114, 117, 145; Convention proposals concerning, 238, 246, 247, 252, 254, 255, 264, 267, 268, 275, 280, 282, 289, 291, 292; Constitution gives Congress power over, 310; Con-

stitution prohibits states from maintaining in time of peace without consent of Congress, 311; Constitution makes President commander in chief of, 313

NECESSARY AND PROPER CLAUSE
Convention proposals, 264, 275–76, 290; Constitution, 310

NEILSON, JOHN (N.J.)
resigns as delegate to Constitutional Convention, 195–96, 196n

NELSON, THOMAS, JR. (Va.)
signer, Declaration of Independence, 76; on committee to draft confederation, 78; resigns as delegate to Constitutional Convention, 195, 198n

NEW HAMPSHIRE
66, 147; ratifies Articles, 101–2, 124; delegates do not attend Annapolis Convention, 177, 183; agrarian discontent in, 178; appoints delegates to Constitutional Convention, 193–94, 223–25, 225n, 232; requires Congress to approve work of Convention, 223; supports increase in powers of Congress, 224; and compromise on trade regulation and slave trade, 242; allotted three Representatives by Constitution, 257, 261, 271, 286, 300, 307; allotted four Representatives after Census of 1790, 300; delegates in Congress (1787), 324

NEW JERSEY
124, 147, 248, 251; supports congressional power to fix western boundaries of states, 54; proposes amendments to Articles, 55–56, 113–18; ratifies Articles, 96, 128–30; delegates to Annapolis Convention, 177, 183; appoints delegates to Constitutional Convention, 193, 195–96, 196n; seeks increase in Congress' power over trade, 196; and compromise on trade regulation and slave trade, 242; allotted four Representatives by Constitution, 257, 261, 271, 286, 300, 307; allotted five Representatives after Census of 1790, 300; delegates in Congress (1787), 324

NEW JERSEY AMENDMENTS
considered and rejected by Constitutional Convention, 234–35, 248, 250–51, 253; text of, 251–53; submitted to Committee of Detail, 255

NEW YORK
147, 248, 251, 323; and Impost of 1783, 66, 189, 190n; vote on independence, 72; ratifies Articles, 111–

13, 124; legislature asks Congress to call a convention (1782), 176; delegates to Annapolis Convention, 177, 182; motion for a constitutional convention in Congress (1787), 179, 186, 187n, 188–89; appoints delegates to Constitutional Convention, 194, 209–13, 232; places limitations on Convention, 194, 210–11; requires Congress to approve work of Convention, 209, 211, 213; allotted six Representatives by Constitution, 257, 261, 271, 286, 300, 307; allotted ten Representatives after Census of 1790, 300; delegates in Congress (1787), 324; opposition to Constitution in, 326, 344, 350; support for Constitution in, 344

NOBILITY, TITLES OF
Draft Articles, 79; Articles prohibit Congress and states from granting, 88; Convention proposals concerning, 265, 268, 276, 281, 290, 291; Constitution prohibits Congress and states from granting, 311

NORTH CAROLINA
124, 147, 208n, 248, 251; ratifies Articles, 96, 124–26; delegates do not attend Annapolis Convention, 177, 183; appoints delegates to Constitutional Convention, 193, 200–2; supports increase in powers of Congress, 200–1; and compromise on trade regulation and slave trade, 242; allotted five Representatives by Constitution, 257, 261, 271, 286, 300, 307; Convention rejects additional representative for, 285; cedes Southwest Territory to Congress, 298; allotted ten Representatives after Census of 1790, 300; delegates in Congress (1787), 324

NORTH VS. SOUTH
See Interstate relations

NORTHWEST ORDINANCE (1787)
as an extra-constitutional act of Congress, 57, 62–63, 333, 341n, 343; background of, 60–62, 168; text of, 168–74. See also Land Ordinance of 1785; Ordinance of 1784; Territory of the United States

NORTHWEST TERRITORY
ceded to Congress by Virginia, 56, 57, 58, 59, 150, 156, 162–63, 173, 333; Ohio Company seeks to buy land in, 60; ordinances for government of, 150–53, 168–74; ordinance for survey and sale of, 156–63; population of, 301; officers of, 352. See also Territory of the United States

OATHS AND AFFIRMATIONS
Draft Articles require clerk of Committee of the States to take oath of secrecy and fidelity, 85; changes proposed in amendments to Articles, 113–14, 117, 144; Northwest Ordinance requires territorial officials to take oath of fidelity and office, 172; Convention proposals concerning, 238–39, 245, 250, 259, 267, 269, 280, 283, 287, 292, 296; Constitution requires of Senate when trying impeachments, 307–8; Constitution requires of President before taking office, 313; Constitution requires of all federal and state officeholders, 316; oath of office to be required of privy councillors in R. H. Lee proposed amendments (1787), 338

OFFICEHOLDERS, REQUIREMENTS AND PROHIBITIONS
Draft Articles, 84; Articles prohibit dual officeholding, 87, 89; proposed changes in Articles, 113–14, 117, 167–68; Massachusetts resolution appointing delegates to Convention prohibits dual officeholding, 205, 207–8; Convention proposals concerning, 243, 243–44, 244, 245, 247, 248, 249, 250, 252, 254–55, 255, 256, 259, 260, 261, 262, 263, 267, 269, 271, 272, 273, 276, 278, 279, 280, 281, 283, 286, 287, 288, 290, 291, 292, 293, 296; Constitution sets minimum ages for President, Representatives, and Senators, 306, 307, 312; Constitution sets citizenship and residency requirements for President, Representatives, and Senators, 306, 307, 312; Constitution provides for impeachment of, 308; Constitution prohibits dual officeholding, 309, 311; Constitution prohibits federal officeholders from serving as presidential Electors, 312; Constitution prohibits religious tests as a requirement of, 316; Constitution requires oaths of all federal and state officeholders to support Constitution, 316

ORDINANCE OF 1784
60, 61, 168; as an extra-constitutional act of Congress, 57, 62–63, 333, 341n, 343; background of, 59, 150–51; publication of, 150–51, 157; text of, 151–53. See also Land Ordinance of 1785; Northwest Ordinance; Territory of the United States

ORIGINAL JURISDICTION
See Judiciary under Constitution

OTTO, LOUIS GUILLAUME (France)
id., 353n
—letter from, 352–53

PACA, WILLIAM (Md.)
217, 222n, 223n; signer, Declaration of Independence, 76

PAINE, ROBERT TREAT (Mass.)
signer, Declaration of Independence, 76

PAINE, THOMAS (Pa.)
calls for a continental convention, 176

PARDONS AND REPRIEVES
Convention proposals concerning, 254, 267, 280, 284, 293; Constitution gives President power to grant except in cases of impeachment, 313

PATENTS
Convention proposals concerning, 275, 289; Constitution gives Congress power to provide for, 310

PATERSON, WILLIAM (N.J.)
delegate, Constitutional Convention, 195, 196, 230; presents New Jersey Amendments, 234, 248, 250; signer, Constitution, 317

PENDLETON, NATHANIEL (Ga.)
delegate, Constitutional Convention, but did not attend, 195, 204, 204n

PENN, JOHN (N.C.)
signer, Declaration of Independence, 76; signer, Articles of Confederation, 94

PENNSYLVANIA
147, 239, 248, 251, 297; supports congressional power to fix western boundaries of states, 54; proposes amendments to Articles, 56, 119; opposes terms of Virginia cession of Northwest Territory, 58–59; ratifies Articles, 118–20, 124; seeks to increase Congress' power over commerce, 153; delegate attends Annapolis Convention, 177, 182; agrarian discontent in, 178; appoints delegates to Constitutional Convention, 193, 199–200, 218; requires Congress to approve work of Convention, 193, 199–200; and compromise on trade regulation and slave trade, 242; allotted eight Representatives by Constitution, 257, 261, 271, 286, 300, 307; allotted thirteen Representatives after Census of 1790, 300; Assembly of receives Constitution, 319, 325; delegates in Congress (1787), 324

PETITION, RIGHT OF
Declaration of Independence denounces British actions on American petitions, 75; R.H. Lee amendments

(1787) propose to include in Constitution, 338

PETTIT, CHARLES (Pa.)
67; on committee to prepare amendments to Articles of Confederation (1786), 163–64

PICKERING, JOHN (N.H.)
delegate, Constitutional Convention, but did not attend, 195, 224

PIERCE, WILLIAM (Ga.)
324; delegate, Constitutional Convention, 204, 230, 322

PINCKNEY, CHARLES (S.C.)
65, 67, 353n; on committee to prepare amendments to Articles of Confederation (1786), 163–64, 168n; calls for a continental convention, 192; delegate, Constitutional Convention, 215, 230, 238, 322; opposes requirement that Congress approve the Constitution, 235; proposes plan of government in Convention, 245–47, 255; signer, Constitution, 317

PINCKNEY, CHARLES COTESWORTH (S.C.)
269n, 298–99, 344–45, 348n, 353n; delegate, Constitutional Convention, 215, 230, 322; in debates in Convention, 234, 241; signer, Constitution, 317

PINCKNEY PLAN
background of, 245; text of, 246–47; submitted to Committee of Detail, 255

PIRACIES
Draft Articles, 82; Articles give Congress power to establish courts for trial of, 89; proposed changes in Articles, 122–23; Convention proposals concerning, 244–45, 247, 252, 264, 275, 281, 289, 294; Constitution gives Congress power to define and punish, 310; Constitution gives judiciary jurisdiction in admiralty and martime cases, 314

POPULATION
Army: Draft Articles, 83; Articles require requisitioning from states according to white population, 91; proposed changes in Articles, 103–4, 104, 116, 117, 119
Census of: Draft Articles requires triennially, 80; proposed changes in Articles, 116, 117, 144, 150; Convention proposals concerning, 241, 258, 265, 276, 286; and apportionment of House of Representatives, 298, 299; Constitution requires every ten years, 306–7
Declaration of Independence denounces efforts to restrict growth

of, 74

Expenses: Draft Articles give Congress power to apportion among states according to population, 54, 56, 64, 66, 80, 83; proposed changes in Articles concerning, 109-10, 110, 148–50; Convention proposals concerning, 240, 251, 297. *See also* Expenses, U.S.

Representation in House of Representatives and Senate: proposals in Convention, 232, 239, 240–41, 243, 249, 258, 261, 271–72, 285, 286, 304; Constitution apportions House of Representatives according to population, 306–7. *See also* Representation in Congress

Statistics of, 297–301

Taxation (capitation and direct): Convention proposals concerning, 251, 264–65, 265, 271–72, 276, 286, 290; Constitution gives Congress power to apportion among states according to population, 306–7, 311. *See also* Taxation

POST OFFICES AND POST ROADS

Draft Articles, 82, 83; Articles give Congress power to establish and regulate, 91; proposed changes in Articles concerning, 119, 144; Convention proposals concerning, 246, 251, 264, 275, 289; Constitution gives Congress power to establish, 310

PREAMBLES: TO ARTICLES AND TO CONSTITUTION

Draft Articles, 79; Articles, 86; Convention proposals, 246, 260–61, 271, 284, 285; Constitution, 306

PRESENTS, EMOLUMENTS, OFFICES, AND TITLES

Draft Articles, 79; Articles prohibit officeholders from accepting from foreign states without consent of Congress, 88; proposed change in Articles concerning, 144; Convention proposals concerning, 276, 290; Constitution declares that federal officeholders may not accept from kings, princes, or foreign states without consent of Congress, 311. *See also* Nobility, titles of

PRESIDENT UNDER CONSTITUTION: OFFICE OF

Convention proposals, 237, 237–38, 238, 238–39, 244, 246, 249, 252, 254, 258, 259, 260, 266, 267, 269, 278, 278–79, 279, 280, 284, 291, 291–92, 292

Convention proposals rejected: election of, by Congress, 237, 237–38,

238, 244, 246, 249, 252, 258, 266, 269, 278, 284; as member of Council of Revision, 244, 246; plural executive, 252; to serve during good behavior, 254; President of Senate to succeed, 254, 267, 280; property qualifications for, 255, 260

Constitution: compensation of, 313; election of, by Electors or by House of Representatives if Electors do not elect, 312; oath of office, 313; qualifications of, 312; successor to be provided by Congress if neither he nor Vice President can serve, 313; term of, 311–12; Vice President to succeed, 312

PRESIDENT UNDER CONSTITUTION: POWERS

Convention proposals, 237, 238, 244, 246, 249, 252, 252–53, 254, 258, 259, 263–64 266, 266–67, 267, 270, 274, 278, 279, 279–80, 280, 284, 284n, 285, 288, 291, 292, 292–93, 293

Convention proposals rejected: to coerce states, 252–53; to appoint heads of executive departments, 254; to correspond with state executives, 266–67, 280

Constitution: to approve or veto acts of Congress, 309; to act as commander in chief of army and navy and of militia when called into service of U.S., 313; may require in writing opinion of heads of executive departments, 313; to grant reprieves and pardons for offenses against U.S., except in cases of impeachment, 313; to make treaties with advice and consent of two-thirds of Senators present, 313; to appoint with advice and consent of Senate, ambassadors, other public ministers and consuls, judges, and all officers established by law, 313; to fill vacancies requiring Senate confirmation while Senate is in recess, 313; to deliver State of the Union message to Congress, 313; to convene both houses of Congress, or either of them, on extraordinary occasions, 313; to adjourn Congress when the two houses cannot agree on a date, 313–14; to receive ambassadors and other public ministers, 314; to execute the laws, 314; to commission all officers of U.S., 314

PRESIDENT UNDER CONSTITUTION: RESTRAINTS

Convention proposals, 244, 245, 249,

249–50, 252, 254, 254–55, 258, 259
262, 263–64, 266, 267, 272, 274, 277,
278, 279, 280, 284, 284n, 285, 286,
287, 288–89, 292, 293
Convention proposals rejected: re-
election prohibited, 244, 249, 252,
258, 259, 266, 278; to be tried by
United States courts on charges
of impeachment, 245, 249, 249–50,
254–55, 259, 267, 280; to be incapable of holding any other office during his term, 252; to be
removed from office by Congress,
252; shall not take command of
military operations in field, 252;
pardons by to be approved by
Senate, 254; shall not grant pardons in cases of treason, 254, 284,
284n
Constitution: shall be removed from
office on charges of impeachment
brought by House and upon conviction by Senate for treason, bribery, and other high crimes and misdemeanors, 307, 307–8, 314; vetoes
can be overridden by two-thirds
vote of Congress, 309; may not
receive any other emolument from
U.S. or the states except compensation as President, 313; may not
grant reprieves and pardons in
cases of impeachment, 313; appointment of ambassadors, other
public ministers and consuls,
judges, and civil officers require
Senate confirmation, 313; advice
and consent of two-thirds of Senators present required to make
treaties, 313
PRESIDENTIAL ELECTORS
See Electors, presidential
PRESS, FREEDOM OF THE
Convention rejects, 285; advocated
in R. H. Lee amendments (1787), 337
PRIMOGENITURE
Northwest Ordinance disallows, 168–
69
PROPERTY QUALIFICATIONS FOR OFFICE-
HOLDING
in Northwest Ordinance, 61–62, 169–
70, 170–71; Convention proposals rejected, 255, 260, 262, 273
PUNISHMENTS, CRUEL AND UNUSUAL
protection from, guaranteed in
Northwest Ordinance 62, 172; R.H.
Lee amendments (1787) propose pro-
tection from, 338

RANDOLPH, EDMUND (Va.)
64, 193; chairman, committee to con-

sider additional powers for Congress
(1781), 143; delegate, Annapolis Convention, 177, 180, 181, 182, 185; delegate, Constitutional Convention, 198,
230; Virginia Resolutions, 232, 243,
248; in debates in Convention, 233–
34, 241, 270, 284, 284n; on Committee of Detail, 242, 255, 260; supports
requirement that Congress approve
the Constitution, 270; refuses to sign
Constitution, 304, 320n
—letter from, 222n
—letter to, 323
RATIFICATION OF CONSTITUTIONS
Draft Articles, 85–86; Articles provide for, 93; Convention proposals
concerning, 233, 235, 245, 250, 259–
60, 269, 270, 283, 296, 317–18; Constitution provides for ratification by
nine states, 316; debates in Congress
on (1787), 323, 327–28, 329, 329–30,
330, 330–33, 334, 334–35, 340, 342, 344,
345, 347, 348, 349, 350, 351, 352.
See also Articles of Confederation;
Constitution, evolution and establishment of
RATIFYING CONVENTIONS
See Conventions, state ,
READ, GEORGE (Del.)
53, 304; signer, Declaration of Independence, 76; delegate, Annapolis
Convention, 177, 182, 185; delegate,
Constitutional Convention, 203, 230;
signer, Constitution, 317
READ, JACOB (S.C.)
on committee to prepare grant of
temporary power to regulate trade
(1784), 153; on committee to prepare
Land Ordinance (1785), 156
REBELLIONS
See Insurrections, domestic
RECALL OF MEMBERS OF CONGRESS
Draft Articles, 81–82; Articles provide for, 87; proposed changes in
Articles concerning, 119, 167; Massachusetts resolution appointing delegates to Convention provides for,
205, 207; Convention proposals concerning, 243. See also Congress under Articles of Confederation: organization
REED, JOSEPH (Pa.)
signer, Articles of Confederation, 94,
118
RELIGION, FREEDOM OF
Northwest Ordinance guarantees,
172; Convention proposals concerning, 283, 296; Constitution prohibits
religious tests as qualification for
office under United States, 316; R. H.

Lee amendments (1787) propose guarantee of, 337

REPRESENTATION IN CONGRESS
Draft Articles, 81–82; Articles provide for by states, 87; proposed changes in Articles, 105, 108, 119, 121, 167–68; Delaware act appointing delegates to Convention prohibits change in method of congressional representation, 203; Massachusetts resolution appointing delegates to Convention prohibits change in method of congressional representation, 205, 207–8; Convention proposals concerning House of Representatives, 232, 239, 240–41, 243, 246, 249, 257–58, 261, 271–72, 285, 286, 297–99, 304; Convention proposals concerning Senate, 232, 239–40, 240, 242, 243, 246, 249, 258, 260, 262, 272, 286, 295, 297; Constitution apportions House of Representatives among states by population, 300–1, 306–7; Constitution provides for and guarantees two Senators from each state, 307, 316; R. H. Lee amendments (1787) propose increase in size of House of Representatives, 339; R. H. Lee amendments (1787) propose that representation in Senate be by population, 339

REPRIEVES
See Pardons and reprieves

REPUBLICAN GOVERNMENTS
governments of territories required to be, 152, 174; Convention proposals concerning, 237, 245, 250, 259, 269, 283, 295; Constitution requires United States to guarantee states a republican form of government, 315

RESERVED POWERS
53; Draft Articles provide that states retain such powers as do not interfere with Articles, 79; Articles provide that states retain every power not expressly delegated to the United States, 86; Convention proposal concerning, 246

RESOLUTIONS OF 24 JULY
background of, 255–56; submitted to Committee of Detail, 255–60, 260; revision of, 260–69

RHODE ISLAND
147, 322, 344, 350; supports congressional power to fix western boundaries of states, 54; proposes amendments to Articles, 55–56, 105–8; refuses to ratify Impost of 1781, 63, 140; rejects three-fifths compromise

in 1783 amendment to share expenses according to population, and refuses to ratify amendment, 66, 149; ratifies Articles, 105–9, 124; delegates of do not attend Annapolis Convention, 177, 183; agrarian discontent in, 178; refuses to appoint delegates to Constitutional Convention, 194, 225–29, 232, 322, 327; allotted one Representative by Constitution, 257, 261, 271, 286, 300, 307; Convention rejects additional Representative for, 285; allotted two Representatives after Census of 1790, 300; unrepresented in Congress (1787), 324; attack on "Leveller" policies of, 331

ROBERDEAU, DANIEL (Pa.)
signer, Articles of Confederation, 94, 118

RODNEY, CAESAR (Del.)
signer, Declaration of Independence, 76
—letter from, 132–33

ROLL CALLS
in Second Continental Congress on Maryland amendments to Articles (1778), 100; in Second Continental Congress on Delaware amendments to Articles (1779), 133–34; in Confederation Congress on calling Convention (1787), 186–87; in New York Assembly on resolution appointing delegates to Convention (1787), 211–12; in Confederation Congress on transmitting Constitution to states (1787), 334

RONALD, WILLIAM (Va.)
delegate, Annapolis Convention, 181

ROSS, DAVID (Md.)
324, 325, 327, 348n

ROSS, DAVID (Va.)
181

ROSS, GEORGE (Pa.)
signer, Declaration of Independence, 76

ROTATION IN OFFICE
Draft Articles, 84; Articles prohibit delegates to Congress from serving more than three years in six, 87, 205, 207–8; proposed changes in Articles, 121; Convention proposal concerning, 246

RUSH, BENJAMIN (Pa.)
53; signer, Declaration of Independence, 76

RUTLEDGE, EDWARD (S.C.)
54, 241; supports Galloway Plan, 52;

signer, Declaration of Independence, 76; on committee to draft confederation, 78

RUTLEDGE, JOHN (S.C.)
53, 64; supports Galloway Plan, 52; on committee on Impost of 1783, 146; favors counting three-fifths of slaves in apportioning expenses (1783), 149, 240; delegate, Constitutional Convention, 215, 230, 322; in debates in Convention, 236, 240, 242; chairman, Committee of Detail, 242, 255, 260, 270; signer, Constitution, 317
—letter from, 353n

RUTLEDGE, JOHN, JR. (S.C.)
—letter to, 353n

ST. CLAIR, ARTHUR (Pa.)
322, 324; appointed governor of Northwest Territory, 352

SALUS POPULI, DOCTRINE OF
debates in Congress (1787), 331–33, 340

SARGENT, WINTHROP (Mass.)
id., 349n; mentioned, 348

SCHOOLS, PUBLIC
provisions for in Northwest Territory, 59, 160, 173

SCHUREMAN, JAMES (N.J.)
324; delegate, Annapolis Convention, 177, 181, 185

SCUDDER, NATHANIEL (N.J.)
signer, Articles of Confederation, 94, 129

SENATE UNDER CONSTITUTION: ORGANIZATION
Convention proposals, 234, 239, 239–40, 240, 242, 243, 243–44, 244, 246, 248, 249, 253–54, 254, 254–55, 255, 256, 258, 259, 260, 261, 262, 263, 266, 267, 269, 271, 272, 273, 274, 276, 277, 278, 279, 279–80, 283, 286, 287, 287–88, 288, 290, 291, 293, 295, 296, 297
Convention proposals rejected: election of, by House of Representatives, 239, 243, 246; reelection of members forbidden until a year after term expires, 244, 248, 256, 263, 273; election of, by electors, 253–54; president of, to succeed President of U.S., 254, 267, 280; impeachment of, 254–55; property qualifications for members, 255, 260, 262, 273; president of, to be elected by members, 262, 272; payment of, by states, 263, 273
Constitution: adjournment of, 308,

313–14; classes of, 307; compensation of, 308; contested elections, 308; discipline of members, 308; election of by state legislatures, 307, 308; journal of, 308; meeting of, 308, 313–14; officers of, 307; President pro tempore of, 307; privileges of members, 308; procedures of, 308; qualifications of members, 307, 308; quorum in, 308; representation in, 307, 316; states guaranteed equal suffrage in, 316; term of members, 307; vacancies in, 307, 313
—restraints upon members: to take oath in trials of impeachment, 308; no dual officeholding, 309; may not accept presents, etc. from foreign nations, 311; cannot serve as presidential Electors, 312; to take oath to support Constitution, 316
—voting in: each Senator to have one vote, 307; Vice President of U.S. may vote only to break tie, 307; two-thirds vote required for conviction in impeachment trials, 308; two-thirds vote required to expel members, 308; yeas and nays to be recorded, 308, 309; two-thirds vote of members present required to approve treaties, 313
See also Congress under Constitution: organization

SENATE UNDER CONSTITUTION: POWERS
Convention proposals, 244, 247, 248, 249, 254, 256, 259, 263, 265, 265–66, 266, 274, 275, 277, 277–78, 278, 279, 280, 287, 288, 291, 292, 293
Convention proposals rejected: to appoint judges, 249, 259, 265, 266, 277; to approve pardons in cases of treason, 254; to declare war, 254; to make treaties, 265, 277; to appoint ambassadors, 265, 277; to provide for settlement of land controversies among states, 265–66, 277–78
Constitution: to try cases of impeachment, 307–8; to alter and amend money bills, 309; to elect Vice President of U.S. if two or more persons receive equal votes of Electors after election of President, 312; to approve appointments of ambassadors, other public ministers and consuls, judges, and all officers established by law, 313; to

approve treaties by two-thirds vote of members present, 313

SENATE UNDER CONSTITUTION: RE-STRAINTS
Convention proposals, 258, 261–62, 272, 287
Convention proposals rejected: not to alter or amend money bills, 258, 261–62, 272
Constitution: judgments in cases of impeachment limited to removal from office and disqualification from any U.S. office, 308

SHALLUS, JACOB (Pa.)
engrosses Constitution, 304

SHAYS'S REBELLION
impact of, 178–79

SHERMAN, ROGER (Conn.)
53; on committee to draft Declaration of Independence, 72; signer, Declaration of Independence, 76; on committee to draft confederation, 78; signer, Articles of Confederation, 94; delegate, Constitutional Convention, 216, 216n, 230; in debates in Convention, 237–38, 239; and drafting of New Jersey Amendments, 250; supports requirement that Congress approve the Constitution, 270; signer, Constitution, 317

SHIPPEN, WILLIAM, JR. (Pa.)
and R. H. Lee amendments, 342n
—letter to, 346

SINNICKSON, THOMAS (N.J.)
—letter to, 341n

SLAVES
54, 56, 61, 62, 64, 150, 300–1; Draft Articles provide for apportionment of expenses according to population, including slaves, 80; proposed changes in Articles concerning, 103, 104, 116, 119, 148–49, 150; prohibited in Northwest Territory, 174; Northwest Ordinance requires return of fugitive slaves, 174; Convention proposals concerning, 240, 241–42, 246, 249, 251, 264–65, 265, 276, 282, 286, 290, 295, 297, 298; Constitution provides for apportioning Representatives and direct taxes according to population, including three-fifths of slaves, 306–7; Constitution provides that importation of slaves may not be prohibited prior to 1808 and limits import duty to ten dollars, 310; Constitution requires return of fugitive slaves, 315

SMALLWOOD, WILLIAM (Md.)
223n

SMITH, JAMES (Pa.)
118; signer, Declaration of Independence, 76

SMITH, JONATHAN BAYARD (Pa.)
signer, Articles of Confederation, 94, 118

SMITH, MELANCTON (N.Y.)
67, 211–12, 324; on committee to prepare amendments to Articles of Confederation (1786), 163–64; on committee to consider Annapolis Convention report, 185; in debates in Congress on Constitution, 343
—notes of debates in Congress on Constitution, 322, 323–24, 327, 328, 329, 330, 330–33, 335–37, 339–40, 341n

SMITH, MERIWETHER (Va.)
180, 181

SOUTH CAROLINA
147, 248, 251, 298, 350; proposes amendments to Articles, 56, 121–23; ratifies Articles, 121–23, 124; agrarian discontent in, 178; appoints delegates to Constitutional Convention, 194, 213–15, 215n; requires Congress to approve work of Convention, 214; seeks increase in powers of Congress, 214; and compromise on trade regulation and slave trade, 242; allotted five Representatives by Constitution, 257, 261, 271, 286, 300, 307; allotted six Representatives after Census of 1790, 300; delegates in Congress (1787), 325

SOUTHWEST TERRITORY
ceded to Congress by North Carolina, 298; population of, 301

SOVEREIGNTY, STATE AND NATIONAL
52, 53, 55, 74, 75, 176–77, 189–90, 190n, 232, 233–35, 236, 236–37, 239–40, 305–6, 328, 329, 331–32, 333, 341n, 343, 349; Articles of Confederation provide that states retain sovereignty and every power not "expressly delegated" to the United States, 86; deletion of word "national" from resolutions submitted to Committee of Detail, 256, 257, 258, 259; Constitution provides that Constitution, laws, and treaties of U.S. "shall be the Supreme Law of the Land," 316. See also States under Articles of Confederation; States under Constitution; Supremacy clause of Constitution

SPAIGHT, RICHARD DOBBS (N.C.)
65; on committee on commercial powers (1785), 155; delegate, Consti-

tutional Convention, 202, 230; signer, Constitution, 317
SPARHAWK, JOHN (N.H.)
225n
SPARKS, JARED
—letter to, 284
STATE, DEPARTMENT OF
Convention proposals concerning,
246, 247, 254
STATES UNDER ARTICLES OF CONFEDERA-
TION
Guarantees to
53, 54–55, 55–56; each state to retain sovereignty and every power,
jurisdiction, and right not expressly delegated to Congress, 86; legislatures to appoint officers of or
under rank of colonel of troops
raised for common defense, 89, 91;
may not be deprived of territory
for the benefit of U.S., 90; to
engage in war to repel invasions or
in case of imminent danger, 88;
each state to have one vote in
Congress, 87; amendments to Articles require unanimous ratification by states, 93; commercial
treaties may not restrain legislatures from imposing the same duties on foreigners their citizens are
subject to, or prohibit the importation or exportation of any goods
or commodities, 89
—proposed changes in Articles (1778–
87), 97–98, 99, 99–100, 106, 108–9,
115–16, 117, 121, 122, 123, 130–31,
133–34, 155–56, 164, 252–53
New states
54, 57–58, 59, 60, 61, 62; Draft Articles provide for admission of, 82;
Articles provide for admission of
Canada but no other colony to be
admitted unless nine states agree,
93; ordinances for Northwest Territory provide for admission of and
for conditions of admission, 150–53,
168–74
—proposed changes in Articles (1778–
87), 127, 128, 145, 253
Obligations of
54, 56, 64, 66, 217, 240, 297; free
inhabitants of each state entitled
to privileges and immunities of
citizens in the several states, 87;
to maintain militia, 88; to raise
share of military forces, 89, 91,
91–92; to pay share of expenses of
United States, 89, 91, 92; to return
criminals fleeing from one state
to another on request of executive
of state having jurisdiction of the
offence, 87; to give full faith and
credit to records, acts, and judicial
proceedings of every other state, 87
—proposed changes in Articles (1778–
87), 97, 99, 103, 103–4, 104, 105–6,
108, 109–10, 110, 114–15, 116, 117,
119, 121, 122, 127, 128, 144, 145,
164–65, 165–66, 251
Powers of
to exercise all powers not expressly
delegated to Congress, 86
Representation in Congress
elect, recall, and replace delegates
at will, 87; each state pays own
delegates, 87; each state represented by not less than two nor more
than seven delegates, 87; no delegate to serve for more than three
years in any six, 87
Restraints upon
may not grant titles of nobility, 88;
may not discriminate against citizens of other states in regulation
of commerce, 87; export and import duties may not interfere with
treaty stipulations, 88; may not
appoint general officers of troops
raised for common defense, 89, 91;
to abide by Articles and acts and
ordinances of Congress, 93; export
and import duties shall not be
discriminatory, 87
—proposed changes in Articles (1781-
87), 63–64, 141–43, 143, 144–45,
145, 164–65, 165–66, 252, 252–53,
333, 341n
Restraints upon, conditional
may not enter into treaties or alliances with foreign powers without consent of Congress, 88; may
not enter into treaties, confederations, and alliances with other
states without consent of Congress,
88; number of peacetime troops
kept by to be determined by Congress, 88; except in emergencies,
may not make war without consent of Congress, 88; may not commission vessels of war except after
a declaration of war by Congress,
88; may not grant letters of
marque and reprisal except after
a declaration of war by Congress,
88; number of vessels of war to
be kept by in peacetime to be determined by Congress, 88
—proposed changes in Articles (1778),
121

STATES UNDER CONSTITUTION

Guarantees to

—Convention proposals, 236–37, 237, 239–40, 245, 246–47, 247, 250, 258, 259, 269, 272, 276, 282, 283, 286, 290, 295

—Convention proposal rejected: Congress to be final resort on appeal in disputes among states, 246–47

—Constitution: each state to have at least one Representative, 307; Congress may not favor ports of one state over another, 311; no new states shall be formed within jurisdiction of any other states except by consent of states concerned and Congress, 315; U.S. guarantees each state a republican form of government, 315; U.S. to protect against invasion and domestic violence, 315; cannot be deprived of equal suffrage in Senate without their consent, 316

New states

—Convention proposals, 241, 245, 247, 250, 253, 259, 268, 268–69, 282, 295

—Convention proposals rejected: two-thirds vote of members present in each house of Congress required for admission of, 268, 282; responsibility of, for public debt, 268–69, 282

—Constitution: provisions for admission of, 315

Obligations of

—Convention proposals, 243, 245, 246, 247, 250, 251, 253, 259, 268, 269, 282, 283, 294, 296

—Convention proposal rejected: to pay share of expenses of United States, 247, 251

—Constitution: full faith and credit shall be given in each state to public acts, records, and judicial proceedings of every other state, 315; citizens of each state to be entitled to privileges and immunities of citizens in the several states, 315; to return criminals fleeing from one state to another on demand of executive of state having jurisdiction of crime, 315; indentured servants and slaves fleeing to another state to be delivered upon request to person claiming their services, 315; state officeholders to take oath to support Constitution, 316

Powers of

—Convention proposals, 233, 234, 235, 245, 246, 247, 248, 250, 251, 254, 255, 256, 259–60, 262, 268 269, 270, 272, 275, 278, 282, 283, 286, 287, 289, 291, 296

—Convention proposals rejected: each state to retain rights not expressly delegated, 246; to levy embargoes in times of scarcity, 246; courts of to have original jurisdiction in federal cases, 247, 251, 254; chief judges of state superior courts to be members of court trying impeachments of federal officeholders, 255

—Constitution: legislatures to elect Senators, 307; legislatures to prescribe times, places, and manner of holding elections for Representatives and Senators, 308; to keep militia, appoint militia officers, and train militiamen according to discipline prescribed by Congress, 310; may engage in war to repel invasions or in case of imminent danger, 311; to appoint Electors to vote for President, 312; nine states required to ratify Constitution, 316; three-fourths of legislatures may require Congress to call convention to propose amendments to Constitution, 316: three-fourths of legislatures required to ratify amendments proposed by Congress or a convention, 316

Representation in Congress

—Convention proposals, 239–40, 240–41, 242, 243, 246, 249, 257, 257–58, 260, 261, 262, 271–72, 272, 276, 285, 286, 295, 304

—Constitution: provisions for apportionment and reapportionment of House of Representatives, 306–7; allotment of Representatives in first House of Representatives, 307; each state to have two Senators, 307; no state to be deprived of equal suffrage in Senate without its consent, 316

Restraints upon

—Convention proposals, 236, 237, 244, 245, 246, 246–47, 247, 249, 252, 252–53, 254, 255, 257, 264, 265, 267, 268, 274, 275, 277, 280, 281, 289, 290, 290–91, 291, 292, 294, 296

—Convention proposals rejected: congressional veto of state laws, 236, 244, 246, 249, 257; may not lay interfering duties, 246; may not keep an army and navy, 246, 255;

President to call forth power of U.S. to enforce laws in, 252–53; state governors to be appointed by general government with power to veto state laws, 255; U.S. to have sole control over militia, 255
—Constitution: Congress to regulate commerce among states, 309; Congress to provide for calling forth militia to execute laws of U.S., 310; Congress to provide for organizing, arming, and disciplining and for governing that part of militia employed in service of U.S., 310; may not enter into treaties, alliances, or confederations, 311; may not grant letters of marque and reprisal, 311; may not coin money, 311; may not emit bills of credit, 311; may not make anything but gold and silver a tender in payment of debts, 311; may not pass bills of attainder, 311; may not pass ex post facto laws, 311; may not pass laws impairing obligations of contracts, 311; may not grant titles of nobility, 311; President to command militia when called into service of U.S., 313; U.S. judiciary to settle controversies between states and/or citizens, 314; laws and constitutions of to be subordinated to Constitution, laws, and treaties of U.S., 316
Restraints upon, conditional
—Convention proposals, 268, 282, 285, 291
—Convention proposals rejected: may not emit bills of credit without consent of Congress, 268, 282; may not make anything but specie a tender in payment of debts without consent of Congress, 268, 282; may not levy import duties without consent of Congress, 268, 282; may not levy export duties without consent of Congress, 282
—Constitution: with consent of Congress may levy export and import duties to execute inspection laws, 311; may not levy tonnage duties without consent of Congress, 311; may not keep peacetime troops without consent of Congress, 311; may not keep ships of war in peacetime without consent of Congress, 311; may not enter into agreements or compacts with other states or foreign powers without consent of Congress, 311; may not engage in war without consent of Congress unless invaded or in imminent danger of invasion, 311

STOCKTON, RICHARD (N.J.) signer, Declaration of Independence, 76

STONE, THOMAS (Md.) 216, 217, 222n; signer, Declaration of Independence, 76; on committee to draft confederation, 78; resigns as delegate to Constitutional Convention, 195, 223n

STRONG, CALEB (Mass.) delegate, Constitutional Convention, 206, 207, 230
—letter to, 346–47

SULLIVAN, JOHN (N.H.) proposes continental convention, 176

SUPREMACY CLAUSE OF CONSTITUTION 350; Convention proposals concerning, 237, 252–53, 255, 257, 265, 277, 296; Constitution declares the Constitution, laws, and treaties of the United States supreme law of the land, 316; debates in Congress concerning, 331–32, 341n

SUPREME COURT See Judiciary under Constitution

SYMMES, JOHN CLEVES (N.J.) on committee to prepare amendments to Articles of Confederation (1786), 163–64

TAXATION 54, 146, 178; Declaration of Independence denounces imposition of taxes without consent, 74; Draft Articles prohibit Congress from imposing taxes or duties except for the post office, 83; Articles permit Congress to charge postage to defray expenses of post office, 91; proposals for changes in Articles concerning, 145, 164–66, 167; provisions for in Northwest Territory, 152, 173; Convention proposals concerning, 245, 247, 249–50, 251, 252, 254, 258, 259, 264, 264–65, 265, 274, 276, 286, 289, 290; Constitution requires capitation and other direct taxes be apportioned among states according to population, 306–7, 311; Constitution gives Congress power to lay and collect taxes, and requires all revenue bills to originate in House of Representatives, 309; Constitution requires Congress to levy taxes uniformly throughout U.S., 309; Constitution prohibits taxes or duties on articles exported from any state, 311. *See also* Export duties; Import duties; Money bills

TAYLER, JOHN (N.Y.) 211–12 ,

TAYLOR, GEORGE (Pa.) signer, Declaration of Independence, 76

TELFAIR, EDWARD (Ga.) signer, Articles of Confederation, 94

TERRITORY OF THE UNITED STATES Cession of, by states: Congress guarantees (1780) that land ceded will become republican states not less than 100 nor more than 150 miles square, 58; Virginia cession of land northwest of Ohio River incorporates congressional guarantees and requires Congress to void prewar purchases from Indians and to guarantee Virginia's remaining territory to her (1781), 58; acceptance of Virginia cession blocked by speculators, 58–59; Congress requests and receives a second Virginia cession (1783–84), 59, 150, 156, 162–63, 333
Ordinance of 1784 provides for government in Northwest Territory and formation of new states, 59, 60, 150–53, 157, 168, 333, 341n, 343
Land Ordinance of 1785 provides for survey and sale of Northwest Territory, 59–60, 61, 151, 156–63, 168, 333, 341n, 343
Northwest Ordinance (1787): 61–62; primogeniture prohibited, 168–69; governor of, 169, 170, 171, 171–72; secretary of, 169, 172; judges of, 169–70, 170, 172; qualifications for officeholding, 169–70, 170–71, 171; laws of, 170, 171; lands and rights of Indians, 170, 173; formation of districts prior to statehood, 170–71; general assembly of, 171, 171–72, 172, 173; legislative council of, 171, 172; oaths for officeholding, 172; delegate to Congress, 172; religious freedom guaranteed, 172; bill of rights, 172; right of eminent domain, 172; protection of property rights, 172–73; public schools, 173; to be part of Union and abide by Articles of Confederation and acts and ordinances of Congress, 173; inhabitants to pay share of public debt and U.S. expenses, 173; districts and states to levy taxes, 173; legislatures may not interfere with land sales by Congress, tax property of U.S., or discriminate against non-resident owners in taxing land, 173; waters leading to Mississippi and St. Lawrence rivers to be kept open and free, 173; three to five states to be formed from territory, 173–74; new states to be admitted to Union on equal basis with old states, 174; slavery and indentured servitude prohibited, 174; return of slaves and indentured servants provided for, 174
Convention proposals concerning, 283, 295
Constitution: Congress may dispose of and govern, but Constitution shall not be construed to prejudice the claims of the U.S., or any state, 315
See also Western lands of states

THOMSON, CHARLES (Pa.) as Secretary of Congress, 151, 157, 163, 163n, 174, 174n, 188n, 229n, 306n, 323, 341n, 342n —letter from, 340

THORNTON, MATTHEW (N.H.) signer, Declaration of Independence, 76

THREE–FIFTHS CLAUSE 64; proposed amendment to Articles to share expenses according to population, including three-fifths of slaves (1783), 148–50; Convention proposals concerning, 240, 241–42, 246, 249, 251, 257, 258, 265, 276, 286, 298; Constitution requires Representatives and direct taxes to be apportioned according to population, including three-fifths of slaves, 306–7

TREASON proposed amendment to Articles concerning, 166–67; Convention proposals concerning, 247, 254, 264, 267, 270, 276, 280, 284, 293, 294; Constitution declares treason grounds for impeachment, 314; Constitution defines treason and requirements for conviction, and gives Congress power to establish limited penalties, 314–15

TREASURY, BOARD OF and sale of western lands, 158–59, 161, 162, 168

TREASURY UNDER CONSTITUTION
Convention proposals concerning, 246, 247, 248, 249, 254, 256, 258, 259, 262, 272, 273, 274, 275, 282, 285, 288, 289, 290, 291; Constitution prohibits drawing money from treasury without appropriations made by law, 311; Constitution requires net produce of state duties on exports and imports to be for the use of the treasury, 311

TREATIES
54, 65, 72, 305, 333, 350; Declaration of Independence declares U.S. has power to conclude peace, contract alliances, and establish commerce, 75; Draft Articles permit states to lay import and export duties which do not interfere with treaties of U.S., 80; Draft Articles, 79, 82, 84; Articles prohibit states from entering into treaties without consent of Congress, 88; Articles give Congress power to make treaties, provided they do not interfere with the commercial powers of the states, 89; Articles require assent of nine states to ratify treaties, 92; proposed changes in Articles concerning, 121, 145, 155–56, 167; Convention proposals concerning, 237, 246, 247, 252, 252–53; 254, 257, 265, 268, 277, 279, 281, 282, 290, 291, 293, 296; Constitution prohibits states from making treaties, 311; Constitution gives President power to make treaties with the advice and consent of two-thirds of members of Senate present, 313; Constitution gives judiciary jurisdiction over cases involving treaties, 314; Constitution makes treaties supreme law of land, 316

TUCKER, ST. GEORGE (Va.)
delegate, Annapolis Convention, 177, 180–82, 185

UNIVERSITY, NATIONAL
Convention proposal concerning, 285

VAN DYKE, NICHOLAS (Del.)
signer, Articles of Confederation, 94, 132

VARNUM, JAMES M. (R.I.)
on committee on coercive powers (1781), 141; on committee on carrying the Confederation into effect (1781), 143; on committee to consider Annapolis Convention report, 185

VERMONT
admitted as state, 298; allotted two Representatives upon admission into Union, 298, 301

VETO POWER
Declaration of Independence condemns king of England for vetoing laws of colonial assemblies, 73; governor of Northwest Territory to have, 171; Convention proposals concerning, 236, 237, 238, 244, 246, 249, 254, 257, 259, 263–64, 274, 285, 288–89; Constitution gives President qualified veto, 309

VICE PRESIDENT, U.S.
Convention proposals concerning, 278, 278–79, 279, 280, 287, 291–92, 292; to serve as President of the Senate and to break tie votes, 307; Constitution provides for four-year term and method of election, 312; Constitution provides for succession to Presidency and for law of succession if there is no Vice President, 312–13; Constitution specifies grounds for impeachment, 314; R. H. Lee amendments (1787) propose abolition of office of, 338

VIRGINIA
147, 239, 248, 251, 297, 344; opposes congressional power to fix boundaries of states, 54–55; opposes state sovereignty, 55; cedes Northwest Territory to Congress, 56–57, 57, 58, 59, 60, 150, 156, 162–63, 173, 333; constitution of and provision for new states, 57; rescinds ratification of Impost of 1781, 63, 140; ratifies Articles, 120, 124; seeks to increase Congress' power over commerce, 153; calls Annapolis Convention, 177, 180–81; delegates attend Annapolis Convention, 177, 182; agrarian discontent in, 178; elects delegates to Constitutional Convention, 178, 193, 195, 196–98, 348, 352; requires Congress to approve work of Convention, 193, 197; impact of its act authorizing election of delegates to Convention, 199, 202n, 203, 208n, 217–18, 222n; influence of Convention delegates, 232; and compromise on trade regulation and slave trade, 242; allotted ten Representatives by Constitution, 257, 261, 271, 286, 300, 307; allotted nineteen Representatives after Census of 1790, 300; delegates in Congress (1787), 325; delegates in Con-

gress divided over Constitution, 326
VIRGINIA RESOLUTIONS
background of, 232, 233–35, 236–37,
238, 239, 243; text of, 243–45; revision of, 248–50
VIRGINIA RESOLUTIONS, AMENDED
background of, 234, 235, 236, 247–48,
253, 255; text of, 248–50; revision
of, 255–60

WALTON, GEORGE (Ga.)
signer, Declaration of Independence,
76; delegate, Constitutional Convention, but did not attend, 195, 204,
204n
WALTON, JOHN (Ga.)
signer, Articles of Confederation, 94
WAR
305; Declaration of Independence declares U.S. has power to levy war,
75; Draft Articles, 81, 82, 84; Articles
prohibit states from engaging in
without consent of Congress unless
invaded or in imminent danger, 88;
Articles give Congress power to engage in with the assent of nine states,
89, 92; proposed change in Articles
concerning, 145; Convention proposals concerning, 254, 264, 268, 275,
282, 289, 291; Constitution gives Congress power to declare, 310; Constitution prohibits states from engaging in unless invaded or in imminent
danger, 311
WAR, DEPARTMENT OF
Convention proposals concerning,
246, 247, 254
WASHINGTON, GEORGE (Va.)
53, 55, 193, 232, 269n, 305–6, 318,
319, 348n; delegate, Constitutional
Convention, 198, 230; elected President, Constitutional Convention,
232; and papers of the Convention,
270, 305; in debates in Convention,
304; signer, Constitution, 317
—letters to, 193, 318, 343–45
—diary of, 319, 320n
WEBSTER, NOAH (Conn., N.Y.)
—diary of, 319
WEIGHTS AND MEASURES
Draft Articles, 83; Articles give Congress power to fix the standard of,
91; Convention proposals concerning, 247, 264, 275, 289; Constitution
gives Congress power to fix the
standards of, 310
WENTWORTH, JOHN, JR. (N.H.)
signer, Articles of Confederation, 94

WEST, BENJAMIN (N.H.)
delegate, Constitutional Convention,
but did not attend, 195, 224
WESTERN LANDS OF STATES
54–55, 55–56, 57–59; Draft Articles
permit only Congress or its representative to purchase Indian lands
not located within the boundaries
of any state, 81; Draft Articles require states to honor state boundaries once established, 81; Draft
Articles give Congress power to adjudicate boundary disputes, limit
boundary claims, and assign territories for new states, 82; Articles
give Congress power to establish
courts to settle disputes among states
over lands and boundaries and controversies concerning private rights
to soil, 89–90, 90–91; proposed changes in Articles concerning, 97–98, 99,
99–100, 106, 108–9, 115–16, 117, 123,
130–31, 133–34, 148; Maryland ratifies Articles but refuses to relinquish
its land claims, 135–37. See also Territory of the United States
WEST INDIES, BRITISH
British trade policies in and impact
on American policy, 153–54
WHIPPLE, WILLIAM (N.H.)
signer, Declaration of Independence,
76
WILLIAMS, JOHN (N.C.)
signer, Articles of Confederation, 94
WILLIAMS, WILLIAM (Conn.)
signer, Declaration of Independence,
76
WILLIAMSON, HUGH (N.C.)
64, 65; on committee on temporary
commercial powers (1784), 153; on
committee on Land Ordinance of
1785, 156; delegate, Constitutional
Convention, 202, 202n, 230; signer,
Constitution, 317
WILSON, JAMES (Pa.)
53, 55, 58–59, 64, 65, 67, 146, 237;
signer, Declaration of Independence,
76; on counting three–fifths of slaves
in apportioning expenses (1783), 149;
delegate, Constitutional Convention,
199–200, 230; in debates in Constitutional Convention, 236, 238, 240,
241–42; on counting three-fifths of
slaves in apportioning representation
(1787), 240, 241–42; copy of Pinckney Plan, 245–47; on Committee of
Detail, 255, 260; delivers Franklin's
last speech in Convention, 304; sign-

er, Constitution, 317
WITHERSPOON, JOHN (N.J.)
signer, Declaration of Independence,
76; signer, Articles of Confederation,
94, 129
WOLCOTT, ERASTUS (Conn.)
resigns as delegate to Constitutional
Convention, 195, 216n
WOLCOTT, OLIVER (Conn.)
signer, Declaration of Independence,
76; signer, Articles of Confederation,
94

WYTHE, GEORGE (Va.)
signer, Declaration of Independence,
76; delegate, Constitutional Convention, 198, 230

YATES, ABRAHAM (N.Y.)
member of Congress (1787), 324
YATES, ROBERT (N.Y.)
delegate, Constitutional Convention,
211–13, 230, 232; and drafting of
New Jersey Amendments, 250
—notes of, 243, 253

THE DOCUMENTARY HISTORY OF THE
RATIFICATION OF THE CONSTITUTION
was composed on the Linotype in
a type face called Baskerville,
and is printed on Warren's Library
Text.